The Outlanders

The Outlanders

Robert Crisp

Mayflower

Granada Publishing Limited
Published in 1974 by Mayflower Books Ltd
Frogmore, St Albans, Herts AL2 2NF

First published in 1964 by Peter Davies Ltd
Copyright © Robert Crisp 1964
Made and printed in Great Britain by
Richard Clay (The Chaucer Press) Ltd
Bungay, Suffolk
Set in Linotype Times

To the librarians of Britain and South Africa, and to all those other keepers of the records, whose ready co-operation has made this book possible.

Preface

I have been concerned in this book to tell a true story: the true story of the alien invasion of the South African Republic which founded the world's greatest gold-mining industry and one of the world's great towns. This is the story of those *Uitlanders* and their Johannesburg, from the discovery of the fabulous gold of the main reef to the surrender of the town to Field-Marshal Lord Roberts in the Boer War. As far as I am concerned everything that happens in these pages, did happen. The men and women who move through them, moved through life. If the conversations they had seem unfamiliar to historians it is, perhaps, because they have hitherto been unrecorded.

I have no wish to anticipate the disbelievers; but because identification of even one palpable untruth could throw doubts on the veracity of the whole story, I would like to extract my version of the actual discovery of the main reef of the Witwatersrand and expose it for analysis here. I accept unreservedly the facts of this episode as revealed by Ethel and James Gray. But it will not escape the notice of South African historians that I have accorded the honour to George Harrison rather than to the generally-accepted George Walker. I believe that after his partner's death, Walker—through aberration of memory or a not unnatural desire to stand for his brief moment in the spotlight of history—adopted Harrison's story as his own. I am convinced this is the truth; and there is no one who can positively contradict me.

There are other instances where my variation of history does not coincide exactly with the accepted version. This has not been done for convenience or to secure a better dramatic effect. The reader may emerge at the end of it feeling that truth is far from absolute; that it is subject, like so many of the verities, to interpretation. I am satisfied my book could be given to the student of history without distorting his facts or his attitude.

Suffolk, England, June 1963.

7

Contents

List of Illustrations

The first outspan
Ferreira's Camp: first organised community on the
Witwatersrand
City and Suburban Mine, 1887
Commissioner Street, Johannesburg, 1887
The first chemist's shop
A view of Johannesburg in 1888
Bendoff comes up for the last round
President Kruger visits Johannesburg, 1887
Portraits of C. J. Rhodes, J. B. Robinson, Abe Bailey,
George Farrar, J. B. Taylor, Barney Barnato
Jameson Raid: At the Reform Office
Boer Commando passing through Johannesburg
Surrender: taking down the South African Republican flag,
31st May 1900

The above are reproduced by courtesy of the editor and pub-
lishers of *The Pictorial History of Johannesburg* (Juta &
Company Ltd), and taken from originals in the Africana
Museum, Johannesburg.

BOOK ONE

The Discovery

CHAPTER ONE

The long line of wagons, sixteen oxen to the span, came slowly, creaking, across the grasslands of the Orange Free State. Just as, in the years before, they had creaked across the arid expanse of the Great Karroo. They travelled at the pace of the ox, thirty miles in a day, leaving behind them a trail of outspan places whose wood-ash and blackened stones were to grow into the 30-mile-apart dorps and townships which dot the rare highways across the South African veld.

Each wagon had its family of emigrant Cape Dutch – soon to be known the world over as the Boers, the Afrikaans word for farmers, which was to become the title of a new nation. They were the Voortrekkers – a people in flight. In flight from the restrictions of an imperial authority which was changing their cherished way of life, pressing down on their spirit, confining them body and soul to the conformities of a great but alien civilization.

In 1834 they had packed their wagons and trekked. Most of the peace and the space they sought eluded them. Confronted always by wild beast and wild man in a wild land, pursued always by the spectre of colonial officialdom, they looked ever northward to the next horizon and the next hope. At last, halted by the dirt-grey waters of a river which they called the Vaal because of its colour, they saw the land rising ahead of them in two long flat steps to a ridge which ran east to west across the whole aphelion.

It was a place they had heard about in the camp-fire stories of the hunters and traders and missionaries who had preceded them ... the watershed which caught and split the summer rains sending some of their bounty cascading south into the Vaal and Orange Rivers and on into the distant Atlantic; diverting the rest northwards to the great rivers which rose God-knew-where in the heart of the wilderness

15

and which found their way by channels still unknown down to the Indian Ocean.

Beyond the ridge lay all of Africa. From the crest they would see it, stretched out in front of them – *for* them.

The long whips cracked, the coloured drivers yelled the names of the patient animals paired along the trek chains ... 'Witman, Vaalpens, Rooikop, Swartbooi!' – each name a distinctive characteristic of the individual oxen. Muscles and chains tautened, the great wheels turned, canvas super-structures lurched and swayed and the slow dust rose to mingle with urgent imprecations and the noise of movement.

One more day and the bearded Boers, matching the shagginess of their ponies, stood on the summit of the last ridge. Behind them in the valleys the wagons moved automatically into the symmetry of a fort that was the pattern of life in a hostile land.

It was as they had imagined. Below them the land sloped in a series of convolutions to the sudden upheaval of the Magaliesberg. Beyond that, sky and earth mingled in the haze-filled vastness of the continent – a koppie-strewn emptiness of bush and plain that stretched across to the deserts of the Kalahari and the western ocean; northwards to the ancient realm of Monomotapa and Prester John enclosed by Limpopo and Zambesi; down to the fevered flats of the low-veld and the Portuguese establishments on the eastern seaboard where breakers seethed on the hot sands of Moçambique.

Standing on the apex of the watershed they surveyed the space that encompassed them. There was no need for the formal recognition. This was what they sought. This was the Promised Land of their faith and their future. The Bible was the word of God, and they were His chosen people. They did not doubt it, ever. Later, when some families were to push on still further north, they came to a sluggish stream through the bush. Sure in their faith they called it the Nylstroom, thinking it to be the headwaters of the mighty Nile and that, if they followed its course, it would lead them through the land of Egypt into Canaan.

Their faith was a lot stronger than their geography; and they had been a long time on the road.

Up there on the divide they heard the music of running water and saw how the streams ran away from their feet in opposite directions. They ran cool and clear, gleaming white and fresh in the rippling sunlight; reminding them, by contrast, of the scores of rivers and spruits they had crossed all the way from the south-west corner of the continent, a thousand miles back ... rivers which were mud-flooded and unfordable in the rains, sandy and stagnant in the long dry spells. They had not seen water like this since they had last knelt down to drink of the cold cascades pouring down the mountains of the old Cape Colony. For a while their minds went back to the valleys of their youth and the high challenge of the peaks of Drakenstein and Hottentots Holland, the Matroosberg, Winterberg and Stormberg.

It was a challenge they had accepted when the valleys closed in on them; that had brought them, after the years of wandering, to the wide and promised land which lay at their feet on this ridge of white waters. And that is what they called it – the *Wit Waters Rand*.

It was these few thousand immigrants who carved out of the wilderness the state which became known as the Transvaal – or, as they were to call it proudly, the South African Republic. They compiled their first constitution, full of the inspiration of the American Declaration of Independence, in 1842. In it they established for a lot longer than they might have thought possible, had they contemplated change at all, the basic inequality under God and within the constitution of the white man and the black man. Ten years later the seal was set on their architecture when the South African Republic was recognized as an independent State by the Parliament of Great Britain.

Of government they knew little and cared less. They were united only by their language, their spirit of independence and their determination to stay independent. The entity was not the State but the family, and it was this small unit which, with the Bible in one hand and a gun always ready to interpret its message in the other, overcame the dangers and hardships by which they were perpetually surrounded and which made the State possible. They came together only under a threat to their common cause, to their common survival. Otherwise they had little sense of responsibility, either to each other or to the constitution they had so bravely composed.

Threats there were in plenty. One native chief after another, glimpsing the future surely, attacked their security

17

and violated the frontiers the Boers had set up for themselves – rightly or wrongly, and not often rightly. Bechuanas in the west, Matabele to the north, Bapedi in the northeast and Zulus in the south-east were in a constant state of war or preparation for war with the infant republic.

While the Transvalers were busy constructing their republic an adventurous young South African, Pieter Marais, set off from Cape Town for the great Californian gold rush of 1849.

One year later, having sold his claim at Yuba for 800 dollars and set himself up as a storekeeper in San Francisco, he stood on a hilltop looking westwards and watched the town burn down. His shop and all his possessions burned with it. Broke, but neither disillusioned nor despairing, he worked his way round the mining camps – Calaveras, Mariposa, Benicia, Nappa, Suscol – for another year before the siren call of gold lured him half-way round the world again to the new discoveries at Bendigo and Ballarat in Australia.

By the end of 1853 he was back again in Cape Town. There he heard and read of the small Boer community that had settled north of the Vaal River.

There was land up there virtually for the asking by anyone who was willing to contribute to the physical and spiritual needs of the new republic ... especially if they had a sound, non-English name like Marais. Young Pieter felt the strong impulse within him; besides, there was always the chance, in a new country, of stumbling across – gold.

He was quite sure, after Benicia and Bendigo, that he would recognize gold even if it was concealed from all other men. He did not know, nor would it have stopped him if he did, that the republican government, jealous of their solitude and their independence and with a high value on the isolation that had cost them so much to find, had passed a law the previous year prohibiting all prospecting for gold and precious stones.

They were impelled towards this curious decision by the discoveries of an English mineralogist, John Henry Davis, who had set out from Maritzburg in July, 1852, on a journey to Marico with the professed intention of finding gold in the Southern Transvaal. This was still a remote region peopled only by a handful of widely-scattered farmers whose livelihood depended almost entirely on their success in hunting the great herds of antelope and the beasts of prey which swarmed over the plains.

Davis's ready eye for the geological circumstances of gold-bearing rock, backed by the sixth sense which is an essential requisite of the prospector, led him unerringly to the high, rocky ridge of the Witwatersrand. There, on its western extremity, he accepted the hospitality of Mr Pretorius, Commandant-General, and owner of the farm Paardekraal (where Krugersdorp now stands). From there he prospected the wild kloofs and krantzes of the district.

One day Davis came into the rough-and-ready living-room of Pretorius's house and dropped a few lumps of rock on the table.

'Gold-bearing quartz, Mr Pretorius. On your farm. And plenty more where that came from, if I'm not much mistaken!'

The old Boer picked up a sample in his hard hands and examined it carefully, squinting through the smoke that curled from the pipe that was almost a part of his features. He put it down thoughtfully.

'Truly; say you so! Is that then gold?'

He did not seem either impressed or believing. But a new look came into his eyes when Davis pulled his hand from his pocket and rolled a few dull pebbles on to the table.

'Pick them up,' he told Pretorius. 'Feel how heavy they are.'

Pretorius gathered them together and felt their weight on his palm. He nodded his head, and asked, 'Where did you find these?'

'Near that deep kloof on your south-eastern boundary. The one with the high waterfall.'

'So; Witpoortjie, huh?'

'That's the place. I tell you, Mr Pretorius, there must be more gold in the klook. In the hills and along the bed of the spruit. It would be well worthwhile to stake some claims in that area.'

'Claims? I do not understand about claims, mynheer. I do not have to claim my own land. Witpoortjie is not my farm. What is on Witpoortjie has nothing to do with me.'

'But, Mr Pretorius . . .'

The Boer held up his hand.

'I will tell you what you must do, Mr Davis. You must

19

take these rocks and your little, heavy stones and go to Potchefstroom. There you will ask to see my kinsman the President of the Republic. You will tell Andries Pretorius I have sent you and of what you have found on Paardekraal and Witpoortjie. Show him these as you have shown me. Then ask him what he would have me do. This is a serious matter, mynheer. Too serious for you and I to settle. The President and the Volksraad must be informed. They will know what is best for the Republic. I have the feeling it may not please you, Mr Davis; but they will know what is best. Now I will tell the kaffir to saddle a horse for you.'

So Davis rode off to Potchefstroom and showed his samples of riches and high expectations to the President and members of the executive.

The bearded patriarchs weighed the rocks in their hands; thoughts passed to and fro among them like millstones. They shook their heads, rumbling away in 'the Taal'. Davis could not understand all of their brief comments, but he deciphered enough to realize that he had come to the end of his trail as far as the Transvaal was concerned. The President turned away from the group and came towards him, serious. He said, quietly and sympathetically:

'Mr Davis, we thank you for the trouble you have taken in bringing these samples before us. Tell my cousin he has acted wisely in sending you here. But there are things more precious than gold, mynheer, and nothing is more valuable to my people than their independence in this land we have taken, with God's help, from the wilderness. We want none of your gold or of the sort of people it would bring to our country. Now, if you will state the price of this gold you have shown us I will instruct the Treasurer to pay you for it. I am sorry, but I must ask you to leave the Republic. I cannot allow you to stay and continue your prospecting.'

Davis, bewildered and hurt, stayed silent. He knew there was nothing he could say that would make them change their minds. He understood their fears and respected them for their decision.

'Very well, Mr President; if that is your wish. As to the value of the gold, it will have to be weighed and properly assessed before I can fix the amount. After that I will go and collect my belongings at Paardekraal and return to Maritzburg within a few days.'

John Davis mounted his horse and rode, a little sadly, out

of the story of Johannesburg – just as Pieter Marais rode briefly into it.

When Marais left Cape Town he headed directly for the Transvaal border, following the deep ruts of the wagons across the Karoo and the Orange Free State to the drift across the Vaal River that would take him into the South African Republic. By the time he reached it he had heard, from a dozen trail-side encounters, of the Volksraad's reaction to Davis and his prospecting. He had also absorbed carefully the gossip and rumours of the discoveries at Paardekraal and Witpoortjie. They supplemented the tales going right back to 1834 of gold finds by wandering ivory hunters in the kloofs of the high ridge on the other side of the Vaal River. Marais decided to look for himself first, and talk to the Volksraad afterwards.

Just north of the Witwatersrand a new village had recently come into existence; the Boers called it Pretoria Philadelphia, in joint admiration of their first president and the people of the United States of America whose successful struggle for freedom had inspired so many of their own wishes and actions. It was a town which at that stage contained almost as many letters in its name as population. It was to Pretoria that Marais decided to go. The track lay straight over the Witwatersrand.

As he crossed the wastershed and began the 30-mile descent to the new village tucked away behind the Magaliesberg range, his eyes flicked here and there across the ridges and down into the kloofs and valley, envisaging alongside them the ravines and foothills of the Rocky Mountains and the geological formations of Western Australia ... comparing, retaining, rejecting. He missed nothing. The granite domes, the quartz outcrops, the rock-carving streams – the essential requirements for gold were all there around him as he rode northward.

Coming to the Jukskei River, half-way between the Witwatersrand and Pretoria, he made an early camp. Before the sun set he had wandered several miles up and down stream and seen enough to make him stay in the locality for another day to continue his explorations over a wider area.

By the end of the next day, after following the Jukskei down to its confluence with the Crocodile River, he had satisfied himself that the region was auriferous, and he knew what he would go and ask of the authorities in the capital at Potchefstroom.

His task with President Pretorius was not as difficult as he might have expected. The Volksraad had had second thoughts about the advantages of finding gold in the Republic, if not about the people who would find it. They had decided that if a sufficient quantity of gold could be discovered it would bring great blessings as well as great evils to their country. They determined to try to make sure of the blessings, while discouraging the evils as much as possible. It was a decision much facilitated by the pressures of the financial situation.

The dilemma of the first Boer Government at Potchefstroom persisted for as long as the South African Republic lasted. It influenced internal and external relationships and was a factor in almost every political dispute with which President and Volksraad had to contend. They never did find an adequate solution, and the problem was resolved for them in the ultimate tragedy of war.

Thus it was that when Pieter Marais reached Potchefstroom he found himself preaching to the more-or-less converted. He not only got a permit to search for gold but was given an official commission to 'find gold mines in the country rich enough to work and which would well reward the men who worked them'.

Members of the Government were delighted that one part of their difficulty had been solved for them. They had found one of their own people who knew all about the finding and working of gold, and it would not be necessary to hire unwanted and dangerous aliens to do the work.

For two years Marais searched for the golden treasure which he was sure lay hidden somewhere beneath the koppies and plains of the Transvaal. He returned again and again to the Jukskei, but it always disappointed him. His only success was at Paardekraal, where John Davis had first revealed the presence of gold to the Volksraad.

Occasionally the newspapers of the day published accounts of Marais' small successes as the official government prospector. He went further afield on his quest – to Rustenburg, Potchefstroom, Lydenburg and away north to Zoutpansberg. Always his reports told of insignificant results but always there was that little bit of gold that kept him searching and his employers hopeful. His last prospecting journey took him west to Marico where, sad and disillusioned, he reported back in March, 1855, that he had 'found nothing deserving the attention of the Volksraad'.

On the other side of the watershed, a few miles south of where Marais wandered in such hope and frustration, the great treasure slumbered on, undisturbed, undreamt of.

But Marais' small revelations, and the brief messages that were picked up from paper to paper as the stage coaches and mail steamers carried them to and around the coast, swelled the inevitable rumours. There are always men who listen to this sort of tale, who do not want to disbelieve it, and who cannot resist its urgent summons. Soon they were wandering northwards from the ports and settlements in the south – the first slow trickle of the flood that was soon to pour across the high-veld.

In Pretoria the Boers watched the new development with mixed feelings. They hoped the newcomers would find gold, but they wanted to make quite sure that the newcomers did not get rich while the country stayed poor. The gold was in the earth of the South African Republic. It was God's gift to the Republic and His people.

Three years after Marais left the Transvaal, the Volksraad passed its first resolution confirming this simple truth. It compelled owners of farms on which minerals were found to sell or lease them to the Government if the Government so desired.

Various ordinances and resolutions succeeded this, none of them rejecting the principle of State ownership but generally making concessions here and there to individuals and property owners. This change of attitude was forced on the Volksraad by their inability to finance anything, and their increasing need for money was revealed in the resolution of 1870 offering a reward of £5,000 to anybody discovering a really rich mine within the borders of the Republic.

The first Gold Law of the Transvaal was passed in 1871. This reserved to the Government all mining rights, excluding those already granted to private individuals. It was also made compulsory for prospectors to have written permission to seek, and to notify the Government of any discovery. Later this section was amended to insist that every person who was not a burgher of the republic had to sign an undertaking to conform to its laws before he could get a licence to prospect.

In the fast-changing situation which built up as each new mineral discovery was made, it was natural enough that regulations should keep pace with development and circumstances. After Gold Law No. 1 of 1871 almost every meeting of the Volksraad discussed an amendment or an addition to it. All of them reflected the essential dilemma of the Boers; needing the income that would come to them from payable gold, yet desperately anxious to maintain the independence and integrity of their way of life – which any major gold discovery would threaten. They reflected, too, the basic conflict in personality and faith between the pastoral, God-fearing burghers and the foreigners who sought rewards measured only in material terms.

For a dozen years after Davis and Marais the new prospectors searched in vain, crossing and recrossing the Witwatersrand as their quest took them further and further into the remote corners of the Transvaal and beyond.

Then, in 1865, a professional elephant hunter named Henry Hartley, in pursuit of ivory far up in the wilds of Mashonaland, stumbled on some ancient ruins in the bush. He had with him on his hunting expedition one of the world's greatest geologists and archaeologists, Carl Mauch.

Mauch saw at once that the crumbling walls and scattered implements and utensils were the ruins of ancient gold workings. It did not take him long to discover that there was a good deal of gold still there. On their way back to the Transvaal, Mauch discovered further gold deposits at Tati, just across the Limpopo River. They returned with this electrifying news to Hartley's Farm, on the Witwatersrand.

CHAPTER TWO

Now men talked about the new gold around camp-fires that began to flicker like rare stars in the black firmament of the African night; they re-told that story of Hartley and Mauch with inspired embellishments in every dockside pub around the coast; soon, as the packet boats and grain ships and barques spread out across the oceans from the 'Tavern of the Seas' at the Cape of Good Hope, they were hearing it in New York and London, Rio, Valparaiso, Sydney and San Francisco. There was always a willing audience. Men who had never heard of South Africa or the Cape Colony now talked familiarly of Mashonaland and the Transvaal and Limpopo. Many of them were fed-up with California and Western Australia. The mining camps were settling down into organized communities with all their restraints on opportunism and irresponsibility.

On the other side of the world was a new land with gold for the finding and with only a half-baked government of half-civilized Boers, who would not know anything about registration of claims, who had few laws demanding obedience and no means of enforcing them, and where there were taxes that nobody could collect. On every vessel calling at Port Natal and Cape Town men came to the new land of opportunity and liberty.

The Boers of the republic gossiped, too. Their government could not afford to buy the arms and bullets that were necessary for the constant Kaffir wars, and the burghers happily refused to make any contribution to the Treasury. Now, if only they could find a rich gold mine; not a few grains of gold in a river bed, but one that would guarantee them a big income for ever. No more need for taxes, then; and as many new rifles and ammunition as they would ever want.

By the time Gold Law No. 1 had been adopted there

could not have been many of the inhabitants of the republic whose minds were completely detached from the possibilities of finding gold or some other precious mineral. Every other farmer became a prospector, each harbouring the hope that his farm would turn out to be a gold mine. The landowners along the Witwatersrand joined in the new activity only a little less hopefully than their fellow-citizens in more favoured areas of the Transvaal.

Financiers in the City of London, always a great source of investment capital for new and exciting ventures, began to take an interest in the South African potential. The London and Limpopo Mining Company was formed in 1868 to exploit Mauch's discovery at Tati. They sent out a well-equipped mining expedition, under the popular explorer Sir John Swinburne and manned by experienced prospectors and miners from the California fields.

The long wagon trail to Moselikatse's country, where Hartley and Mauch had made their finds, passed through Potchefstroom, and there Swinburne halted his expedition for a few days to talk a little business with the President and members of the Volksraad. He offered them £50,000 in cash for exclusive rights to all the minerals in the South African Republic.

Fifty thousand pounds! It was a lot of money in any terms. To the near-bankrupt government it represented more than a fortune, it was salvation. They debated the matter long and earnestly. Then they turned it down. It was a courageous decision, for at that time there was only the most superficial evidence that their republic possessed any mineral wealth at all. On what the London and Limpopo based its offer is not known. Undoubtedly, if it had been accepted it would have been the greatest speculative bargain in the history of the human race. Within twenty years of Swinburne's offer being rejected the newly-opened Witwatersrand mines were producing nearly £1,000,000 of gold a year; by 1910, this figure had risen to £32,000,000. (Just one mine, Crown Mines, on the outskirts of modern Johannesburg, which started operations in 1887, has produced between that date and 1960 more than 42,000,000 ounces of gold.)

The trickle of treasure-seekers and adventurers was now a steady stream of immigrants. But they were essentially pick-and-shovel men: uncouth, uneducated, irresponsible, polyglot, unscrupulous and often desperate. There were few of the geologists and engineers who were needed to find and exploit the deep secret of the golden hoard. These others only succeeded in scratching the surface, looking for the easy pickings. It was all they knew how to do. They found the likely-looking outcrops and alluvial deposits, crushed the rock with their primitive implements, shovelled the dirt into their riffled basins watching hopefully for the first specks of 'colour' at the bottom of the washed gravel. Very few found it. Most of them lived on hope, their wits and kaffir-corn meal, plus whatever meat they were able to shoot.

Nothing that had happened or was happening seemed likely to ease the mounting economic difficulties of the new republic. Then came the news that made every digger in Africa pack up his tools and join the stampede converging on a barren piece of ground a few square miles in extent on the undefined western border of the Orange Free State.

Diamonds!

From all corners of the earth they came rushing to this flat no-man's-land, inhabited by a strange, mixed race who called themselves, complacently, the Bastards.

Deep down in the earth, when the planet was cooling, blue clay had captured and compressed the pure, incandescent moments of prehistoric time, forcing them upwards to the surface in volcanic pipes, spewing them out on the visible soil where they lay through aeons of waiting for the first avaricious touch of man.

The diggers followed the pipes down into the earth, hauling the blue soil with its precious content to the surface by relays of buckets, until they had dug themselves the biggest hole in the world. Alongside it rose the town they called Kimberley.

As always happens on such occasions there were a hundred failures and disillusions for every success. But the diamonds and Kimberley had already played their essential part in the story of a Johannesburg that was so non-existent as to be beyond anybody's wildest dreams – at a time when wild dreams were a part of every digger's night.

Kimberley not only supplied the vital reservoir of men which would be needed when the moment came; it not only threw up the diamonds which insured the imperative finance;

it produced the individuals of genius and the pattern of organization which they conceived and perfected at the diamond diggings for the vastly more complicated task of extracting gold from deep down in the earth in a way that had never been attempted before. Rhodes, Barnato, Robinson, Beit, the Joels ... these were the giants of finance of the world's greatest industry on the Witwatersrand; the multi-millionaires who, from their burrowings into the soil and rock of the Transvaal high-veld, built a city of gold. All of them cut their teeth on the diamonds of Kimberley.

Competing with the news of finds of big stones at Kimberley came fresh rumours of gold strikes in the Eastern Transvaal. For the established diggers, the ones with the payable claims which were even then being bought up and amalgamated by the financiers, these rumours were just food for gossip. But for many hundreds who had not struck it rich they offered new hope, new opportunity. They gathered their gear together again and headed back into the republic, making for the distant mountains of the Portuguese border where the great step of the plateau drops down to the fevered low-veld.

To and fro across the watershed of the Witwatersrand the gold-seekers and their camp-followers passed. After Tati came Eersteling, Lydenburg and the brief glory of Pilgrim's Rest. It was from Lydenburg that Edward Button was the first to claim the Boer Government's reward of £5,000 for the finder of a rich gold mine. The application was rejected – a decision which does not stand up to the judgment of history, since the Lydenburg Mining Estates, subsequently known as the Transvaal Gold Mining Estates, developed into the largest mine outside the Johannesburg district.

The whole country was gripped in a high fever of excitement. Anything was possible, and men looked with a new regard at the stubborn earth that so often had resisted their desperate efforts to make it produce food and livelihood. As stories filtered through from Kimberley of big stones, and from the Eastern Transvaal of bigger nuggets, almost the whole population, in spirit if not in body, became diggers. Gold and diamonds were potentially in everybody's back yard.

From Pilgrim's Rest the diggers, swelled by the new influx from America and Australia and Britain, and harried by the Boer government, spread out through the peaks and valleys. Some struck it rich, most of them made just enough to live on.

But it was still not much more than scratching the surface. And all the time, as the wagon wheels turned and the whips cracked and the jaded feet plodded on, as the air crackled with ancient Anglo-Saxon oaths and the new blasphemies of Australia and the American West, the greatest buried treasure on earth lay somnolent beneath the passing fortune-hunters.

They had their eyes fixed on a bright and distant gleam. They failed to see the subtle smile flickering where the sunlight caught the quartz outcrops that bent and twisted the trail all along the ridge of white waters.

In the background glowered the owners of the republic. The Boers were sullen and suspicious. Rising among them was their new Commandant-General, Paul Kruger, who seemed to concentrate in his own personality all the hatred of and resistance to an intrusion which they seemed powerless to prevent once they had let it start.

But the Boers were also poor; nor were they any more immune than other men to the temptations of sudden wealth. The owners of farms in the Pretoria and Heidelberg Districts which enclosed the greater part of the Witwatersrand ridge were especially susceptible to such thoughts engendered by the superficial discoveries of Davis and Marais. Groups of them joined forces to prospect along the line of their own farms and those of their friends.

The local farmers, lacking specialized knowledge and equipment, were ill-rewarded for their diligence and labour. While they roamed hopefully over the summits and along the wide valleys the delegated burghers grumbled and debated in their new capital at Pretoria, waiting for the miracle, which their God would surely perform, that would rid them of these unwelcome *Uitlanders* – foreigners – and at the same time resolve their other difficulties. The essence of their problem was that, unless there was a miracle, the only hope of solvency lay in the intruders they did not want.

It seemed a pretty dim hope, and the members of the Volksraad did not know whether to be glad or sorry at the disappointing news from Lydenburg and Pilgrim's Rest where hungry, desperate diggers were making trouble on every possible occasion. In July, 1873, the Volksraad issued

29

a formal notice to whatever newspapers they could reach at the time – to the *Transvaal Advertiser* and *De Volkstem* in Pretoria, and then by way of stage coaches to the established papers around the coast. It said without much sorrow:

'The Transvaal Government has officially notified that people ought not to go to Lydenburg to look for gold if they do not wish to lose money in their search after the auriferous treasures of the locality.'

Nobody was more upset by this gentle discouragement than Albert Gottheimer, the Baron Grant. This colourful character was, without doubt, projected into the second half of the nineteenth century for the specific purpose of promoting companies.

His first venture was the Emma silver mine – a project which repaid investors one shilling for each of their £20 shares. This did not damage the esteem in which he was held by the public enough to prevent him being elected Member of Parliament for Kidderminster.

Obviously this was a convertible asset, and he made use of it to persuade the London Metropolitan Board of Works to sell him the rather neglected little open space near Trafalgar Square, known as Leicester Fields, for £30,000. With the assistance of a few gardeners he converted this into a public garden which he renamed Leicester Square. To add the necessary tone and dignity Baron Grant then had a copy made of Scheemaker's statue of Shakespeare in Westminster Abbey and placed it in his square, where it still ponders silently the passing taxis and cinema-goers and those in search of stimulating literature just across the road.

There has always been argument about Baron Grant's real intentions in handling an enterprise which was apparently without profit to himself. The most charitable interpretation of his investing £30,000 in a project showing no return is that he put a high value on his personal popularity and prestige, and it is a rather sad commentary on the cynicism of the times that on the occasion of the unveiling of the Shakespeare statue which was to formally open Leicester Square to the public, a ballad was being sold in the streets which attempted to explain the whole performance by suggesting that, for once, the Baron wanted his name to be associated with 'something square'.

The fact that the day after the ceremony he was unseated

as a Member of Parliament for bribery in his constituency is a tribute to his sense of timing.

He must have felt that a move was necessary and, surveying the world, he could not have failed to notice favourably the new South African Republic. It was remote, its form of government seemed a little haphazard, the liberty of the individual was held superior to the civic authority and, above all, the indiscriminate organization of the new goldfields required a man of his imaginative talent.

The talent was real enough and his imagination, if introspective, foresaw the possibilities and opportunities in a clearer light than most of his contemporaries. Not long after his arrival in Lydenburg he knew exactly what he wanted to do.

The diggers and their claims were scattered over a wide area. There was no continuity or control, and no proper geological investigation had been carried out of any of the surrounding districts. It was evident that much of the country was gold-bearing and Grant's plan was to buy up all the ground not yet developed and as many of the occupied claims as he could to bring the gold recovery under a single, strong hand. He would do for the Eastern Transvaal goldfields what Rhodes, Barnato and Robinson were in process of doing with the diamond diggings at Kimberley.

There was never any small-mindedness about Baron Grant. He went straight to President Burgers of the Republic to enlist his support and, if possible, to secure his partnership.

The Transvaal administration was in a chaotic state, with its Treasury practically bankrupt. The President saw in Grant the answer to some of his prayers. They not only discussed the possibilities of centralized development of the eastern gold-fields but various other ways of opening up the country and turning its natural resources to profitable account.

These included the construction of a railway line from the port at Delagoa Bay in Portuguese East Africa to the capital at Pretoria. Baron Grant undertook to arrange the finance and construction, with the President's active help.

It was no wild-cat scheme. An outlet to the sea at the nearest point was an essential if the republic was to progress and prosper. Grant, however, was not quite the person to raise capital for a highly technical project in which such rewards as gold or silver nuggets could not be dangled temptingly before wide-eyed investors.

But he was able to persuade Burgers – who did not need much persuading – that it was an opportune moment for a presidential visit to London and Europe to raise the £300,000 which they considered necessary for the first phase of their schemes. It was a typically Grant touch that the President should have purchased a large Lydenburg nugget for £470 and had a number of coins to the value of a sovereign struck from it. He presented one to each member of the Volksraad and sent one to the head of each European State that had recognized the South African Republic. The remainder he took with him as visiting-cards on his journey and as demonstrable evidence of the truth of his sales-talk.

The combination of president and promoter was ill-fated. Burgers was able to raise only £90,000, and the machinery and equipment for the railway on which he spent most of it was to lie rusting and rotting at Delagoa Bay for lack of funds to pay the freight charges.

Baron Grant after a career of some fluctuations in the gold-fields was to end up with his mining company insolvent and himself pursued through the bankruptcy courts. What can be fittingly described as his epitaph appeared appropriately enough in the *Transvaal Advertiser* for Friday, August 7, 1885:

'Baron Grant, whose connection with the Lisbon-Berlyn Company in this country is well known, appears as a bankrupt in the *London Gazette*.'

He retired to Bognor where he lived long enough to read of the fabulous discoveries on the Witwatersrand that laid the foundations of the great city they called Johannesburg. It was only a name in a newspaper to Baron Grant; yet in many ways he was the first Johannesburger.

CHAPTER THREE

Environment has a decisive influence on the character and personality of everything which grows. Johannesburg, in the circumstances of its growth and incredible development, was bound to acquire highly individualistic characteristics – some good, some bad, but all dynamic, energetic, kaleidoscopic and full of a magnificent unscrupulousness.

There was plenty of environment, all right, but few towns in the world have grown up with such a complete disregard of what went on around it, or of conventional patterns of behaviour. Rather, the potent influences went outwards from this lusty, precocious infant – and changed the history of three nations.

The most significant of the original environmental factors were political and personal. Obviously, since the motive force of the Great Trek was the overwhelming desire to get away from the authority of an alien government, any intrusion of that authority into the affairs of the Transvaal Republic was bitterly resented. There existed an almost permanent state of suspicion and resentment among the majority of the Boer inhabitants, though this was never allowed to smother the natural hospitality of their race towards the stranger and traveller.

The Keate Award of 1871, resulting in the annexation by Great Britain of Griqualand West and the diamond fields around Kimberley, further embittered relations between the Imperial Government and a republican population who saw in the diamond fields the solution of their impoverishment.

The immediate consequence had been the resignation, under pressure of popular disapproval, of President Pretorius, and the election in his place of the Reverend Burgers, who seemed to the Transvalers to fulfil their ideal of a sophisticated man of the world, well-versed in the devious procedures of international diplomacy. He was to play his part, as much as any individual, in the circumstances which made Johannesburg possible.

Burgers had the essential characteristics of unorthodoxy, confidence, enthusiasm and vision. But if they were essential for the progress of his country it was not long before they aroused the antagonism of his ultra-conservative countrymen.

He envisaged a federal republic embracing all the Boer States and settlements, with an outlet at the port of Delagoa Bay 'free from the trammels of British ports and influence'. His insistence on equal rights for all civilized men – there is no indication that anybody included the native inhabitants in this definition – did nothing to make him popular with his electorate. But he saw that he would have to offer these rights to the new influx of population attracted to the Transvaal by the gold discoveries in the north and east. Between 1854 and 1875 the population of the Transvaal had increased from 15,000 to 40,000.

But Burgers, as we have seen from the incident with Baron Grant, was over-impressionable and susceptible. He lacked stability and strength of character. He never got the wholehearted support of the Volksraad and could not, like Kruger who succeeded him, impose his will upon it. A disastrous little war against a native chief, Secocoeni, so depleted the Treasury that it was unable to pay the interest on a £66,000 loan from the Cape Commercial Bank, who threatened to foreclose. When he tried to organize the gold industry, and tried to placate the diggers by offering them full rights of citizenship in order to ensure some contribution towards the costs of running the republic, his own supporters turned against him.

During Burgers' absence in Europe in quest of funds for the railway and other projects, the Transvaal got itself into such a mess politically and economically, and was threatened by native uprisings on so many borders, that an impression was created that it would be just as well if it too was annexed by Britain.

The militant diggers made the most of the situation, and it was not really a surprise to anyone when the Imperial Government decided to intervene in the interests of South African stability and sent Sir Theophilus Shepstone up from Natal in 1877 to hoist the Queen's flag at Pretoria.

The annexation lasted little more than three years. At the

34

end of 1880 the Boers of the Transvaal rose in revolt. They attacked the meagre British garrisons and sent a strong force to the Natal border. There, at Majuba Hill, they defended a hastily-prepared and badly-commanded British expedition. A Liberal government under Gladstone completed the débâcle of Majuba by ordering an armistice to be concluded, and by the end of March the Transvaal was once again the South African Republic, though with theoretical acknowledgment of the suzerainty of the Crown.

The reaction in South Africa was as might have been expected. The Boers were jubilant and arrogant; the English-speaking section – South Africans, Englishmen, Scots, Australians and most of the Americans – furious and disgusted.

It is no part of Johannesburg's story to pass judgment on the rights and wrongs of this historic incident. It is enough to say that it established the relationship between Briton and Afrikaner which has persisted to this day. The Boer War, which was to begin less than twenty years later, really began in men's minds in March, 1881. Thereafter the diggers, the Uitlanders, developed as a separate and inimical State within the State. It was an attitude of mind which crystallized in the first tents on the Witwatersrand which grew into the first shacks which grew into the great, concrete edifice of Johannesburg. It was an attitude that is only now beginning to change.

The annexation was the end of President Burgers. He had had his brief and essential moment on the stage: essential, because it was Burgers who gave gold-digging and gold-diggers whatever status they had in the republic. It was Burgers who had contrived to merge, however unsatisfactorily, the hesitations and fears of the present with the needs of the future in the first gold laws. For these he had relied heavily on the advice and information supplied by the brothers Harry and Fred Struben, well known in the republic as geologists, prospectors and farmers.

The Strubens' draft of rules for the guidance of the *Volksraad* (the republican Parliament) was compounded of extracts from the mining legislation of Australia and California with modifications which they thought suitable for the Transvaal's peculiar conditions. They were not asked to express any opinion on the political and patriotic influences which were a decisive element in the relationship between State and miners.

35

The Strubens, having performed their first – but by no means last – task for the republic, went about their business of seeking gold. While the majority of prospectors hurried off to Tati or Eersteling or Lydenburg, Fred Struben became fascinated by the rock formation of the long ridge that ran east and west some thirty miles south of the capital at Pretoria.

He chipped away with his hammer at the line of outcrop quartz, and was not surprised at the tail of gold when he panned his crushed samples. Beneath the outcrop, he felt sure, lay the beds of gold-bearing reef. But how deep were they, and did they contain enough gold to make it worthwhile to dig down to them? A whole lot of things, including Johannesburg, lay in the answer to that question.

Fred Struben was not only the first man to appreciate the sort of riches that might be concealed below the Witwatersrand; he realized immediately that their recovery was going to be a different and more difficult technical proposition to anything that had ever been attempted in mining before.

During the short period of the annexation Struben had taken advantage of the opportunity of a more sympathetic hearing from the British administration, and had persuaded Shepstone to invite an American mining engineer, Alfred Watson Armfield, to come to the Transvaal to investigate its mineral potential. Struben wanted him particularly to examine the Witwatersrand formation. Armfield was given the official title of Inspector of Goldfields, and his duties were defined as 'to provide for the systematic exploration of the mineral resources of the country; and to prevent needless excitement, premature rushes and disappointment'.

His instructions reveal clearly that at that stage the administration, conscious of the burden on the State of a disillusioned community of diggers, was as much concerned with the disadvantages of such a frustrated and uncompromising horde as with expectations of discovery.

Armfield seemed to share this view. Certainly, his reports are unlikely to have caused any excitement or premature rushes. Of disappointment there was plenty.

His first estimate of the possibilities reached the Government on August 18, 1878, in this form:

'I have been engaged with my party in prospecting the country comprised within the main range of the Witwatersrand, commencing at Badenhorst's farm and continuing my

36

researches as far as Sterkfontein ... Having satisfied myself that, to find gold in sufficient quantities to pay, I should have to abandon my exploration of the Witwatersrand, I struck across country to Rustenburg.'

A couple of months later he was in the Heidelberg District, some miles south of the main ridge. In that locality, as in so many others, fitful prospecting had been going on ever since the days of Davis and Marais – chiefly by hopeful farm-owners. There had been some evidence that gold-bearing reefs existed in the district. The American expert, obviously not a very talkative man, did not agree with this assessment. In November of the same year he was reporting to the Government again: 'I am of the opinion that this district, the subject of this report, is not a field for the prospector.'

Convinced of the futility of further exploration along the high watershed, Armfield did not hesitate long when word was brought to him of a rich gold strike on the Selati River in the low-veld to the east of Zoutpansberg. Bored stiff with his unrewarding task in the central district, he packed his instruments and belongings into a wagon and set off on the now well-worn trail to the north-eastern Transvaal. There, like so many others who valued the chance of wealth above the chance of life, he was struck down by fever and died.

Once again the great treasure trove, astonishingly, had escaped discovery. Armfield had come and gone, joining the increasing company of pioneer prospectors who had been literally within a few feet of the very fortune for which they were so avidly seeking; who had not only passed by, but walked over it time and time again.

But the Strubens carried on, secure in their faith and sustained by their knowledge. For five years Fred searched along the northern face of the ridge of white waters, chipping at the pink outcrops that gleamed through the yellow winter grass of the high-veld, confirming or rejecting the reports of haphazard prospectors who had preceded him. He and his brother traced the hidden flow of the reef under the rugged surface until, at the beginning of 1884, they felt certain enough of its course to buy up the chain of farms under which it ran.

In March of that year the Struben brothers formed the Sterkfontein Junction Syndicate. It was the Rand's first real gold-mining company.

But the picks and shovels of Struben's labourers only bit into the edge of truth. Reality, as it so often does, lay just over the hill.

Fred Struben did not think he was guessing, or that he was wrong; but he wanted to be sure, before revealing his discovery to the world. He decided, for the time being, to keep silent.

In October, the *Pall Mall Gazette* was publishing for the entertainment of its rather cynical subscribers an account of a public meeting in the City of London at which our premature Johannesburger, Baron Grant, had magically persuaded the disillusioned shareholders of his Lisbon-Berlyn mining company to part with another £50,000 'to carry on operations in the Eastern Transvaal gold-fields'. The *Gazette* ended with this comment:

'We believe what we have said all through will prove correct. There is plenty of gold in the Transvaal to pay for economical working, but nothing that is known at present can justify extravagant ideas of fabulous wealth. That wealth may be there, or it may not; at present it has not been found.'

Fred Struben thought he had found it. He had a clear picture in his mind of an underground system of gold-bearing reefs running downwards through the rocks of the Witwatersrand. He was as confident as a prospector can be, but he did not realize that he was prising open the door of a treasure house that would make 'extravagant ideas of fabulous wealth' sound like a major understatement.

Like the writer in the *Pall Mall Gazette*, a lot of people in the Transvaal thought they were on the edge of great discoveries that would make them rich overnight. Nearly all of them were looking in the wrong places – at the farms Kromdraai and Blaauwbank to the north of the ridge, near Heidelberg to the south.

Like Struben, they were looking in the wrong places. Between Heidelberg and Rustenburg flowed the great reefs of conglomerate with their burden of gold. Compared with that aureate stream, Struben and his contemporaries were but dipping their fingers in the unrewarding sand of a dried-up creak. Yet all the time the prodding and the chipping went on.

All over Southern Africa men talked endlessly about gold

and diamonds and other valuable minerals and stones. If they mentioned the Witwatersrand at all it was usually as the half-way stage between the diamonds of Kimberley and the gold of Barberton; it was the place where you got headaches and breathlessness from the altitude; the ridge of cold nights, no trees, no firewood; a place to go to in the hot summer when the deadly low-veld fever swept through the mining camps – no one knew how or why.

There was so much else to gossip and complain about. The sell-out by the British Government after the annexation remained the chief inspiration for disparaging comment among the disgruntled diggers and other foreigners. The attitude and actions of the new President, Paul Kruger, gave them new material for vilification of the republic and its burghers. For it became clear that President and Volksraad were flagrantly disregarding the terms of the recently-signed London Convention giving to all Europeans in the Transvaal equal rights with the burghers of the republic, and equal taxation.

There is some justification for the argument that the London Convention, from the Boer point of view, was an immoral document, and that the question of ethics did not enter into an arrangement between the representatives of two groups who distrusted each other so completely. Enough at this stage to emphasize that the fires of revolt and repression smouldered continuously in the South African Republic, alongside an almost constant campaign to secure imperial intervention – on behalf of the diggers, and to restore British sovereignty. With considerable prescience the historian Froude wrote a letter to the London *Times* dealing with the explosive situation being created in the sub-continent:

'If the Imperial Government interposes on its own authority, the Dutch of the Cape Colony will consider the cause of the Transvaal to be their own cause and each step will bring us nearer to the point when we shall have either to reconquer South Africa or abandon it altogether . . .'

The scramble for Africa had begun. The names of Livingstone and Stanley were familiar in every household in Britain. The focus of public attention was General Gordon's progress up the Nile in the Sudan campaign against the Mahdi.

In the United States the Americans were exclusively involved in the process of electing another President.

Throughout 1884 and through the first half of 1885 the names of Struben and the Witwatersrand did not once appear in newspaper print – not even in South African newspapers. And if they were mentioned by word of mouth, as they must have been, it was usually in accents of mockery or disbelief.

It did not particularly worry Fred Struben. He went on digging.

CHAPTER FOUR

The light four-wheeler, its single horse sweating as it trotted over the grass *middelmannetjie* of the track, swung left off the main Pretoria–Potchefstroom road and headed for the homestead under the cliffs at the head of the valley. The occupant of the cart looked about him with great interest and satisfaction as he passed the trenches and mounds of quartz, crude winding gear and sluices, primitive rock-crushing implements. It was because of this that the State Attorney of the South African Republic, Dr E. J. P. Jorissen, was paying a visit to Fred Struben at Wilgespruit.

As the cart pulled up and its occupant became recognizable, a white man detached himself from the small group of natives clustered round a winch. Struben knew and liked Jorissen, though the latter was not popular with the Boer inhabitants. He was one of Burgers' importations from Holland at a time when the President had found it impossible to carry on an effective administration with the semi-literate, unsophisticated and unwilling human material at his disposal in the republic. Jorissen was intelligent and far-sighted; but he was a Hollander and therefore an Uitlander, as intolerable as any other alien in a position of authority over the independent-minded Boers. Now Paul Kruger had replaced Burgers as president, and Jorissen, along with other 'Burgers' importations and innovations, was soon to go.

The two men shook hands and went into the house, where a cookboy soon placed before them the inevitable mugs of coffee.

For a while they talked about the weather, the mealie crop and the prospects for the cattle due to return shortly from their winter sojourn in the low-veld. Struben spoke in the dialectic Afrikaans, just emerging as the language of the Voortrekkers, while Jorissen slowed down his quick Hol-

41

lands to be more clearly understood.

'Mynheer Struben; as you know, I have not come all the way from Pretoria this morning to discuss the weather – which is so much the same every day that it is hardly worth talking about.'

'I did not think you had come to talk about the weather, Doctor.'

Jorissen leaned forward, abrupt and serious.

'The finances of the republic are in an impossible state. We cannot meet our commitments and we are unable to pay all salaries in full. We have heard that you have struck gold in reef form and that you believe it to be in payable quantities. Can you confirm that to me now?'

Struben took a few puffs on his pipe. He was quite sure in his own mind, but that was a little different to producing evidence that would support his claim before world opinion.

'I would like a little more time, Doctor. I am certain myself that the Witwatersrand will produce a very considerable quantity of gold. But the technical problems are new, and likely to be difficult. I need more evidence.'

'What sort of evidence?'

'The only evidence that anybody will believe – gold, and proof that it is here in worthwhile quantity.'

'Let me explain the position more exactly, mynheer. The Pretoria Government, with the greatest difficulty, has managed to raise a loan of £5,000 from the Standard Bank. That is its total cash resources. When that is exhausted, the State will be bankrupt. If we can make known immediately the existence of new and substantial gold deposits, more substantial and less speculative than in the Eastern Transvaal, our reputation and our credit will be restored – and the Republic will be saved.'

'It is a very serious position, Doctor.'

'It's a desperate position, Mr Struben. I must urge you – and it will be in your own interests – to make a statement that can be given to the newspapers as soon as possible. It is President Kruger's earnest desire.'

'Has it struck you that the State would also be saved by returning to the protection of the British Crown? Just a minute, Doctor; I know what you are going to say. There is no need. I cannot lie about the gold. It is here! Give me another month; then I or my brother will come to Pretoria with the proof you need. You can invite the newspapers to see it – and the President, and the whole Volksraad, if you like.'

Jorissen jumped to his feet and grabbed Struben's hand.

'You will save the Republic, mynheer!'

'I'm not so sure about that,' Struben said in phlegmatic contrast. 'But keep in touch with my brother in Pretoria. I'll leave all the arrangements to him.'

He watched the State Attorney drive off. Then, with an expressive shrug, he walked over to the newest heap of rock dragged up from the deep trench.

In the last week of May, 1885, Harry Struben sat at a desk in his home near the capital and scribbled a note to his brother. A native runner took it across to the mine on the northern edge of the Witwatersrand. It said:

'Have arranged for the President and Members of the Volksraad to attend an exhibition of gold and rock samples from Wilgespruit in the Union Club on June 5. Dawson, the Government assayer, will do a report on the samples and weigh the gold. He says he will need everything the day before so suggests you bring it all over as early as possible on the 4th, or the night before that if possible. We can fix up the exhibition just before they are due to appear. Kruger and the Volksraad people will be along about 11. *The Advertiser* and *De Volkstem* are each sending a representative and there is a young man from the *Cape Argus* who has recently arrived in Pretoria.'

The runner came back to Pretoria late the same night with a message from Fred which said that he would leave it all to Harry, that he didn't care much for exhibitions of that sort, and that he would see that the gold and rock samples got to Pretoria in good time. It was just the reply Harry had expected.

Shortly after eleven o'clock on the morning of June 5, the President of the South African Republic, attended by the chairman of the Volksraad and half a dozen members, walked over from Kruger's ramshackle bungalow with its wide stoep on which the President conducted business with his burghers.

From the entrance to the Union Club, Harry Struben watched them approach against the background of Church Square with its somnolent wagons and the long spans of oxen through which the bearded, slouch-hatted farmers moved while bonneted, shapeless women greeted each other with immediate gossip.

There was little difference to be seen in the distinguished party strolling over to the club. They looked like any collection of farmers in from their farms and ranches for market or for the religious festival of *nagmaal*. Only Kruger stood out among them; and not only because of the top-hat he wore like a badge of office.

Here was the man who was more than President of the Republic. He was the will and the destiny of the Republic; the concentrated purpose and resolve of his people. It was visible in the man – shaped and carved to be immovable. The great block of the body; the face moulded round a magnificent obstinacy of nose and mouth; square chin supporting full mouth; thick eyebrows overhanging small, shrewd eyes sunk in perpetual watchfulness behind the bulwarks of great, round pouches which seemed to fill the top half of his face. All framed in white beard which rimmed the line of the jaw from ear to ear.

There was no concealing the strength of the man, and it was confirmed and enlarged by the deep rumble of the voice. It boomed like a double bass among the flimsier instruments of his fellows. In anger or frustration it bellowed like a bull. No plump, domesticated bull; a bull buffalo – massive, courageous, cunning, untameable; at its most dangerous when hurt or cornered.

Paul Kruger, in experience and suffering, was an old man by the time he was twenty-two; and widowed, too. Now, at sixty, walking down the main street of his capital, of his Republic, he looked what he was: a patriarch of patriarchs, the old bull, but still the leader and inspiration of the herd.

Struben watched them. The government of a country, the representatives of a handful of poverty-stricken people who in the bush and on the grasslands between the mountains were founding a new State and a new nation: it was not easy to see it in them as they came solidly along, sucking at their pipes, raising small puffs of dust from the road surface with ruminant expectoration. But they gave an impression of crude strength, of an obstinate faith – in themselves and in the square, top-hatted figure at their head – which was almost tangible. A thick book was tucked under the President's arm, seeming to nestle there as easily as a well-worn slipper fits the foot. It was his only literature, his encyclopaedia of all knowledge, the source of his strength, the real inspiration of his judgment and his actions. It was the Holy Bible.

Struben greeted them formally at the club entrance and they moved in, curious and voluble. Few of them bothered to remove their hats; for a moment Struben contemplated with some surprise the fact that he had never yet seen the top of the President's head.

In the dining-room the tables had been set out in two long rows with a cluster of chairs at one end. The quartz samples, the crushed rock and two containers of some gleaming material over which a State policeman mounted impressive guard, were laid out in orderly sequence. At a table next to the wall sat a small group of reporters. Dawson, nearby, consulted a scribbled column of figures.

Struben conducted the delegation the length of the display, explaining briefly the geological nature of the exhibits. At the second table Kruger picked up a knobbly bit of stone, balancing it in his hand. He examined it curiously, half-smiling.

'This looks a funny sort of rock, Mr Struben. Is this what the gold comes from?'

'That is what the prospectors call "rotten reef", Your Honour. It is a conglomerate, a mixture. We are not yet sure about it. Some of it is undoubtedly gold-bearing; some of it is not. It is a new type of rock-formation in my experience, and there are indications of several reefs composed of this conglomerate running through the Witwatersrand. If they prove to contain payable gold it may mean the beginning of a very large gold-field. But we do not know yet, and this exhibition is not concerned with rotten reef but with the quartz reefs on Wilgespruit.'

Paul Kruger held up the mottled piece of rock for the others to see, pointing out the pebbled reef of rounded, water-worn fragments embedded in a cementlike matrix of sand and silica.

'See, gentlemen,' he rumbled. 'This is what Mr Struben calls "the conglomerate". Some call it "rotten reef". There may be gold in it. What does it look like to you? Do you not see this is truly a pudding stone? Look, the pebbles are the almonds sitting in the pudding. It is just like the pudding our wives make – the dish we call "banket". Our country is to be saved by a piece of banket!'

45

They all laughed, and pressed round Kruger and the lump of conglomerate, ejaculating their agreement.

'Truly, it is a piece of banket ... I must take some home for my children to suck ... It is surely not a *cheap* kind of sweet...!'

They went down the line of exhibits, chuckling and happy as schoolboys on a half-holiday excursion. Then they reached the small containers at the end of the table, their laughter and joking subsided. Now their eyes gleamed with a pleasure more than merriment.

'Well, gentlemen,' Struben said. 'If you will be seated, I will ask Mr Dawson to show you what the quartz holds.'

They slumped into the chairs, silent now; leaned forward, fascinated, as the assayer took a few pieces of reef, explaining how these had been specially selected because of their richness, showing them how the gold particles nestled sparkling in the quartz. He went through a simple process of crushing and smelting, the vapour from the crucible mingling with the thick, pungent fumes of raw pipe tobacco. At the end of his demonstration he had in the bottom of the crucible a small button of gold and silver amalgam.

Harry Struben picked it out carefully, holding it aloft between thumb and forefinger, like a magician at the end of a conjuring trick. He emphasized that it was an exceptional sample that could yield so much gold, and that the average reef was nothing like as rich. He passed the gleaming marble to the President. Kruger took it in the palm of his hand, astonished at its sudden weight.

'It is too heavy, Mr Struben. It is not natural for such a small thing to be so heavy.'

'The weight is the measure of its value, Your Honour. It must be heavy and strong to support the burden of all the world's trade that rests on it.'

'A small sin can weigh as heavily as that sometimes, mynheer. Let us hope that it does not increase the burden on my shoulders. We have seen what it can make of men in the Eastern Transvaal, and what sort of men it can bring into my country. Now you must tell us more about it.'

Struben described how the gold-bearing reef ran under the surface of the ground, showing itself in quartz outcrops, then dipping into the earth – how deep, no man knew. He told them of the work done by his brother, prospecting and mining along the whole length of the Witwatersrand for sixteen months. Fred Struben had traced the reef over the three farms they owned in a continuous line for a distance of twelve miles. A number of shafts had been sunk, some as deep as seventy feet. Tunnels had been dug from the shafts, and where they intersected the reef it had shown a greater content of gold at the lowest depths than at the surface; in some places it increased in width as it went down. The angles ranged from sixty to eighty degrees of dip.

Struben went on to tell his audience that he and his brother intended to work as many of the properties in their possession as they could at their own cost. Machinery had been ordered and would soon be out. He recommended those who could manage it to open up their properties and farms either individually or in small workable companies of moderate capital. In that way they would keep the money in the country and not hand everything over to speculators who formed gigantic companies with foreign capital – which, the Eastern Transvaal had shown, did not pay dividends, and brought the country into disrepute.

'And now, Your Honour and gentlemen,' said Harry Struben, 'I must take this opportunity of impressing on you the duty of the government to foster and protect the mining industry, in the era which is opening up before us, by wise legislation ...

'I trust that the Raad will so legislate this session upon the important question of the revision of the Gold Law that proprietary rights will be fully defined, acknowledged and protected and no excessive duties or royalties will be levied that will cripple the mining industry.'

The men before Struben shifted a little uneasily in their chairs, their eyes on the bulky, top-hatted figure in their centre. Kruger's little eyes flickered to and fro beneath the porch of his hat, avoiding direct contact with Struben who was looking hard at him.

'It is going to be a very expensive business, this gold-mining on the Witwatersrand,' said Struben bluntly. 'There will be nothing easy about it. But if you look after it, it will look after you. The digger, the man who exploits the mineral resources and consumes the agricultural produce of the country, should be encouraged and protected as long as he proves himself a law-abiding citizen.

'It is at this moment that I urge the President and the Volksraad with all my heart to abolish the system of con-

47

cessions and throw the government lands open to the digger. And to express the thoughts of my brother and me in the future of this region, we intend to call our discovery the Confidence Reef.'

Harry Struben sat down in a silence as heavy as the sombre faces before him. There was no applause. Kruger slumped in his chair, chin sunk on chest in the characteristic pose of misleading somnolence.

That's shaken them (thought Struben); I hope I haven't overdone it. But somebody had to tell them, and there'll never be a better opportunity outside the Volksraad.

He kept his eyes on the President who, looking briefly about him with that slow, shifting glance, was getting ponderously to his feet, leaning heavily on the arms of his chair. Without raising his eyes from the golden pebble lying on the table before him, he said, evenly and impassively:

'On behalf of the Volksraad and the people of the South African Republic I would like to thank Mr Struben for the exhibition of the wealth of the country and for his statement. It may be that he and I have different ideas about the ownership of that wealth and the rights of the Uitlanders who come here in the hope of making themselves rich without very much thought for enriching the country; but I assure him that he can depend upon the protection and assistance of the government for those who intend to develop the mining wealth of the State.'

CHAPTER FIVE

Down in Kimberley, where most of the shrewdest, many of the most unscrupulous and some of the greatest brains in the country were concentrated, the small voices of the Strubens were overwhelmed by the shouting from Barberton and the ever-present din from the diamond diggings. But they did not pass altogether unheard. One day, shortly after the Union Club demonstration, a telegram arrived at the Kimberley Club addressed to J. B. Robinson, one of the town's leading citizens and one of the sharpest and most fearless operators South Africa has ever produced. It read:

DISCOVERY MADE ABOUT THIRTY MILES PRE-
TORIA OF CONGLOMERATE SHEDDING GOLD
STOP THINK IT WORTH YOUR WHILE YOU
COME AND SEE STOP ENDS

It was a hard gem in the rubbish of rumour which poured into Kimberley from wherever men searched for and found the treasure of the earth. But it was all sieved and selected, and the choicest items inevitably reached the ears of Cecil John Rhodes, who had arrived on the diamond fields in 1871 as a lanky, fair-haired anaemic boy of eighteen and in ten years had risen to control the De Beers Mining Company.

At a time when reports from the Witwatersrand were beginning to attract attention, Rhodes was locked in a struggle for control of the diamond fields. Opposite him was ranged the Kimberley Mine, its shareholders headed by Barney Barnato. Barnato was a young Whitechapel Jew who had arrived in South Africa in 1872 and whose first public appearance had been heralded by this notice in the *Cape Argus* of September 17, under the headline SIGNOR BARNATO:

'This wizard performed last night in the Mutual Hall before a tolerably full house, and at once made himself a favourite with the audience. Some of his tricks were very clever and elicited continuous applause. We recommend all to see him.'

Barney Barnato had got into the act on his first evening in South Africa. He was never to get out of it. With the proceeds of his tolerably full house he bought himself a stock of cigars, and headed for the diamond fields. Exchanging his cigars by devious processes for shares and claims he gradually acquired control of the Kimberley Mine, so that by 1880 he and Rhodes stood face to face in the final struggle for virtual control of the world's diamond market.

There was never any doubt about who would win. Barnato wanted money and position for their own sakes. To Rhodes they were essential assets in the attainment of that great imperial vision which had come to him as he contemplated the vastness and emptiness of Africa which stretched to every horizon around the diggings. He would fill these great barren spaces on the map of Africa with massive daubs of red – a bright, Victorian, pillar-box red all the way from Cape to Cairo. His interpretation of the Divine Plan in which he believed implicitly – and in himself as its chosen instrument – was that 'the British are the first race in the world, and the more of the world we inhabit the better it is for the human race'.

Diamonds were but the stepping-stones to his grand objective; so were the people who supported or opposed him. If he could not deal with them – and the means were always quite insignificant compared with the end – he crushed them just as coldly and impersonally.

Among the men who stood in his way to the north was Paul Kruger, the new President of the South African Republic. Unlike most of the others who milled around the colossus of Kimberley, Kruger believed as firmly if less arrogantly as Rhodes in his own Divine mission as the chosen leader of God's chosen people – the Afrikaners. Their meeting was a meeting of the irresistible force and the immovable object – an apt enough description of the two personalities – though the historic recognition of their opposed destinies was missing from their first brief encounter in Bechuanaland, where the Boers looked as though they would establish themselves across the road to Matabeleland and Mashonaland.

'That young man,' Kruger subsequently told his friends, 'will cause me trouble if he does not leave politics alone and turn to something else. Well, the racehorse is swifter than the ox, but the ox can draw the greater loads. We shall see.'

Rhodes left no recorded comment on a fateful moment in time.

As reports of the Strubens' activities and other discoveries on the Witwatersrand percolated through, Rhodes was inclined to be sceptical and disinterested. His mind was concentrated on the struggle with Barnato and the great amalgamation that was to end in the formation of De Beers Consolidated. It was a struggle that lasted two years. In the meantime Johannesburg had been born with Rhodes, almost against his will, attending at the confinement.

It was out of curiosity more than anything else that Rhodes, in August, 1885, sent Gardner Williams, an American mining engineer in his employ, to see the Strubens and inspect their Confidence Reef. He rode briefly, and a little contemptuously, over the line of outcrops on Wilgespruit, Sterkfontein and Kromdraai; he examined the rock the Strubens were busy crushing; then he went back to Kimberley and wrote out an adverse report. Rhodes, for the time being, put gold and the Witwatersrand out of his mind.

The only practical result of the Union Club exhibition was the signing of a deed of concession by the Transvaal Government granting to Fred Struben the mining rights on 3,000 acres of the farm Wilgespruit for an annual payment of £550, with the right to commute payment to a royalty of two-and-a-half per cent of the value of metals or minerals recovered. As a mining concession it proved to be worthless; Struben was wrong, and although he showed the way to the Witwatersrand gold-fields, the ultimate truth was not his revelation. There was no payable gold in Wilgespruit.

On the high-veld, of which the tumbled ridge of white waters was the central feature, the green of the summer grass faded to yellow and sparkled whitely with the first frosts; valley and plain filled with the hazy aftermath of the annual veld-burning. The Boers continued their pastoral lives – hunting, herding their long-horned cattle, preparing the unwilling soil for the next planting of mealies. In between they filled the slow minutes of coffee-drinking gossip with clouds of pipe-smoke and speculation about the rocky reefs which ran through their farms and which had suddenly acquired a meaning which the good earth had never held for them before.

All through the winter of 1885 the main stream of the gold-seekers passed as quickly as they could over the bitter ridges of the watershed to the warmth and excitement and easier pickings of Barberton and the De Kaap valley – booming like a Californian gold-rush.

At Wilgespruit, Fred Struben pursued his conviction down into the rock and soil. But doubts were stirring in his mind as he waited for the five-stamp battery he had ordered to come and crush out the truth.

Among the visitors who came regularly to learn or to advise was Jan Meyer, Government appointed *Veld Kornet* in the Heidelberg District. He examined the rock-pile ready for the crushing plant, and told Struben bluntly that he had got hold of the wrong stuff, that he would find much higher values in the rotten reef – or 'banket', which had become the popular name for the conglomerate outcrops.

By the end of the year another battery was pounding away on the farm Steynskraal, just south of Heidelberg. A few months before that, Veld-Kornet Meyer, who combined prospecting freely and ideally with his official duties of census-taking, surveying and erecting beacons, had approached Mr Bezuidenhout, owner of the farm Doornfontein, and tried to get from him a prospecting licence for the high ridge running through his farm where the densely populated suburb of Berea now lifts its skycraping buildings above the line of the hills. Bezuidenhout turned him down.

The year 1885 marked the end of the old order of things on the Witwatersrand and in the South African Republic. The rock-strewn hills, the bush-covered kloofs and the wide valleys would never be the same again; neither would the people who lived in them. It was a gradual, almost a subconscious process and it went on virtually unrecognized by the republican government or by the outside world.

Throughout the first half of 1886 it was the Eastern

Transvaal and Barberton in particular that stole the head-lines in newspapers all round the world. Pockets of fabulous wealth were revealed almost every week in the wild hills above Swaziland, and the location of fairly extensive reefs, with some prospect of a longer life than the alluvial offered, induced a considerable inflow of investment moneys.

Advertisements appearing in the coastal and more south-erly newspapers, quoting fares by stage-coach from Kim-berley to the Transvaal gold-fields, made no mention of the Witwatersrand. Struben and his Confidence Reef, the demonstration before the President, all were forgotten. From Kimberley to Potchefstroom, £7; from Potchefstroom to Pretoria, £3-10-0; from Pretoria to Barberton, £8-10-0. Half-way between Potchefstroom and Pretoria the gold-seekers, lurching and swaying and cursing their discomfort, passed over the greatest gold deposit in the world.

In the City of London news from the Eastern Transvaal excited a fresh burst of speculation and buying on the Stock Exchange – but the Witwatersrand was never mentioned. By the beginning of December, 1885, an exceptional interest had developed in Transvaal shares, and rapid advances had been made in prices of almost every enterprise – mining, industrial and commercial – connected with the republic.

An investigation conducted by the financial correspon-dent of the *Weekly Review* in the City revealed some signi-ficant and unexpected explanations. One was that the bank-rupt condition of the South African Republic and the diffi-culties being experienced by President Kruger in raising money would make it impossible for the government to carry on. This factor, allied to the return to power of Lord Salisbury following the collapse of the Gladstone ministry and the swing to Conservatism throughout England, en-couraged investors to believe that the South African Repub-lic would soon revert to the British Crown, voluntarily or under compulsion. Share prices rose accordingly.

Still there was no mention of the Witwatersrand, whose golden reefs were to invalidate the economic reasons for the return of the republic to the stable administration of the Crown at the same time as they were to make the republic infinitely more worth having.

CHAPTER SIX

The year 1885 had not been a good one for the South African Republic and its inhabitants. Paul Kruger and his government were glad when it came to an end.

On the Western frontier a vassal chieftain at the head of the Koranna tribe had refused to pay taxes and had virtually rebelled against the central authority in Pretoria. In the punitive action which followed under Commandant-General Joubert the Boers had lost fourteen men killed and over thirty wounded. It was a high percentage. The Koranna had suffered heavy losses and the tribe had been broken up.

The President was worried about the slow progress being made in his obessive scheme for the railway line linking his capital with Delagoa Bay that would seal his independence of the British and their South African colonies. Three railway lines had snaked up to the borders of his republic through Natal, the Orange Free State and the northern Cape. He refused them all permission to enter the Transvaal. Yet his own railway was barely inching its way out of the low-veld of the Portuguese territory in the east.

Money was the big difficulty. Kruger could hardly remember the time when it had not been. The finances of the republic could not have been in a worse condition. The Standard Bank's credit – and probably its patience – was exhausted, and its directors refused to advance any more funds without adequate security.

The President himself made several circular tours through his far-flung communities urging his dispirited and poverty-stricken countrymen not to lose courage, enabling them by direct contact to share his own massive faith and indomitable will.

The year 1886 stretched ahead of them with all its fears and bleak uncertainty, mounting pressure from within and without. Kruger's message was always the same. The Lord had led them through the perils of the wilderness to their promised land. He would not forsake them now, as long as they had faith.

The year 1886 ...

As Paul Kruger rattled and jolted back to Pretoria in his mule cart he must have prayed hard for the miracle that would change all those minuses in the State budget into plusses. Yet, when the miracle happened, it was the wrong one.

Deep in the heart of the year the barren ridges of the Witwatersrand would at last unlock their secret, revealing the greatest treasure on earth.

The wrong miracle?

That was how Paul Kruger and many of his associates saw it. In 1902 Kruger – a broken, tired old man dragging out his last years in the sanctuary of Holland, to which he had fled at the end of his grim struggle with the might of the British Empire in the Boer War – asked his biographer:

'Can we look upon the discovery of the Witwatersrand gold-fields as fortunate for the Republic?'

He answered the question himself: 'I tell you, "No!" Gold and the embittered feelings left behind by the British annexation of 1877 are the causes of the present misery in South Africa. Of the two, gold was the worst influence. It is quite certain that had no gold been found in the Transvaal there would have been no war. No matter how great the influx of Englishmen and other Uitlanders to the Republic, no matter how varied and manifold their complaints, the British Government would not have lifted a finger in their defence had they not been tempted by the wealth of the country. The question of the franchise which in reality caused no hardship to foreigners was made use of by intriguers to further their plans. I was myself with General Joubert when a burgher came along, bursting with the news that a new gold-reef had been discovered. I remember the General's words – "Instead of rejoicing," he said, "you would do better to weep; for this gold will cause our country to be soaked in blood." I tell you, Joubert knew the heart of man; and he knew the English.'

The year 1886 ... The tangled threads of destiny were being detached from the spinning-wheel to form a first vague pattern that was suddenly to leap into violent life as

55

Johannesburg. In the confused web of events and personalities two threads converged with a moment of time and fate to produce one of the accidents that determine the future of man.

The lives of George Harrison and George Walker were insignificant in themselves. They were products of a century of change in which many of the great secrets of the world were being opened up by the explorers, and made ready for exploitation by the materialist society of the industrial revolution. It was the age of the adventurers, and whether they were great men or great rogues or just camp-followers depended essentially on the quality of their inspiration and the magnitude of their ruthlessness and unscrupulousness.

Walker and Harrison could never hope to be anything but camp-followers; their ambitions in dishonesty never rose much beyond the 'findings-takings' class, or the occasional tall story for the sake of temporary gain.

In this respect they were outclassed by the men whose fate was so closely linked with their own – the great Rand-lords, as they came to be known, who built empires of money and men and land – but who all had to wait for Harrison and Walker.

The obscurity of these two lives is reflected in the little that is known of them before their brief meeting with history. Harrison was an Australian gold-digger who found his chosen career so spasmodically rewarding that he had to develop other talents to stay alive. He became a jack-of-all-trades and a competent mason. In January, 1876, he makes an appearance on the record which he might well have preferred to be without even if he had known how indispensable it was to history.

He had gone to New York from the West with the proceeds of six months' prospecting in his pocket. Down in the waterfront saloons and gambling dens he had drunk too much, which was excusable; and flashed too much money around, which was not. Lurching along the dark alleyways of the docks area he had been an easy prey for the hoodlums of the district. He regained consciousness in the forecastle of a sailing ship, well out to sea and penniless.

Harrison had no love for the sea or its sailing ships. To him it was just a lot of water inconveniently separating the gold-bearing places of the earth. He liked the feel of a pick or hammer and the solid rock beneath them – with a fortune waiting at the end of every blow. He would jump ship at the first port of call . . .

When Harrison saw the great, flat mass of rock come up over the eastward horizon he knew it was Cape Town, and was glad. South Africa was a country he could use, and which could use him. It was not difficult. He just walked off the ship and kept on walking, setting his feet on the long trail to the north that was to end in a great new city and the birth of a nation.

The other George – Walker – was no different from millions of his fellow men. He was born in Wigan, Lancashire, in 1853, and like so many others who were fed up with the soul-destroying life of the labourer and mill-hand in England, had emigrated to South Africa in his early twenties after reports of diamonds at Kimberley and gold in the Eastern Transvaal had begun to appear in the papers.

Walker, ill-equipped with knowledge, skill and the indispensable luck, became what many became when their dream of easy wealth had faded into the reality of hunger. From prospecting and digging he turned to odd jobs, hanging around the successful claims, pursuing the latest strike or rumours of strikes, earning enough to eat a little and drink a little more, to keep his boots repaired for the next long walk.

It was at the beginning of December, 1885, that George Walker set off from the Free State farm where he had been resting following a long spell down on the Swaziland border. He was broke again, and it was time to go back to the diggings and the new boom town of Barberton. Perhaps this would be the time; perhaps this time he'd strike it rich.

He headed north for the long range of the Witwatersrand where the road from Kimberley to the gold-fields dropped down through the Boer capital at Pretoria. That was the best chance of getting a lift on one of the numerous supply wagons.

At about the same time as Walker set off on his return to Barberton, George Harrison packed his few belongings and his handyman's kit that would do just as well for building a wall as digging a mine, and threw them on to an ox-wagon that was leaving Kimberley for Pretoria.

He was finished with the diamond diggings. There was no room at Kimberley for the small man. Those two fellows from England, Rhodes and Barnato, were buying up every claim in sight. Pretty soon they would own the whole place and everybody in it. Besides, if he was going to dig for anything, it would be gold. Diamonds were for women. He would go back to the Eastern Transvaal where the gold was, where the jobs were.

The wagon carrying Harrison and his kit arrived at the last outspan before Pretoria. George curled up in his blanket that night a little more cosily than usual, already aware, though it was nearly mid-summer, of the cold night air at 6,000 feet. He hoped he would soon find transport on to Barberton. He had just about enough money left to get him there; he couldn't afford to hang about.

Just as he was dropping off to sleep he heard the stranger arrive at the outspan, and the gruff but hospitable exchange of greetings, the inevitable invitation to have a cup of coffee – prelude to the rumble of subdued gossip as news of people and events were exchanged.

The first noise of the morning – the 'boys' calling the names of the oxen as they were marshalled into their positions on either side of the long trek chains – awoke the outspan. The early mist of a high-veld morning mingled with the first smoke of the camp-fire, for which the wood had been carried all the way from the Vaal River to this treeless upland.

Harrison pulled on his boots, rubbed his eyes and scratched his head reflectively at the prospect of another day and an uncertain future. He fumbled in his kitbag for his mug and then moved slowly over to the fire where two or three men stood sucking alternately at their coffee and their pipes, filling the air with the aroma of both.

'Well, damn me!' said a voice still resonant of Lancashire. 'It's George Harrison. What brings you here?'

'Walker! Blimey, where've you been, cobber? Last I heard of you, you were half-dead of that low-veld fever. How are you?'

The two men shook hands warmly. They were of the status of friends in misfortune since neither had had the luck – nor the ability and determination to make the luck come to them. They shared a lost hope, a dwindling sense of purpose. Their independence had gone, along with their dreams and illusions. They had become the hirelings of other men – for a month or a day, a year or an hour. It was in this that their comradeship lay. They had no awareness of the part they had been selected to play and for which they had been led to this meeting-place.

Standing there by the fire, away from the smoke drift, their hands clasped round steaming mugs, they bartered reminiscence for reminiscence, restoring the balance of experience each with the other, discovering their common intention of crossing the watershed and returning to the goldfields.

Their tongues and thoughts fastened on the latest gossip that afforded profitable conjecture. Down in Kimberley, and to a lesser extent in the other Afrikaner republic of the Orange Free State, rumours had been percolating for months of gold at Rustenburg and Heidelberg and, lately, on the ridge of the Witwatersrand. The activities of the Strubens were well-known, and the recent proclamation of the farm Kromdraai as a public diggings had lent some sort of official confirmation to stories that nobody quite believed. Attention, in Britain as well as in South Africa, was still focused on the big strikes at Barberton and in the De Kaap valley. The Witwatersrand was just not the sort of place to find gold.

As the talk drifted around the wood-smoke, the sun came up over the flat rim of the plateau, clear and with a warm promise of the heat of the day to come.

'Y'see where yon sun's coming up, George,' said Walker. 'That's about where Barberton is.'

'It's a bloody long way, all right.'

'And what do we do when we get there?' Walker went on. 'Work twelve hours a ruddy day for somebody like as not who won't be able to pay us at the end of the month!'

'Oh, I dunno, cobber. What was that bloke in Kimberley telling me a few weeks back? About all them nuggets in the De Kaap. Thousands of quids' worth in one hour off of one claim. Said he read it in the papers. Still, it's a bloody long way to Barberton.'

'Hullo!' Walker said suddenly. 'Look over yonder, George. That weren't here last time we passed.'

He pointed off to the north-west, where through a cleft in the ridge they could see a shack with smoking chimney near a curious structure around which men were moving busily.

The transport rider came and stood alongside them.

'That's Wilgespruit – Fred Struben's place,' he told them. 'That must be the new five-stamp battery that arrived for him a week or two ago. I brought the first parts up for him myself. He's got a heap of reef there waiting to be crushed. Reckon he'll make a fortune out of it. They tell me he's having a devil of a time getting that battery erected. Nobody except Fred himself knows how to put it together.'

'A five-stamp battery,' Walker murmured, half to himself. 'That's a big mill, for a place where there isn't supposed to be any gold.'

He turned to Harrison.

'George, we can put a battery together. How about it? Shall we try Struben? It'll save us a bit of a walk, and the grub won't be any worse.'

'Not me, cobber. That sort of stuff's not in my line. Digging, yes. Bricks and mortar, yes. But no clambering up and down those girders.'

'Hell, there's nothing like that about it, George. We're not making a bridge. Just a matter of tightening up some nuts and bolts and putting a bit of corrugated iron over the top.'

Harrison hesitated a little; then he said: 'Well, if you've made up your mind to go to Struben's I might as well come along. He could probably find something for me to do.'

The transport rider said quickly: 'If you're a mason, Mr Harrison, I know somebody who's looking for one. If you go on to Langlaagte, the widow Oosthuizen wants to put up a house for her son. He rode over the last time I came through to ask if I knew anybody who could do it. Of course, that was about a month ago. She may have found somebody by now.'

'How far is Langlaagte?' Harrison asked.

'About ten miles due east. You walk that way for about two hours and then start asking for the widow Oosthuizen's farm. Her name's Petronella, I think. The son's called Hendrik. But she's the one with the money. It's her you want to see.'

'That sounds a good proposition to me,' Harrison said. He turned to Walker. 'Tell you what, George. You go over to that Struben place, and I'll go and see Petronella. Then if you don't get fixed up, come on over to Langlaagte. If there's nothing doing with the widow, I'll join you at Struben's.'

Walker nodded. 'If we don't see each other for a bit we'll know we're both at work.'

'That's it. Well, no use mucking about here. I'll be getting along. You know where to find me, cobber. Drop over for tea one day.'

The two men gathered their bundles together, hefted them on their backs, shook hands with the transport rider, gave each other a brief salute and strode off in opposite directions into the morning.

Now a train of events had been set in motion which was immutable and inexorable. Time and place had been determined, and the instruments chosen. Still the shadows cast before stayed unrecognized though their presence was felt by all on whom they fell. The fever infected the staid inhabitants of the Witwatersrand as they blundered about the farms and kloofs, pecking at the pink and black oxidized outcrops which they had been told were the surface indications of hidden gold.

It was an attitude of mind rather than a pursuit of reality, and its first impact was on the restrictive clauses in the Gold Law which discouraged prospectors from searching and landowners from encouraging prospectors.

The centre of the new activity was Heidelberg, where Veld-Kornet Meyer had convinced the Boers in his Ward that the yellow grass which provided such meagre fodder for their cattle was sprung from a soil rich in the yellow metal which would make them independent of cattle and crops for the rest of their lives. The words 'banket' and 'rotten reef' replaced the weather and mealies as standard topics of conversation among the Witwatersrand farmers.

Meyer began to instruct them in the intricacies of the Gold Law and its recent amendments. As a result they started to put pressure on Kruger and his executive to allow them to operate more freely.

But banket and rotten reef were still no substitute for the visible gold of the Eastern Transvaal. Johannesburg would have to wait.

Down in the low-veld the diggers were getting more and more irascible. Now their anger and frustration were concerned more with practical grievances than with the political bitterness which had inspired their discontent after the annexation, and which would do so again.

The eastern gold-fields had become an important asset of the republic. So had the diggers, and others whom the diggers attracted. This was acknowledged, however reluctantly, by all Boers to whom the new population offered a profitable outlet for their produce.

During the last quarter of 1884 government revenue from diggers' licences was £46. In the last quarter of 1885 the same source had supplied £1,900. In July, 1885, the republic's account with the Standard Bank had been overdrawn to the extent of £34,000 and all payments from the Treasury had been stopped. By the end of December the overdraft had been reduced to £5,000; a month later the Government was out of the red – and beginning to count the gold.

President and administration knew full well where the money was coming from. They had taken good care of that. If Uitlanders wanted to come and look for gold, they had to pay for the privilege; if they wanted to eat and drink, that was a privilege too – as were all their other requirements. High tariffs on everything that came across the borders, plus cash from the sale of concessions for retailing them and on local manufacture, assured a steady stream of money into the coffers of the republic; and a steady stream of complaints and blasphemies from the diggings and the new towns the diggings brought to life.

Kruger wasn't really worried about the petitions which began to come in from Heidelberg and Klip River and Paardekraal. They were his own burghers and, besides, the possibilities were still based on rumour. The Strubens had not produced anything of value to the country. The banket reefs were still of less worth than kitchen banket – which could at least be eaten.

It was from the Eastern Transvaal that the money and the complaints were coming, and it was to Barberton that the President set off in his mule cart one day in March, 1886. On Langlaagte, at the same time, George Harrison had just about finished the new house for the widow Oosthuizen's son, Hendrik.

Kruger arrived at Barberton on the evening of March 16. At 9 o'clock the next morning he attended a public meeting at which the Diggers' Committee laid before him a list of the community's most urgent needs:

1. The amendment of the Gold Law of 1885 to further facilitate prospecting and the development of mining.

2. Representation of the gold-fields in the Volksraad.

3. The holding of regular circuit courts in the Fields.

4. Reduction of excessive taxation, and especially that on

timber for mining purposes.

5. Introduction of a law against pegging out claims by power of attorney.

6. A more secure tenure of ground on which capital had been expended.

Kruger listened, solemn and poker-faced, as the members of the committee made their case. Beyond the shade of the great wild-fig tree under which the table and chairs had been placed, the diggers stood orderly in the strong sunlight as the shadows of the peaks withdrew from the motley huts and stores and rubbled shafts of Barberton. Occasionally they rumbled away in an alliance of articulate approval. Even at Barberton, nine o'clock in the morning was a little early to be drunk.

When the delegates had had their say the President rose to a great burst of applause. He stood there unsmiling, not conceding anything to this alien crowd. He spoke briefly, in Hollands, addressing himself to the interpreter rather than to the meeting.

'His Honour assures you of his warmest support and assistance – in everything except the reduction of taxation.'

Kruger waited, head bowed not in humility but like a buffalo ready to charge, as waves of disapproval and dissent beat against the rock of his presence. Committee members waved their hands for silence as they saw slow anger mounting to his face. As the noise subsided the President looked up, expecting the silence. When it came his voice rolled over the crowd – in English:

'You must not ask me to work for you and cut off my hands at the same time!'

He lowered himself back into his chair. For a few moments the tension of uncertainty hung heavy in the air. The committee looked anxious, waiting for the first insult that would inspire the first brick. That would be the end of them and of their diggings, the start of God-knows-what. One of the delegates, called Browning, rose to his feet.

'Gentlemen,' he called loudly. 'Before the meeting ends I propose the toast of "The Ladies".'

The diggers roared their delight and acclamation. Unfortunately, there were no ladies present.

It was nearing the end of the month when Kruger, completing his slow round of outlying farms on his way back from the low-veld, came in sight once more of the rugged skyline of the Witwatersrand. Where the road forked, offering the choice of Pretoria or Heidelberg, the mule cart halted. Now that he had made his contact with the diggers and explained to their leaders some of the financial necessities of the republic, his thoughts were switched to the new prospects opened up by recent petitions and the reports of Veld-Kornet Meyer.

These were his own people. Was this then the miracle which the Lord would surely send to deliver them? He would go and see for himself. The mules' heads turned south-west along the track to Heidelberg.

That night the President met Meyer and others of his officials together with representatives of the farming community. The evidence was accumulating that the district was gold-bearing. Outcrops of rotten reef had been traced along a regular line, and assays had confirmed their gold content. But did the burghers really want their land proclaimed as a gold-field with all that it implied in diggers and touts, the rape of their Transvaal earth?

By this time most of the burghers had either turned prospectors themselves or were partners in small syndicates eager to investigate and exploit the golden potential of the whole area. They left him in no doubt that they had no objections whatever.

What they did not want was a repetition of the consequences of previous proclamations, such as that at Kromdraai where the prospector and digger had virtually been eliminated by the restrictive clauses in the Gold Law. Nor were there many farmers in a position to pay in advance the fee of five shillings per morgen which was the annual charge for a mining lease from the government.

Kruger, anticipating the course of events, advised them to send a petition to the Volksraad stating their grievances and the remedies they suggested. Once again he assured his listeners of full and sympathetic consideration.

On the same day – Wednesday, March 31 – Kruger left Heidelberg to return to Pretoria. He instructed the landdrost to send a telegram to the State Secretary informing the executive of his departure and that he would arrive in the capital at 10.30 a.m. on Friday morning. He would spend the intervening night at the widow Strydom's farm on the Witwatersrand. The President was very conscious of the honours due to his high office, and he was giving the State Secretary plenty of opportunity of providing them.

That night Mrs Strydom told Kruger of the discovery on Langlaagte....

CHAPTER SEVEN

It was the first Sunday morning of that March. George Harrison sat on top of a koppie which rose out of the flat valley of Langlaagte. Directly below him lay the stone walls and hollow-eyed windows of the new house. He lifted his gaze across the long flats of waving grass, the brief green of the summer rain already disappearing with the sap, and saw how the land fell away down the steps of the Klip River Berg and Heidelberg to the broken country where the Vaal River had carved its course all the way to the Orange and the Atlantic. Beyond the Vaal was the Free State, and beyond that the Cape Province. Just behind him rose the main ridge of the Witwatersrand, cutting out further contemplation of the infinity of empty land and empty sky.

Harrison knew that if he glanced over his right shoulder he would see the nek through which the track ran to the Strubens' place at Wilgespruit. He had heard they were packing up there. The reef was not payable. Perhaps it was all just talk. Underground streams of gold: those early Boers may have been right – they would rather have streams of water.

Now the story was that Struben was interested in Braamfontein, the big farm almost adjoining Langlaagte on the north. Poor George Walker hadn't lasted long with Struben. Still, old George was a bit of a lead-swinger, all right! That would be him now, coming over the brow of the rise at the western end of Doornfontein ...

Harrison looked down on the Oosthuizen house that had sprung from the rock and earth and his own hands. The triangles of the roof timbers were in place and the sheets of corrugated iron lay in ready piles.

'I should have got a bottle of brandy from the widow,' Harrison murmured, 'to christen the roof. It would have

66

been just right for today. But George'll have some, for sure.'

He stood up, stretched himself and started a quick descent of the koppie timed to arrive at the farmhouse just ahead of Walker from the other side. It was a little too quick for legs which had lost their nimbleness. At the bottom of the slope he tripped over a boulder concealed beneath the grass, and fell headlong.

Ponderous and blaspheming, he struggled to his feet and saw the dislodged piece of rock. Furious, he lifted it up and dashed it against its parent outcrop. He was about to give one of the fragments a kick when his foot was stayed by the yellow sparkle which blinked up at him.

'Iron pyrites,' he said aloud. 'That fool's gold can't fool *this* digger any more.'

Nevertheless he bent down and picked up the offending rock, holding it obliquely to the sun. It flashed back at him like a message from a heliograph. To Harrison the message was unmistakable.

'By God! *It's gold!*'

He scrabbled around furiously in the grass for the other segments, studying each piece carefully in a mounting excitement. Then, with a lump in each hand, he ran to the house where Walker was waiting for him, puzzled and expectant.

'What happened, George? I saw you fall. Did you hurt —'

'Take a look at this. Tell me what you think of it.'

Walker took the out-thrust rock and examined it critically from every angle. A low whistle escaped his lips as he looked up at Harrison, who could not restrain himself when he saw the confirmation on his friend's face.

'Have you ever seen anything like it?' he blurted out.

'Can't be; it can't be!' Walker kept saying. 'It must be pyrites —'

'I tell you it's gold! You think I can't tell the difference by now? Anyway, I can see you know what it is.'

'Well, I've never seen this amount in reef before. But we can soon find out. Where'd this come from?'

Harrison pointed to the outcrop sticking out of the veld about 200 yards away.

'Then let's take some more samples,' said Walker, 'and crush and pan them. You get your hammer.'

Harrison went to one of the empty rooms of the house in which he had rigged up a rough shelter. From his kit he took his geologist's hammer, and together the two men walked across to the spot where the Australian had fallen. For a quarter of an hour they moved about chipping at the solid outcrops and picking up the flaked rock that surrounded them. With hands and pockets and shirt fronts bulging they went back to the farmhouse.

'The next thing,' said Walker, 'is crushing it. Got any tools?'

'We'll find something. There's plenty of junk lying around.'

They went off in opposite directions to search the farmyard. In a few minutes they were back, Harrison with an old plough-share and Walker with a large, rusted bolt. They made a careful selection of some of the more promising bits of reef and placed them in the curve of the share. Hammering away with alternate blows it took them a good half-hour to reduce the rock to a suitable mixture of gravel and powder.

'Now what?' Walker asked. 'How do we pan it?'

'My frying-pan. I'll make a few kinks in the side. That'll do the trick.'

Soon Harrison was back with frying-pan and a bucket of water. They tipped the crushed rock into the pan and filled it with water. Harrison's hands and muscles, with the volition of long usage, went into the culminating movements of the prospector's quest. Round and round went the pan in intermittent circles, discharging at each stop its content of superfluous muck, pausing for the fresh water, then round and round again.

Both men held their breath as Harrison tipped out the last cupful of mud-saturated water. This was the moment before the moment. This was when they would know everything or nothing, when all of the future was condensed in one second of present time. They bent over the pan. Walker was the first to break the silence.

'God Almighty!' he whispered.

'I've never seen anything like it,' muttered Harrison. 'Not here, not in Australia, not in California. *Never anything like it.*'

He tilted the pan slowly from side to side. From the gilded bottom, where left-over grease from the morning's breakfast had caught and held the precious grains, the sun splashed back on two unbelieving faces. From the end of the last handful of rubbish was a tail of gold as long and thick as Harrison's middle finger.

BOOK TWO

The Raid

CHAPTER EIGHT

The year 1886 had come and gone; Johannesburg was taking shape on the ground at a pace just a little slower than the concept of it in men's minds. The surveyor's blueprint with its static, immutable lines was inadequate to deal with the influx of humanity that followed in the wake of the grain ships and packet boats which carried rumour and report round the globe ... was unequal to the earth and its deep streams of gold and the men who were determined to capture that yellow metal.

To the Witwatersrand had come not only the legions of gold-seekers, but men of great wealth, intelligence and vision who could see clearly that the nature and extent of the reefs guaranteed permanence to the structure of whatever community established itself along the outcrops.

Machinery and men in vast quantities would be needed, and with them all the paraphernalia of civilization and society. But even the men of vision could not see, at that stage, beyond a few hundred feet of underground gold and a few thousand men to dig it out of the reluctant conglomerate.

Nevertheless this concept of permanence made Johannesburg, from its very beginning, different to every other mining camp in the world. While the gold attracted every human element from every corner of the earth, its peculiarities demanded an organized operation and an organized community which could only function and prosper in conditions of law and order and under accepted rules of behaviour. At the top of the list of essentials, above the gold itself, were such things as food and water, health, housing, light, waste disposal and the civilizing links of good communications.

Since the Government, for its own reasons, would not at first give Johannesburg the benefit of recognition as an established community entitled to the protection of the State, the men on the spot had to make their own arrangements. The first manifestation of their intention and their determination, following a pattern adopted at Barberton and Kimberley, was the election of a Diggers' Committee. As this was, in effect, Johannesburg's first Town Council, their names deserve acknowledgment:

I. P. Ferriera (96 votes), J. S. Harrison (87), H. J. Morkel (74), Dr Hans Sauer (73), W. P. Fraser (64), J. E. Eloff (64), J. G. Maynard (65), T. Y. Sherwell (56), W. Bisset (54).

This established an area of contact and negotiation between Johannesburg and Pretoria which, while friendly enough on most occasions, emphasized the fundamental differences between the two institutions; differences of background, outlook, objectives, religion, philosophy, language, desires and appetites. There was no point of mutuality or understanding. The arrangement had nothing to do with liking or disliking. On a personal level there was a good deal more amity than discord, and a jovial camaraderie between Boer and digger that might have been the basis of a more complete fraternization if both sides had moved towards each other, or if they had not been caught up, because of the gold of the Witwatersrand, in the overwhelming pressure of world events.

The Mining Commissioner, Carl von Brandis, was the ideal man for the job of interpreting the Government's orders to the new population. They were as hard and conglomerate as the rock which imprisoned the gold, but they gave him their loyalty and respect in return for his. It was only behind von Brandis that the nebulous shape of the republic rose, unapproachable, alien, inimical, cause of all misfortune, target of all abuse. The executive felt much the same way about the Uitlanders.

It was in this sphere that the Press, as it so often has done, distilled and exaggerated the essence of disagreement and fomented the disgruntled mutterings of the mining community into something that was to become potent and explosive. As early as January, 1887, when Johannesburg was still in its swaddling clothes, the correspondent of the *Transvaal Advertiser* was writing:

'I see the members of the Volksraad are paid; in fact their patriotism and public spirit are to be measured by their fees, and I cannot for the life of me see why the nine elected members of the Diggers' Committee should not be paid by the State too. They expend a great deal more time on their duties than the nonentities who sit in the Volksraad.

'What a pity it is the Government authorities cannot do the graceful and initiate all these reforms which are being howled into their ears week after week instead of sitting stolidly by. These feeble-brained politicians had far better go back to their farms and their coffee and make room for more intelligent men who understand the wants of the nineteenth century, who comprehend the blessings of modern civilization, who know how to effect reforms and who are able to keep pace with this go-ahead age of steam and bustle.'

A more sophisticated and cynical society would not have paid much attention to this sort of diatribe. To Kruger and his burghers it was intolerable and, although he made no attempt to muzzle a freedom of expression which was one of the genuine tenets of the republic, the offence to his dignity and the insult to the State contained in these jibes accumulated to a mountain of resentment which, if it did not lead to the war, made the prevention of war impossible. The reaction of the Boers was fortified by the conviction that what they had done to the British at Majuba in 1881 they could do again at Johannesburg or anywhere else.

Although the Diggers' Committee had few powers, the Pretoria Government recognized its authority in matters of water rights and other local disputes, provided its members took the oath of allegiance to the South African Republic. This was done, in most cases, quite willingly.

There was plenty to do of a practical nature, but their real responsibility was limited to advising the Mining Commissioner and to carrying out the wishes and instructions which came through von Brandis from the central government.

But no restrictive legislation could deny the diggers the power to complain – and they had a good deal to complain about. The diggers, the great majority of whom came from countries where the democratic rights of the individual were well defined and acknowledged, made their demands known in voices loud enough to reach well beyond the Transvaal capital. They wanted revision of the Gold Law, cheaper licences, lower customs duties on food and machinery, adequate postal services; they wanted proper protection against increasing lawlessness, and a share of the revenue which was pouring into Pretoria from the mining community; and they wanted parliamentary representation.

Whatever Paul Kruger thought of the Witwatersrand population, and whatever he wished upon it, he could hardly continue to ignore its existence. All the forces of evil were undoubtedly congregating along the ridge of white waters – but the devils were proving highly remunerative! In 1884 the total Treasury revenue had been £161,595 and the expenditure £184,822. By the end of 1886, when the Witwatersrand gold-fields had begun to make their contribution, the comparative figures were £380,433 and £211,829. The changing situation, and the Government's opportunism, is vividly reflected in revenue returns for the first quarter of 1886 alongside those for the same period of 1887:

	1886	1887
Import Duties	£18,218	£43,608
Licences	£6,270	£13,698
Diggers' Licences	£1,331	£22,158
Prospectors' Licences	£40	£4,956
Stand Licences	—	£5,597
Mining Lease Tax	—	£2,528

When Kruger decided to pay an official visit to Johannesburg in February, 1887, it set the seal as far as the Government was concerned on its existence. Cut off from the new community by the Magaliesberg range and an unbridgeable gulf of the mind, the President could never quite believe that all this was really happening, or that Johannesburg was really there – thirty miles away.

Had he not passed across the barren ridges the previous winter? Little more than six months before! The farms had been empty then, the mealie fields bleak with stubble. The only changes he could visualize on the treeless flats of the high-veld were that the cattle would now be back on the summer grass and the brown patches of overturned earth hidden beneath the tall green of mealies sprouting their feathered head-dress. He could not conceive of the great city that would spring from the rubbled earth, or that the trenches which disfigured his beloved veld would be the foundations of tall buildings making canyons of the dusty streets.

Sometimes the President, sitting on his stoep with the future spread out before him, must have hoped that it was all a dream and that one morning he would be able to inspan his mules and drive again to Heidelberg and see only the scars of an alien invasion, see cattle grazing again among the debris of avarice and materialism; see only the wagons and scattered farmhouses of the Boers; hear only the familiar vowels and lazy consonants of 'the Taal'.

But the facts and figures were a new kind of dream, a reality of prosperity that the Voortrekkers could not have imagined – and probably would have turned aside from, if they had. Now they were no longer Voortrekkers. When you were trekking you did not need money; only guns and ammunition, grass and water, food and life. Now there was the Republic and the burghers; the State. And for that you had to have money. You would lose the State you had created if you could not pay to maintain it. You would lose it to the bankers and the Power behind the banks, whose representatives would walk in like bailiffs.

Well, the Boers now had the miracle they had been waiting for. And it was as much in humble recognition of the workings of the Lord who would deliver his people, as well as to make certain that the Uitlanders knew on which side the Lord was, that Kruger decided to make his call on the new gold-fields.

As the stream of fortune-seekers poured into the Transvaal from all points of the compass except the empty north, they gravitated to the new township not only because it was the Mecca of their hopes but because it was the only place on the Witwatersrand where they could hire a bed and buy a meal.

Johannesburg expanded naturally to accommodate them and their needs and weaknesses. By the time republican officials were riding round the many-peopled plains and ridges putting up notices heralding the Presidential visit, Johannesburg was already growing old in experience and was a hundred years ahead of the Boer capital in sophistication.

As the reed tents fell and the static wagons moved on, houses went up and womenfolk moved in with their men and families. Soon a community hall and school were paying their tribute to domesticity, fecundity and permanence.

Johannesburg had celebrated its first Christmas and New Year with an uninhibited Anglo-Saxon fervour that could almost be heard in the quiet, devout churches of Pretoria and Heidelberg; the storm that hit the township on New Year's Day, demolishing half the newly-erected buildings and scattering unsubstantial tin and canvas, was regarded by the rest of the republic as a demonstration of just retribution.

Johannesburg had had its first race meeting and its first cricket match, in which a Langlaagte eleven easily beat a team from Ferreira's Camp, and in doing so aroused a mixture of bewilderment and boredom among the Boer and American spectators which has survived to this day. Among the recorded onlookers was Mr Alfred Beit of Kimberley, who had come to the Rand to supervise the dissolution of his partnership with J. B. Robinson and to acquire some interests of his own.

If the surrounding farmers did not understand cricket or approve of other hobbies of the Uitlanders, they were not slow to appreciate some of their constant requirements. One of the first installations of the new administration was the morning market, and on February 1 the Market Master, Mr Papenfus, held his first sale.

Wagons streamed in from every district of the Transvaal, with mealies and mealie meal, onions, carrots, potatoes, forage and firewood. With mealies fetching 7s 9d a bag and firewood 28s a load, the Boers were delighted – particularly as they no longer had to make the long and arduous trek to Kimberley or Barberton to get rid of their produce.

They were incredulous, too, at the physical changes to the old farms Braamfontein, Doornfontein and Langlaagte, where they had been used to dropping-in on nephew Bezuidenhout or old uncle Oosthuizen for a cup of coffee and an hour of slow-moving talk. Now there were streets with names like Commissioner, Eloff, Rissik; buildings of brick and stone that made right-angled corners around which the long spans of oxen, as goggle-eyed with wonder as the small, black piccanins at their heads, swung awkwardly. Pretty soon, the Diggers' Committee thought, they would have to introduce traffic regulations and keep-to-the-left. It was a pity the planners had not made the streets wider.

Only in Commissioner Street was there room to make a full swing with a 16-ox span.

As the population and activity concentrated on Johannesburg, so the original camps disintegrated or were replaced by private-enterprise townships. The process of attrition was considerably speeded up by the new regulation that a canteen proprietor had to pay a licence fee of £50.

It was not long before the first club was formed. This was the Rand Club, one of the world's great meeting-places, whose present international reputation is in no small measure due to the fact that it has one of the longest bar-counters in the world. Even in the original brick and thatch club-house, there was plenty of elbow room.

The club was another Rhodes conception. Preferring always the company of men, and especially that of his social and financial equals, he found it most easily in the exclusively masculine atmosphere of a club such as he had set up in Kimberley.

Although Rhodes had missed his biggest opportunity on the Witwatersrand (through leaving there to go to the death-bed of a friend at the very moment Sauer was trying to persuade him to buy a big block of claims), the increasing activity in the new gold-fields of men like Robinson, Beit and Barnato had compelled him, still slightly doubtful, to become more active himself.

He paid frequent visits to the Rand and at the time of the sale of stands on Randjeslaagte his visionary mind had assessed part of the possibilities in the new discoveries. By February he had planned the details of his first gold-mining company, and dispatched Rudd to England to arrange the vast financial backing that he saw would be needed. He wrote to Rudd:

'Barberton has smashed up but Witwater is all right – there is little doubt that discovery of good things has only commenced – the belief in the Rand is increasing daily – Beit is here and so is Porges from Paris. They are investing heavily and have, with Robinson, driven up all prices and it is very difficult to purchase anything worth having; Robinson has given £16,000 for a property called Randfontein beyond Witpoort.

'Your business will be (1) to get as much money as you can, (2) to order a large quantity of machinery, (3) to draw a trust deed with very wide powers, (4) to obtain us a good remuneration or else the Company is not worth working for.'

Three days after the auction of stands Rhodes walked through the newly laid-out site of the township with Hans Sauer. The streets were still only avenues of alternate dust and mud between the posts and pegs marking sites and intersections, but already enterprising merchants and hoteliers were carting in building materials and adding new trenches for foundations to the questing holes of the prospectors. The two men walked along Commissioner Street, surrounded by the evidence of expansion and permanence. It looked as though Johannesburg was there to stay all right. Well, if it was, they ought to have a club.

At a street intersection near the Market Square Rhodes tapped Sauer on the arm and stopped.

'This is the place, Hans. This corner will do. Find out who owns these four stands, and buy them.'

Two of the stands belonged to Ikey Sonnenberg, one of the great band of Jews who pioneered the Transvaal and the Witwatersrand. The other two belonged to Marshall – a Scotsman who can be regarded as the Rand's first property magnate.

It was the Jew who gave his stands to Sauer free of charge; the Scotsman got the full price of £72, which is what he had paid for them plus a few pounds profit.

It is small tribute to that early act of generosity that the Rand Club, ever since, has been a stronghold of anti-Semitism. If this has been resented by the Jewish community of Johannesburg it has not been reflected in the constant endeavours of wealthy and influential Jews to secure membership. A few have succeeded.

The club was also, unashamedly, a stronghold of the imperial tradition – a British enclave within the great financial fortress of Johannesburg against which the republican nationalism of the founders of the State beat in vain. But with an ever-increasing insistence.

A great deal of the spirit and body of Johannesburg emanated from that exclusive coterie of original members of the Rand Club. Many of the things that are characteristic of the city – its magnanimity and spontaneous, slightly bogus charity; the devotion to sport and gambling; its separate sense of values; its latent hardness and happy unscrupulousness – could be found concentrated in the individuals who gathered there daily to plan their ventures, deal in stocks and shares, and organize their entertainment. Most of it was to the great benefit of the whole community – though this was not often foremost in their thoughts.

There had been share dealings of a sort on the Witwatersrand ever since Struben first revealed it as a potential goldfield. But most of these transactions were done on a personal basis, and a lot of them were pure confidence tricks. Now as the big syndicates and individuals moved in and as the nature of the reefs became apparent, it was clear that the gold-getting operation was beyond the resources of personal wealth, and the public were asked to subscribe the vast sums necessary for development.

The first public sale of shares in Witwatersrand gold mines took place on January 26, 1887, at the Transvaal Auction Mart, Johannesburg, when 150 shares of the Kromdraai Gold Mining Company changed hands. It was the prelude to large-scale stock and share transactions which could no longer be confined to the confidential negotiation of the club or an exclusive group of privileged individuals. The Johannesburg Stock Exchange was an inevitable outcome, though it was to go through some strange metamorphoses before it became established in integrity and independent authority.

In the meantime there were the pressing practical needs of the swelling population and the embryo mining companies. Everything was waiting for the machinery. All along the discernible banket reefs the first tentative trenches had grown into ditches and from the ditches had probed the shafts following the tilt of the reef. As the excavation proceeded, great mounds of conglomerate piled up on the surface waiting for the plodding wagons and their burden of stamp batteries, water wheels, turbines, steam engines, amalgamators, concentrators, and for the fitters and mechanics and technicians to go with them. It took thirty-three ox-wagons and three weeks to bring Knight's equipment and plant from the railhead at Kimberley to the Witwatersrand.

By the end of February crushing had started at Knights, on the Tarkastad property and on Turffontein and Langlaagte. It opened up a new era of activity and hope – and a new era of headaches. For it was soon evident that the processes of milling and extraction operating successfully on the richer ores of California and Australia were wholly inadequate for the comparatively low yields of the Witwatersrand series.

This was a factor which had not been wholly overlooked by engineers on the spot, and it was one of the reasons why some experts had rejected the whole idea of mining such 'ten-penny-weight stuff'. It was reckoned that from the first crushings up to two-thirds of the gold was lost in the extraction.

New machinery and new methods were needed, new chemical processes to complete profitably the work of the mechanical operation. The gold was there, in vast quantities. It was a matter of getting it out in ways which had never been tried before.

Nobody, except some of the experts who came and departed hurriedly, ever doubted that the way would be found. Johannesburg grew on that ignorant faith – and grew fast. First the stores and hotels, then the offices, then the houses and halls and churches. Mud and wattle replacing canvas, wood and iron replacing mud and wattle, stone and brick replacing wood and iron. The face of the township changed overnight every night. So did the stand values. Within two months of the first auction, selected sites bought originally for a few pounds were selling for more than £1,000 each. And every week the wagon trains arrived with more hundreds to be provided for and accommodated.

There was a shortage of everything, and when Mr van Rensburg arrived from Colesberg in the Cape Colony and discovered the sort of prices that were being offered for oxen he sold the span that had dragged him all the way up and went hurrying back to his farm for more.

He could not, of course, take his wagon back, so he left it behind Morkel's auctioneer's office for safe keeping. Mr Morkel was not in the office at the time, and the clerk with whom van Rensburg left a message forgot all about it. Six weeks later, when van Rensburg returned to Johannesburg, he found that the open space behind the auction room had been completely built over except for the few square yards occupied by his wagon. He had to dismantle it on the spot and carry each piece out through the front door of Mr Morkel's office.

As the town expanded so the pressure on the Government for social and civic recognition increased. Not long before President Kruger's visit, and probably because of it,

Mr von Brandis was able to tell the Diggers' Committee of a number of executive decisions.

The Government had agreed to subscribe £500 towards the erection of a hospital, and had appointed Dr Hans Sauer as district surgeon; there was a further grant of £500 for the repair of roads and bridges on the Rand, and Johannesburg was to be connected with Potchefstroom and the outside world by telegraph; the Mining Commissioner had been instructed to select a site for a cemetery, and to treat for the purchase of the water rights on the adjoining farm of Braamfontein.

Although this all fell a good deal short of demand and expectation it was adjudged a beginning to the road along which the Johannesburgers were determined to push the Government if they could not lead them. The proposal to provide a water supply for the township was particularly welcome, as two young Englishmen, recent arrivals who had been missing for a week or two, were found at the bottom of a well from which many of the inhabitants drew their drinking-water. The bodies were in a pretty advanced stage of decomposition.

Thus, after less than three months' existence, Johannesburg was a substantial town and a substantial community. It was the centre of a new population of Uitlanders who were rapidly approaching numerical equality with the republic's burghers in the rest of the Transvaal, and who, in material and intellectual resources, were vastly superior.

The high air was stimulating of expectation and endeavour, the weather was wonderful in between thunderstorms, the grass was green, the present was fun and the future full of promise and potential. Dogs barked a good deal more than was necessary, rare and precious donkeys brayed their self-importance and so, perhaps, did too many humans. The rain and warmth brought out a deadly assortment of snakes and scorpions. There was a strange shortage of cats.

The Diggers' Committee, more aware than the rest of the community of the need for the goodwill and co-operation of the Pretoria Government, were determined to make a good impression on Kruger. They had a huge triumphal archway of evergreen branches constructed across the roadway in front of the Mining Commissioner's office, surmounted by two-foot high lettering:

WELCOME
LONG LIVE THE PRESIDENT

For weeks members of the Committee had been compiling, receiving, amending and rejecting addresses of welcome from various sectional interests and individuals. They were anxious to strike the right note of enthusiasm and pleasure, desperate that no offence should be given, yet resolved that by the time he left the Witwatersrand Oom Paul would have a good idea of what was bothering its inhabitants.

They had notices posted up all over the district, wherever there was a tent and a trench, urging the populace to come and greet the President and inviting anybody who had a horse or a horse and cart to ride out to meet him on the Pretoria Road.

It was a hot and sultry morning, with early promise of an afternoon thunderstorm, as a cavalcade of some 400 diggers, town residents and burghers headed out to Grobelaar's farm, where they met the Presidential coach and smothered it in dust and good humour. Then the whole procession rode noisily back to Johannesburg, the mounted troopers of the Staats Artillerie making a brave escort beneath the flanking *vierkleurs* – flags of the South African Republic – at the head of the convoy.

Kruger, who had set off on this journey as though preparing for a visit to a foreign and unfriendly State, was surprised at the warmth of the welcome but unrelenting in his suspicion of the whole flamboyant outfit. He drove through the archway with a brief acknowledgment of the effort, and stepped bulkily from his coach on to a prepared platform in front of the Commissioner's office.

As he heaved himself erect and the familiar beaver, frock-coat and blue-green sash became visible above them, a great cheer went up from the crowd of some 3,000 people which filled every available space within 100 yards' radius of the platform. Jubilant voices roared 'Long live Paul Kruger! Long live the President!' and, while the members of the Committee prayed that no silly fool would start singing 'God Save the Queen', Kruger lifted his hat and waved it to the crowd in a rare gesture of response. He probably surprised himself most of all.

The addresses of welcome were presented to him. One from the official reception committee, one from the burghers resident in the area, a third from the merchants and townspeople of Johannesburg.

Von Brandis read each of them aloud to Kruger, who sat there portentous and dignified, inclining his head occasionally as each compliment preceded a request. The last address was one from the Diggers' Committee and the crowd pressed closer together, anxious to hear the words that carried the burden of their complaints. The voice of the Mining Commissioner droned on, but as he came to the end of it a restless movement rippled through the crowd and a low murmuring drifted up to the platform as men spoke to each other in anger and disappointment at the emptiness and obsequious tone of their address. That was not how they felt. What was all that about *ad valorem* duties and fixity of tenure? They wanted their rights, not soft soap. And what about the vote? Not one word about the vote. To hell with the Diggers' Committee! And Kruger!

The change in atmosphere was immediately apparent to the group on the platform. Von Brandis, only too well aware of the unpredictable temper of the citizens, was silently thankful that he had closed the bars for the day.

Then Kruger rose to his feet and stood there massive above the crowd – just as he had done at Barberton. The subdued rumble in the heart of the gathering subsided as that bass voice rolled across them.

'This is not the time or the place for an argument.' He spoke in Dutch, aware that the delayed action of the interpretation would assist his purpose. 'I am glad that I came to Johannesburg, and thank you for your welcome. I want to come and hear for myself all about the Rand. For that reason I will hold a public meeting this afternoon and after that I will meet a deputation representing Johannesburg so that we may go more deeply into these matters. No man can talk properly with three thousand people at a time. There are, however, one or two things I would like to say, before we get down to business.'

As the interpreter began to give the English version of the last sentence Kruger made a gesture with his hand and went straight on in rapid Dutch. Not many of them could understand what he was saying, but the men behind him on the platform could, and so could the burghers in the crowd. Perhaps that was enough. He didn't want to start a riot on the spot. But his words would get around soon enough.

'You must know,' he told them, 'that I have the welfare of the community at heart, and I will see justice is done to all irrespective of nationality. The people of Barberton are well satisfied with the way things are going and I am happy to be able to call them my children. In regard to the Witwatersrand I cannot say that I am quite so satisfied inasmuch as there is a section of the community here who are inclined to overstep the boundaries of the law.'

The group on the platform, including von Brandis, glanced quickly at each other and shifted uneasily in their chairs. Kruger went on deliberately:

'I have my spies here, as at Barberton, and I know those who are loyal to the Government and those who are not. In fact, I know everything of importance going on at the goldfields. Should any troubles arise in the future I will not at first deal with them myself but I will call the Diggers' Committee together and get the law-abiding diggers to settle the matter themselves. But if this should not prove satisfactory I will be compelled to call up the burghers, and then I will have to call the diggers rebels – and deal with them accordingly.'

Now the faces on the platform showed astonishment and dismay. Von Brandis could not conceal his surprise and disappointment. What on earth had Kruger been listening to? One or two Boers in the audience rumbled 'Hoor, hoor!', and a low murmuring, gradually swelling, ran through the crowd as the President's words were translated and passed on from mouth to mouth. Kruger held up his hand and continued obstinately.

'I believe the diggers to be honest and law-abiding people and I wholly understand that in a country like this there will be some who want to overrule law and order. It is like having a large herd of sheep. Most of the sheep are good, healthy sheep and each season deliver a good crop of wool to the farmer. But some of the sheep are scabby or lame, and some will stray all the time taking the others with them. These are the sheep that must be got rid of so that the whole flock may thrive and the farmer prosper. I do not say that you are my sheep, but I hope I will be able to call you, like the diggers at Barberton, my children.'

It was over. One or two remarks came shouted up from the crowd like the first scattered shots before a volley. But the greater part of the audience remained uncomprehending. There was no applause until one of the committee members, sensing the need for mass exclamation, stepped up beside Kruger and called for three cheers for the President.

These were given generously enough, and as the platform party went off-stage into the Commissioner's office the crowd dispersed in gesticulating groups through the township, scattering dust and argument over the streets and on the surrounding veld.

The most worried man on the diggings that afternoon was Carl von Brandis. He felt keenly his responsibility for the success of the Presidential visit, and he knew as well as the syndicates what could happen to the vast capital investment already made in the area if Kruger was maltreated in any way. He had closed the canteens, but many of the diggers had their own resources – as was evident in the township as the day wore on. Rumour and hyperbole were already embellishing Kruger's speech with wild exaggeration and insult. Von Brandis looked up at the gathering black nimbus clouds and prayed for rain as fervently as any drought-stricken farmer.

Shortly before three o'clock, as the truculent crowds began to gather for the afternoon meeting, a whiplash of lightning split the sky and the crash of thunder shook huge drops of rain from overburdened clouds. One more cosmic collision and the rain came cascading down right where the Commissioner had asked for it – on Johannesburg. The crowd, with full experience of a high-veld thunderstorm, had not waited. The first flash of lightning had sent them scattering for shelter.

It ended all possibility of direct contact between President and populace. By the next morning the humour of the town had changed. It is very difficult to be bad-tempered in a clear, rain-washed Transvaal morning.

Kruger gave the delegations an assurance that all their complaints would receive attention. He wanted a railway-line as much as anyone. The matter of the roads to and in the district was being attended to, and so were postal arrangements. A new telegraph would be a great help to them. He could not make any promises about a Municipality for Johannesburg until the next session of the Volksraad. As for parliamentary representation, that would have to wait until they could all see the future more clearly.

Well, that was that. Not very much perhaps, but a little better than many had expected. And thank God, no disasters. In a good mood again, the President was taken off to lunch with about fifty leading citizens including Mr J. X. Merriman and Mr C. J. Rhodes, both of whom were to become Prime Ministers of the Cape Colony.

Kruger's visit left behind a mixture of satisfaction and discontent. The satisfaction, as usual, soon wore off, leaving only the discontent. The insult to the community, whether it was meant as such or not, could not be lightly forgotten. It rumbled away in the intestines of the township – in the canteens and in the shafts sloping down the reefs.

But Kruger had no need of spies in Johannesburg. The affairs of the township were being freely reported in every newspaper in South Africa. In Pretoria the *Transvaal Advertiser* and *De Volkstem* were as well informed as the Government, and published their information with admirable unrestraint and impartiality.

There were obvious opportunities on the Rand for an enterprising publisher. Already the area contained the biggest concentration of population in the Transvaal and showed every sign of becoming one of the most populous communities in the whole continent.

There was no lack of news and no lack of people to read it. And the enormous appetite of the mining community for the ordinary essentials of living, and most of the extraordinary non-essentials, plus the specialized requirements of the developing mines, guaranteed a handsome advertising revenue.

Two groups of people got the same idea at the same time. The publishers of the embryo *Transvaal Mining Argus*, to be produced in Pretoria for general distribution around the high-veld, asked a Johannesburg firm to print some handouts announcing the date of publication of the first edition of the *Argus* as February 25. It was just the information the Johannesburg printers wanted. They produced the handouts – and the first edition of *The Diggers' News* – on February 24.

The human stream continued to pour into the catchment area of the Witwatersrand. Every day a few hundreds were added to the total and a new building was completed in the township. The population was further increased, and its problems multiplied, by the steady influx of Africans from the surrounding territories in search of work and wages – both of which were new to them.

On every railway-line and road the trucks and wagons pressed north with their burdens of machinery and equipment. Along the Rand the skeletons of headgears stuck out of the veld like rows of unconnected pylons, and heaps of ore rose to dwarf both them and the iron sheds which were being erected everywhere to house the approaching crushing-mills. For fifty miles, plain and valley and ridge were a shambles of trenches, rubble and jagged silhouette.

As the weeks and months passed it seemed as though the crawling wagons would never catch up with the growing mounds of exhumed reef. But bits and pieces began to arrive as wagon-trains creaked wearily through the diggings. Soon the quiet air was shattered by the constant pounding of the mills as the rock went through them. The whole Transvaal waited breathlessly for the first results. It was generally accepted that an average yield of one ounce per ton of reef would prove payable, and this was, no doubt the figure that experts like Gardner Williams had in mind when they contemptuously described the Witwatersrand deposits as tenpennyweight stuff.

The first company to make an official announcement of a crushing result was Wemmer's Extension, who came out in the second half of May with the astonishing statement that the first two tons of banket through their mills had produced twenty-two ounces of gold.

The Wemmer Company was not trying to fool the public or boost its share capital with false values. It was an exceptional yield because there was an inclination on all the early mines to select only the most promising-looking sections of reef; all managements like to show high yields and good results.

The reaction to the Wemmer announcement, supported by very satisfactory yields from other mines where crushing had begun, was inevitable. There was a frantic resurgence of speculative interest in the Witwatersrand, and some thirty or forty gold-mining companies mushroomed into existence overnight, in addition to the ventures with secured capital.

But London and other European sources of investment finance had been scared out of Transvaal gold by the operations of Barberton speculators like Baron Grant. The capital for developing the gold of the Rand had to be found elsewhere, and most of it came from Kimberley – from diamonds.

The one exception was Rhodes' new company, Gold Fields of South Africa, Ltd., which, for a long time, was the only Transvaal mining company with its head office in London. It says much for the magic of his name and the persuasive powers of Rudd that the first share offer, as early as February, 1887, and months before any mills were functioning, was heavily over-subscribed in the City.

Although they could not but benefit, on paper, from the new surge of optimism and cupidity which swept through the country, it did not delude the experts or the more responsible financiers. For them the one big conundrum remained to be solved. It hung in the sky over the Transvaal like a cosmic question-mark, dominating the whole future of Johannesburg and the history of South Africa . . .

How deep did the golden reefs go?

Hundreds of thousands of pounds had been poured into the land, into the trenches and pits and the first prying shafts. Millions more would be necessary to release the golden stream from its confining rock. It would only be worthwhile if the reefs went deep: deeper than anybody believed was possible.

It was not a thought that penetrated the surface buoyancy and enthusiasm of the Johannesburgers. They were not supplying the capital, they were sharing in it. But Joseph Robinson, for all his instinctive faith, was beginning to lose some of his certainty. He was the first to appreciate the supreme importance of finding out the extent, in depth, of the banket reefs. His was the first significant attempt to do so. But he was by no means alone in his fears and reservations.

By September of that year Robinson's shaft on Langlaagte had gone down beyond 250 feet without encountering the reef. He was spending more and more time out at the widow Petronella's old farmhouse – urging on his workmen to greater effort, giving each of them shares in his mining company as an additional incentive, supervising the erection of the milling plant that had just arrived; or just sitting on the stoep watching the untidy heaps of rock piling up expenditure.

One afternoon, as he was sitting there trying not to think

about his position if some of the experts were right in saying that there could not be any depth to the reefs, his foreman came up to him looking distinctly gloomy.

'We've struck a reef of conglomerate, sir. But when we panned it we drew a blank. Not a speck of colour.'

'Are you sure?' Robinson wouldn't believe it. 'You couldn't have taken a proper sample. I'll come and see for myself.'

Together they walked across to the inclined shaft, fear gnawing at Robinson's heart. A bin full of conglomerate had just been winched to the surface as the two men reached the pithead. Robinson examined it briefly and then scrambled down the sloping tunnel to where the men were hacking away at the rock and soil dislodged by the last blast of dynamite. There he saw the strip of pebbled rock they had encountered. He took one look at it, and felt the fear lift off his shoulders.

'That's not the reef,' he told them. 'That's only a stringer. You're not deep enough yet. Go on digging!'

But his confidence and assurance were not enough to remove the disappointment and doubts of his workers. As soon as they finished work for the day they went into Johannesburg and sold the shares they had been given. There was no difficulty in selling. The shareholders in Wemmer's were refusing offers of over 30s. for their £1 shares; rumours of high values from the Jubilee Company's crushing, which was still proceeding, had pushed their share prices up to 50s.

Another month and Robinson was still waiting for his shaft to strike the reef. Every day he expected the news that would transform his own life and that of the whole country. Then, as he sipped his habitual cup of coffee at the house one morning, he saw a figure leave the mouth of the shaft and coming running towards him.

Fifty yards from the house the foreman started shouting, his words so mixed up with his own excitement and exertions that they were unintelligible. Robinson walked quickly out to meet him.

'Stop shouting, man,' he said urgently. 'What is it?'

'We've found it, sir. We've hit it. We've hit the reef, the true reef. It's real jam!'

Robinson was caught up in the excitement. They ran back to the shaft together. They found the place deserted. Robin-

91

son stopped in astonishment.

'Where the devil are the workmen?'

'Hell, sir, they've all gone off to buy their shares back. And no wonder. Here's some of the stuff we've just brought up. Pan it for yourself, and see.'

Ten minutes later, as Robinson looked down at the last handful of muck and saw the bright tail of gold semicircling the pan he knew that he was right, knew that George Harrison's outcrop was but one visible bubble from a cauldron of rock and sand and gold that had flowed across this high plateau during the hot travail of earth and which had been congealed in this petrified stream. He raised his eyes from the witnessing dish and followed the run of the range to the westward. As far as the horizon and over it the underground rivers of untold wealth ran. And a lot of it already belonged to him.

The business of living in a more or less civilized fashion while they made as much money as quickly as possible preoccupied the Uitlander population in the first four years of Johannesburg to an extent which overshadowed other aspects of political agitation.

When President Kruger dropped in at the end of 1887, on his way to Bloemfontein to discuss the extension of the railway with the Government of the neighbouring Orange Free State, the inevitable reception committee reminded him that since his February visit Johannesburg had become a substantial town of some 6,000 inhabitants, who looked forward to living in civilized conditions and 'taking that part in the making of laws which prudence and justice alike dictate and which are essential to the true happiness of a people and a republic'.

The address ended with another reminder that the wonderful progress the town was making could only be maintained in conditions of law and order – which twenty-five policemen could not possibly enforce.

But Kruger had railways on his mind, not policemen. So that, apart from pointing out that if the community was as law-abiding and free from crime as the reception committee had suggested there was hardly any need to increase the police force, he did nothing about it.

Four months later there were still only twenty-five policemen on the Witwatersrand.

*

It was another Sunday morning in Johannesburg. And a miserably wet one. Most of those who had beds were still asleep in them. Those who didn't had found what shelter they could in tents, abandoned reed huts or unfinished buildings permanently in course of erection. A few native houseboys and Cape Coloured workers had crawled out of their miserable sackcloth and were heading for their places of employment to begin the morning clean-up. At least fifty per cent of the population would wake up with a hangover.

Yet this Sunday, February 13, 1888, was to be slightly different. The difference first became apparent when an early-rising citizen living next to the Roman Catholic Church looked out of his bedroom window and saw a white man lying in the pathway which led up to the church door.

Another disgusting drunk, was his first thought. And in front of the Lord's house, at that! But the man was not lying like a drunk would have fallen, and the strange inertness of the body sent the householder out in his pyjamas and oilskin for a closer look.

The first thing he noticed was that the man, face down in the mud, had only one arm. Then he saw the crushed skull, the congealed blood, the two neat slits in the neck. He touched the body gingerly and found it not quite stiff.

Feeling distinctly queasy he looked around for help and, finding none, hurried along the road to the police station. The night duty men were preparing their breakfast when they got the news and were not at all pleased when the sergeant sent two of them off with a stretcher to the Roman Catholic Church. Corpses were not so rare that they couldn't wait until breakfast was finished. Still, as the sergeant said, they'd better clear up the mess before early Mass.

As soon as the two policemen saw the body with its missing arm, now surrounded by a shocked and curious group, they recognized it as George Graham's. He had been the billiard-marker at the Kimberley Bar and, as everybody who had ever had a drink there knew only too well, had lost his arm from an assegai thrust in one of the Kaffir wars.

Thrusting the onlookers back, the two policemen lifted the body on to the stretcher and started back to the station. Along Commissioner Street they were surprised to see two of their colleagues approaching them carrying another stretcher.

'Hey! Where are you off to? We've got the stiff here. That sergeant must be going loco.'

'Consider yourself lucky you've only got one to carry. We've to go and pick up two more!'

The two pairs went off in opposite directions, one lot leaving deep imprints in the soft earth, the other hurrying as far as the Rand Club where they turned along Fox Street and squelched across Marshall's Square to a littered building site next to the property office. There they found a Hottentot, face pressed hard into the slush and with his ankles tied tightly together with a strip of rawhide. The side of the skull was bruised and bloody and there was a long, incised wound in the neck.

At the entrance to a road leading off the square an agitated cluster of people revealed where the third corpse lay. The policemen, the stretcher laden between them, hurried across to find the body of a Kaffir sprawled where it had been felled by a heavy blow on the head. Blood which had oozed from several knife wounds in the neck showed how the work of the bludgeon had been finished off. They made room on the stretcher and lifted the Kaffir alongside the Hottentot. This one, said the policeman, was still warm.

The grim processions converged on the police station, each heavy stretcher attracting the townsfolk like a magnet attracts filings. At the station the three bodies were put in an anteroom to await identification, while the crowd outside multiplied with each rumour that spread through the township and the surrounding mining camps.

A steady file of citizens passed steadily all morning through the improvised mortuary, ostensibly to assist identification, but actually to share personally in the excitement and horror. It was a fine Sabbatical alternative and only the most God-fearing and superstitious – who had long awaited some positive sign of the Lord's displeasure – attended Church that morning to hear the hurriedly-revised texts and portentous messages.

It had been quite a night. In addition to the triple murder and the apparent robbery of all three victims, evidence gradually built up of considerable nocturnal operations. The Central Hotel had been broken into and money and watches stolen from guests while they slept; Steytler's store had been entered and shelves stripped of paint pots, under the impression, judging by the mess, that they contained jam and other groceries; a dozen other store-keepers and hoteliers reported attempts to force doors, and a window at the back of the Club had been smashed; almost every boarding-house keeper in town reported visits from strangers and loafers during the night, asking for help and demanding something to eat; travellers coming into Johannesburg during the hours of darkness reported that they had been stopped on the outskirts by small gangs of three or four men and forced to hand over cash and valuables – one man complaining that he had been robbed of £200.

By midday several theories had found partisan acceptance at different levels of intelligence and information in various pubs which, in spite of repeated attempts to close them after 10 a.m. on Sundays, were doing very much better business than the pulpits on this day.

The widest consensus of opinion was that the 'Irish Brigade' was responsible. This was a gang of wild Irishmen who had achieved the quite remarkable distinction of being socially unacceptable even in Barberton; they had been driven out of the Eastern Transvaal by what can be described euphemistically as pressure of public opinion.

Now, a few days after their appearance on the Witwatersrand, the fear was that they had recognized the inadequacy both in numbers and efficiency of the police force, and were systematically imposing a reign of terror on the town in order to take what they could from it before being compelled to move on again.

It was also agreed that the two murdered coloured men had been witnesses of the first murder, had been followed and silenced. It was pointed out that the three bodies had lain in a dead straight line over several hundred yards and that a trail of blood led from corpse to corpse. Here was no haphazard encounter in the night; it was deliberate pursuit.

In the Kimberley Bar, where one-armed Graham was a familiar figure and not very highly respected even in that dissolute company, there were men who had seen him leaving the race-meeting on Saturday afternoon staggering drunk. He had also been observed in a tented brothel near the Catholic Church – which was convenient for those seeking the opportunity of early absolution. In that tent a number of coloured women made themselves available at economic rates to the lower income groups.

The majority opinion among the Kimberley Club customers, many of whom were also customers of the coloured girls, was that Graham had been beaten up and stabbed to death in the brothel and his body dumped outside the church; the Hottentot and Kaffir had seen it all and their evidence suppressed in the only way that could guarantee silence.

In the Rand Club, where conjecture was on a higher intellectual level, rumour was fortified by the report of Dr Sauer who had performed the post-mortem on the three bodies. He was convinced that the murders were the work of a single killer, and one who had a knowledge of anatomy and how to kill quickly.

The influential and professional members of the Club stiffened their whisky tots and decided that something must be done immediately, before the situation got out of hand. The hot breath of panic was wafting through the township and could be felt seeping in through the dignified windows of the Club. They decided to hold a public meeting the next afternoon at which, as Dr Sauer said, 'the public can express their indignation and horror and initiate a movement for the better protection of life and property in the district'.

The murmur of speculation and gossip in the bars and hotels of Johannesburg that night drowned the distant thudding of the stamp batteries which were crushing night and day to overtake the mounting dumps of ore. In private houses doors were locked and windows boarded up as fearful householders peopled the night with gangsters and homicidal maniacs. Everybody hoped the morning would come quickly.

Shortly before five o'clock the next afternoon, with the heat of the day dwindling, more than 1,000 people clustered in the open space in Commissioner Street opposite the Rand Club – the focal point of leadership and authority when the Uitlander populace was deeply concerned. Mr H. S. Caldecott was voted to the Chair, which he promptly stepped on to in order to quieten the murmurous crowd.

'The people of Johannesburg,' he began, shouting to reach the rim of his audience, 'have been called together on a most important and solemn occasion to express their horror and detestation of the dastardly and cruel crime which has been committed in the midst of the community, and to ask the Government to take steps for the better protection of life and property in this town.

96

'Hitherto Johannesburg has had the reputation of being one of the most law-abiding and peaceful places in South Africa, but now a most fearful crime has been perpetrated. People at a distance will be shocked at the news and will come to regard the town as unsafe and be afraid to set foot in it.'

Mr Caldecott than called on a number of the gentlemen ranged behind him on the club veranda to put their resolutions to the meeting.

A number of these followed, all expressing 'profound horror' and a determination to assist the authorities in the discovery of 'the base and cruel perpetrators'. All were received with enthusiastic demonstrations from the gathering.

One speaker expressed the feelings of the community more accurately when he blamed the shortage of policemen and their inefficiency as the direct cause of the crime. He wanted a public funeral for the victims, which the whole town should attend as a mark of protest – an idea which could not be pursued, as the three men had already been buried, with somewhat indecent haste, by the police.

Dr Matthews, who proposed that a committee be formed to collect funds so that a more suitable reward could be offered for the discovery of the murderers, told the crowd that he had lately returned from the United States. He had read in the newspapers there of many cases of a similar nature occurring in the Western states and that the whole community rose as one man, found out the murderers and strung them to the nearest tree. He held up a slip of paper and read from it:

'I have got here a cutting from a leading American newspaper which says that in 1882 there were 1,266 reported murders in the United States. Of this number only 93 were convicted and executed while 118 were lynched. I am giving you these figures to show that when properly constituted authority fails to protect the public then the citizens cannot be blamed for losing patience and taking the law into their own hands. I am beginning to think that if the people of Johannesburg take the same sort of action it will do more to maintain law and order than all the public executions – what there are of them.'

This got the biggest hand of the meeting. From a rooftop on the edge of the crowd a man yelled across: 'We're with you on that, Doctor. But where the hell do we find a bloody tree?' A moment of ugliness passed into laughter.

The fund-raising committee was then elected, including among its twenty-seven members names which were to become familiar throughout South Africa and Britain as they grew in magnitude with the town and the gold-mining industry. Most of the pioneer financiers were represented, and the list marked the first public appearance of a new arrival from Barberton called Abe Bailey.

It occurred to someone that twenty-seven such formidable men were rather wasted on a brief fund-raising effort, and amid scenes of great enthusiasm it was decided that they should continue in office indefinitely as a Vigilance Committee.

When Mr Caldecott announced that the Committee had decided to increase the reward by £500, the meeting dispersed, happy in the knowledge that they were approaching a better-organized existence. Not everybody, of course, was happy.

Within a week Paul Kruger had his first communication from the Johannesburg Vigilance Committee. He had heard it all before, and read it all before. But there was a new urgency in the demands for adequate protection, and a new authority which added influential sanction to the complaints and reports which poured into Pretoria from the Witwatersrand.

That Pretoria did not react more vigorously was due largely to the fact that they did not know how to, and had none of the organization or mechanical means required to cope with such a situation.

Lacking adequate administrative capacity, the President was compelled to adopt various expedients. First he had to continue the policy of his predecessor, President Burgers, and import what he was short of among his burghers – men who could read and write. He so mistrusted the English that he would not even employ his own stock, the Dutch in the Cape Colony, because of their contamination by British rule. He brought in large numbers of Hollanders, who soon established a bureaucratic ruling class which came to be almost as unpopular with the Boers as with the Uitlanders. Nominally each department was under the direction of a Transvaal Afrikaner who, though with enough common sense and native shrewdness to exert overall influence, was completely at the mercy of his Hollander clerks when it came to correspondence and the framing of reports and directives. It was a system which was open to considerable abuse – and got it, one way and another.

In the circumstances there was no great objection to the top jobs going to old companions or men who had served the republic faithfully in the hazardous days of its foundation. One such old friend came to Kruger for help.

'Oom Paul,' he said, 'the rinderpest has killed all my cattle, the drought has ruined nearly all my mealie crop and the locusts have got the rest. The farm will no longer provide enough food for me or my family. Now you must get me an appointment in the government.'

'I will do what I can for you, old friend. Come back tomorrow and I will let you know if there is anything.'

When the farmer returned next day Kruger had to explain to his great regret that no vacancies suitable to the old man's talents were available.

'But surely there must be some post you can give me?'

'I am sorry, Oom Gert. I have tried all the departments. All the chief positions and even the deputy-chief positions are filled. There is not one vacancy.'

'Then there is certainly a place as a clerk available somewhere, Oom Paul!'

'But you must know, Oom Gert, that you are too stupid to be a clerk...'

CHAPTER NINE

It was this simple lack – of people who could read, write and add up a column of figures – which determined not only the fiscal policy of the Transvaal Government but on which so much of Krugerism was founded.

Direct taxation was unknown in a community of widely scattered ranchers and hunters, few of whom had ever heard of taxable revenue and would certainly not have parted with any if they had had it. Most of them were ignorant of the fact that it costs money to run a country. The Executive of the South African Republic, since its inception, had been faced with two basic problems – how to create administrative as well as legislative machinery, and how to pay for it.

The first was solved by the importation of a Hollander bureaucracy. As for the second, Kruger and his Volksraad had little doubt about who should be made to supply the cash ... the people who were extracting wealth from the earth of their beloved republic would certainly have to hand a good deal of it back to its rightful owners.

Years before the discovery of the Witwatersrand goldfields the prospectors and diggers and the new mining companies were contributing the bulk of the country's revenue through licences and customs dues on essential machinery and supplies.

After the retrocession of the republic in 1881, following the brief British occupation, Kruger resolved his increasing financial and administrative problems by the introduction of an almost universal concessions policy.

He sold or rented to individuals and companies the exclusive right to supply commodities and services to the Transvaal population and all its enterprises.

It is clear that in the circumstances Kruger had little choice, and the sale of concessions must have seemed to him the ideal solution. It produced revenue, either in lump sums or at regular intervals, and it required a minimum of administrative machinery.

This was not something which the President was likely to have thought up quickly by himself, even if an absence of acceptable alternatives would eventually have compelled him to it. The real inspiration of the concession and monopoly policy came from Samuel Marks. Marks was an early Jewish immigrant to the Barberton fields, whence he emerged with a partner, Isaac Lewis, a fortune, and an ability to speak Afrikaans better than English.

Partly on the strength of a £5,000 loan to the Pretoria Government when it was in one of its initial periods of financial stringency, and partly because of a genuine affinity of opposites, he became a trusted friend and adviser of Paul Kruger. The fervent Calvinist and the worldly Hebrew found unlikely common ground in their widely diverse faiths, and their intimacy and regard for each other's qualities was founded, as much as anything else, in the long religious arguments they had. Kruger once told Dr Leyds: 'If there is one man in the whole Transvaal I like, it is Sammy Marks. And I will yet convert him!'

With the Presidential ear at his disposal it would have been unnatural for Marks not to have made use of it. But it is fair to say that he had the Republic's interests at heart as much as his own. It was he who pointed out to Kruger that the only solution to the financial, administrative and industrial problems which were besetting the country with the development of the Witwatersrand and the influx of new population was the creation of a system of concessions.

It was inevitable, of course, that Marks would get a number of them for himself. In this way he acquired monopoly rights for a variety of commodities including liquor, jam and leather. In each case the Boers benefited by the ready market he created for their produce. The Transvaal was undoubtedly good for Sammy Marks; with equal truth it can be said that Sammy Marks was good for the Transvaal.

In the forefront of Kruger's intentions, too, was the promotion of the industrial development of his country and the hastening of the day when the republic would be, as far as possible, self-sufficient. Some years later, when opposition to the concessions system was reaching its peak in 1893, he told the Volksraad: 'It is simply murdering the erection of

101

factories to say there shall be no concessions. I say that factories cannot be erected without them! If the Raad wishes to throw out concessions, well and good. That simply means the fostering of industries in other countries and loss of income for ourselves.'

The monopoly formula had the additional, if dubious, advantage of enabling the Government to distribute favours to friends and relatives and to those who deserved well of their country. It was a system which, even from the best of motives, was wide open to abuse and exploitation. Most of the concessionaires were well aware of the opportunities and, from the start, made the fullest use of them.

The revelation of the Main Reef gold and the startling growth of Johannesburg magnified these opportunities a thousandfold. Competition was deliberately banned by legislation, and every consumer and user in the country, whether of jam or mining machinery, bricks, brandy, leather or paper, had to pay the monopoly price or bear the burden of prohibitive tariffs on competitive goods.

The procedure of concession followed a fairly well-defined pattern. The individual secured the concession from the President by influence, favour or nepotism. The rights it conferred would then, more often than not, be sold to a syndicate. The syndicate would then float a company with or without the intention of exploiting their monopoly – the flotation was the profit-making factor in which they were interested. Very seldom, with the possible exception of Marks' companies, was anything produced other than a prospectus; in 1895, when a Volksraad committee was appointed to report on the scores of industrial concessions granted since 1881, all except four – liquor, dynamite, leather and bricks – were found to have lapsed.

The only serious blemish on the record of Marks' association with the President was his association with Edward Lippert in the creation of the iniquitous dynamite monopoly, in which every weakness and opportunity for corrupt exploitation of the concession system was concentrated and exposed, and which, in the ill-feeling and frustration it aroused, was as potent a factor as any other in precipitating that conflict of ideas and emotions which was to end in war.

Edward Lippert was undoubtedly the most mistrusted man in the South African Republic. 'Oh, Lippert E., Lippert

E., what crimes are committed in thy name!' was a popular parody in all the pubs and clubs. He was an intelligent, cultured, charming and thoroughly unscrupulous German, whose numerous enemies never ceased to believe that he was a spy for the Fatherland. There is some evidence, in fact, that although his first objective was money, a good deal of his time was spent in trying to thwart British intentions in the scramble for Africa which was in progress and which, in the southern half of the continent, revolved around the gold of the Transvaal.

Lippert flitted like a red-bearded shadow through almost every chapter of Transvaal history that led up to the Boer War. He it was who conceived the idea of a dynamite monopoly; Marks it was who recommended it to Kruger.

In this solitary aspect the meeting between Marks and Lippert was pregnant with destiny for the republic and the nation, though such a thought could not have been in the minds of either. Lippert had taken his idea to Marks in Pretoria and, the perfunctory introduction over, he came straight to the point.

'Mr Marks, I have a scheme that will make us both a great deal of money.'

'Mr Lippert,' Marks said, 'up to now I am very interested.'

'It must be obvious to you, Mr Marks, and to anybody else, that the Witwatersrand mines as they go deeper are going to need enormous quantities of dynamite for their underground shafts and tunnels. So far all dynamite has been imported under permit. I want the concession for making it here.'

Marks pricked up his ears. Now, why hadn't he thought of that himself? He asked casually:

'And where do I come in?'

'I want you to take me to Kruger and help me put over the idea.'

'Yes, Mr Lippert?'

'For a quarter share in the monopoly company to be formed.'

'And for the Government?'

'A royalty on each case of dynamite sold.'

Marks thought hard for a few minutes. It was a hell of a good idea, all right! There was a fortune in it. But why should he make it easy for Lippert?

'I don't think,' he said finally, 'that will be enough for Kruger and the Volksraad. These concessions all have to be ratified by the Raad, you know. But I'll tell you what we'll do. We'll undertake to make dynamite in the republic and take over that gunpowder factory that's just about come to a standstill. It's gunpowder that Paul Kruger's interested in, not dynamite.'

'Splendid, Mr Marks. Splendid! Then you'll take me to the President?'

'For twenty-five per cent, why not?'

'There is one other thing,' Lippert paused for a few moments, contemplating his finger-nails. 'I am not acting entirely on my own initiative. You will appreciate that for this business to proceed successfully contacts with overseas interests, and all their technical and expert knowledge, are essential. I am the sole representative of those interests and the transaction can only continue in my name. I am sure I need not say any more.'

'I quite understand, Mr Lippert. My interests do not lie outside the Transvaal. Your terms are acceptable. Well then, when shall we go and see Oom Paul? Would tomorrow morning suit you?'

Kruger needed no persuading. He could see that the dynamic forces contending against his and the republic's way of life would only increase in intensity and purpose. At the end of his vision was unavoidable war. He did not fear it, nor did his countrymen. But war was bullets and shells; more than they had ever had before. Bullets and shells needed gunpowder. And he would get the Uitlanders, the ultimate enemy, to pay all expenses. He gave Lippert the dynamite concession on condition that he operated the gunpowder factory. All that Lippert had to do was pay the Government a small royalty on each 50-lb case of dynamite sold.

The Transvaal was not the only country in which a dynamite monopoly existed. Virtually all the world's trade in this explosive was monopolized by two European rings – one French, the other Anglo-German dominated by Nobels.

Lippert took his concession to a firm in the German ring who turned it down because, they said, it would not be possible to manufacture dynamite in the republic at less than the maximum price stipulated by the Volksraad. Lippert could see clearly enough what they were after, so he took his contract to a member of the French monopoly. They behaved in a far more realistic manner.

A subsidiary company was formed in Pretoria, of which the agent of the Netherlands Bank, L. G. Vorstman, was appointed managing director. He was a close friend of Dr Leyds. Lippert, as the only salesman, got twelve-and-a-half per cent commission, and Sammy Marks was, in his own words, taken on as part of the concession, though at a somewhat lower rate. The price fixed by the company was £5-2-6 a case – nearly 200 per cent higher than the price at which it had previously been imported.

What annoyed the mining companies more than the price was the poor quality of the dynamite – and this was not because it was manufactured in the Transvaal. The French contractors went through the motions of setting up a factory and starting production, but ninety per cent of the end product was imported. They were able to get away with this for two years – after which even the Volksraad, or a majority of them, could no longer tolerate the blatant contempt of the terms of concession. Two years had meant a lot of dynamite...

None of the Transvaal Government's concessions was more significant, politically or financially, than the one granted, in spite of Lippert's distributed enticements, to a Netherlands syndicate to construct and operate all railway lines which, in effect, were to connect the republic to a seaport.

It was one of Kruger's major obsessions, inherited from his predecessor Burgers, that the rail link between the Witwatersrand and the coast should be made at Delagoa Bay in Portuguese East Africa. This was not only the shortest way to the sea, it was the only route by which he could avoid all contact with British territory and British officialdom.

By the beginning of the nineties three railway lines were poised to penetrate the republic from the south – one from Natal, one across the Orange Free State from the Cape Province which had already reached Bloemfontein, and a third which was probing northward from Kimberley in the footsteps of the Rhodesian pioneers, along the western boundary of the Transvaal.

Kruger blocked them all on his borders, determined that

none of them would reach his capital before the Delagoa Bay line was completed. He was greatly fortified in this resolve by the Boers, many of whom were dependent for their income on transport riding. This traffic would inevitably be lost to the new railways and it was no easy matter to persuade the Volksraad to sanction any construction work at all.

When, shortly after the Main Reef was located, vast coal deposits were discovered some thirty miles east of Johannesburg, it became essential that the gold-fields should be connected by rail with the new coal mines. The consent of the Raad was only obtained when the scheme was presented to them as a steam tramway instead of a railway line. By the end of 1890 the Rand Steam Tram was running the length of the reef from the coal mines at Boksburg to beyond Krugersdorp.

This 'Tramway' was built by the Netherlands South African Railway Company, which had finally found enough capital to form a company in June, 1887, to take up the concession and begin its main objective of constructing the Pretoria–Delagoa Bay line.

The capital of £166,666 was subscribed for by three groups in rather curious ratio: a German group acquired 819 shares carrying 30 votes; the Hollanders had 518 shares carrying 76 votes; the Government of the Repulic paid for 600 shares carrying 6 votes.

If the Volksraad wondered what it was all about they said and did nothing, but it was impossible to prevent the citizens of Johannesburg linking these developments with the recent appointment of Dr Leyds as State Attorney at the same time as he was regarded as the agent in Pretoria of the Dutch concessionaires. He found himself, in fact, in the happy position of drawing up the terms of the concession and the company's contract, and piloting it successfully through the Raad.

Nearly 1,000 Hollanders were imported each year as labourers to work on the line during the six months of the low-veld dry season. As soon as the weather became hot all of them were shipped back to Holland at the republic's expense.

Another item which could be defined as eccentric was the importation – over 7,000 miles by ship, rail and ox-wagon – of hundreds of tons of dressed stone from Holland for the construction of the bridge over the Komati River, which runs through some of the most rock-strewn areas on the face of the earth.

In spite of all this activity and expenditure – including an item of £124,000 for construction before any work had started – not a single yard of track had been laid between Pretoria and the coast by 1890. By that time other influences, irresistible and largely beyond the control of President and legislature, played their part in compelling Kruger to change the whole basis of his railway policy.

The third concession of significance – significant not for any intrinsic quality but for its after-effects on the mining industry and the Uitlander community – was the liquor monopoly.

It is unlikely that Marks and his partner Lewis knew what they were letting the Witwatersrand in for when they took over the factory outside Pretoria with its exclusive rights for the manufacture of spirituous liquors. For this they paid the Government £1,000 a year, and the rate of expansion of the business can be judged from the fact that in 1892 the partnership sold the monopoly to a company for £120,000.

Unfortunately, this rapid rise in the popularity of the company's products was almost solely due to increased and illicit consumption of them by the thousands of native mine-workers whose palates were probably less discerning than those of the European population.

Although there is no evidence that the monopoly company encouraged the sale of liquor to natives, or that it had any connection with the chain of canteen-keepers from whom the native mine-workers made all their purchases, its directors consistently made representations to Kruger whenever pressure of public opinion led to attempts to restrict the sale of liquor. Just as consistently, Kruger gave them his support – which may have been surprising from one who was a total abstainer, but which did not surprise those who knew how many of the President's relatives and favoured supporters stood at the crossroads of the devious routes by which liquor from the factory reached the natives.

Although it was estimated that the number of native mine-workers permanently incapacitated by the effects of drink varied from fifteen to thirty per cent of the total labour force, this was not as devastating a consequence as the atrocious crimes it led to, the occupational accidents and the deterioration in morals and character of the Witwatersrand's African population.

By the mid-nineties it was reckoned that these and a score of other concessions were costing the mining industry alone well over £2,000,000 a year, which they regarded as extortion.

CHAPTER TEN

One of the commonest sights in Africa, and still one of its mysteries, is the gathering of the vultures. Deep in the heart of the bush a lion will make its nocturnal kill. By morning the half-eaten carcase will be left to the camp-followers – the jackals and hyenas. Then, coming from blue invisibility, the first vulture will glide across the sky and begin its slow circling.

Immediately the dark specks float swiftly, one by one, across the canopy, taking shape on their downward glide from some intangible perch in space; converging above the kill in concentric, patient circles, each circumvolution a little lower than the one before; as silent and inexorable as the approach of death itself.

To Paul Kruger, watching the skies above the Witwatersrand from his stoep in Pretoria, it must have seemed that the vultures were gathering over the Transvaal. When they were done, he wondered, would the clean-picked corpse be all that was left of his South African Republic?

They were not all vultures. Carrion and predators came indiscriminately to the gargantuan feast; and among them some free-flying eagles with eyries already established on pinnacles of wealth but with appetites of ambition and greed still unsatisfied.

The news that came up on the winch from the bottom of Robinson's shaft was what the big money had been waiting for. With the main reef intersected at 360 feet the period of surface scratching came to an end, and so did the doubts of financiers who could now see that there was more to be taken out of the Witwatersrand than they could ever put in. The prospector and digger had played their parts. Now was the time for the speculator and investor, the group holdings, the engineers, the scientists, the miners. And the stock-broker.

*

The elections for the Cape Legislative Assembly were held in November, 1888. The most hotly contested seat in the whole province was Kimberley, which returned four members. Among the candidates was Barney Barnato.

He had come a long way from the travelling salesman touting cigars and braces around the diamond diggings, buying up claims with the money he made from music-hall turns and the winning share of prize-fight purses.

Like so many members of a race which has been oppressed and scorned for centuries, Barnato recognized the one sure way by which he could reach the position of power and social acceptance to which his ambition and ability aspired. The means was money. He must make himself rich. And then make himself richer. One million pounds would not be enough; one would lead to two, and two to ten; with each million his stature and his status would increase. He would reach out and take every luxury and indulgence his spirit and body craved. His money would open every door, reserve a place for him at every table in the land. *Any* land.

Diamonds had shown him the way with a brilliant, many-faceted light. They had made him his first million. They had led him to Cecil John Rhodes and membership of the exclusive Kimberley Club as part of the price Rhodes had to pay for the great De Beers amalgamation. Now here was the Whitechapel Jew standing for the Cape Parliament under the sponsorship of Rhodes. It was another part of the bargain. When the result of the election was announced, Barney Barnato was top of the poll.

Barney Barnato, Member of the Legislative Assembly, was on the crest of the wave. But where was it taking him? Alongside Cecil Rhodes, he was a director of De Beers diamond monopoly, with a couple of million pounds in his bank account; there were no more diamond mines to develop, no more claims to float into companies into corporations. His work in Kimberley was finished, there was nothing left there for his ambition to pursue. Without the dreams of Rhodes or the philanthropy of Beit to sustain him, Barnato's inner resources were limited by selfishness and vanity to the pursuit of money and the recognition of his fellow-men. In the Kimberley Club one evening, he discussed his immediate future with Rhodes ...

'I suppose you'll be going down for the next session soon, C.J.'

'Yes, within the week. You coming with me?'

'No. I think I'll let the dust settle a bit. Ain't no use hurrying this sort of thing. I want to find my feet, study the form as the racing men say, before I start talking in the House.'

'I think that may be the wisest course, Barney. What'll you do in the meantime?'

'I dunno. Nothing for me here. You've got the diamonds. Can't get any more out of you. Anyway, I'd like to get out of Kimberley for a bit.'

'Tell you what, Barney. Why don't you go to the Rand?'

'Ah yes, the Rand. Matter of fact I've been thinking of that. You know I was up there over a year ago. Took two of our blooming mining experts with me, an' all. Experts! Know what they told me?'

Rhodes knew exactly what they had told Barnato. They had told him the same thing. But he did not interrupt.

' "Oh," they said, "there's gold present in the outcrop all right, but the reef's just the elevated bed of an old water-course and therefore the auriferous rock cannot possibly extend to any depth." That's it, word for word. I had to ask them what "auriferous" meant. Elevated backsides! But I believed 'em. Just like you did earlier. Now J. B. Robinson's got proof that the reefs go down 400 feet and maybe a lot more. Strikes me I've missed the boat!'

'You haven't missed it yet. There's still a lot to be had, if my information is as sound as I think it is. And not only gold. There are wonderful opportunities for investment on the Rand – businesses, property, public services, development schemes. Why d'you think I formed the Gold Fields Company?'

'To get other people to finance your gold mines, of course.'

Rhodes gave a little smile. He was pretty well used to Barnato by now.

'Only partly. I'm turning it into a big holding company, and I'd say most of our capital will be invested in other things than gold.'

'Yes, and how much profit did your first year show? Loss, wasn't it?'

'An anticipated loss. But we're showing very satisfactory

profits now, I can tell you.'

'You had a shareholders' meeting in London a month or two ago, didn't you? I hear you got the bird.'

'I don't know about the bird, as you put it. The shareholders were a little disappointed that the gold-mining side hadn't developed more quickly; but the Chairman knew what to say. He told them that gold production from the Witwatersrand area had increased from 11,000 ounces in January to well over 21,000 ounces in August. And it's still going up. And when the gold output goes up like that, Barney, everything goes up with it. You don't want to leave it too late. You don't want to leave it all to Robinson and Beit!'

'What does Alfred think about things up there?'

'He's had a good look round. He tells me that the Rand is the biggest thing that ever happened. Bigger than Kimberley.'

'That I won't believe. Not until I see it with my own eyes.'

'Well, you know he and Robinson have split up . . .'

'Had to. Couldn't last. Chalk and cheese. Impossible chap, Robinson. Never had much time for him. Couldn't understand him. Couldn't get him to like me. But what happened with Beit? Robinson pick a quarrel? Had something good he didn't want to share?'

'As far as I know, Barney, there was no quarrel. The partnership ended, as they say, amicably. Robinson wanted to go west along the reef. Beit thought the best prospects lay in the other direction. So they did a deal. Beit bought J.B.'s share of the Robinson mine, which is in production, for £50,000; they formed a joint company to operate Langlaagte; everything west of that was Robinson's, everything east went to Beit.'

'I'll lay you six to four Beit comes best out of that. That Beit! If I had his reputation for honesty I could double my millions overnight.'

'You could still double them, Barney. But you'd have to risk them first. There are no diamonds on the Rand. It's like burying your capital in a damn great pit and waiting for it to sprout sovereigns. Capital, and more capital. That's what the Rand needs. Beit had to bring in Wernher to support him. They've opened an office in Johannesburg, with Hermann Eckstein, J. B. Taylor and Lionel Phillips to run it for

112

them. Three very good men. I've seen some of the first returns. Exceptional, exceptional...'

'Well, if it's all right with Alfred Beit it's all right with me. And never mind the figures. But what about you, C.J.? That's where you should be, isn't it? There's nothing more for you in Kimberley. You've got the lot.'

'Well, what about me, Barney? What do you think of me?'

Surprised at the question Barnato took a mouthful of brandy and swilled it round his mouth. Then he looked Rhodes straight in the eye.

'I think this. I think that if Barney Barnato had had the education of C. J. Rhodes there would have been no Cecil John Rhodes. You don't believe that, do you? But I do. Why don't you come up to Johannesburg with me? We'll buy up the whole Witwatersrand – lock, stock and barrel. Then you can sell it to Queen Victoria, if you like. But only forty-nine per cent!'

Rhodes, a little put out at first, relaxed into his high-pitched laugh. Then he grew serious, and his eyes – as they so often did – seemed to look through the walls of the club into the far, far distance.

'I can't come with you this time, Barney. I'm expecting a message almost any hour now. From Rudd up in Matabeleland. It's going to tell me that I've got a mineral concession from Lobengula for the whole of his kingdom. From Limpopo to Zambesi.'

'Matabeleland! Lobengula! I can't understand you, C.J. ... You want to leave that place to the Kaffirs and the elephants. Me, I'm off to Johannesburg...'

The Johannesburg that Barnato came to in November, 1888, was a perpetual source of shock and amazement not only to the daily invasion of newcomers but to all the regular inhabitants who woke up to a new visual or emotional experience almost every morning. Not that Johannesburg ever slept. There was not one hour in the twenty-four when it could be said that the town was asleep. Somewhere, sometime, somebody was making money, spending money, stealing money. All the time.

And there was not an hour, throughout the day or night, when the toot-toot-tra-la of a post-horn was not announcing the arrival of a coach with passengers or mail. All roads led to Johannesburg. No roads led from it. And the hungry maw of the town absorbed everything the roads carried – the express passenger coaches with their ten-mile full-gallop stages; the weary, wide-eyed pedestrians seeing their holy grail in the rising mine dumps that were the new foothills of the Witwatersrand; the slow ox-wagons, padding to market through the dust of the night.

It was a town with a reputation that was spreading to every country in the world. Men talked about Jo'burg and the Rand in every waterfront bar from San Francisco to Sydney; they gossiped about it in Russian and French almost as much as they did in English and German. When the Sanitary Board took a superficial census five years later they found among the inhabitants 3,335 Russian Jews, 2,262 Germans, 992 Australians, 819 Hollanders, 754 Americans, 402 Frenchmen, and 16 other nationalities.

Johannesburg's day began at the Market Square. That's where the wagons converged, drawn through the night behind their plodding oxen, burdened with meat and maize, vegetables, firewood and the buxom Boer women with baskets of eggs and butter and bundles of flowers.

There, too, converged the townsfolk in search of wholesale bargains for their stomachs, while the clear sun rose to light up a chaos of oxen, mules, donkeys, wagons, merchanise and men.

Into this uproar Louis Cohen stepped carefully between the ruts and pot-holes, ignoring the tramps and toughs demanding sixpences and shillings for their essential first brandy, giving knowing greeting to the ladies of the dawn as they returned from their night's engagements – well dressed, well paid.

Louis Cohen had been a partner of Barnato in the early Kimberley days, but he had found the pace and Barney a little too hot for him. He had joined in the 1887 exodus from the diamond diggings to the Witwatersrand, and there, like so many others, found there was more immediate gold to be made out of the gullibility and greed of his fellow-man than out of the ground.

Now, on this morning of November 22 one year later, he wanted to make sure of the ingredients for a very special lunch. He was not sure whether the guest would be there; but just in case . . .

Half an hour later he had sent his purchases off in a cab

114

and sauntered back to his hotel as the last of the milkmen, horses anxious to get home, cantered out of the township. He stopped to buy a copy of *The Diggers' News*.

Tramps, vagabonds, thugs, harlots, newsboys, milkmen – the harbingers of civilization's awakening, dawn outposts of society preparing the way for frock-coats and top-hats, bowlers and boaters, for rich-noised silks, for muslin veils and lace, wasp-waists and waistcoats, patent leather making careful prints in the alien dust on determined British consti-tutional or, thrust into stirrups, transplanting Rotten Row to Commissioner Street. What matter if very few had ever set eyes on Rotten Row, let alone ridden in it? In Johan-nesburg you were what you said you were.

Before he reached his hotel Cohen saw the township blos-som into brief carnival as womenfolk and servants des-cended on the flower market, bearing away their burdens of scent and colour to the Victorian vases of their hidden, velvet domesticity.

The hotel veranda was rustling with newspapers when he reached it, and single-room celibates were emerging to bask like flies in the first sun and buzz their gossip across the print. Breakfast was ham and eggs, toast and apricot jam, share prices, racing tips and coffee while the streets outside began to fill with men in a hurry. Always in a hurry. Hurry-ing to the Stock Exchange, by way of the house on the corner where Hermann Eckstein performed his proconsular duties for Wernher and Beit. From there would come the seeds of information which, when skilfully planted in that fecund soil, would sprout sudden sixpences and shillings as rumour stimulated growth and share prices rose to meet hands ready to pluck them.

Cohen joined the throng which was congregating outside the Corner House. It filled the block-long space between Market and Commissioner Streets with a noisy, gesticulat-ing, mobile mass. Brokers and dealers, crooks, beggars and touts, merchants, hotel-keepers, clerks and messengers, the curious, the knowledgeable, the idle, the damned and the blessed. This was where the 'killings' were made, and where the left-overs were available for quick-witted scavengers. This was where predators mingled with carrion – and it was not always possible to distinguish between them. This was where Johannesburg expressed itself, visibly and volubly.

Cohen was arguing heatedly, as people usually did, with

115

the two Lillienfeld brothers – a well-known pair of Cape Colony merchants who had set themselves up as brokers at an early stage on the gold-fields and made things as tough as possible for any intruders on their domain. It was they who had bought the 'Star of Africa' diamond for £11,200 – and passed it on eventually to the Earl of Dudley for £25,000.

'No, Louis!' Arthur Lillienfeld was saying in his heavy, Teuton voice. 'I am taking two-thirds of the commission. Take it or leave it. If you ... Hullo! Look who's coming. Your old friend Barney. The great Barnato, M.L.A. ... Such a surprise!'

'It's a surprise, all right,' said Cohen. 'He hardly gave his agent time to organize that welcoming committee this morning – three top-hats and a bouquet. And who d'you think called three cheers for Barney Barnato?'

'Well, aren't you going across to meet him?'

'Not me. He'll probably cut me dead anyway.'

'Cut you? But I thought you were old friends?'

'Let's say I know him too well. Like a brother, perhaps. But that's not it. He asked me to go down to Kimberley to help him in the election. I wouldn't do it. He'll not forgive me for that.'

Barnato was making a royal progress from Height's Hotel. He walked along jauntily, his immaculate frock-coat swinging away from narrow striped trousers. White carnation. Butterfly collar poised over gleaming silk cravat; gold chain and fob. Pale leather gloves matching pale leather shoes. Gold-rimmed pince-nez magnifying the sparkle behind; full moustache with waxed ends framing the rosy cheeks of good health and good success. Top-hat doffed frequently in magnanimous response, revealing the hair parted straight down the middle, falling like eaves on each side of the dome of the forehead. An intelligent piece of tinsel made durable by diamonds, substantial by gold, formidable by personality and courage: Barney Barnato had come to Johannesburg.

On his back-slapping walk a trail of men attached themselves to his wake like asteroids to a comet. As he blazed along Commissioner Street towards the Stock Exchange everybody joined in, nine out of ten trying to sell him something. At the corner of Simmonds Street he was stopped by the wall of people and a row of wooden posts across the intersection. Above the heads of the men who closed around him he got a quick glimpse of Lou Cohen and the hulking Lillienfelds, and cleaved a way towards them.

'Lou!' he yelled, when he was ten men away. 'Lou Cohen! You old bastard! Come here!'

Cohen, surprised and relieved, pressed towards him and grabbed the outstretched hand.

'Get me out of here – away from this lot. And those Lillienfelds. Before they rob me ... Where can we go for a drink?'

'There's the Stock Exchange bar. It'll be quieter there, but not much.'

Cohen turned about and with Barnato pushing genially and forcefully behind him they cleaved a way to the Stock Exchange, the irrepressible staccato of Barnato's chatter peppering his ears.

'You wouldn't do nothing for me in the election. Ungrateful. You should have stuck to your old partner. But you see I beat those Kimberley bastards. Nobody didn't want me in. Not even Rhodes, though he was on my side. He had to be, had to be. I know he doesn't like me. He looks down on me because I never been to college like him. But I beat him all the way in Kimberley. He had a stone in 'and, but I won in a canter.'

Cohen, who knew differently, was not disposed to argue. You couldn't argue with Barnato. He was his own logic and his facts were words ... words of all shapes and sizes fired from all angles of truth. The comparative peace of the Stock Exchange bar brought little respite.

'Is this the Stock Exchange? No wonder they want to do their business in the street. We must change that, Lou. We'll put up a building big enough for all of 'em, and posh. Every convenience. They'll be glad to pay to come inside. That's it. My own Stock Exchange. Let's have a drink. Champagne. Never touch anything else; bad to mix your drinks. Put it down to me ... well then, you pay for it. Lend me a fiver. You owe me ten. Yes, you do, Lou. Always settle your racing debts. Thanks, that'll be five you owe me. Now a bottle. Fine. Tell me, Lou, how long has that crowd been outside there? What do they do there?'

'Well, you can see the Exchange building's too small to hold them. It's been like that ever since Alfred Beit put Hermann Eckstein in that office in the corner house. They follow Hermann and Alfred more than anybody else around here – including Rhodes.'

'So they should, so they should. But what's the idea of them posts? Do they have to close 'em in like that?'

Cohen laughed as Barnato poured out the champagne.

'That's not to keep them in, it's to keep the horse carriages out. They had accidents every day before old von Brandis put the posts across the road; though if you ask me, there was more danger of the horses being trampled to death by the dealers than the other way about. We had to get Kruger's permission, you know. What he'd like to do, of course, is put iron bars around the whole lot of us.'

'Can you blame him? Trouble with you people, you don't understand Kruger. How d'you set about seeing a president, Lou? Like seeing a king or a queen? I mean an audience, that sort of thing?'

'Well, you shouldn't have much difficulty,' Cohen said, smiling, 'now that you're a member of the Cape Parliament.'

'Ah, yes; I'd almost forgotten that. What the devil are those blokes doing?'

He pointed along the bar counter, where half a dozen members were standing each with a lump of sugar on a gold sovereign in front of him.

'That's the fly game,' Cohen told him. 'You scoop the pool the first time a fly settles on your lump of sugar.'

'Well, that shouldn't take long. Never seen so many flies. But tell me, who are the big operators around here now? Who are the people I'll have to deal with? Not just shares. Property, mines, everything. Let's see that paper. Bailey, Bailey. That's a new one for a start. He's got a list of about eighty mining shares here.'

'That's a young fellow called Abe Bailey. Came up from Barberton. Bright fellow, beginning to launch out in other directions. I should think he's worth keeping an eye on.'

'All right; Bailey. Who else?'

'Your old pals Robinson and Beit.'

'Ah, yes. They don't like me up here. Upsets their little applecart. I know 'em too well. But I'll leave them alone for the time being. What about all these square-heads? Lillienfelds, Hanau – decent chap, Hanau – the Lippert brothers. I'd like to give that red beard a bit of a twist. Concessions! What a way to make a living – bribery and corruption for a

118

solid month and then no more work for the rest of your life. Blooming theft by false pretences, that's what it is. Wish I had a few.'

'There's going to be hell to pay about that dynamite monopoly, they tell me, Barney. But Lippert's got the government in his pocket, so they say.'

'I'll make you a lot of money, Lou. Tons of it. Order another bottle. Never mix it. How's your wife? Not for you the money; for your family. You wouldn't help me at Kimberley. Why should I make you rich? I'm a fool. Tell me, where can I hire a horse and cart? Will you see to that for me, Lou? Tomorrow, first thing. At the hotel.'

'What are you going to do with a horse and cart, then?'

'Just have a good look round. See for myself. Only trust my own opinion. What's all this about deep levels? Never mind. Find out for myself!'

'I'll get you the horse and cart, Barney. But I won't be paying for it. And what after that? You've told me everything except what you're doing here.'

'Shall I tell you? Well, why not? They'll all know soon enough. I've come to buy up Johannesburg. All of it. Just a minute – need a match. You got a match? I'll borrow one...'

Barnato was away from Johannesburg for a week. He could not stay away longer because he had accepted an invitation to be the principal guest of the Scottish community at their St Andrew's Night banquet and he had also promised to play the leading part in *Ticket of Leave Man* which was being put on at the Globe Theatre to raise funds for Johannesburg's first synagogue. This was the building, its huge dome dominating the Johannesburg skyline, which President Kruger, with commendable impartiality but curious theology, later declared open 'in the name of our Lord Jesus Christ'.

Barnato spent the week travelling up and down the length of the Main Reef, examining outcrop and development properties, questioning miners, mine managers, geologists and engineers. By St Andrew's Day he was convinced that even the wildest and most optimistic rumours were right and that he was on to something in the Witwatersrand that was bigger than his beloved Kimberley and its diamonds. The sky was the limit as far as he was concerned, and it was not long before he was telling that to anybody who would listen. The banquet provided him with an opportunity he was not likely to miss. He began his response to the toast of 'Our Guests' with a whopping great lie.

'I came to Johannesburg with one object, and that was recreation; for I have gone through many troubles lately and encountered much opposition.

'As you know, I was here some ten months ago and did not then form a very high opinion of the Witwatersrand gold-fields. Now things are altered. I do not wish you to be led away by my opinion, but I can assure you that it is my firm opinion that the gold-field of the Transvaal will be to South Africa generally what Kimberley has been to the Cape Colony. I am now willing to pay a good price for Rand stocks today.

'I can tell you that when I arrived here a few days ago I felt simply paralysed at the sight of what has been done. The mail left for England today, and if some of you had only been able to look over my shoulder and read what I wrote to some of the leading financiers at home about the prospects of these gold-fields, you would have been astonished.'

It was, in fact, an astonishing speech for anybody who was about to engage in a large-scale buying operation of stocks and properties. It is explicable only if it is remembered that Barney Barnato always liked to please his audience – and that he might have already bought a good deal of stock which he would not be averse to selling at a higher price.

His pince-nez flashed his pleasure as the applause rippled round the white sea of table-cloth and napkins and starched shirt-fronts. He held up his hand for quiet.

'. . . The report which appeared in a Kimberley newspaper a day or two after my arrival here to the effect that I had bought out all Mr J. B. Robinson's gold interests is untrue and without the slightest shadow of foundation. I assure you,' he added amid the general laughter, 'I haven't got that much money. Anyway, I'm not competing against Mr Alfred Beit. There are many other Main Reef properties which under similar able management as the Robinson and Langlaagte Estate will give equally good results. I have no hesitation in giving my opinion that in the near future Johannesburg will rival, in fact surpass, any gold centre the world has yet seen. I look forward to Johannesburg becoming the financial Gibraltar of South Africa.'

Johannesburg loved it, and they loved Barney Barnato. He responded eagerly to this avid courtship. By the end of the year he had become the biggest claim-holder on the Witwatersrand; he determined in his mind what would be the business centre of the thriving town, and bought every vacant site he could lay his hands on; control of the Johannesburg Estate and Chambers Company enabled him to proceed with his plans for a great new Exchange building and a block of 100 office suites and shops (to be called, of course, Barnato Buildings); the Johannesburg Consolidated Investment Company was formed to handle his land and property deals; the Johannesburg Waterworks Company and its potential in all sorts of directions attracted his interest; and he produced blueprints, as a final gesture of faith and personal identification, of a palatial residence he was going to have erected for himself on top of one of the high ridges to the north of the town.

In three months Barnato had bought up stock and property to the value of more than £2,000,000, and was looking round for more. He had acquired or floated six mining concerns, a vast number of claims on what he hoped would be the extensions of the reefs, three large real-estate companies through which he controlled the business heart of Johannesburg; he had got control of the Stock Exchange and of the town's water supply.

More and more people were remembering and quoting his phrase 'the financial Gibraltar of South Africa'. It sounded like Cecil Rhodes. Were Rhodes and Barnato working together? Had Rhodes sent Barnato to build a citadel of Johannesburg from which the republic could be smashed? But if Barnato was ever aware of the full allusion of his metaphor – which is unlikely – it was entirely as a personal fortress. If it was to be directed against anybody it would not be at Kruger, but at Rhodes.

He had seen what Kimberley had made of Cecil Rhodes, and he recognized the impelling motive behind his great contemporary. He knew, better than anyone else except Beit, that the Witwatersrand gold had made the Transvaal essential to the vision, and that the empire-builder could no longer be content with the Bechuanaland by-pass on his way to Cairo.

Barnato's own ambition did not extend beyond the material and personal. He had few, if any, political prejudices or preferences. His candidature for the Cape Parliament was inspired by the same motives of egotism and justification which inspired his quest for wealth. Money, with the position it bought him, was an end in itself. It did not matter to him whether the Transvaal was a republic or a British colony. He saw no difference that affected him between President Kruger and Queen Victoria.

To Rhodes, money was the essential means to the great end he had set himself in Africa. The Witwatersrand goldfields and his early stake in them were, at first, not much more than a supplement to Kimberley and De Beers. He wanted the gold as he wanted the diamonds, and for the same purpose – to finance the flotation of his stupendous intention to make the continent of Africa a British stock company.

Later, just about the time of Barnato's arrival in Johannesburg, a completely new factor had been introduced into South African politics; it changed all Rhodes' immediate plans, and in its moment of revelation marked the doom of the republic. This was the disclosure of the fantastic extent and potential of the Transvaal gold-reefs.

Almost overnight the South African Republic changed from a bankrupt, nondescript attempt at a State into the richest country in the world. Until then Rhodes had been content to wait for the republic to join his concept of federation as part of an inevitable South African economic and political process. It could, if necessary, wait until that obstinate old so-and-so Kruger died: give him ... another ten years? The foundation of Rhodesia, the exploitation of its gold – that was the immediate task, and then the wrapping-up of the Transvaal would be complete.

Now, with inexhaustible resources of wealth at their disposal, Kruger and his burghers, from temporary nuisance, loomed suddenly as a menace to the grand vision. Rhodes, who was himself using money to build an empire, was only too conscious of the power this placed in the hands of the ageing President. With it he could buy men and guns and turn them into armies; with it he could make new allies of the European Powers who were scrambling for slices of the great carve-up of Africa, and who would leap at any excuse for an intervention or alliance that would embarrass Britain. French, German, Dutch; all had their feet in the door. By the beginning of 1889 the Transvaal, from Rhodes' point of view, could not be allowed to continue as a republic much longer.

Barney Barnato, who knew Rhodes well enough to sense the motives which actuated him, must have been aware that Johannesburg and not Pretoria held the key to the unfolding situation, to the unfolding map which Rhodes' pudgy hands were spreading over Africa. The greatest moment in Barnato's life had been the all-night bargaining with Cecil Rhodes over the amalgamation of the diamond diggings. He, the Whitechapel Jew, had been the victor then. He had forced Rhodes to pay his price.

Now he looked forward to the next encounter – for control of the Witwatersrand and Johannesburg. He had chosen his positions carefully. He had got his gold-producing mines and his stakes in the future of the deep levels. Next would be the Stock Exchange, the visible translation of the underground treasure, with every dealer and broker a tenant. At the heart of his financial empire, Barnato's Buildings; and his finger on the pulse of Johannesburg and the gold industry. What else? Ah, yes – the essentials of the industrial and commercial life of the community must be cornered. Electricity? Gas? All in the hands of concessionaires under the authority of the Volksraad. Too late. But what about water? The town and the mines could not live a day without water. That Waterworks Company. Easy to buy control of that, and make it into something efficient and therefore potent. He would like to see Robinson or Beit or Rhodes – especially Rhodes – coming to ask him for a little water in their taps.

CHAPTER ELEVEN

Barnato was a man in a hurry. The bus was in motion and he was determined not to miss it. His determination was founded on complete confidence in the future of the gold-mining industry and Johannesburg; but he responded readily to less substantial stimuli which whirled about him like neutrons round an electron. His new Stock Exchange, for instance, was inspired largely by a moment of incandescence.

He came into the Exchange hall one morning to find the two Lillienfeld brothers in the middle of a violent altercation with Louis Cohen. They loomed large as they argued, hands waving, fingers jabbing, guttural voices booming. Barnato walked straight between them, the light of battle in his normally placid blue eyes.

'What's this, what's this? Are they hammering you, Lou? What are you two up to, hey? Don't give them a penny, Lou. Not a penny more than the normal commission. I know these Lillienfelds!'

'You keep out of this, you cheap little Yid: get back to the East End, where you belong!'

'Ah, so that's the way of it! Shall we, Lou? Shall we see what sort of pork their noses are made of?'

He took off his pince-nez as he spoke, handed them carefully to one of the crowd of members who had gathered round the four men. Barnato, his eyes blinking a little as they adjusted the focus, did not wait for Cohen's reply. He squared up to Arthur Lillienfeld, aware of the first bets being offered among the onlookers as they made a quick appraisal of the form ... 'It's two to one on the Germans; they've got about ten stone in hand between 'em!'

'Come on, you square-headed bastard!' Barnato yelled, loud enough for all to hear. 'Let's see who's going home: me to the East End or you to your Prussian pigsty!'

The two Lillienfelds came blundering forward together, arms flailing, to be met by the practised fists of Barnato and the ready, if less expert, opposition of Cohen. There was little room for manoeuvre and it is more than likely, in a plain slugging match, that the two smaller men would have been severely mauled. But now various members of the Exchange committee had been summoned, and with the assistance of some of the onlookers who were not involved in the speculative aspect and could therefore be deemed impartial, they quickly broke up the fight.

After the subsequent post-mortem, all four contestants were asked to apologize to the committee and to each other. Barnato refused to do so, and it was immediately suggested that he should resign.

'Resign? How can I resign?' he told the wide-eyed committee. 'I own the place!'

He had bought up enough shares to give him control. Instead of resigning, he gave orders for the building to be pulled down and a new Exchange, financed by his Estate and Chambers Company, to be erected in its place. While dealings went on unabated outside in the street, the hall was demolished and a new one put up by three shifts of men working continuously night and day.

In an incredibly short space of time Jan Eloff, the Mining Commissioner, laid the foundation stone, and, almost overnight it seemed, prices and orders were being shouted across the floor of the big Exchange building which was to be the centre of South Africa's financial activity for the next fifteen years.

By 1890 the geologists and mining engineers were getting a pretty clear, if limited, picture of the phenomena they were probing. They had traced a conglomerate outcrop for a distance of about 150 miles in a vast semicircle, with the thirty miles of the Witwatersrand gold-fields, stretching from Boksburg to Robinson's newest mine at Randfontein, in the centre of the arc. This outcrop, they thought, was the northern rim of a vast lake of molten conglomerate that had petrified under the enormous pressures of the globe's cooling, and been tilted up until its perimeter had broken through the surface of the earth at the foot of the ridge of the Witwatersrand. From the outcrop the banket reefs dipped southward in a long incline and at varying angles of depression – no man knew how far or how deep.

It was on this interpretation that millions of investment capital were staked and from which Johannesburg grew out of the few stores and bars of the conventional mining camp. It was less knowledge than educated faith, and fortunately there were men like Robinson, Rhodes, Beit and Barnato who sensed the full possibilities long before the geologists confirmed them – and backed their faith with their fortunes.

But while the geologists contemplated the incredible, speculative interest was content to venture just a few hundred feet below the surface and a few hundred yards south of the Main Reef outcrop. That was more than enough to promote another boom in what were known as the South Dip claims.

In the early days, when the nature of the formation was quite unknown to the prospectors and diggers, claims on all the proclaimed farms had been pegged out by the hundred and sold and re-sold by speculators who followed up the first rush. As the reefs were traced along an east–west line, most of the claims away from the outcrop were abandoned as worthless or were held by the mining companies as valueless assets, available to anybody who wanted them at a nominal sum.

At the beginning of '89 a minor gold rush took place for these off-beat claims – a paper rush of promoters, since the digger had long disappeared in search of more rewarding digging. These claims were soon as valuable as any along the outcrop, and a whole new series of 'deep-level' companies were floated to operate the South Dip down to a few hundred feet. That watchdog of Johannesburg, *The Standard*, felt compelled to warn its readers against over-enthusiasm and exploitation:

'Already some schemes are on foot to float ground which has very little chance of catching the reefs, even if they existed, at a depth less than 3,000 feet. Now, that must not be permitted. The deep levels are all right when in close proximity to the reefs, but it does not follow that every claim so long as it lies to the south of the Main Reef will be of value. If frauds are not allowed to go unchallenged we again repeat that the deep-level mining will be a benefit to the mining industry in general.'

In the light of subsequent developments that last phrase could be assessed as the major understatement of the nineteenth century; but at the time, this restrained and conservative attitude to the Witwatersrand discoveries was shared by nearly all expert and responsible opinion.

If the Transvaal company promoters were having a high old time it was as nothing compared to some of the fraudulent flotations which were put over on the London Stock Exchange, where shares were lapped up by a gullible and excited public. There is no doubt that most of these flotations were deliberate swindles; but, unknown to promoters and sharedealers and the public they battened on, events taking place deep underground were catching up with the prospectuses of even the most imaginative financiers. The introduction of the diamond drill made boreholes possible at depths well beyond the contemplation of the first probers in the disappearing reefs. Still, it was to be a long time before fact overtook fancy; time enough for the feverish activity in the stock markets to be succeeded by the inevitable reaction of slump and despair.

Nobody was thinking of slump when the first English cricket team, sponsored by Major Warton, visited South Africa and arrived at Johannesburg at the end of January, 1889. The skipper was C. Aubrey Smith, a young Sussex amateur who was beginning to make a reputation for himself as an actor. Long after his cricketing days were over, Hollywood and motion pictures were to ensure his fame to two succeeding generations.

The boom in market values was at its peak. The whole population of Johannesburg seemed to concentrate at certain hours between Market and Commissioner Streets in the enclosed section of roadway known universally as 'Between the Chains'.

Boom or no boom, even this frantic arena of speculation was bare and deserted while the community flocked to the Wanderers ground to watch and entertain the England cricketers.

The inhabitants of Johannesburg, pound for pound, were probably the most sports-minded collection of human beings on the face of the earth. The first thing they did after pegging out their claims was to look around for a space that was big enough and level enough to accommodate cricket or football. The next thing they did was to lay out a race-track.

They wanted a one-and-a-half-mile track and, as it was

127

impossible to find a course over that distance that did not intrude on somebody's pegged-out claim, the horses in the early meetings had to pursue a somewhat zigzag course to the winning-post. Later the race-course was established permanently on the farm Turffontein, an appropriate coincidence which could hardly have been foreseen by the original Boer settler who had given that name to his ranch.

The pursuit of cricket and racing has been characteristic of every English establishment around the globe. Since these are both pastimes that require a considerable area of ground it might be interesting for some historian to speculate upon the part this factor has played in the Englishman's unique propensity for annexing territory. The 'Sporting Club' can be found in every exotic corner of the earth where the British have settled, permanently or temporarily; no one can say that it has not been a beneficent and civilizing influence and an instrument of peace and goodwill.

The Johannesburgers were no exception; at the end of the 1888 football season, when the thoughts of all loyal subjects of the Queen turned inevitably to cricket, a group of prominent citizens decided to approach Kruger for a grant of Government land on the northern outskirts of the township. They got thirty acres on a ninety-nine-year lease for a yearly rental of £25. A committee was formed, and the Wanderers Club was born.

They raised £5,000 by the sale of 1,000 £5 debentures, and set about preparing a site and a pavilion in time for the arrival of Major Warton's cricketers. Within three months 2,000 tons of earth had been excavated and carted away, the front portion of a pavilion with seating accommodation, dressing-rooms and bar had been erected, plans had been drawn for one of the most comprehensive sporting clubs in the world, and the £5 debentures were changing hands readily at £12. It was a successful diversion of the enormous energy which is latent in Johannesburg and its people and which is normally concentrated on the making and spending of as much money as possible in the shortest possible time.

When the England team arrived it was decided that, to meet an obvious disparity in skill, Johannesburg would play twenty-two men against the visitors' eleven.

About 3,000 spectators, most of whom objected bitterly to the high entrance charges, paid for admission to the ground and pavilion enclosure. The disproportion in numbers did not make itself evident in the home team's batting; only four of the twenty-two reached double figures, and after being sixty for four wickets at lunch-time on the first day, the remaining seventeen Johannesburg wickets fell for the addition of only seventy-eight runs.

Approaching their task a little light-heartedly perhaps, the England batsmen soon found themselves confronted by a situation for which neither the mechanics of the game nor the technique of the players made any provision – twenty-two men fielding. The classic repertoire of strokes and the great experience of the batsmen were insufficient to penetrate such a human barrier. The only way the ball could reach the boundary was by being hit over it; and the re-adjustment to this primitive approach to batsmanship came too late. The England XI, to the dismay of the many who had taken the odds laid on them, were all out for sixty.

Considerably shaken by this experience, the visitors went to bed early on the intervening Sunday night for the first time on the tour. They came into the arena of the Wanderers on Monday morning like gladiators, with the result that ten of the Johannesburg representatives failed to score at all and the remaining twelve managed only fifty-eight runs between them.

This left Major Warton's team 137 runs to get to win and, with memories of Saturday's débâcle fresh in the minds of all who had witnessed it, it was reckoned that they did not have a better than even-money chance of doing it. These odds, freely offered, were snapped up eagerly by the visiting players, who sent in two of the greatest batsmen in England – Hearne and Abel – to redeem the honour of their country and a couple of dozen betting slips.

Whether any of the Johannesburg side also backed England is not officially recorded, but there was a sharp decline in the standard of fielding and catching which, combined with some inspired batting, enabled Hearne and Abel to knock off the runs required without being separated.

On the whole everybody except the bookmakers was well pleased with this result, as it would not have done the prestige of either England or the Uitlanders any good in Pretoria if the English representatives had been beaten. Every field of encounter in which Britain was involved in those days tended to be another form of Majuba.

Off the field the tourists had to cope with Johannesburg's already fabulous hospitality, which began when the reception committee ('accompanied by the ladies') drove to meet their coach from Kimberley outside the town.

A full programme of promenade concerts, smoking concerts, theatrical performances at The Globe and the Theatre Royal, and a luncheon party at the Jumpers Mine culminated in a grand ball for the cricketers given by the ladies of Johannesburg. It was a roaring success, the only people not attending it, apparently, being the English cricketers. They had put in a brief appearance and had quick visual proof of the fact that the population of Johannesburg at that time consisted of approximately 7,000 adult white males and 3,000 adult white females, nearly all of whom were married or about to be married. With a quick assessment of the odds against them, plus the possibility of having to listen to more soprano solos during the course of the evening, the cricketers had slipped away in small groups to see something of the less-organized night life of the town.

CHAPTER TWELVE

The tough and pugnacious citizens of early Johannesburg, unlike those of the American West with their gun-fights, got rid of their frustrations and settled their frequent differences of opinion with their fists. In Tombstone and Tucson it may well have been advisable to be quick on the draw; in Johannesburg, if you couldn't talk your way out of an argument, you usually had to slug your way out. Barnato's ability and reputation in this respect always stood him in good stead, and among the leading amateur boxers of the Rand in the eighties and nineties was the young stockbroker and property dealer from Barberton – Abe Bailey.

There was a great demand among the more civilized section of the populace for a knowledge of the art of self-defence. To satisfy it a school of boxing was opened by J. R. Couper, a quiet and gentle Scot who almost against his will had fought and won the championship of South Africa in Kimberley a year or two previously. Most of the 'aristocracy' of the town became his customers, and they showed their regard for him by making him a member of the Stock Exchange.

One day in February, 1889, a well-known English prize-fighter stepped off the mail steamer at Cape Town. His name was Woolf Bendoff, and he was on his way back home after fighting a draw in Australia with the great Jack Burke.

Within a few days of his arrival the newspapers were publishing a challenge:

'Woolf Bendoff, recently arrived in this country, hearing of the boxing abilities of Professor J. R. Couper, champion of South Africa, would like to box him in any style he likes, for £1,000 up to £5,000 a side. Bendoff hopes he will come to the point like a solid man and defend his title.'

The sport-loving citizens of Johannesburg were on to this

morsel like bees on to nectar, and soon the hive was buzzing with rumours, the most popular of them being that Barney Barnato had imported Bendoff to settle profitably a little dispute with Abe Bailey on the merits of Couper.

Whether this was true or not, Barnato lost no time in getting in touch with Bendoff and bringing him up to the Rand. Then he went in search of Cohen.

'Lou, this Bendoff is good. I know his uncle well. One of the cleverest men in England, he was. Bendoff's staying in that place opposite Height's Hotel. Go round and see him. See what shape he's in. Tell him I'll guarantee his purse. He'll need a backer or two if he's thinking in thousands. Couper won't be short of backers. Bailey's bound to have a go. I'd like to take a couple of thou' off Bailey.'

'Look, Barney. I know Bendoff's record. He's fought most of the best men in England. Jimmy Couper's a friend of mine. I wouldn't like to see him beaten senseless.'

'Well, Lou, let's leave that part of it to Couper. If he's as good as Bailey says he is, I don't see what you've got to worry about.'

Abe Bailey was having his usual morning sparring session when the news was brought of Bendoff's challenge.

'D'you know this Bendoff, Jimmy?' he asked Couper, as they rubbed down after a couple of brisk rounds. 'Is he good?'

'I've heard about him. He's got a useful record. But I'll find out about him from my pals in England. Out of my weight, I reckon. Must be a couple of stone heavier.'

'What about this challenge? Shall we take him on?'

'*We*; Mr Bailey?'

'Certainly. I'll back you if you're willing to fight him. And I've got a pretty good idea where Woolf Bendoff'll find his stake money.'

'Well, you know I've announced that I've finished with prize-fighting. And two stone's a lot to give away. But I know what they'll all be saying if I refuse this challenge. How much are you willing to put up, Mr Bailey?'

Bailey slapped the boxer on the shoulder.

'Good man, Jimmy. I was sure you couldn't refuse a challenge. Tell you what we'll do. I'll get a couple of pals and we'll tell Bendoff we're willing to put up £2,000 to his £2,500 – winner take all. Now, we'll work out a reply to this challenge.'

In due course the terms of acceptance were published:

'J. R. Couper, though having advertised for some time his retirement from the pugilistic profession, would say in answer to Mr Bendoff's pressing challenge that he would be glad to meet him in a light boxing match with small gloves to a finish for any stake or for £2,000 on condition that J. R. Couper, whose weight is 144 lb, gives no more than 8 lb away.'

As might have been expected this brought forth a few sarcastic and derogatory remarks from the opposite camp and the issue quickly became one not of who would win but whether Couper was afraid to fight or not.

'Well, Mr Bailey,' Couper said, a few days after their first discussion, 'it's as I expected. If I don't fight him they'll say I'm frightened.'

'That's about the size of it, Jim. Of course, I know you're not. But that won't make the others change their mind, especially as Barnato has already taken odds on Bendoff. What're you going to do?'

'I've had a look at Bendoff. He's not fit, and he's not built to be fast. Nothing below the waist. I'll fight him – and I'll beat him.'

'What about the weight?'

'The heavier he is the slower he'll be and the better I'll like it. But don't tell anybody.'

As soon as the committee was informed of Couper's acceptance, they made their arrangements for the fight. It was fixed to take place on July 26 at a place known as Eagle's Nest about six miles from the township. It was billed in the manner of fight promoters anywhere, any time, as a contest for the heavyweight championship of the world. It was to be fought under London prize-ring rules and the purse of £4,500 was, at that time, the highest ever offered for a prize-fight.

The two men went into training immediately on opposite sides of Johannesburg – Couper at the Half Way House on the road to Pretoria, Bendoff a few miles out on the western side of the town.

Lou Cohen, who had been appointed umpire for Bendoff, did not much like the idea of opposing his friend Couper and was convinced the latter had no chance against the strength, weight and wider experience of the other. Bendoff's sparring partners were complaining bitterly about the weight of his punches. And what had Bendoff told him?

'I tell you, Mr Cohen, I'm quite willing to go into a room with Couper with one hand tied behind my back until only one man can walk out. And it won't be Couper!'

Cohen, uneasy in his conscience and annoyed with Barnato over the whole affair, had travelled out to the Half Way House to see his friend.

'Look here, Jimmy, I've decided I'm not going to have anything to do with this fight, because I couldn't possibly back you. I think the other man's sure to win. That being the case, I'll have no bet.'

'I'm sorry you feel like that, Lou. I think I've got a very good chance. But if you won't back me, why not back the other man? What are the latest odds?'

'It's six to four against you and evens Bendoff, if you can get it.'

'Then why not have a good bet on Bendoff at evens, and have a saver on me? Though I'm warning you, you'll make more money the other way round.'

'Well, if it's all right with you, Jimmy, I'll go ahead and back my fancy. But I don't like it. I don't like it.'

He went off shaking his head. The next day he put a thousand on Bendoff to win. The easiest and worst thousand, he said to himself, he had ever made in his life.

Out at Eagle's Nest an enclosure 100 feet square had been formed of corrugated iron nine feet high to keep out the vast crowd of spectators expected who would not be willing to pay the £5 entrance fee. But there was still one major difficulty to be overcome. Kruger was known to disapprove violently of prize-fighting. It was more than likely that he would order his 'Zarps' (South African Republican Police) to break up this one, if he had not already done so. The committee decided to send one of their number who had long been in the employ of the republic over to Pretoria to sound out Oom Paul.

'Mr President,' the visitor began, as he sipped his coffee on the long stoep of Kruger's house, 'there's a big Englishman in Johannesburg who says he can thrash any man in the Transvaal – burgher or Uitlander. What would you do with a man like that?'

Kruger took the pipe out of his mouth and spat accurately over the veranda railing.

'Shoot him,' he said gruffly.

'Well, Mr President, that's surely a good idea, but it is against the law. Besides, it is not necessary. We've got a Transvaler who can thrash this Englishman.'

The man from Johannesburg then went on to explain how they were planning to do this on July 26. It seemed very much to the President's liking, and he forthwith signed an order to the head of the police force in Johannesburg instructing him not to interfere with the fight.

The morning of July 26, like every other July morning on the Witwatersrand, dawned clear and bright and cold. As the sun rose it lit up the first walking queues as they left the town, boots crunching into the frosted, yellow grass or raising little puffs from the long-dry dust. They had started off in semi-darkness on their six-mile tramp to be at the ring before 7.30 – the time at which the fight was scheduled to begin.

Soon the noisy marchers were being passed by a stream of vehicles which varied in shape and size with the financial and social status of their occupants. It was apparent by seven o'clock that the greater part of the adult male population of Johannesburg was on the road and spreading over the veld heading for Eagle's Nest. Even the Stock Exchange was closed.

It was also apparent that very few of them would get anywhere near the fight. The enclosure had been built to accommodate five or six hundred without being more congested than the high price of tickets warranted. There were at least six times that number leaving the township.

Back in Johannesburg Louis Cohen was busy, at an early hour, spending part of the £1,000 and more which he expected to collect after Bendoff had won. He had arranged a sumptuous luncheon at his house for the various friends he had put on to this good thing, and before he left for Eagle's Nest he supervized the laying of the table and the preparation of the food and wine to which they would return in triumph. Poor Jamie Couper, thought Cohen; he would ask him along as a friendly gesture, though he doubted he would be able to eat anything.

Cohen was rather surprised when Woolf Joel arrived at the front door and offered him a lift out in his post-chaise. It was not often that anybody had the company of Barnato's charming and able nephew to himself, and Cohen immediately accepted. They shared a half-bottle of champagne, well chilled by the cold air, and then set off through a town grown strangely quiet with the exodus of all its men. Joel did not waste any time.

'I hear you've got a lot of money on Bendoff, Lou," he said, as soon as they were seated in the carriage. 'Wouldn't you like to lay some of it off?'

'I've got plenty on him, all right. But not as much as I'd like to have.'

'Is he as big a certainty as that?' Joel murmured.

'I feel really bad about it, Woolfie. Jamie Couper's my friend. I don't like to think of what's going to happen to him in the next couple of hours.'

'You shouldn't let a friend of yours fight without any of your money on him. It'll bring bad luck to both of you.'

'With Bendoff, I should worry about luck! One thousand pounds without working for it is not my idea of *bad* luck!'

'Well then, if you won't back Couper with me, you should lay off a bit of what you've got on Bendoff. What did you get? Six to four on? I'm offering five hundred of mine to two-fifty of yours.'

'Two to one on! I tell you Woolfie, this is a twenty to one shot. That poor Couper.'

'Well, I'll tell you, Lou. I'd like to have a little money on this fight. Makes it more interesting. I haven't got a penny on either man. Like going to the races without backing a horse.'

Joel felt in his breast pocket and pulled out a neat, crisp bundle of notes.

'Here, Lou. This £500 on Bendoff to £200 of yours. You surely can't be so stupid as not...'

'Nothing doing, Woolfie. Why don't you ask your Uncle Barney to lay off some of his bet at five to two?'

This brought the conversation to a sudden end. The postchaise was now weaving its way through the trudging crowds and the clumsier carts and wagons that were converging on the ringside.

The 12-foot corrugated iron walls of the prepared enclosure rose like a breakwater out of the sea of humans. This was, in fact, the main purpose of the wood and iron walls, but not only to keep out the crowds. There was always the possibility that a section of the Volksraad would

136

make Kruger change his mind about such ungodly activity, so that the barrier which surrounded the ring was designed first and foremost to keep out the police until the fight was over.

Inside the enclosure a level, close-cut square of turf had been roped off and around this the acknowledged gentry and wealth of Johannesburg were jostling each other in high good spirits, making last-minute bets with the odds against Couper gradually increasing with every big wager.

It was not until nine o'clock that shouting from the crowd outside announced the arrival of the South African champion. He came straight along the passage squeezed out for him through the press of men, with his trainer and seconds struggling to prevent his well-wishers from thumping the breath out of him. He tossed his cap into the ring to a great cheer, and went to his corner. He stood there, a little fine-drawn in the face, but smiling and confident-looking, as Lowenthal and Bailey got him ready for the fight. Lou Cohen, as Bendoff's umpire, took a supervisory interest in the proceedings. There was still no sign of Bendoff. Lowenthal said to Cohen:

'Lou, your man's too late. If he's not here soon we'll claim the fight and the stake money.'

'You'll get yourself lynched if you do! Anyway, our man turned up here before eight and went away again. It was Couper who was late.'

The argument was cut short by a loud splintering crack and a great roar from outside as a hole was torn in the enclosure and the crowd started to pour through. Half a dozen fights started immediately as the men inside turned to meet the intruders. Barnato and Bailey, never reluctant to display their ability, strode purposefully from their place at the ringside. They were quickly intercepted by Woolf Joel.

'Don't be a fool, Barney,' he urged. 'And you, Abe. We can't lick that lot. They'll trample the place down and us with it! Let enough of them in to keep the rest out, and we'll have them on our side.'

'Woolfie's right,' Bailey agreed. 'We can't fight that lot.'

It was the only solution. About 200 men were let in and distributed around the inside perimeter. A group at the breach undertook to let no more come in. The crowd outside accepted the situation with a few pithy comments and dispersed to the nearby koppies and hilltops where they had a comprehensive, if distant, view of the proceedings. While these negotiations and disposals were being concluded another great roar heralded the arrival of Bendoff. He threw his cap into the ring and stepped jauntily across to Couper to shake hands.

It was after 9.30 when Mr Clem Webb, the referee, stepped into the centre of the ring to make the introductions.

'Gentlemen; we have assembled here today to witness a contest for the championship of the world, to take place between Woolf Bendoff of London and J. R. Couper of Johannesburg!'

He waited a few moments for the cheering to subside.

'I may tell you that we have a strong representative Press here today, and I can only hope there will be no necessity for these gentlemen to note anything that is unfair —'

'There bloody well will be, if you don't stop jabbering and get on with it!'

Webb continued, 'The stakes fought for today are the largest that have ever been fought for in the world. I shall now introduce J. R. Couper of Johannesburg, on my left. And Woolf Bendoff of London, on my right. And I hope the best man will win.'

As the referee summoned the two men to the scratch, Couper turned briefly, took out his false teeth and handed them to one of his seconds.

'Look after them carefully. I'll be a little hungry by lunchtime.'

The fighters shook hands, the brief salutation ending in a swinging left from Bendoff to Couper's body. Quick as lightning the smaller man brought over his right full on Bendoff's nose. The sudden look of surprise on Bendoff's face was augmented by the rapid blinking of his eyes as they smarted under the blow. He stepped back a pace as though he wanted to explain to Couper that he hadn't come 7,000 miles for that sort of thing, then he drove forward with all the weight and power of his body. Couper dodged quickly, but could not avoid the blow altogether. It caught him on the shoulder with enough force to knock him to the grass, bringing the round to an end. He jumped up nimbly, but as Bendoff turned towards his corner the crowd could see the slow trickle seeping from his nose to the corner of his mouth. A great shout went up: 'Couper's drawn first blood!'

The course of the fight was reflected accurately enough by the ringside betting. Up till the end of the fifth round the odds were still on the visitor. By the end of the tenth it was even money the two of them. Then, with every succeeding round, the odds against Bendoff grew longer until nobody was willing to bet on him at all.

But every blow that Bendoff swung contained the power to put an end to the fight, and several times Couper was forced to drop to the ground to avoid massive blows, or was crushed through the ropes as Bendoff's fists thudded into him. Yet every round marked out a little more obviously the pattern of pain that Couper was weaving on the face opposite him.

At the end of the thirteenth round the challenger staggered back to his corner, and, as he sat panting on Cohen's knee, groped around for the sponge lying in the bucket of water by his side.

Cohen was quick to spot his intention.

'You can't throw in the sponge now!' he hissed in Bendoff's ear, as he pushed the bucket out of reach. 'You've still got a chance. What d'you think'll happen to me if I let you give in now? There's too much money on you – including a lot of mine. You go on fighting!'

For seven more rounds Bendoff stayed in there. But Couper showed no sign of losing his speed or his head or his tactical efficiency, and from the twentieth round onwards the Londoner was at his mercy.

Now the shouts were all for Couper, and it was Bendoff who was forced to retire to his corner or go to the ground to evade punishment. Occasionally, though, he would charge forward like a blundering bull and force Couper through the ropes by sheer weight.

Couper was smiling as broadly as his supporters even as he skipped round the ring to avoid the other's rushes or crashed left and right punches into Bendoff's face.

At last, in the twenty-sixth round, Bendoff stepped suddenly back from a clinch, holding his left arm above the elbow, his contorted face contriving somehow an extra grimace of agony. Following up swiftly, Couper connected with a smashing right to the jaw which buckled Bendoff's knees and drooped him over the ropes in his own corner.

'My arm's gone,' he groaned to Cohen. 'I can't go on.'

Lou Cohen, who had said good-bye to his thousand

139

pounds many rounds before and who reckoned that even the Johannesburg crowd had had enough of blood and the humiliation of Bendoff, nodded his head and reached into the bucket. He pulled out the sponge and, with a sad shrug of his shoulders, tossed it into the middle of the ring.

Nobody turned up to Lou Cohen's lunch. Not even Lou Cohen.

CHAPTER THIRTEEN

There could not have been a better beginning to a year than 1889.

The Johannesburg share market was in a state of apparently perpetual multiplication, with infinite permutations of profit offered by over 140 quoted gold-mining companies; new revelations of underground possibilities constantly magnified the opportunities for surface exploitation; Barnato was still buying and beginning to build; Beit and Robinson, their confidence justified by more certain knowledge, were proceeding methodically to expand and consolidate their great financial enterprises; Rhodes was wrapped up in the acquisition of Mashonaland and Matabeleland in the north, but his Consolidated Goldfields was actively increasing its holdings on the Rand; the favourite had won the Summer Handicap.

To its inhabitants, Johannesburg was undoubtedly the greatest boom town in the world. In less than four years the population had increased from a single farming family to 10,331 whites (of whom 3,000 were female). No one had attempted to count the shifting herds of natives who drifted in from the distant plains and mountains with their blankets and assegais, and went back six months later as miners, cooks and house-boys in smart suits and with new shoes strung around their necks to prevent wear on the long walk home.

There were hotels and theatres, schools and convents, a public library, a general hospital and a general post office, three clubs, several parks, a permanent circus and menagerie, half a dozen churches and the biggest concentration of gold mines, bars and brothels on earth.

Johannesburg even had its own special currency. Every mining company on the Witwatersrand, whether they intended to do any mining or not, was printing it. A company

141

would be floated with a capital of, say, £20,000. It would strike a reef of high yield or acquire some fabulous South Dip claims – or it would merely suggest that it had. The £1 shares would rise to £10 and by selling 5,000 shares at the right moment the promoters could obtain £50,000 for a capital increase of £5,000. Sometimes this money was used for development; most of the time it was not – chiefly because there was nothing to develop.

As long as that currency continued to increase in value, irrespective of its intrinsic worth, there were no serious problems.

The Johannesburg Stock Exchange functioned for a good deal of the time on hectic reaction to inspired rumour. If the transactions coincidentally supplied capital for development, this was far from the thoughts of ninety per cent of the people who supplied it. Outcrops, banket reefs, deep levels, the South Dip ... these were all mysterious natural phenomena which, by some process of alchemy, made share prices rise.

But there came a time when even the most detached and ignorant speculator could perceive that the gold he was making out of the new companies' printed scrip was unsupported by any gold from the ground.

Doubts and fears were translated into selling orders, swelling rapidly from the first hesitant trickle to an irresistible onrush which flooded the stock exchanges with unwanted shares and which the flimsy paper barriers of worthless scrip could not contain.

The town went from boom to slump almost overnight, the whole process being speeded up by the revelation of persistent fraud practised by the promoters and share jobbers. New ideas in swindling had been thought up every week. Nobody had cared very much so long as share values had kept rising. But the day of reckoning could not be postponed for ever, and when people began to take a close look at what they had bought, what they saw scared them stiff. By the end of April the collapse was complete. Reaction in London was particularly drastic: the Stock Exchange virtually ceased dealing in Transvaal gold shares. The Witwatersrand Chamber of Mines urged London brokers not to deal in shares of companies which were not recommended by the Chamber, in the hope of restoring confidence in those they did recommend. But thereafter the City's attitude to the Witwatersrand was always tainted by suspicion.

The crash which had begun in March had nothing to do with gold production or the gold capacity of the mines. Output, which had built up the previous year to a steady average of 1,000 ounces a day by December, had shown a slight drop in the first three months of '89, but the influences were seasonal and explicable.

The disaster would have been much worse had it not been for the indulgence of the commercial banks, bolstered by the unshaken confidence of the genuine financiers and investors, who were less susceptible to market fluctuations and who could see plainly enough that the gold was there.

'All we've got to do,' Barney Barnato kept on telling everybody, 'is get it out!'

Early Johannesburg was a town that was never short of drink but always short of water. One of the first official organizations in the population was the Licensed Victuallers Association, and as early as January, 1888, its chairman was complaining that out of 320 members of the trade in town only thirty-seven belonged to the Association. Few of them, alas, regarded water as an essential for their customers.

The streams of rippling, white-foamed waters were such an unaccustomed sight to the hot, tired eyes of the Voortrekkers after the blistering journeys across the Karroo and Orange Free State that the choice of *Witwatersrand* as the name for the long ridge from which the streams flowed was understandable. But what had been an adequate water supply for a few farms and a few thousand head of cattle proved totally unequal to the needs of a concentrated and continually expanding population.

The selection of Randjeslaagte as the site for the new township had not helped matters. It had been chosen for a variety of reasons quite unrelated to the needs of the community which would inhabit it, and without any conception of the vast conglomeration of humanity and concrete which, in an incredibly short space of time, was to obliterate the veld.

A single small spruit ran along the north-west edge of the site, and at an early stage its banks were lined by rows of brickmakers – who could be said to have moulded Johannesburg out of the earth with their bare hands, but who provided nothing for themselves except a filthy collection of hovels and holes in the ground.

This stream was the township's principal source of water. It was also the natural drainage channel, so that after heavy rain all the accumulated rubbish and other less pleasant forms of pollution were washed into it.

A number of wells provided a temporary solution, but it needed little foresight to see that even if the diggers were not particularly interested in the social uses of water, the town and the mining industry could not hope to expand without it. And there was money to be made out of it.

The Johannesburg Waterworks Company, of which Barnato had bought control, was floated (if that is the right word) in July, 1887, to construct a reservoir and pipe a water supply to the township. Its first object was to acquire the inevitable concession, which had been given to James Sivewright, a Cape Town merchant, by the Pretoria government 'for the purpose of laying pipes through the streets of Johannesburg in order to supply the inhabitants thereof with water'. The only thing that Mr Sivewright failed to supply was the water to run through the pipes.

The site chosen by the company for the construction of a small reservoir was a spring emerging from a steep ridge on the northern boundary of the farm Doornfontein. It was one-and-a-half miles from the edge of the township, with the advantage of a 55-foot head of natural gravitation.

The progress of the Waterworks Company followed the contemporary pattern. First the acquisition of the concession, then the capital subscription, the flotation of the public company, the swift appreciation in value of shares. These were the primary objectives in most enterprises of the time.

Although Mrs von Brandis laid the foundation stone of the new reservoir early in 1888, it was not until Barney Barnato secured control towards the end of that year that any impetus was given to the actual work of construction. It was not finished in time to cope with the drought of 1889.

The rainy reason on the Transvaal high-veld is comparatively brief, spasmodic and violent, with a certainty that for at least four months of the rest of the year not a drop of rain will fall. Thus, without proper storage facilities, failure of the summer rains was followed by inevitable hardship.

During the hectic Stock Exchange summer which spanned

1888 and 1889 few people were even aware of any water shortage. Then, as human buoyancy sank with the falling market, Johannesburg suddenly realized they were in the middle of a drought.

The parched earth would yield no nourishment to crops or beasts, and fears of famine grew alongside the minor inconveniences of a shortage of drinking- and washing-water.

Ankle-deep in the dust, townspeople waited each morning for the wagons that never arrived. Anything eatable that came trickling in was snapped up at fantastic prices and satisfied only the hunger of the rich. Potatoes were sold at £6 a bag; sugar rose to five and six shillings a pound. Mealie meal, the staple diet of the native mineworkers, soared from £1 to £5 a bag, and managements were faced with an urgent problem of finding enough food for their 'boys' or sending them home to their kraals. A deputation from the Chamber of Mines went to Pretoria early in October to tell Paul Kruger that they would have to close the mines if they could not get provisions quickly.

Kruger was genuinely sympathetic, and concerned at the thought of losing the bulk of the State revenue. He sent for Sammy Marks and gravely explained the situation confronting Johannesburg and the gold mines.

'What would you do, Mynheer Marks, if you were president?'

'I'll tell you what I'd do, Oom Paul. I'd offer a prize to each wagon carrying a load of, say, two tons of food that reached Johannesburg before a certain date.'

The President ruminated on this between two sips of coffee.

'That sounds like a good idea. But it also sounds like a race meeting. I could not give my consent to anything ungodly. We'll have to think of something else.'

'Well then, Oom Paul, you can give them a bonus instead of a prize. You know what bonus means? It means good. Not even the God of Israel would object to that. Offer your Boers a bonus of £200 each for every wagon that brings in two tons of food!'

'*Vragtig*, Sammy! Do you want to ruin the republic? There will be 10,000 wagons going to Johannesburg Market Square within a month: I doubt whether the Volksraad will consider the Uitlanders worth that much!'

'Now you are making jokes, Oom Paul. But I see the point. All right, then, do it this way ... A bonus of £20 for each of the first 250 wagons arriving in Johannesburg with two tons of foodstuffs.'

'A wagon can carry much more than two tons, mynheer. We will make that three tons. Then the people will be better fed and we will get better value for our money.'

The announcement of the bonus offer, as Kruger anticipated, precipitated a rush of wagons to the Witwatersrand. Farmers in the outlying districts who got the news last had the worst of the start but were compensated by having the most food stocks, as the countryside nearest the mines had already been scoured by foraging parties.

The newspapers published daily bulletins recording the progress of the wagon trains moving as fast as the plodding oxen could pull them towards the hungry town. By the end of November the £5,000 had been paid out and the immediate crisis was over.

But still the rains did not come. Drought was something which the Boers had learned to contend with as an act of God; and God, in His wisdom, would bring an end to it in His own good time. Yet the presence of the Uitlanders added a new sort of problem to the normal pastoral hazards. Secure in their faith, they passed the difficulty on to the Almighty: Kruger and his Executive set aside a day of prayer for rain.

It did not occasion the burghers any great surprise when rain fell during the ensuing week to end the drought, and it was no credit to the Johannesburgers that the consensus of comment in that cynical town was that the Boers would far rather pray for rain than work hard to produce food.

Kruger and his colleagues had other reasons for wishing for a speedy end to drought and famine and the depression in the share markets. What was worrying the President was that the hardships of the situation, unrelieved by good cheer from the Stock Exchange, were making the Johannesburg population far too concerned with their physical and political circumstances. This was made manifest when the citizens combined in the middle of the year to send a memorial to the Volksraad asking for the establishment of a municipality in Johannesburg to enable them to levy taxes to provide a proper organization and adequate services for the town.

When the memorial was rejected, Johannesburg was furious. As long as the streets were paved with gold it didn't matter much how muddy or dusty or pot-holed they were; as long as the champagne flowed in, did it matter where it flowed out? It always evaporated, didn't it, or seeped away? True, the smell was a bit unpleasant at times, especially when the wind blew from the cesspits behind Braamfontein, or when the night carts were late on their noxious rounds. But it was no match for the heady smell of easy money that filled the air 'Between the Chains' when the market was booming.

Now that the golden world had collapsed, the desert tracks that were the streets were seen to be paved with nothing but garbage and sewage. There was no lighting and no drainage. Johannesburg was a dump; a rubbish dump. A place fit enough for the flies which swarmed all over it – flies which bred in millions in the cesspits and flew over, heavy-winged, to regurgitate their threat of pestilence through the town.

It was all right for those bloody Boers over in Pretoria. The smell didn't carry that far, anyway. As long as they could tax the trousers off Johannesburg, why should *they* worry? Well, it was about time somebody gave them something to worry about...

The Rand Club was the focal point of Uitlander dissatisfaction. On this peak the grumblings and rumblings of the populace collected like snowstorms, accumulating glaciers of discontent from which cold winds of anger and frustration swept down on Pretoria.

The members of the Club were not in the best of tempers at this time. Their new premises were a long time building, and although the enlarged bungalow they occupied wasn't all that bad – it provided for 170 dinners every day – they were impatient for the conveniences and luxuries with which the new building would supply them.

There was a bar, of course, but it was not always easy for lesser members or newcomers to get past the phalanx of founders or the recognized leaders of the community who had established their right to favoured position and privileged treatment.

The Corner House group held a fairly regular pre-lunch session at the bar counter. With Eckstein away in England trying to restore overseas confidence in the shattered gold market, Alfred Beit had come to Johannesburg to direct the affairs of his firm through the crisis; surrounded by his own youthful associates – Lionel Phillips, Percy FitzPatrick and J. B. Taylor – Beit proved a sure magnet for other leading Rand personalities as they drifted, singly or in pairs, into the Club. Soon there were gathered about him men like J. B. Robinson, Abe Bailey and Hans Sauer, Carl Jeppe, Charles Leonard (the town's most prominent lawyer and an outspoken advocate of the Uitlanders' political rights) and Edward Lippert – who normally would have had difficulty in getting through the club doors, but who was in the middle of some concession negotiations with Beit's firm.

It was a garrulous cross-section of the men who made the Rand, each in his separate way possessing the qualities, good and bad, which the time, place and circumstances needed.

Abe Bailey, signalling to the Indian barman to put another bottle of whisky on the counter, produced a copy of *The Diggers' News*, and said to Beit:

'Have you read the leading article today, Alfred? No? It's good stuff. Just what's wanted. Here, Charles, you're the educated one here. Read it out to us.'

Leonard skimmed through the article while he waited for their undivided attention.

'Here's a good bit. Listen. "Johannesburg has nothing it requires to make it fairly habitable or ordinarily safe or healthy. The attempt to make it so by self-taxation and local control is denied. Nothing remains at present but to await the issue of the promises made by the President and if they are not satisfactory a stronger, more continual and louder demand must be made for that which is universally granted in other civilized communities." Not bad, eh?'

'Sanitation's not the only thing. The place is getting more and more difficult to live in – and we've made it one of the most flourishing countries in the world.'

'*Who's* flourishing?' Bailey demanded. 'Have you seen the latest prices? But *I'll* tell you who's flourishing. The Government. They've just about doubled every official's salary in the short time I've been here. And there's plenty left over in the bank.'

'It's true, I'm afraid,' Carl Jeppe told them. 'I know the rough figures. Back in 1886, when the reef was found, fixed salaries in the administration came to a little more than

£50,000 a year altogether. This year they're well over £300,000.'

Even Beit whistled.

'Of course,' Jeppe went on, 'you've got to remember the Government was short of trained or even educated officials in the early days. Bringing in all these Hollanders was bound to be expensive . . .'

'They didn't have to. There were plenty of good enough men in South Africa.'

'I can tell you,' Robinson joined the discussion, 'old Kruger is very annoyed at all these suggestions that we doubt his word or that he's broken his promises.'

'For God's sake, J.B.!,' Leonard interrupted. 'We wouldn't doubt his word if he'd *done* anything about it! Does he think we're a bunch of schoolboys to be scolded when he's cross with us? Does he think we can be put off with a lollipop when we ask to be allowed to run our own lives, our own business? What about this railway line he's been promising for years? Where is it? Exactly where it was three years ago – nowhere! And we pouring money down the drain of that Netherlands Company with nothing to show for it.'

'The Company certainly seems to be misusing its opportunities,' Beit said judicially. 'We really ought to do something to try and get things changed. What are the chances in the Volksraad, Carl?'

Jeppe shook his head emphatically.

'Not a hope. This is the way Kruger wants it and the way he's going to get it. With a few exceptions he's got the Raad behind him. They'd do without railways altogether if they had their way. They reckon that as it's only you Uitlanders that'll get any benefit from them you should do all the paying that has to be done. Broadly speaking that's his attitude to most of the things the mines require – including dynamite.'

Everybody looked at Lippert, who grinned amiably back at them and raised his glass in a toast: 'To dynamite,' he said blandly, and held up his hand to stop the torrent of protest he could see forming on their lips. FitzPatrick, who had invited Lippert in for a drink, shuffled uneasily and cleared his throat.

'I know exactly what you are thinking, gentlemen,' Lippert said happily. 'And what you would like to say. Profiteering, bribery, corruption? All those things, no? Let me tell you a little story about the dynamite concession.'

Lippert finished his whisky and wiped his pointed red beard. 'You know, you do a grave injustice to the Volksraad by thinking that you can buy their votes. In my experience, and I have a good deal of experience, these men are not for sale as is so often suggested.'

Percy FitzPatrick laughed. 'What you mean, Edward, is that you only hire them for a limited time, and then hire them again for the next job.'

Lippert said gravely, 'What I mean is that, from the President downwards, they are honestly convinced of the rightness of their case and not influenced by bribes. You remember Stoffeltosen?'

They had all read about Stoffeltosen. He had made a strange and wild outburst in the Volksraad, during the debate on the dynamite monopoly, claiming that during the previous night he had had a vision and heard the voice of the Lord saying to him: 'Stoffeltosen, Stoffeltosen! If you sacrifice the dynamite monopoly, the country will lose its independence!' It was a decisive contribution to the debate, an intervention of Providence which the anti-monopolists could not hope to withstand. Lippert went on:

'Now, it is true that Stoffeltosen is a rather ignorant and bad-tempered old man, but there is no doubting his sincerity, or that he believed every word he said. ... Just a moment! I know what you are thinking. That he was bribed and that it was I who bribed him. But you are wrong, for I happen to know that Stoffeltosen's story is true.'

Lippert said this with such an air of conviction that it halted the rude guffaws of disbelief. They waited, incredulous, while he refilled his glass.

'Are you trying to tell us,' Bailey asked finally, 'that the Lord appeared to this man and actually spoke those words to him?'

'I do not pretend to be an authority on such matters, gentlemen, therefore I cannot state positively that it was the Lord's voice that spoke to Stoffeltosen. But I do know that he heard these words, the very words he repeated in the Volksraad the next afternoon. Because – I heard them myself.'

This time they could not check their laughter. But Lippert went on unperturbed: 'Of course, you must be wondering how I know all this. It's quite simple. Whenever I am in Pretoria I always stay at the Transvaal Hotel. That's where I meet all the people I want to see and who, perhaps, can be er ... useful to me. On that particular night there were, as usual, a number of Volksraad members staying at the hotel – including Stoffeltosen. As a matter of fact he had the room next to mine.

'They are small rooms, as you know, with the walls made of ceiling board. Quite comfortable and reasonably priced, but not soundproof. Thus it was that I can support Stoffeltosen's testimony and say that he did hear the words he told the Raad he had heard.'

Lippert paused to take a sip of his drink. His audience took side-long glances at each other while disbelief twisted their mouths and arched their eyebrows.

'It was a very disturbing experience, as you can imagine,' Lippert said. 'But there is just one thing that baffles me. I never knew that God Almighty spoke Low Dutch with a German accent ... just like mine.'

There was a moment of astonished silence, then the party burst into roars of laughter. It was some minutes before the normal flow of conversation could be resumed. Charles Leonard restored the earlier seriousness.

'A lot of our troubles would disappear if old Kruger could be persuaded to retire and let some of the Liberals in. He won't take any heed of public opinion; he never reads the newspapers; he won't take advice from the more far-seeing men around him. People like General Joubert, or Louis Botha, or Esselen, for instance —' Francis Dormer of *The Star* came bustling into the group. He seemed excited.

'Have you heard?' Dormer grabbed the bottle and poured himself out a stiff measure. 'Bill Brown of *The Standard* was arrested early this morning!'

For a moment the scene froze. Glasses hung in mid-air between counter and lip, words stopped in mid-sentence, the cloth in the busy hands of the barman came to a dead stop in a puddle of beer, even the scotch which Hans Sauer was tilting over his glass seemed to suspend its flow. Then the babbled chorus of questions: Dormer held up his hand, like a judge calling for silence.

'For lese-majesty!'

'Lese-majesty?' Bailey was heard to say. 'But we haven't *got* a majesty in the Transvaal!'

151

Dormer went on: 'You remember that article in *The Standard* last month? I think it was titled "Reform or Revolution". That's what did it.'

Carl Jeppe shook his head. 'I thought there'd be trouble. With all due respect to you, Francis, it often seems the Johannesburg papers forget they're published in an independent republic and not in a part of the British Empire.'

'I thought it was fair enough comment in places,' Beit said equably. 'Mind you, I do not think the mines have much to complain about except in so far as these monopolies are operating. But the Pretoria Government cannot reasonably expect to go on treating this great town that is growing up here like a little backveld village indefinitely. What d'you think, J.B.?'

Robinson looked round the little circle. He enjoyed any opportunity of disagreeing with Alfred Beit, especially in public.

'Well, since you ask me, I think Kruger's quite right. How could he have acted otherwise? That article was an incitement to rebellion. What we must remember, as Carl said, is that we're all foreigners here. I know we pay nearly all the revenue of the State and we haven't got a vote and we've no language rights, but you know as well as I do that we don't have to live in the Transvaal. If we don't like it we can leave it. Well, why don't we? I'll tell you why: because each one of us has got a better chance of making a fortune here in Johannesburg than anywhere else in the world. Why must we pretend it's our political rights that are so important to us?'

'May I remind you, Mr Robinson,' FitzPatrick said, 'that I have just lost every bit of capital I possessed. But that's not the point. Most of us here have been brought up in the belief that the individual has certain rights. If we're fit to be taxed then we're fit to take part in the government of the country, and we're certainly fit to govern our own community in Johannesburg. As for being compelled to use Dutch...'

Leonard held up his hand.

'Let's not start on all that, Percy. We're getting away from the subject.'

He turned to Dormer: 'What about Bill Brown, Francis? Where is he now? They haven't put him in Pretoria gaol, have they?'

152

'No, he's out on his own recognizances, as you lawyers say. He's publishing a denial to the charges in tomorrow's paper, I believe. Claims they're untrue and unfounded and that the article contained nothing that could cause sedition or high treason. So we'd better keep our opinions to ourselves, J.B.! He also maintains that the article was written in the general public interest and is therefore justifiable criticism as is allowed in every free State.'

There was a chorus of 'Hear, hears' from all round the crowded bar-room. Leonard concluded:

'I think it would be wiser, gentlemen, as this matter can now be considered *sub judice*, if we refrained from further comment.' He looked round the room deliberately. 'You never know who's listening, these days . . .'

Representation, taxation and language were the inflammable elements smouldering in the rubble of the share market collapse.

The original constitution on which the Republic was founded declared that 'the territory is open for every foreigner who obeys the laws of the Republic', and up to 1882 any immigrant could acquire the electoral franchise after a residence of two years. The discovery of gold in the Transvaal greatly increased the number of foreigners entering the country, and very few of them gave the appearance of being either permanent or desirable citizens. In order that most of the more transient and obnoxious types should be disqualified the residential period was raised to five years in 1882.

The enormous inrush of population which followed the discovery of the Witwatersrand reefs created a new problem, for which the answer was not difficult to find – even for a president who had had no schooling. In five years' time the electorally qualified Uitlanders would equal the Boer population; in ten years the burghers would be outnumbered.

As Kruger saw it, the whole future of the republic was at stake in the franchise law. Before the end of the century, he could see plainly, the Uitlanders could have a majority in the Volksraad and legislate for any form of government they wanted. It would be the end of his South African Republic, and of his great dream of a new Afrikaner nation covering the whole of the southern half of the continent.

In 1887 he rushed a bill through the Volksraad, without

153

opposition, raising the residential qualification from five to fifteen years. That would disenfranchise the whole of the new population on the Rand until he had worked out an electoral plan that could somehow contrive to give the Uitlanders a vote without giving them power to run the country.

As soon as the new measure was promulgated, the row started. But the dispute was political and artificial. The diggers were not by nature either political or social creatures. They couldn't have cared less for President or Queen, for Parliament or Volksraad or any other form of constitutional authority. The vote mattered less to them than a bottle of whisky or gin.

They were fundamentally 'agin the Government', wherever they were, and it was not difficult for them in their interminable glass-thumping arguments to blame the Pretoria administration for the Stock Exchange disasters, their bad luck and every other irritation that came festering to the surface as the fever of discontent mounted.

Most irritating of all was the language question. By law, the use of Dutch was compulsory in all Courts and Government offices, including the market places. In a Dutch-speaking republic this was not altogether unreasonable, but when applied uncompromisingly to Johannesburg in which much less than one per cent of the inhabitants could claim Dutch as their mother tongue, it produced irksome and incongruous situations.

Naturally, the commercial life of the town was conducted in English, but the absurdity of the situation was constantly emphasized in any transactions involving Government officials – and emphasized every morning at the early market when produce brought in by farmers was sold by auction.

Bidding was always in English, this being the only language most of the buyers could speak. Then some fervent patriot would take exception to the fact that the Market Master, an official of the Republic, offered the produce of Transvaal farms to Uitlanders in a foreign tongue. Off would go a complaint to Pretoria and back would come an instruction to the Market Master that the law regarding the use of Dutch in public institutions must be strictly adhered to.

The auctioneers had to comply. For a time everything brought in from the farms was offered and described in

Dutch. The townsfolk retaliated by not understanding a word of it, so that the only bids made, which had to be accepted, were from isolated Afrikaners. This always brought bitter complaints from the farmers at the low prices their produce obtained, and a demand for the return of English as the medium for morning market transactions – until the next patriot came along.

Although Kruger's approach to this problem, with the enthusiastic encouragement of the majority of the Volksraad, was narrow-minded and unimaginative, his concern was not the discomfiture of the Uitlanders but, as always, the continued existence as an Afrikaner entity of the Republic.

The Dutch language, slowly evolving into exclusively South African *Afrikaans*, was one of the anchors which Kruger threw out to secure his ship of state. Although none of them was able to prevent imminent shipwreck in the storms that were mounting in and around the republic, the anchor of the Afrikaans language stayed secure. When the tempest of war subsided with the Transvaal obliterated as an independent state, that anchor remained for the next generation of Afrikaners to cling to. None of today's South Africans would be prepared to say that Kruger's language policy was shortsighted.

Kruger was well aware of the immense forces of public opinion building up against his administration on the Witwatersrand and overseas. He had learnt his lesson from the events leading up to the British annexation of 1887. He would give the Uitlanders, from time to time, a little of what they wanted. He would give them an occasional lick of the lollipop.

On October 23 the *Staatscourant*, the official Government gazette, published a proclamation which conferred powers on the Johannesburg Sanitary Board which made it, in everything but name, the municipality its citizens were clamouring for. With the recognition went the right to levy a rate of 2d. in the £.

Although this decision was welcomed in the Press as a Johannesburg victory over the forces of reaction, the majority of the citizens were far more interested in the draw for half-a-dozen different sweepstakes which took place every month and especially as Christmas drew nearer. Vast sums were conjured up by the impecunious citizens for these lotteries, and prizes totalling several hundred thousand pounds were regularly competed for.

Such ungodliness was not to the liking of the Volksraad, who ran a constant campaign to force the Executive to make horse-racing and sweepstakes illegal. In one session of the Raad a member asked Kruger point blank why he did not suppress these evils.

'It is very true,' the President rumbled, 'that these things are evil and against the Word of God. But it is also the duty of man to have exercise and to exercise his horses. It is for that reason that we have thought it advisable not to legislate against horse-racing.'

'But what about sweepstakes?'

'What is the difference?' the President asked blandly, closing the discussion with a question which, they all knew, he did not want anyone to answer.

Kruger knew his Volksraad, and he was beginning to know his Uitlanders. If he was determined to cork up one outlet of the volcano by denying them political rights in order to safeguard the republic, he would allow them to let off as much steam as they liked in other directions where they could only harm themselves.

As the year came to its end the members of the Cape Assembly heard John X. Merriman telling them that there was at that time £108,000,000 of British capital invested in Transvaal gold-fields. If the greater part of the Johannesburg population had lost contact with any portion of this vast sum, it was not going to destroy their capacity for enjoying themselves or forgetting their distress. One of the first duties of the newly-empowered Sanitary Board was to renew 550 bar licences and to listen to over 100 new applications.

The decade came to an end in a great burst of desperate gaiety spread between Johannesburg's Christmas and New Year. For a few nostalgic moments the sweet music of carols filled the unlikely midsummer nights; then the hymns and organ peals were drowned by the brassy blare of the new materialism which had invaded the plains and hills. To Paul Kruger and his burghers, kneeling in prayer in the devout simplicity of their reformed churches, it must have sounded like the trumpets of doom.

It was impossible for anybody to imagine that five years ago Johannesburg was undreamt of – an unwanted strip of veld squeezed between vast, empty acres of ranchland. Now a great town and a community numbered in tens of thousands stood on the brink of a new decade, a decade that was to prove one of the most fateful in the history of a continent and of the nations that were entangled in the drama of its awakening.

There were all those millions of black men, too; but nobody thought of them as a nation – not even the black men.

The ageing President, a gnarled and bearded buffalo in a top-hat, looked down the last years of the century and of his life from lowering eyes. He could not live for ever; nor, he knew with the fatalism of age, could his country. But he would live as long as his republic and, with God's help, the republic would live as long as he.

Sadly and angrily he confronted the dilemma before him. He resolved in his own mind that if the Uitlanders wanted his country, they would have to take it from him by force. He would not give it to them. 'They can have it,' he told Dr Leyds, 'over my dead body.'

The law could be changed, and changed again, to deny them the rights they demanded. Then if they broke the law he could act against them in support of the law.

But the republic also wanted much from the Uitlanders. It wanted a share of the riches they were digging from its very heart. In a way these Uitlanders were employees of the South African Republic. That was it – employees! So they must be kept happy and well paid. Proper public services, street-lighting, policemen, even railways. All these they could have. But no shares in the company. That was their stock-exchange language, wasn't it? No voice in the board-room among the directors, except perhaps the illusion of a voice. Yes, a voice without a vote. He would let them have a vote – but only to a second Volksraad. He would let them vote their heads off! But he would never let them run the country.

Paul Kruger was not a man to run away from a dilemma or any other form of danger. He preferred to walk towards it – with his bible in one hand and his gun, loaded, in the other. He would go and face the Uitlanders and tell them of his plans for their future and their welfare.

There was to be a meeting on the Vaal River early in 1890 with the new British High Commissioner in South

Africa, Sir Henry Loch. It would be a good idea to spend a little time in Johannesburg on the way. He could listen to all their complaints yet again, and to the hypocrisy of all those addresses of welcome; they would hardly expect him to discuss the Government's policy with them before he had had a chance of talking to the High Commissioner.

CHAPTER FOURTEEN

Shortly after six o'clock on the morning of March 4, 1890, the four-striped banner of the South African Republic was run up on the flagstaffs of every Government building in Johannesburg. It was an example followed with hardly less enthusiasm by the tradesmen and businessmen as they opened their premises, so that by noon almost every building in the township was fluttering with flags and bunting.

The Stock Exchange and the banks closed their doors at eleven, followed an hour later by the shops and offices. The bars, unfortunately, stayed open.

At noon some 300 armed and mounted burghers rode in from the Klip River district and paraded in the Market Square under the leadership of Jan Meyer, the Rand's first Veld-Kornet, and now the Member of the Volksraad for Johannesburg.

The gathering crowd of onlookers stared fascinated at this motley commando of Afrikaners and their four standard-bearers. Greybeard and beardless boys; muskets, carbines, umbrellas; boots, rough-hewn veldskoens, barefooted youths gripping stirrups with their toes; some in jackets, some in waistcoats; many without either, slack-legged on despondent ponies – ponies that would have been rejected from an auction sale for want of condition, but which could and did carry their riders across deserts, over mountains and swollen rivers, through tsetse-fly-infested bush where a thoroughbred would not have lasted twenty-four hours.

It was a collection of shaggy men and shaggy animals that invited coarse comment. But the whole array was impregnated with such a positive air of dignity and self-sufficiency that the crowd of diggers and miners, not naturally respectful, were restricted to incredulous murmurs, remembering that these were the people who had opened up a savage wilderness, the same men who had defeated the red-coated regulars at Majuba Hill.

The throng of Uitlanders, having conceded the Boers their tribute of silent curiosity and respect, turned to the better opportunities of the gathering parade in front of the Post Office.

There the carriage which was to convey the Special Land-drost and the Mining Commissioner to greet the President on the outskirts of the suburbs was waiting, drawn by Mr Casey's magnificent pair of Flemish stallions. Behind this vehicle other conveyances assembled, carrying anybody who thought himself significant enough to be a representative of the community. All the civic dignitaries and the officials of various boards and associations and chambers were assembled, and around these the crowd accumulated, shouting appropriate slogans and epithets depending on nationality and status of the recipient.

It was a good-natured crowd, warmed up by the late summer sun and early alcohol. They gave a big hand to the walnut-sized carriage, belonging to Mr Ross, drawn by six Shetland ponies which, alongside the stallions and other horses, looked no larger than medium-sized dogs. But this was nothing to the cheering which greeted the Mosenthals, Barney Barnato and Woolfie Joel as they drove up in a fabulous landau which gleamed and glittered like the Lord Mayor's coach. The general opinion, freely expressed, was that if this was not Oom Paul's turn-out it blooming well ought to be.

The new clock on the Post Office struck 12.30. This was the signal for the whole procession to move off – clanking mounted police at the head, followed by the carriages with the slouch-hatted host of Boers cantering and tripling in their wheel-tracks. Behind, and barely visible in the moving cloud of dust, rode a heterogeneous cavalry of citizens and diggers and anybody else who could borrow or steal a horse. Finally, like bedraggled inverted commas putting an end to an untidy conversation piece, came a gay humility of donkeys and mules and their coloured and native riders.

The Presidential coach, escorted by a troop of the State Artillery, had stopped just short of the hostelry at Orange Grove to change horses and to await the arrival of the reception committee from the other side of the high ridges of the Witwatersrand.

160

At two o'clock the cavalcade of citizens and Boers arrived at Orange Grove and immediately split up into three groups. The burgher commando took up their positions on each side of the road, forming an avenue of loyalty and security through which Oom Paul could drive; the opulent carriages went on with their official greeting for the President; the crowd of Johannesburgers got no further than the hostelry and the ready hospitality of its bars and verandas.

It was another hour before the whole column moved off on the return to Johannesburg. Kruger had brought Dr Leyds with him for the High Commissioner's conference, and these two for the sake of greater comfort over the rough approaches to the town, had moved into the Landdrost's more manoeuvrable vehicle. He had prudently put a dust-coat over the frock-coat and riband of his office; but the top-hat was unmistakable.

As they lurched and swayed along the pass that took the road over the ridges and valleys of the Rand, the unspoken thought was present in every vehicle: if the bruises on the Presidential backside did not subsequently remind the Head of State to vote some funds for maintaining the roads in and around Johannesburg, nothing ever would.

The reception committee had another fear – that the animosity which the Uitlanders felt towards the Government would manifest itself in a deliberate boycott of the President. They need not have worried.

As the leading carriage came over the brow of Hospital Hill even the horses seemed to stop in surprise at the sudden scene below. Kruger stood upright in the coach in his astonishment. He had not seen Johannesburg for three years. He had heard all about it, of course, but his memory had no comparative image on which he could picture reality. Now it was spread out at his feet.

He saw squares crowded with buildings; roads, which looked like kloofs in the cliffs of the town, emerging as tracks leading out to suburbs of elegant gables and gardens with colonnaded stoeps gleaming through young eucalyptus, pine and other quick-growing trees with which the wealthy had surrounded their homes. He saw the spreading huddle of shacks and shanties in which filth and misery were concealed by distance; the background of smoke-stacks, headgears and vast barns of corrugated iron from which the

161

wind bore a perpetual rumble of the crushing batteries; slow-growing dumps of reef and rubble that marched over the horizons to east and west parallel with the mountains ... the whole vast canvas set in motion as the westerly wind fluttered the reds, whites, blues, the oranges and greens of patriotic bunting which covered the town. Beyond it all the encompassing veld was sprinkled with converging plumes of dust as late-arriving farmers and storekeepers whipped up their horses to reach Johannesburg before Oom Paul.

The President stared straight down into the bowl of the Wanderers Ground where the red earth of the cricket field was obliterated by the mass of humanity gathered there. Even as he watched, the predominant tone of khaki and dust was transmuted magically as every face turned upwards towards the carriage on the crest and the silhouette of a top-hat.

As the breeze caught the quick cheer and blew it up the hillside to Kruger, he spat largely and appreciatively over the side of the coach, and gave the signal to drive on. Dr Leyds, who did not always approve of the President's habits, showed by his expression that he was glad the wind was unfavourable; otherwise the gesture of satisfaction might have been carried on to the heads of the waiting Uitlanders – where it would, no doubt, have been misinterpreted.

At the Wanderers Pavilion a platform had been erected at the foot of the centre of the grandstand, the covered portion behind being reserved for various civilian and Government officials and a selected group of about fifty ladies. Inside the pavilion enclosure were gathered the club members, their friends and families – separated from the commonalty on the ground by a fragile wooden fence buttressed by a rank of hefty State Police.

A great surge of humanity flooded in as the Presidential procession came to the foot of Hospital Hill and turned into the club gates. With over 10,000 people jammed into the cricket field it was not long before those at the back were pressing forward to positions from which they could see and hear Paul Kruger. On the inner perimeter of the pavilion railings there were frequent scuffles between police and interlopers – until concerted action replaced individual enterprise and the enclosure gates were rushed.

The six 'Zarps' on duty there, massive though they were,

could not match the build-up of pressure concentrated on this narrow apex. The officer in command, after a few words with members of the Club committee, wisely conceded the inevitable and let the public come in so that they would form their own bulwark against themselves.

At this moment a mellow but active digger managed to clamber up on the bandstand where the Police Band were playing inoffensive music to entertain the crowd. He snatched the conductor's baton, waved it up and down crazily, and began to sing 'Rule, Britannia'.

The near assembly took up the refrain and spread it from mouth to mouth until the whole multitude, with the exception of the few pockets of burghers and those foreigners who owed no allegiance to Queen Victoria, were singing it. As the long drawn out 'slaves' ended the stanza, the whole mob burst spontaneously into 'God Save the Queen', ignoring frantic appeals for silence from the platform whence officials could see the President approaching.

Complete disaster was avoided by the energetic action of the bandmaster, who gave the offending digger a shove which precipitated him on to the heads of the crowd below, and led his musicians noisily into the *Volkslied* – the new hymn of Afrikanerdom.

The confusion of tune and supplication, which must have been as confusing to a Britannic deity as it was to the singers, moved into a moment of competition when the outcome hung in the balance. Then, with bewildering impartiality, the throng joined enthusiastically in the Dutch chorus of the republican anthem.

In the same minute a standard-bearer walked on to the platform, the broad stripes of the *Vierkleur* billowing out over the heads of the nearest audience. The singing switched dramatically into a great roar of welcome as, immediately behind the flag, Paul Kruger came up the steps.

At the front of the platform he paused and took off his top-hat in acknowledgment. Then, as cheer after cheer beat about him, the hard look on his face relaxed into a smile that he himself had never expected.

Considering that he was the Government representative on the Sanitary Board and the President's nephew, Jan Eloff did pretty well by the Uitlanders in identifying himself with the grievances contained in the address of welcome which he read out to Kruger; and applause for Eloff's speech swelled into a great cheer as the crowd saw Kruger getting to his feet. The President took a large handkerchief from his pocket, and blew his nose like an elephant trumpeting. The ladies behind him looked startled. Then he placed his hat carefully on the vacant chair and took a few plank-creaking paces to the front of the platform.

For a moment or two he loomed large above them, filling the silence with his bulk and his hostility. The Republic in person: Canute before the alien ocean: his harsh voice gave unintended harshness to his words.

'Subjects and friends, I wish —'

As though by prearrangement a group of young Englishmen immediately started to sing 'Rule, Britannia'. Kruger stopped as though he had been hit in the mouth. Then, pointing straight at the singers while the angry blood coloured his face, he roared *'Bly stil!* – Be silent!' in such a voice that the crowd grew hushed and fidgety like a rowdy class of schoolboys interrupted by the headmaster.

'You must keep silent if you wish to hear me speak,' he told them abruptly, and then started off again:

'Burghers, subjects and foreigners; I thank you for the welcome accorded me. As you are aware, for four years I have laboured with difficulties in getting the railway into the interior of this country —'

The mixture of cheers, laughter and booing which greeted this brought him momentarily to a stop. He raised his voice above the din, determined to get it over quickly.

'The greatest of these difficulties has been surmounted, and the railway is already proceeding from Delagoa Bay . . .'

This time there were no cheers.

'How much are the Portuguese paying you?' they yelled. 'What's Doctor Leyds getting out of this from the Hollanders?'

'What about the Cape Railway? What about the line from Natal?'

'Put your hat on – you've got sunstroke!'

They heckled him and shouted at him from all corners of the ground, while the burghers in the crowd grouped together to cheer him and yell encouragement. Behind the President, members of the Sanitary Board and Captain von Brandis were making frantic signals for silence.

For a few moments, as Kruger's fists clenched into knotted clubs, it looked as though he was going to come down among them. Then he pulled himself together and addressed himself directly to the people at his feet who had been showing obvious disapproval of the demonstration.

'I shall lay the Bloemfontein extension of the Cape line before the Volksraad at the next session so that it may be proceeded with at once. The railway will come over Johannesburg to Pretoria. I shall now retire to meet the deputa--tions.'

Abruptly he turned his back on the crowd, a broad and studied insult. He walked to this chair, picked up his hat and rammed it on his head and, without another glance, stamped angrily off the platform, followed by a flustered collection of officials and representatives.

The abandoned throng on the cricket field did not know whether to cheer or jeer, and did both. They sped the President on his way to Carl von Brandis' house, where he was to spend the night, with 'God Save the Queen' and other patriotic songs of England, the notes and words following the clatter of hoofbeats all the way up Rissik Street.

There were ten thousand people left behind on the Wanderers Ground. They had come to hear the President. And tell the President. They had seen him for five minutes and told him nothing except that Britannia ruled the waves. He had given them a few phrases about non-existent railway lines – phrases they had been hearing for four years. What about taxation and concessions, what about the vote and their language rights? When were they going to get decent sanitation? It wasn't a Sanitary Board they wanted, but sanitary living conditions. They felt slighted and cheated.

A rollicking digger pushed his way up on the platform, the fashionably-dressed women shying like startled fillies from his rough progress.

'Are we going to stand for this?' he roared. 'To hell with Kruger! We haven't finished with him yet – we've got a few messages for him to take back to Pretoria. But how can we give them to him? Where's the old bastard got to?'

'He's at the Government Buildings,' they shouted back at him.

'Well then, what are we waiting for? To the Government Buildings!'

'To the Government Buildings!' The crowd took up the chant as they poured out of the exits of the Wanderers Club, filling each street with rivers of people and noise as they flowed towards the Market Square.

Not a policeman was in sight as the square gradually filled. Impromptu orators jumped up on packing cases and wagons, shouted their expletives and exhortations, and were as quickly pushed off again or pelted with the ungarnered residue of that morning's market.

But as the sun sank, colouring sky and crowd with its afterglow of crimson, the mood of the multitude changed ominously. They had achieved nothing. Kruger was somewhere, invisible but potent still, listening to the endless addresses of polite deputations, hearing all and saying nothing. Now, like children, they were suddenly weary of their fun and games. There was a spontaneous move towards the Special Landdrost's office at one end of the Government Buildings. In front of it stood the flagstaff with the broad colours of the republic flaunting its authority in the last of the sunset.

In the Landdrost's offices two Court Messengers, McMaster and Oosthuizen, watched the movement of the crowd with apprehension.

'You know what I think, Hendrik?' McMaster said as they peered through a window, 'I think they're going to pull down the *Vierkleur*. Who's that young fellow there – the tall one in front?'

'That's Leo Rogaly. Not a bad sort – a little too clever. That's Reid next to him; the other's a remittance man I've never seen sober yet.'

'There's Rogaly getting up on the stoep. Looks as though he's going to make a speech. Keep your eye on him, Hendrik.'

As McMaster moved through the empty building he heard quick cheers punctuating the inaudible speech. He came out of the front door to hear Rogaly shouting:

'What d'you say, then? Shall we pull down the flag?'

There was a yell of approval, but a man near the front said: 'Don't be a fool, Rogaly. You'll get at least five years!'

'Here's a fellow,' Rogaly told them loudly, 'who says I'll get at least five years. Well, they can't put us *all* in gaol, can they?'

Oosthuizen joined McMaster in the doorway.

'What'll we do if they pull down the flag, Ernest?'

'Don't worry, man. Let them try. We'll know who did it. But if things get too rough, you'd better run off and see if you can find the police lieutenant.'

'Come on then,' they heard Rogaly shout. 'What are we waiting for? Let's pull the bloody thing down!'

The sudden surge of men heaved Rogaly and Reid up to the foot of the flagpole just as McMaster and Oosthuizen leapt forward to block them. Reid reached up and pulled on the rope so that the flag was half-way down before McMaster pushed him aside and tried to hoist it again. Someone grabbed McMaster round the waist and tried to pull him away from the pole.

'Let me go, you drunken bastard!' McMaster hissed.

'And what if I don't?'

'I'll knock your blasted head off!'

'You hear that?' the man shouted. 'This Irish Dutchman's going to knock my head off! Get a knife somebody, cut the rope while I hold him!'

A score of men swarmed round: McMaster was beaten to the ground and trampled into insensibility. A knife flashed in the fading light and the *Vierkleur* came tumbling down, wrapping its folds around the heads below. With a yell of triumph a dozen pairs of hands seized it and ripped it into jagged shreds, scattering the fragments in the air.

Oosthuizen and one or two others fought their way through the press of bodies and dragged out the battered McMaster. Then he sent one man running for a doctor while another messenger went to von Brandis' house to give the Landdrost a full report.

In a room in that house, Kruger was listening to Mr Leonard and George Farrar, one of three brothers who had recently arrived in Johannesburg and who were rapidly making a name for themselves in the mining and political world. Kruger was sitting in a customary pose – staring at a point where wall and ceiling met – as the deputation listed their grievances and requirements. He shifted a little uneasily in his chair and then held up his hand.

'You want me to withdraw many of the duties and then you ask me for large sums of money. Taxes must be removed, you say, and more spent on public works. The new Government Buildings on Market Square cost over a hundred thousand pounds; the bridge over the Vaal River will cost more than three hundred thousand; there are all your roads and lighting; the Sanitary Board never stops asking me for money. Where is it all to come from, if you do not pay taxes?'

'It is hardly fair, Your Honour,' Leonard pointed out, 'that the present inhabitants should bear the whole burden of costs for roads and bridges and buildings that will be used by many future generations.'

'The following generations will have enough to pay for on their own account, Mynheer Leonard.' The President leaned forward in his chair. 'What was that noise?'

'It is only the crowd in the Market Square, celebrating Your Honour's presence in Johannesburg,' George Farrar told him. 'Is there anything you can add, Mr President, to what you said this afternoon about railways?'

'I was about to say, in connection with the railways, that whatever happens it will be impossible for the line to reach Johannesburg this year. It is on this account that I want you to see that there are enough men and animals and wagons to carry food if, perhaps, there has to be another time of scarcity. I will assist you in this with all my heart, as I do not want another famine here again.'

Out in the Market Square, just a few hundred yards away from where Kruger was holding audience, scraps of *Vierkleur* were being bought and sold like valuables at an auction sale. The crowd showed no signs of dispersing and was constantly being reinforced by contingents from the encircling bars and shebeens. Only the principals in the flag incident had slipped away into the night.

'We want Kruger!' became the new war-cry, and as the chanting swelled to a roar a mob of men set off along Pritchard Street to Captain von Brandis' house, mingling their calls for Kruger with the jingo songs of Empire.

The house was surrounded by a low wooden fence and at one corner the Transvaal flag drooped from a tall mast. At a gate in the fence three or four policemen stopped the leading group, and against this human bulwark the mob accumulated, shouting demands and insults.

In the front the ring-leaders gave insolent orders to the 'Zarps' to go and fetch Kruger so that he could hear what they had to say. With great foresight the Landdrost had stipulated that only English-speaking members of the force should be on duty in Johannesburg that day; the provocation of a language barrier was not added to other difficulties of communication and persuasion.

Nevertheless, the worried policemen could sense the ugly

mood that was replacing the first good-natured ribaldry. A corporal went into the house and emerged a few minutes later with a message that if the crowd dispersed in an orderly manner the President would receive one of their number to hear their complaints.

This news was received with cheers, and the crowd's choice fell on a thrustful German auctioneer called Liebman who was even more articulate and obstreperous than his profession required him to be. He was also rather drunk.

Liebman was escorted inside and shown into a room where the President still sat with various citizen delegates. As soon as Kruger saw him he growled, 'Take that man out of here. I will not hear him.'

Liebman took a pace forward, unsteady but aggressive.

'You listen to me, Paul Kruger!' he said gutturally. 'I represent the people of Johannesburg. D'you know you're insulting the people of Johannesburg? We demand —'

'No!' Kruger bellowed, half-rising, his big fists gripping the chair's side. 'I did not know that. But I know that I am insulting *you*. Now *voetsak*! Clear out!'

Captain von Brandis nodded to the watchful policeman. Liebman was grabbed by the arm and propelled out of the door, hurling oaths over his shoulder.

'They kicked me out!' he yelled to the crowd. 'He told me to *voetsak*, like a dog! It's an insult to Johannesburg! Are we going to let these bloody Dutchmen insult us?'

'No!' roared the mob back at him, and as Liebman was pushed down the steps and out of the gate they sang 'For he's a jolly good fellow' followed by the all too familiar and singularly inappropriate tribute of 'Rule, Britannia'.

The policemen at the gate were having a rough time. Had they been Afrikaners it is more than likely that the Boer War would have started nine years earlier than it did. It became clear that the fence would not stand up indefinitely against the mounting pressure. Von Brandis came out on to the stoep to persuade them to disperse. He had done it often enough, in the past few years; but tonight it was different. There was some cheering for him, but it was past time for reason or respect.

'Bring out Kruger!' they yelled. '*We want Kruger!*'

The Landdrost shook his head emphatically and said something to one of the policemen. Together the two of them went inside.

The crowd felt this was another small victory, and gave another forward surge. There was a loud crack as the gate-post and a length of fencing gave way. The police sentries were forced back to the steps of the veranda, and looked like being overwhelmed; they drew their revolvers and threatened to shoot any man who came a step nearer.

Confronted by the grim muzzles, the front ranks pressed back against the thrust, reaching a state of precarious equilibrium along the line of the fence. On the outskirts groups of men broke away to return armed with piles of bricks and wooden staves, which they distributed gleefully.

One man, seeking the bubble reputation, lurched through the gap of the gate and made for the flagpole. A policeman, anticipating his intent, got there just before him. As the man saw the revolver pointing straight at him he stopped dead in his tracks.

'If you touch this rope I'll shoot you,' the policeman said loudly, his words carrying beyond the man to those behind who were urging him on. A brick came sailing out of the night to land with a crash on the woodwork of the stoep, missing the constable near the flagpole by a few feet. He pointed his gun in the air and fired a single shot.

The shock of the detonation stilled the noise of the mob, and in the few seconds of sudden silence the whole event froze into immobility. At the foot of the flagstaff stood the 'Zarp'. From the muzzle of his gun wispy smoke curled upwards as it levelled out again in line with the digger's stomach. The digger himself had recoiled from the explosion and its meaning and now stood open-mouthed and with hands half-raised. Behind them lamplight from the veranda lit up the front ranks of the mob, their expressions frozen in astonishment and indecision. In the background, the shadowy mass of the crowd – a many-faced animal waiting for the unanimous thought that would lead to unanimous action. On the steps, held in the same rigid grip, the small pyramid of policemen aimed their revolvers and wondered whence would come the sudden movement, the quick shout that would release the monster. One more brick, one more shot, one puff of wind to unfold the somnolent *Vierkleur*...

The white rectangle of the doorway filled with movement and sudden silhouettes, and out on to the veranda streamed some thirty fully-armed policemen. They came straight down the steps with carbines at the ready and lined up inside the fence facing the mob.

Out in the anonymous dark somebody started singing 'God Save the Queen'. Soon the whole crowd had taken it up, respectfully, ridiculously standing bareheaded in what was not a tribute to their sovereign but an insult to their president. Groups of men broke away and drifted off to bars, brothels, doss-houses; others, more energetic, roamed the streets and squares in search of republican bunting on which to vent their frustration and, often enough, their bladders. For the rest of the night gangs of revellers came and went before the Landdrost's house, taunting the stolid line of 'Zarps', hurling their epithets through the windows where the aged President talked on with von Brandis, sipping endless cups of coffee through clouds of pipe-smoke, contemptuous of the external noises and of the men who made them.

'You know what these people remind me of, Carl? They remind me of an old baboon chained up in my yard. I have had this animal for a long time and we are good friends. I was out feeding it the other day when it got its tail by accident in the Kaffir's fire. It immediately jumped at me and bit me in the hand. The hand that had just been feeding it. Tomorrow, Carl, you can tell your Uitlander friends that even if they are not baboons, they sometimes behave like baboons. And you can also tell them that I will never set foot in Johannesburg again.'

Kruger liked the baboon story so much that he retold it to Sir Henry Loch a few days after, at the Vaal River conference. But he did come back to Johannesburg – two years later, when Sammy Marks persuaded him to open the new Jewish Synagogue.

CHAPTER FIFTEEN

Kruger's first major political move of 1890 was to secure passage through the Volksraad of a law establishing the Second Chamber, and in which the voting rights of the new population were so defined that it made virtually certain that present and future generations of Uitlanders could be disfranchised for ever.

That political dissension became a predominant factor in the grievances of the Johannesburgers was largely due to this sort of mishandling of the situation by the Pretoria Government. Their fear of numerical and political preponderance was real and understandable, but they were bad psychologists.

The polyglot population of the Witwatersrand were not fundamentally opposed to the President and the republican authority. The majority were quite prepared to become citizens of the Boer State, share its responsibilities and contribute to its proper maintenance – provided they could also share the rights and privileges of its burghers. In every denial of democratic rights to the Uitlanders, however, the President was ensuring his own and his country's destruction.

It was in this atmosphere, accentuated by the demonstrations during Kruger's visit to the town, that the Transvaal National Union came into being to bring about constitutional and parochial reforms. The Union did not represent any particular section or interest, and the capitalist class – for the first few years – held aloof. The embryo mining magnates, the Randlords, saw clearly the dangers of the situation that was being created, and that their operations and profits were dependent in the first place on maintaining good relations with President and Raad.

Later, confronted with the increasing intractability of the Government party, the financiers and the mining companies perceived that their survival depended as much on a changed and reformed environment as on the goodwill which it did not seem possible to get. They began to contribute funds and other resources to the National Union and to the stimulation of a Progressive Party in the First Volksraad. This liberalizing role has never since been wholly abandoned by the great mining houses.

From this association of the National Union and high finance the full Reform Movement grew and flourished until it represented the whole Uitlander community and became the militant organization, ably led and well founded, which eventually felt itself strong enough to oppose the Government directly.

Although it started in spontaneous demonstrations, the full political consciousness of the Uitlander movement can be said to have grown from the top downwards. Most significantly it coincided with the determined resolve of Cecil Rhodes that the Boer Republic must be brought into the community of a united South Africa if his dreams for a greater community within the British Empire were to succeed. Rhodes did not want the gold mines: he wanted the Republic. It was the Republic's possession of the gold mines that was enabling Kruger to thwart his imperial plans.

Before that stage was reached, time and circumstance were conspiring against Oom Paul and his Boers. The first manifestation of this occurred when the President found himself unable to continue with the construction of the Delagoa Bay line because of a shortage of funds.

Three factors contributed: the depressed state of the mining industry, the weakness of the money market in Europe and a growing disbelief in the political and financial stability of the Transvaal. The Netherlands Railway Company had no money to carry on the work, and could extract no more, with all their ingenuity, from the Government.

By the time Kruger set off to meet the High Commissioner he had come to the conclusion that the Witwatersrand could not wait indefinitely for its railway. At the meeting it was agreed, therefore, that the existing line from Cape Town to Bloemfontein, owned by the Cape Government, should be extended to the Vaal River where it would connect with a projected Transvaal line from Johannesburg.

On September 15, 1892, the first train steamed into Park Station, Johannesburg. It had been preceded the previous evening by a pilot engine and a few trucks which slunk in unobtrusively in the darkness so as not to mar the official arrival next morning.

Pretoria refused to give recognition to the event, determined to celebrate only the advent of the first train at the capital from Delagoa Bay. Nevertheless, over 2,000 Johannesburgers were present at Park Station as noon approached, and thousands more lined the last ten miles of the line from Germiston.

The train, its six coaches jammed with passengers, was due at 11.43. Punctually at 11.41 it puffed round the bend at Doornfontein and pulled up, smothered in bunting, steam and the cheers of the crowd at the end of its thousand-mile journey. Johannesburg was now only two days, fourteen hours and seventeen minutes from Cape Town and the sea.

In the meantime, very important changes had taken place in the techniques of the mining industry. Largely as a result of the introduction of the Scott-Forrest cyanide process of gold extraction, the yield of gold from the reef ore had been increased enormously.

For the first four years of Johannesburg's existence the only method of extraction was by crushing and amalgamation which, under the most favourable circumstances, recovered only fifty per cent of the precious metal.

As experiment continued and specialized knowledge increased, other processes were added; by 1891 the leading mines on the Rand were producing results like this:

Gold saved by amalgamation	50 per cent
Gold saved by chlorination	12 per cent
Gold saved by cyanide process	28 per cent
Gold remaining in tailings	10 per cent

With each new process recovering a little more gold from each ton of reef, mines found their income rising against steady costs, and even those mines operating on low-grade ore were given new hope of life at a time when many of them had decided to close down.

Then the scientists and engineers began to tackle the last residue of gold in the discarded tailings. In March, 1891, the first gold recovered from tailings was won at the Robinson Mine. By the end of another year twenty-two of the mining companies were treating tailings and concentrates and the yield from these sources had risen from 42,954 ounces in 1891 to 211,865 ounces in 1892.

The influence of the various factors on gold production was clearly illustrated by the Chamber of Mines output figures for the first six years. In 1887 this was 23,155 ounces; the first revelation that the outcrop reef extended to deeper levels in 1889 produced a production surge which took the figure to 382,364; introduction of the cyanide process, which made hitherto unpayable reefs workable, with the addition of waste-gold recovered, swelled the annual total by the end of 1892 to a startling 1,210,869 ounces. Undoubtedly this figure would have been even higher had the mining companies found an effective way of preventing the continual thieving and illicit buying of gold.

But it was a slow business and the extra development and plant entailed made it an expensive one. It proceeded quietly, almost unobtrusively. Only the end figures were sensational, and the absence of excitement kept the disillusioned and still battered speculators away and the share market only steady.

Nobody talked about deep levels and south dips any more. But the big financiers, Beit and Robinson in particular and some of the newcomers like the Joels, George Albu and the Rothschilds, went ahead with their purchases of claims well south of the original outcrop, many of which had been thrown on the market or abandoned as useless after the big slump.

The financial world overseas was still suspicious and sceptical of the Witwatersrand, and without vast capital backing the deep levels were unreachable. The conservative London banking houses kept their safes shut; the essential support came from French and German investment companies, whose association with and confidence in Messrs Wernher and Beit placed at the disposal of the Johannesburg firm the then staggering sum of nearly £150,000,000. It was undoubtedly this factor and the brilliant administration and foresight of all the partners that enabled the Rand to develop with such terrific momentum.

It seems almost unbelievable now that in 1891 it was still possible to get in on what might be described as 'the ground floor' of the deep-level mines. Nobody was thinking of working much beyond a few hundred feet or perhaps, in wild flights of optimism, up to a thousand. They did not think it would be possible to operate at depths beyond that, and they did not believe the golden banket would be found if they ever got there.

CHAPTER SIXTEEN

The whole Witwatersrand was like a gigantic boiler: spasmodic eruptions of violence acted as safety valves to forestall the major explosion, revealing in their reckless energy something of the nature of the forces at work beneath ...

On Thursday, January 14, 1892, a Reuter telegram was rushed to the offices of *The Star* just as the first edition was about to go to press. It announced the death in London of the Duke of Clarence.

The event was not unexpected, and all that Dormer had to do was change the leading article he had written that morning to one on the Duke which his assistant editor had recently composed. He altered the heading from 'The Dying Duke' to 'The Dead Duke', and went off to lunch at the Rand Club.

He was mildly surprised half an hour later when various members drew his attention to the questionable taste of that day's editorial; he had to confess that he had not read it very thoroughly. He was shown the offensive paragraphs:

'Like his cousin, the present Emperor of Germany, he was glaringly out of touch with his fellow-men ... The Prince, his father, would have been glad to have welcomed a little wholesome sin in him, just to keep his virtue sweet.'

Dormer agreed that a certain lack of taste was evident, but would not concede that the article in general was offensive or untrue. Nevertheless, in the face of rising protest from Club members, he was persuaded to make one or two alterations for the latest edition. By the time that reached the streets the damage had been done; Dormer, to his astonishment, found his newspaper and himself at the centre of a storm of popular disapproval.

He attempted to quieten this by a statement in which he disclaimed personal responsibility for the article though acknowledging his responsibility for publishing it. It was sadly ineffective.

That evening Dormer went to see the performance at the Standard Theatre. During the interval he left his box and went, as was the usual custom, to the theatre bar for a drink. Before he had time to order his Scotch, he was set upon by three men and beaten up. In spite of his screams for help nobody came to his assistance, and it was only when the manager came running from his office that Dormer was able to extricate himself from the fists and feet of his attackers and, sheltered by the manager, stagger to the stage door and make his escape – battered, and stripped of most of his clothing.

The manager got Dormer away in a cab; returning to resume his duties, he found himself rebuked by one of the theatre's directors for going to the help of 'such a despicable person'.

At 4 o'clock on Saturday afternoon several thousand people assembled on the Market Square, where they heard a Major Robertson tell them from the improvised platform of an ox-wagon that they had come together to express the disgust that was felt for 'that cowardly wretch, Dormer'.

'I do not consider,' said the Major, 'that Dormer is fitting society to breathe the same atmosphere as white men. I hope this meeting will make a sufficient pretext to cause Dormer to clear out from among us!'

When the cheers for this had died down another gallant gentleman, in the person of Captain Hinton, proposed the first resolution – an essential adjunct of all public meetings on the gold-fields.

'The only object of this meeting,' he shouted as though the Market Square was a parade ground, 'is to get rid of the venomous viper who lives in our midst. . . .'

Speaker after speaker continued in similar strain, all urging the dismissal of Dormer and his banishment from the community. The editor of the *Mining Argus*, who had printed a virulent attack on Dormer in his paper – and been served with a writ for libel as a result – did not lose the opportunity to bolster his case. He moved that 'in the opinion of this meeting it is best for Johannesburg that Mr Francis Dormer is no longer a fit and proper person to live in this community'.

Each speech served to inflame the temper of the gathering more, and Major Robertson delivered his peroration in mounting uproar.

'This man Dormer should be stoned out of the place!' he yelled at them. 'It is not for me to make such a proposition, but if Dormer is still in this town tomorrow let him be tarred and feathered!'

That did it.

But since this was essentially a patriotic demonstration the violence that was burgeoning in that mass mind had to be properly sanctioned by the national anthem 'God save the Queen' – from such scum as Francis Dormer! That this was not all as spontaneous as it may have appeared was proved by the appearance of an effigy, skilfully dressed to represent the editor of *The Star*.

'Let's get Dormer!' they yelled.

A man jumped up on the wagon, wild-eyed.

'What are we waiting for? We know where Dormer is! Let's go and get him! To *The Star*!'

'To *The Star*!' a thousand voices bellowed. They put the dummy on a wooden bench, and with this at their head the whole mass moved off along Pritchard Street to the offices and printing works of the newspaper. By this time the crowd had swelled to about 5,000.

At the entrance to *The Star* the head of the column encountered half-a-dozen mounted police, a few foot policemen and the station officer, Lieutenant Heugh. In the wide portico of the building the newspaper staff – printers and journalists – formed a solid human barricade, and behind these a cluster of Zulu employees, the light of battle in their eyes, flourished knobkerries while their feet stamped out a joyous war-dance. Other men guarded a narrow passage that gave access to a side entrance. Deeper in the building compositors were still at work on the late edition, all determined to get it out on the streets. Every few minutes a reporter would rush up to them with a scribbled account of the scene outside.

While the mob deployed itself to fill the space around the building and up and down the road, their ring-leaders dumped the effigy on the pavement and set light to it. The horses of the mounted police, startled by the sudden flames and smoke, reared and backed away from the entrance. This was the signal for half-a-dozen men to pick up the burning bench and rush the front door, the angry chorus of the mob urging them on.

Twice the blazing effigy was forced through the doors. Twice it was hurled back on the heads of the near attackers so that screams of pain were added to other brute voices of violence. A barrel of wood shavings was poured on the fire to keep it going, and men lit staves of wood in the flames and hurled them through windows, spraying the battle with splinters of flame and glass. Inside, the Zulus picked up the burning spears and hurled them back, giving yelps of pure enjoyment as they did so.

As the fire died out, the windows became the crowd's next target. They were big windows, dark-painted with gold lettering. A score or more of them fronted printing house, counting house and shop. It took a lot of bricks and stones before the demolition was complete, and the crowd had the additional pleasure of seeing their missiles shattering showcases, furniture and equipment beyond the gaping windows. They roared their appreciation the louder whenever one of the hard-pressed defenders was felled.

Casualties were treated inside the sanctum of the editor's office. They included George Sheffield, one of the local directors of the Argus Company who owned the paper, who came in with his head streaming blood. It was a glancing blow, and he was soon back organizing the defence, his chief concern being to restrain some of his printers who wanted to use the revolvers they had with them.

Every stone, brick and other object that came crashing through the windows was ammunition to the men inside. Everything was sent hurtling back into a target that could not be missed. The roadway soon began to look like a battlefield; the foot police were able to regroup in front of the doorway, and the position there could now be regarded as secure.

By this time, too, the mounted police had regained control of their horses and made a short charge into the mob to clear part of the road before the building. One of them, receiving a painful blow on the thigh from a length of wood, attempted to draw his sabre to retaliate. As the bright steel glittered, a dozen hands seized him and jerked him from his horse.

His colleagues rushed to his assistance and, in a violent flurry of horses and humans, the policeman was extricated together with two men who were placed under arrest and hustled into custody inside the newspaper office where, not surprisingly, they suffered further damage from irate printers.

The direction of the attack switched dramatically, and sudden calls for help came from the narrow passage where the few defenders had been forced back by concentrated pressure.

Summoning his Zulus, George Sheffield roared into the fray with a war-cry which would not have disgraced the *impis* of Chaka. Blood still oozed from the bandage round his head, smearing his face with a carmine mask. Confronted by this savage apparition and the unholy delight on the faces of the Zulus behind it, the attackers in the passage turned about and began a panic scramble to escape, fighting each other just as enthusiastically to get out as they had fought the printers to get in. When they finally managed to get clear of the passage, four of their number lay unconscious on the concrete. Sheffield wedged himself firmly in the narrow entrance – as much to keep the Zulus in as to keep the mob out.

In the pause which followed this repulse Jan Eloff arrived and was passed through the crowd and the sentries into the newspaper office. After a brief consultation he was propped up on a windowsill to address the crowd; but the influence of his official presence was somewhat weakened by the sympathy he expressed for the demonstration.

Major Robertson again attempted to take over the leadership, but could not get a hearing. The fickle crowd began to shout for George Sheffield. Measuring the moment, Sheffield had a chair pushed through the front door, and on to this he clambered, bandage, blood and all, to tell them what he thought of them. The crowd pressed about him, surging and swaying against his narrow platform as restless and involuntary as the sea. Twice he was brought down, only to be pushed upright good-humouredly by hands which, only a few minutes before, had been intent on punching his face in.

No one could tell which way the temper of the crowd would break. It was as finely balanced as the bulk of George Sheffield on his chair. Then a loud cheer started at the back of the crowd and flowed through it – Carl von Brandis, escorted by two policemen, was forcing a passage to *The*

Star building. Sheffield gladly gave up his platform to the Special Landdrost, and for a full minute von Brandis stood there, his long white beard billowing like a peace banner, as he waited for his welcome to cease.

It was a familiar role for him, among these Johannesburgers. He spoke to them firmly but without malice.

'Look here, I haven't come for an argument. I don't even want to talk about that article in *The Star*. Whatever your feelings about that, you ought to be ashamed of yourselves as men and Englishmen for what you are doing now. Damaging property, endangering lives, assaulting the police—'

'Give us Dormer,' a voice shouted, 'and we'll damage *him* instead!'

When von Brandis heard the genuine laughter which greeted this, he recognized the change of temper in the mob.

'If it's Dormer you're after,' he told them, 'he's not here. He's at his home, still injured. And it's no use you going there because the place is surrounded by armed police. With orders to fire if necessary. You've done enough mischief, and you must now disperse – otherwise you might find that the mischief will be done to yourselves. If you'll look over towards the Square you'll see that police reinforcements have arrived ... I don't want to call on them and I hope you won't compel me to. Now, why don't you all go home? Or to the circus?' He looked at his watch. 'The first performance begins in half an hour.'

It was all over. There were cheers for the Captain, and this was the signal for dispersal. One small group stopped off at the company's shop in Commissioner Street to hurl a brick through the window, but when they were reminded by the manager that it was not Mr Dormer they were harming but innocent men with wives and families to support, the individual who had thrown the brick came forward to apologize almost in tears, and promised to pay for the damage.

At a Rand Club post-mortem during the solemnity of Sunday lunch it was agreed that although this was in part a demonstration against Dormer and *The Star* as the mouthpiece of capitalism and 'the bosses', it was also another manifestation of the spirit of revolt and upheaval that was smouldering continuously at the heart of the whole Uitlander community – a condition created and maintained by the stubborn policies of the Pretoria Government.

Francis Dormer won his libel action against the editor of the *Mining Argus*, but the Court did not agree that the injury to his reputation was as great as the claim for £5,000 suggested. They awarded him damages of £25.

CHAPTER SEVENTEEN

From the political cauldron that was developing, Barney Barnato held aloof. He could be impartial because he was basically disinterested. His eyes were still fixed on the main objectives – the next million, and financial control of the Witwatersrand. He didn't particularly care who had political control as long as it did not stop his upward flight. Because he was not diverted by political distractions, he could concentrate on his money-making and the expansion of his own little empire.

Alfred Beit had got himself firmly hitched to Rhodes' soaring star. If that ever came plunging it could easily bring all of the Corner House plunging with it. It all depended who won – Rhodes, or Kruger...

Barnato didn't care much who won. All this political unrest was damn bad for the market, of course. But even in bad times the market could be stimulated a little here and there. If he occasionally put over a fast one on the speculative public it was largely the result of a fertile imagination picturing perhaps a little too enthusiastically the enormous potential of the underground reefs. He was sure in his own mind that one day fact would catch up with imagination – even with *his* imagination.

But they were all still amateurs playing with the most complicated mining proposition in the world. It needed the best brains and the best engineering skill before all that gold – which might well be unlimited – could be extracted profitably. Barney talked the matter over with his brother Henry. They decided to find the world's greatest mining engineer and hire him.

'Price is no object, Henry,' Barnato said. 'For every million we have to pay him, he'll be able to make us an extra million.'

The man they chose was John Hays Hammond, an

American mining engineer who, although still under forty, had established a tremendous reputation in the great mining booms of the Western States. (Later he was to become Vice-President of the United States.)

Barnato waited only to see Paul Kruger re-elected President in 1892, and then cabled Hammond in Nevada setting out his proposal and inviting him to a conference in London – all expenses paid, of course.

The two men, with brother Henry sitting in, met in Hammond's suite in a London hotel in April, 1893. It was difficult for the hard-bitten engineer, who had primed himself well on Barney and his activities, to imagine that this perky, thick-set little man, blond and rosy as a Cupid (as Hammond described him) was one of the shrewdest and toughest operators in the world.

'Good morning, Mr Hammond. I hope that's right. Or do you prefer Hays-Hammond? Is there a hyphen? I hope you've had a pleasant trip. You've come a long way to see me. But then, I've come a long way to see you!'

'Hammond's the name, Mr Barnato. The Hays comes from my mother's side. I've had a very good journey, thank you, though a little tiring. And I hope both'll prove worthwhile.'

'This is my brother Henry. The only business associate I can trust, ha-ha! Now, what are your immediate plans, Mr Hammond? How long are you planning —'

'I've booked a return passage for the end of the week.'

'The end of the week! I wonder if that'll give us enough time to finish our business . . .'

'Mr Barnato, I figure that if we cannot agree on the fundamentals of our relationship in half an hour, there will not be much point in continuing the discussion. Let's get down to business?'

Barney nodded his head appreciatively. Behind the pince-nez his eyes took on a slightly different gleam.

'I've been told,' Hammond went on, 'you've often engineered the market for your stocks. That's not my kind of engineering. Before we discuss any terms it must be clearly understood that my professional reputation is not to be used for the purpose of rigging the market for your mining securities.'

Henry was just about to say something when Barney stopped him.

185

'I'm delighted to hear you say that, Mr Hammond. If you'd do whatever I told you to, what use would you be to me? Why, you'd be just as likely to do the same for anybody else, if he made it worth your while. I'm very glad to hear you talk like that.'

He looked across at his brother who, quite clearly, was not all that pleased with Hays Hammond.

'Henry and I have talked this over very carefully. We've decided to offer you a salary, in your kind of money, of twenty-five thousand dollars a year to take control of the mining side of my interests. I might say, Mr Hammond, that twenty-five thousand dollars is the biggest salary any American engineer has ever been paid in South Africa. And we've had some of the best, the very best. There are people like . . .'

'I'm sorry, Mr Barnato, I'm not interested at that figure. I'm doing much better than that at home.'

'How much do you want?'

'Double it.'

Again the quick look towards brother Henry, the brief nod back.

'All right then, Mr Hammond. That's satisfactory to us.'

'There are one or two other things, Mr Barnato. Just so there's no loophole for misunderstanding. You're going to spend many millions of dollars in developing your mines. I believe I can increase the efficiency and introduce economies that will amount yearly to many times my salary.'

Barnato nodded happily.

'We don't expect to pay you that sort of salary for nothing, Mr Hammond.'

'Therefore,' Hammond went on, 'I shall accept your offer of fifty thousand only until such time as I have been able to convince you, as a good businessman, that my services are worth a great deal more to you. When that time comes you must be prepared to accept from me a request for a much higher salary.'

Barney took this in his stride.

'I expect to have to pay you what you're worth, Mr Hammond. If you can do what you claim you'll be earning it.'

To Hammond, who was expecting a tough bit of horse-trading, Barnato's ready acceptance of everything came as a tremendous surprise. They agreed that a form of contract should be drawn up for signature the following day.

'And now, Mr Hammond, I'm sure you'll want to rest after your long journey. I hope you'll dine with me tonight? Good. We'll meet you here at eight, if that suits you. Till tonight, then.'

The two brothers shook hands with Hammond; the door was hardly closed behind them when Barney held out his hand again.

'Give me the fiver, Henry. I told you we'd get him for fifty thousand dollars at the most. It's a bargain – we've got the best man on the business! Wait till Rhodes hears about this! Let's go and have a bottle, Henry.'

Barnato, a raincoat over his pyjamas, was down at Park Station to meet the Hammond family – wife, sister and two sons – when they arrived in Johannesburg on the early train six months later. He drove them from the station to their hotel.

'Just for a day or two. Then we'll fix you up with a house in the suburbs. Servants a problem. Drop you at the hotel, then you must come to breakfast. Mrs Banato's famous for her breakfasts.'

The Barnato breakfasts were indeed famous. They had set an original fashion in entertaining, and not only provided Mrs Barnato with an opportunity to exploit her gifts as a hostess but Barney with an opportunity of organizing each morning's share market tactics. Woolf Joel was a regular guest, as was Lou Cohen – a sort of Mercury to Barnato's Cupid of high finance, dispensing the darting arrows of gossip and rumour that started swift upward flights of share prices, or just as swift downward swoops.

As they entered the Barnato home guests were invariably greeted by a green parrot, perched near the door in a gilded cage – which *might* have been the solid gold Barney always claimed it was. Every time the front door opened, the parrot would screech: 'Barney, what price Primrose today?'

Primrose Mine was Barnato's favourite possession, though the fact that it was an excellent gold producer seemed to interest him less than the opportunities it gave him of manipulating the market.

John Hays Hammond, with his own great reputation and invested with so much authority by Barnato, found himself thrust straight away into a position of considerable prominence in the town. This he was not reluctant to assume. He was overwhelmed, too, by the immense potential of the Witwatersrand gold-fields – a potential far beyond anything he had imagined possible.

As a super-efficient engineer he was appalled at the antagonistic attitude of the Pretoria Government and the way in which this was retarding development. He saw that the efficiency and payability of the whole mining industry depended as much on political changes as on good management and scientific development, and found himself caught up inevitably in the potent political forces that were fomenting the thoughts and actions of the Uitlander population. For year succeeded year without any attempt to redress their grievances, or to grant them the rights which they claimed and which they were beginning to demand with greater and greater insistence.

The association of Barney Barnato and Hays Hammond was not a success. This was hardly Hammond's fault. He repeatedly urged his employer to secure properties on the largely undeveloped East Rand where Wernher and Beit were increasingly active. He tried to convince him of the great possibilities of really deep-level mining, and that he should buy up every surface claim that remained available south of the outcrop.

But Barnato was a speculator first, and attached more importance to the advice of his stockbroker associates than to that of his mining engineer. Hammond was hurt and angry when his recommendations were so casually ignored, and he was frequently annoyed at Barney's inability to keep appointments. His professional and natural vanity were offended by the reputation he was getting as 'Barney's White Elephant'. At the end of six months he resigned.

He was immediately offered a number of top-level appointments. The only one he was interested in came in a telegram from Cape Town. It invited Hammond to meet Cecil Rhodes, now Prime Minister of the Cape Colony, at Groote Schuur – the lovely gabled house which Rhodes had just completed and which he was to leave to the nation as the official residence of South Africa's Premiers.

The meeting, thick with destiny for Johannesburg, took place on the slopes of Devil's Peak in the spring of 1894. The two men sat side by side on a wooden bench looking out over the pine woods and the sweep of Table Bay to the forest of masts and rigging in the harbour.

'Mr Hammond, I take it you are not in South Africa for your health.'

'No, Mr Rhodes. With due appreciation of the climate of this wonderful country, I prefer that of California.'

'Well then; how would the idea appeal to you of taking charge of all my mining interests? Name your own salary.'

'Seventy-five thousand dollars a year and a participation in the profits would suit me.'

'All right. Now tell me. You've seen my properties on the Rand. What do you think of them?'

'Not very much, to be truthful, Mr Rhodes. But with your backing I'm sure I could improve your investments without any difficulty.'

Rhodes searched round in his pockets and pulled out an old envelope. He glanced briefly at the address and postmark, then scribbled on the back:

'Mr Hays Hammond is authorized to make any purchases for going ahead and has full authority, provided he informs me of it and gets no protest. C.J.R.'

He handed this to Hammond.

'Take this back to Johannesburg with you ... and use it. I want you to investigate the Witwatersrand thoroughly. Let me know the full possibilities. Especially how long they're likely to last. After that, a little later in the year, I'll want you to come up to Matabeleland and Mashonaland with me.'

It was October, 1894. For a month Rhodes, Hammond and Dr Jameson had been travelling round the new domains of the British South Africa Company between the Limpopo and the Zambesi. The Matabele War was over and its instigator and inevitable victor, Jameson, was riding high in popularity and self-confidence. Now was the time for consolidation and development.

The three men had visited the foundling settlements and the lonely outposts; they had scrabbled with their hands and their imaginations among the litter of ancient workings whence a forgotten race had, perhaps, smelted gold for Solomon and Sheba.

They were searching, searching. And there was no doubt what Rhodes wanted to find. He wanted to find another

Main Reef, another Witwatersrand, another Johannesburg, in his own country. Now they were at the end of their search and Hammond had to tell him that he would never find it; that there was plenty of gold but no main reef; that there would be only one Johannesburg, and that one in the Transvaal. Kruger's Transvaal.

They sat around the camp-fire in the heart of Matabeleland. The leaping flames threw shadows on the rocks that rose between mopani trees and endless thornbush. For Rhodes it was a moment of realization and disillusion. He had to meet his Chartered Company shareholders in London in January. The shares had been rising steadily in expectation of his engineer's report on their Charterland.

Now they would hear the truth from Hammond: and they would not like it. Rhodes stared into the fire. He would paint another picture for his shareholders. A picture of a great federation of African States in which they would be shareholders with the Crown and all the peoples of Empire: in which they would share in the wealth of the Transvaal. In Mashonaland and Matabeleland he had hoped to find the golden weapons with which he could destroy the South African Republic in a bloodless victory – a mammoth take-over bid in which Kruger and his burghers could not hope to match him. Now he would have to find other weapons. Nothing would prevent the fulfilment of the dream.

In the distance a lion roared, and the challenge was answered from the other side of the night. The bush shivered gently as the reverberations rolled across the silence. Rhodes turned to Hammond.

'Are you absolutely sure about the Rand? Johannesburg'll die without the mines. How long do you think they'll last?'

'Geologically, Mr Rhodes, there's no reason why the Rand should not last a very long time. If you want to pin me down more precisely, I'd say at least fifty years and probably more.'

Both men looked at him in astonishment. Hammond went on quickly.

'Let me put it this way. The reefs have been exposed along the outcrop for more than forty miles. It's my belief they'll be found to extend a good deal further. But, for the sake of this argument, let's cut down the length of the gold-bearing reefs to thirty miles. Now, I'm quite positive that the slope of the reef will be within the reach of the economic mining operations over several miles of the South Dip; but let's cut that down again to *one* mile. So we then have thirty square miles of reef. Agreed?'

Rhodes and Jameson nodded in unison.

'Right! I'm going to assume an average thickness of five feet of payable banket through the reef, and I assure you that's putting it low. According to fairly recent Chamber of Mines figures the average yield of the Rand ores is twelve-and-a-half pennyweights per ton. It is a figure which will inevitably be improved with improved methods. But never mind that. We'll bring it down to eight pennyweights of extractable gold. Then, unless my arithmetic is very wrong, the Rand will produce a minimum of a hundred and thirty million ounces of gold worth, say, four hundred and fifty million pounds at today's prices. Even with the producing power of the mines reaching ten million pounds per annum – which it'll do very soon if the Pretoria Government doesn't discourage it – you can see that this'll mean a life of forty-five years.'

Rhodes sat in silence for a few moments, watching the shadows play hide-and-seek in the great rocks. Then he asked:

'Supposing that, with good government, the output was increased to twenty or even thirty million pounds a year?'

'Not at all an unreasonable figure, Mr Rhodes. But we've been talking about thirty square miles of the Witwatersrand. What if I were to base my estimate on a hundred and fifty square miles of reef, with mines operating at depths up to five thousand feet vertically —'

'Five thousand feet straight down!' Jameson was incredulous.

'Sure, Doc. It's true we don't know exactly how far down mining is practicable, but the Comstock Lode in Nevada is now being worked below three thousand, and in Cornwall the Dolcoath tin mine is about the same depth without any uncomfortable increase in temperature. On the Rand I reckon the two biggest difficulties will be ventilation and water. It's a power problem; and with all that coal more or less next door it should be easily answered.'

Hammond took out his drawing-pad and made a number of rough sketches explaining the geology of the reef formation and his belief in the continuity in depth of the banket. He scribbled in some figures showing the yield per acre of the outcrop companies already in production, their costs and the resultant profits.

'This is the point, Mr Rhodes. You can't buy the outcrop companies now at any price – but you can still get the claims over the South Dip cheaply, and they can be worked to several thousand feet of vertical depth at a cost only slightly above that of the outcrop mines. I'm quite satisfied, gentlemen, that large profits can be made by buying up the land, sinking shafts to strike the ore bearing reef and milling according to the methods of the outcrop companies.'

'Why would it not be good business,' Rhodes asked, 'to sell our holdings in the outcrop companies, buy all available deep-level claims along the strike of the reef and start deep-level mining – using the cash we get from the sale of our outcrop shares?'

'That's exactly my idea,' Hammond told him. 'That's just what I recommended to Barnato. But he was too much engaged in other affairs. He wouldn't listen. So I left him.'

'Poor Barney,' Rhodes murmured, smiling at the thought of past encounters. 'A tremendous character, but his own worst enemy. And his own best friend. But never mind Barney ... You're sure, are you, Hammond, that your geology is sound on this deep-level theory of yours?'

'I'll stake my reputation on it. And I'm not the only one who's convinced of it. Your friend Alfred Beit has been buying a lot of South Dip claims over the past couple of years. Fortunately he's been more interested in the East Rand – not that the prospects aren't just as exciting out there.'

There was a pause while Jameson and Hammond watched Rhodes in silence. He picked a stick out of the fire and, when the flame at its end burned out and the slow, blue smoke curled upwards, the two men could sense the effort of will and imagination to make, out of the unsubstantial wisps of the present, a reality of the future.

'All right, then,' he said at last. 'Let us send a cablegram to London at once. Write this down on your pad, Hammond: "Have decided best policy for company would be to sell out our entire holdings in outcrop companies stop do this at once Hammond approves cable reply Rhodes." Address that to Consolidated Goldfields in London.'

'The nearest telegraph office is at Mafeking, Cecil,' Jameson pointed out. 'How are we going to get it there?'

'My secretary, Fiennes, can take it,' Hammond said. 'He's probably been asleep for some hours by now. He can start first thing in the morning.'

'What's the time now?' Rhodes asked.

'Nearly two o'clock.'

'Then let him start right away. He's got a five-hundred-mile ride ahead of him.'

Hammond went across to a small tent where the fourth white member of the party was sound asleep. Eustace Fiennes, later to become Governor of the Leeward Islands, survived a brief moment of bewilderment, and then got dressed. Jameson meanwhile had called to the boys to saddle a horse, and within half-an-hour Fiennes was on his way south, hastily-gulped coffee still warm in his stomach. In a few seconds horse and rider were swallowed up by the night.

The three men went back to the fire, still holding their mugs of coffee.

'We've made a big decision, Hammond,' Rhodes said quietly. 'I hope it works out well for you.'

'It's geologically and financially sound, Mr Rhodes. All we need is good government in the Transvaal, and the Rand could be the treasure-house of the entire world.'

'Ah; good government! And how d'you think you can get good government, Hammond?'

'Let's hope old Kruger'll see sense. Otherwise he'll have to have some sense knocked into him. Nobody concerned with the progress of the Rand mines can afford to stand aloof from the political implications. The issues are too mixed up.'

Hammond paused to finish his coffee, tilting the dregs out on to the sand. He looked at his watch.

'Three o'clock! I'm off to get a little sleep. We'll remember this night, I believe, Mr Rhodes, as the beginning of big things for your Gold Fields Company. Good night; and good night to you, Doctor.'

Rhodes and Jameson murmured their good nights as Hammond moved off to the tent where Fiennes had been sleeping.

'No, don't go, Jim.' Rhodes threw another branch on the fire, sending sparks cascading upwards through the smoke. 'Let's talk awhile.'

Jameson waited. He knew what was coming.

'Well, it's not so good, is it, Jim? Your little Matabele war didn't solve all the problems we hoped it would, did it? Lobengula wasn't sitting on a gold-reef, after all. Now how're we going to get the shareholders to pay for a railway line?'

'At least it showed us how certain problems can be re-solved – by direct action.'

Rhodes looked up quickly at his friend – aware, not for the first time, of the strange accord between them that made it unnecessary to discuss their thoughts or even, at times, the plans that preceded action. When Rhodes spoke again it was as though he had just been asked a question.

'No; not that way. Not yet. Step by step. Better to keep in step with the feelings and demands of the people as a whole. It took me twenty years to amalgamate the diamond industry. That's what South Africa needs. Amalgamation. A union of the people and of the land within the greater union of Empire. But under the Crown; not under the Colonial Secretary! Kruger's the obstacle. Kruger and his republic. And his gold mines. Good government's what the mines want. That's what Hammond said. It's something Kruger can't give because he'll never have it. *I* can give it to them: through amalgation!'

His cold, blue eyes, fixed on their distant vision, glowed with the earthy warmth of the camp-fire as they flicked back to Jameson.

'If only I had Johannesburg, Jim! If I had Johannesburg I could unite the whole country tomorrow. Then you'd have a great commonwealth here in Africa; a union of states and nations. Then, I think, apart from my mother country, there would be no place on earth to compete with South Africa. There's no place to touch this for the beauty of its climate and the variety of its products. Yet here we all are, quarrelling over things like equality of rights, instead of thinking of the great country that's been given us!'

'Give me a few hundred mounted police and a column of our pioneers, and I'll make you a present of Johannesburg,' Dr Jameson said urgently. 'We'd have fifty thousand Uit-landers on our side. The Boers 'd pack up overnight!'

Rhodes shook his head.

'The Boers are not Matabele, Jim. And the Uitlanders have no arms. All the same, if the Johannesburg population . . .' He paused in mid-sentence.

'. . . if the Johannesburg population were to rise in revolt against the Government, that might be the moment. First of all restore law and order, then invite the High Commissioner to intervene. He could initiate and supervise a referendum open to every adult male in the Transvaal. That's the way it *could* happen.' Rhodes nodded slowly. 'It looks very much, Jim, as though you and I had better call on some friends in Johannesburg.'

CHAPTER EIGHTEEN

Hammond's assessment of the Rand's fantastic potential was by no means prophetic. He had studied earlier reports, including the brilliant analysis by his countryman Hamilton Smith. But his predictions were based more than anything else on an event in June which not only had confirmed all the theories which most people were finding so difficult to believe, but had provided the final proof, to those who were waiting for it, of the almost inexhaustible nature of the underground streams of gold.

For an entire year Messrs Tracey, English and Beatty had been probing deep down into the earth with their new diamond-faced drill. They had set it up on the open veld nearly a mile south of the outcrop on the Simmer and Jack Mine, east of Johannesburg. For days and weeks and months the drill cut through the familiar strata of the Witwatersrand formation, carving out of the varied rock a plain story for the men on the surface who examined the slim, smooth core which the drill excreted. Then, one day, they read in the revelation of the rock the first few phrases that were to mean a new chapter in the story of Johannesburg and the South African Republic. The drill had bitten into another stratum – and this time it was conglomerate. But was it the Main Reef? A few more days of tense probing produced the evidence the experts needed. The Main Reef had been intersected at 2,397 feet. It was nine feet thick, and the lower three feet assayed an extremely satisfactory thirty-five pennyweights.

Still only a comparatively few men perceived the real significance. Hammond was one; but even backed by this irrefutable testimony he had failed to persuade Barnato of the enormous possibilities of the deep levels. There was no rush either to buy claims or to buy shares in the deep-level companies.

For Barnato and the speculators the proposition held out little prospect of quick development, quick profit. It was simply not speculative enough. The Stock Exchange just did not think in terms of mining at depths of 2,000 feet and more: it was not their line. The market stayed dull and uninspired and the South Dip claims lay as abandoned as orphans – except for the careful, selective buying of Wernher, Beit and the later intrusion of Rhodes and Hammond.

In 1892 a total of £1,149,768 was paid by Witwatersrand gold mines in dividends, on a production of 1,210,865 ounces of gold. The output for 1893 was nearly 1½ million ounces; but even this failed to produce any reaction in a community which was far more interested in quick capital gains than annual dividends.

The State profited with the mines. In the last quarter of 1892 revenue totalled £331,663. Of this £305,779 came from import dutics, transfer dues, licences and other taxes which only the Uitlander class had to pay; £16,579 came from taxes on natives; and £9,285 from other taxation to which the burghers were the chief contributors. The agile mathematicians of Johannesburg were not slow to calculate that about ninety-two and a half per cent of total taxation was borne by the mining community and the civilian population of the Rand, about five per cent by the native inhabitants, and little more than two and a half per cent by the rulers of the republic.

The rulers could see nothing wrong with this arrangement, particularly as the Uitlanders showed no disposition to depart from the land of their oppression. On the contrary they swarmed in by the hundred every day. But the Uitlander population liked money too much to part with it in such disproportion – particularly as it wouldn't even buy them a vote. Without any deep sense of spiritual values, and with very flexible patriotic affiliations, it is doubtful whether they believed in anything enough to fight for it – certainly not to die for it. But, under a variety of pressures, they were becoming malleable material for the potent forces of history which were massing, by the end of 1894, all round the boundaries of Kruger's Transvaal.

All this had been dramatically demonstrated in the crisis of the Malaboch affair half-way through the year.

Malaboch was a petty native chief living in a remote and mountainous corner of the north-western Transvaal. He had been in arrears with his taxes for nearly fifteen years and was becoming the focal point for feelings of unrest and rebellion which were latent in all the native tribes which the Boers had either subjugated or pushed into the border no-man's-land. Systematic gun-running to the tribes had increased the dangers to the republic.

It was decided to make an example of Malaboch. From Pietersburg a small force under the district commandant was sent to extract payment from the chief. Secure in his mountain fortress, with the slopes and surrounding hills filled with armed supporters, he laughed at the handful of Boers, stole half their horses and sent them insulting messages.

The Boers were forced to withdraw to Pietersburg without their taxes, and the Volksraad decided on a full-scale effort against Malaboch. They ordered 'commandeering' – the Boer equivalent of selective mobilization – to begin throughout the republic. According to an 1883 Act all inhabitants aged from sixteen to sixty were liable for service when summoned; anybody so selected had to drop everything, saddle his horse, equip himself with gun, ammunition and food, and ride off to the designated assembly point.

Badly advised, Kruger made a fundamental error in authorizing the commandeering of a number of British subjects in Pretoria. Although it could be argued that the expedition was being made as much for the protection of the Uitlanders as of the Boers, the Government's case was weakened by their continued denial of citizen rights to the new population, and the fact that, of all the nationalities represented in the Transvaal, only the British had no treaty of exemption from commando service.

No Johannesburg residents were involved in the commandeering, but when a number of Pretoria Britons were thrown into gaol on their refusal to join the Boers, or were taken up to Malaboch's country under escort, the militant Johannesburgers made this cause their own.

The National Union immediately promised financial and legal assistance to any Uitlander who disobeyed the commandeering order. When a High Court judgment upheld the rights of the Volksraad, they appealed to the High Commissioner in Cape Town. Sir Henry Loch cabled the Colonial Office. There, Lord Ripon found himself in a bit of a spot. He had to admit that British subjects could not claim exemption from commando duties in the Transvaal on strict grounds of law, but found it insupportable that other nationals should be excused 'and that Her Majesty's subjects should remain in a position of such marked disadvantage'.

He instructed the High Commissioner to make a protest on behalf of the British Government – but to do it courteously. Loch, who also had the matter of the native territory of Swaziland to discuss with Kruger, found it opportune to visit Pretoria and deliver the protest in person.

Feelings in Johannesburg ran high. Plans were discussed for raiding Pretoria gaol and releasing the British prisoners. These were dropped when it was pointed out that the capital was full of armed Boers mobilizing for the Malaboch affair. The National Union were disappointed that the intervention had not been more decisive; but at least the British High Commissioner was coming to Pretoria, and they were determined to make the most of him.

When Loch's train arrived at Pretoria Station on the morning of Monday, June 25, there were ten times as many Johannesburgers there to greet him as local inhabitants. They had been coming in by train, cart and on horseback since before daylight, and the streets and Market Square were filled with excited men and women wearing red-white-and-blue rosettes and flourishing home-made patriotism in a thousand flags. By half-past eight, when President Kruger arrived in his State coach, over 3,000 Uitlanders had gathered outside the station.

A double rank of volunteer infantry blocked the entrance to the plaform, and behind this the presidential party took what shelter they could from the hooting and booing of the crowd. This did not cease until an Uitlander arrived with a Union Jack mounted on a tall, bamboo pole, and managed to insinuate himself through the escort to take up a position on the platform next to Kruger as the train steamed in.

When Loch stepped up to the President and shook his hand, a band played 'God Save the Queen', the slow notes being taken up by the voices of the crowd outside. When the music changed to the *Volkslied* of the Republic, the crowd went right on with the British anthem and repeated cheers for the Queen and High Commissioner.

The tumult rose to a point of hysteria as Kruger and Loch appeared in front of the station and climbed into the coach. The tall stranger with the Union Jack vaulted on to the driver's box and waved his banner to and fro while the crowd yelled their delight. The cordon of the escort broke under the pressure, and a score of men surged towards the coach. While a few pulled down the hood of the brougham, laughing off Kruger's protests, the rest quickly unharnessed the horses and, seizing hold of the traces, began to drag the coach away down Market Street to the Transvaal Hotel where the visitors were to stay.

Loch was plainly embarrassed by the whole performance and kept turning to Kruger as though he wanted to apologize for the unseemly behaviour of Her Majesty's subjects. He was silenced each time by the studied impassivity of the President, who had obviously steeled himself to meet a patriotic exhibition and a display of Uitlander bad manners. Only when the flag, caught in a gust of wind, draped itself around his shoulders, did he relax his self-control. He lifted his silver-headed walking-stick and struck viciously at the offensive bunting; for a moment he looked as though he would strike at the standard-bearer too. Then he felt Loch's restraining hand on his arm, nodded briefly in acknowledgment and resumed his stoic immobility as the procession moved on to another welcoming throng outside the hotel.

There the High Commissioner was met by the official reception committee of British residents, who presented him with an address of welcome which did not omit reference to the latest difficulties. Loch thanked them formally and then, conscious of the massive, lonely figure in the coach, added:

'There is one thing I wish you to do; that is, if you respect the Queen, and myself as her representative. I am here as the guest of President Kruger —'

The loud groans and boos which greeted the name made him pause and hold up his hands in a gesture for silence which was nearly a gesture of surrender. He went on more loudly:

'I ask you to respect my position here in a State which maintains the friendliest relations with Her Majesty's Government. By complying with my wish you will assist me in looking after your interests and those of the country I represent and to which you belong. I ask you, in all sincerity, to join with me in cheers for the President.'

It was no good. The response was so feeble, the cheers so soon drowned in jeers, that Loch regretted his conscientious impulse. He shook hands with Kruger and went into the hotel, leaving the old man in his horseless carriage surrounded by a host of jubilant foreigners. Although he could see groups of Boers gathering on the outskirts of the crowd, needing only a signal from him to unsling the rifles from their shoulders, Kruger kept his impenetrable dignity until a dozen burghers came and towed him away.

In the *Volksraad* a secret session on Monday afternoon discussed a motion asking for an inquiry into the circumstances in which the South African Republic and its President was allowed to be insulted by aliens, and urging the Government to take immediate steps to have the rioters punished. An address to the President was prepared and signed by many English-speaking residents of Pretoria, expressing disapproval of the demonstration. A similar move was made among the mining houses of the Witwatersrand; and the Cape Parliament resolved 'that this House desires to express regret and disapproval at the unseemly display of disrespect towards the President and Government of the Transvaal by individuals representing themselves to be British subjects . . .'

The Prime Minister, Mr Rhodes, said they were all deeply sorry for what had occurred, and hoped that the reports in the newspapers had been exaggerated.

A number of Members expressed their concern at the High Commissioner going over to Johannesburg. Serious consequences, they said, could ensue if Sir Henry by his presence inflamed the dangerous temper of the populace. Sir John Merriman urged that the High Commissioner should be recalled immediately.

It was a situation which responsible Johannesburgers did not underestimate. With armed Boers streaming into the capital after Monday's events, they felt themselves sitting on a powder keg which could, by exploding prematurely, blow all their golden dreams to dust. Lionel Phillips came home from the Transvaal Hotel on that first evening serious-faced and filled with an anxiety which he could not conceal from his wife.

'What is it, Lionel?' she asked as soon as she saw him. 'What's gone wrong?'

Phillips looked steadily at her for a few moments.

'Listen, Flo. If I tell you to leave the place with the children, even if it's at an hour's notice, will you do it?'

201

'If you really want me to. But what's it all about?'

'There's the devil to pay in Pretoria. A shocking insult to the President. The Boers are hopping mad – and I can't blame them. They're parading the town in armed groups with guns loaded, looking as if they'd willingly shoot down every man, woman and child wearing a red-white-and-blue rosette.'

'What about Sir Henry, Lionel? Couldn't he do anything about it?'

'He did his best in the circumstances, I suppose. But I'm not at all sure of Loch. I believe it wouldn't take much to make him intervene here.'

'Well, who wouldn't? He's every right to!'

'It's not as simple as that, my dear. You must realize that intervention could mean a war between Britain and the Transvaal. And then where'd Johannesburg be? Or the Corner House, come to that.'

'Surely it wouldn't come to war. They wouldn't dare...'

'I wouldn't bet on that, Flo. They dared once before, you know. At Majuba.'

'Majuba! Majuba! That's all those Boers think about. If there'd been a Johannesburg then, and fifty thousand Uitlanders, it would have been a very different story.'

'Well, perhaps. But we're not ready for that sort of thing yet. The Turf Club's invited Loch over for next Saturday's race meeting. I wish they hadn't and I hope Loch has the sense to refuse. Almost anything could happen if he sets foot in Johannesburg this week. There's a rumour that five hundred Boers have been sent to Orange Grove. They're in a nasty mood – talking about making the *rooineks* pay, and so on.'

'Well, there's nothing much you can do about it, Lionel. Except to buy a rifle and some bullets. We've got one pistol in the house. Don't you think we ought to be a little more prepared?'

'I think we all ought to be. You're right, Flo. I'll get a rifle during the week. But there's something I *can* do, you know. I can stop Loch!'

In Pretoria the High Commissioner was playing a deep and devious game. Behind the public protestations of friendship, and his restraint of the more hot-headed demonstrators, even while he was addressing the Volksraad in the most cordial terms he was busy inquiring into the strength of the Uitlander element in Pretoria and Johannesburg and the possibilities of revolt. He made no effort to conceal his thoughts when Phillips came over for his second interview. In the High Commissioner's suite at the Transvaal Hotel the two men talked alone.

'Well, Mr Phillips!' Loch ended a long period of question and answer. 'After what you've told me I must agree that it would be unwise to visit Johannesburg at this juncture. It may interest you to know that I have had several telegrams from the Cape, including one from Rhodes, advising a postponement. At the same time, as Her Majesty's representative, I feel it is my duty that I should make direct contact with British subjects on the Rand.'

'I can support that wholeheartedly, Your Excellency,' Phillips said, with evident relief. 'May I add that I am most grateful for your understanding approach to this problem.'

'In that case you will be glad to know that I have already telegraphed the chairman of the National Union informing them of my reasons for not accepting their invitation and that of the Turf Club, and suggesting that they send a small deputation of, say, a dozen people to meet me here in Pretoria.'

Phillips nodded his agreement and appreciation. He stood up, ready to take his leave, feeling that his mission had been accomplished.

'One moment, Mr Phillips,' Loch motioned him to sit down. 'There are one or two other matters on which I'd appreciate your advice. You understand that in a situation like this I have to take into account every factor, every possibility. The Colonial Secretary and the Government rely on me to keep them fully informed of every development, I might almost say every movement. I cannot always do that through official channels. You understand?'

Phillips understood, all right. He leaned forward in his chair as Loch went on.

'Very well, then. My inquiries among British residents in Pretoria have elicited the information that there are fewer than a thousand rifles among them in the whole town and district, and probably not more than five hundred. Would you agree with that?'

'I would say that's putting it very high. That figure probably includes every sort of firearm – rifles, shot-guns, revolvers – even air-guns.'

'Quite, quite. Whatever it is, it struck me that it would be singularly inadequate if a situation arose in which these Britons – my countrymen and yours, Mr Phillips – in which they found it necessary to defend themselves against, shall we say, a Boer counter-attack.'

'A Boer counter-attack!' Phillips, for all Loch's careful approach, was incredulous. Loch held up a reassuring hand.

'Mr Phillips, I have tried to convey to you that my questions are purely hypothetical. I am in search of information. One hypothesis which a man in my position cannot ignore is that, under extreme pressure, there may be a rising of Uitlanders in Pretoria and Johannesburg. As far as Pretoria is concerned it is fairly clear that the possibility can be ruled out. Now, Mr Phillips, what about Johannesburg – the second hypothesis? For the purposes of this hypothetical uprising in Johannesburg I am led to believe that some seven thousand rifles would be available. Can you confirm that?'

'Absolutely not!' Phillips was emphatic. 'I shouldn't think there are one thousand – and not more than ten thousand rounds of ammunition.'

'I am glad to see you are keeping yourself well informed. But are there not prospects of increasing that number? Prospects which are even now materializing?'

'I am obviously not as well-informed as Your Excellency thinks, if you'll forgive me for saying so. As far as I know the prospects you refer to are still only prospects.'

Loch looked very put out.

'I'd heard differently. In fact, my information led me to believe that Johannesburg could hold out for five or six days in the event of a rising. It would require five or six days, of course, for any practical intervention to prove effective.'

'Sir Henry.' Phillips had obviously come to a sudden decision. 'Perhaps I ought to make my position clear. As you know, I am President of the Chamber of Mines. I assure you that there is no more loyal subject of the Queen on the whole Witwatersrand, and nobody more aware of the grievances of the Uitlander population or the disastrous effects of Kruger's policy on the mining industry. But we – that is the majority of members of the Chamber – feel sure there must be a peaceful way of solving our problems, and that any resort to violence could be catastrophic for the industry and for our shareholders.'

'Then I can take it, Mr Phillips,' Loch said icily, 'that the mining industry was not represented in the demonstration on Monday, or in the loyal addresses?'

'Well, Your Excellency,' Phillips replied, a little uneasily, 'I must tell you that the Chamber of Mines has already prepared an address to the President deploring Monday's incidents and disclaiming any association with them. At the same time we have pointed out very firmly indeed that such things are a direct result of the Government's policy and would not occur if he gave Johannesburg some redress of justifiable grievances.'

'But that's the whole point, Mr Phillips, if I may say so. Supposing you get no redress? What then? Are you and your associates going to allow present conditions to continue indefinitely, and probably worsen?'

'Not at all; but the responsibility would then be Kruger's, not ours.'

'I fully understand your position, Mr Phillips. Naturally you feel your first duty is to your gold mines and your shareholders. But you all have another duty, too, you know. Your duty to your country and your countrymen.'

Loch paused for a moment to study the dust drifting through a shaft of lazy afternoon sunlight. Then he said casually:

'Incidentally, I have prolonged that Swaziland agreement for another six months. I suppose in six months Johannesburg could be better prepared than it is now. Shall we leave it at that?'

Late in October, 1894, Rhodes and Jameson entered the South African Republic on their return from 'Charterland' by way of Delagoa Bay. That railway to Pretoria had at last been completed, and these two men, ironically enough, were among the first passengers on a line which, in linking the republic independently with the outside world, had constructed a barrier as tangible as its iron rails and embankments against closer union with the south.

Rhodes had never ceased to believe that to his imperial edifice the railways from the Cape Colony were as essential as steel reinforcing. Now every beat of the wheels, every thrust of the labouring pistons, must have hammered home the message of Kruger's tactical triumph: which was, after all, why the Delagoa Bay railway had been built.

Rhodes had no difficulty in foreseeing that rates on the line which was now carrying him to Pretoria would soon discriminate so heavily against its competitors that most of the import traffic would be diverted. He would go and see Kruger when he reached the capital, and warn him of the dangers of starting a tariff war. He would make one last attempt to get Kruger to co-operate in the concept of a federation of South African States. The Transvaal he *must have*. 'If only one had a Johannesburg, one could unite the whole country tomorrow....' He would rather get it by negotiation, or even by purchase if necessary; but he was going to get it, anyway.

When they reached Pretoria, Rhodes sent Jameson on to Johannesburg to start discussions with the leaders of the Uitlander community, while he himself arranged his interview with the President.

The two men met in the *voorkamer* of the homely bungalow near Church Square and it was a vital conversation that has been lost to the story of Johannesburg. Only Rhodes' parting words to Kruger are on record to provide inadmissible evidence of what must have been spoken but went unheard by eavesdropping history.

'If you do not take care,' Rhodes said to the grim old man as they came out on to the stoep and the State Artillery sentries stamped to attention, 'you will have the whole of South Africa against you. You are a very strong man, but there are things you may do which will bring the whole of the Cape Colony and indeed the whole of South Africa against you, and in such strength that you will not be able to stand against it.'

The President's heavy jaw set immobile as a rock, barring the entrance to his mind. It was, perhaps, just as well that Rhodes could not penetrate it. For Kruger has left no doubt what he was thinking of his great adversary at that moment – and all the time.

'Cecil Rhodes,' he told his biographer when it was all over and he was just a broken old man in Holland, waiting to die, 'is the man who bore by far the most prominent part in the disaster that has struck my country. In spite of the high praise passed upon him by his friends and his countrymen he was one of the most unscrupulous characters that have ever existed.'

There was another character who could be described as unscrupulous if history is to be judged – or recorded – scrupulously. To Jameson in Johannesburg Rhodes hurried as fast as a four-horse Cape cart would take him. It was useless trying to argue with Paul Kruger. Now the plan that had been born during the long, firelit nights in Matabeleland, and up on the Zambesi watershed, would have to be put into operation.

It was a simple one. First the Uitlanders must be stimulated and hardened into threatening direct action against the Boer Government. For this they would require organization and money. The Transvaal National Union was a ready-made breeding ground for the seeds of revolt. But it was too spontaneous, too lacking in purpose; and it needed too the big financiers and capitalists who, fearful of their fortunes, had declined thus far to get entangled in its politics. So Rhodes persuaded Beit with same difficulty to support the movement; and once Beit was involved, most of the others followed in various degrees of enthusiasm or reluctance. Two notable exceptions were J. B. Robinson and Barney Barnato, who were more or less immune to political partiality, and who would anyway have felt that something had gone out of their lives if they had found themselves on the same side as Rhodes and Beit on any kind of issue.

In addition, none of the Randlords could trust each other; or, if they could, they didn't. They were united with Rhodes and Loch in their eagerness to get rid of Kruger and his form of government, but Rhodes had good reason for thinking that they were just as enthusiastic about maintaining a republican authority under their own direction as Rhodes was on expanding the federal territories of the Crown. That would create a situation that he would not be able to deal with as easily as he hoped to cope with Kruger. After all, although most of the mining magnates behaved as though they were more patriotically British than the British, many of them sang 'Rule, Britannia' in guttural accents, and the greater part of their finance originated in Germany and France. The threat of German intervention was a permanent factor in Transvaal politics.

From this visit of Rhodes and Jameson to Johannesburg the Reform Movement was to emerge, to concentrate and spearhead the Uitlander assault on the citadels of the Republic. It was primarily a psychological assault and it was to give the psychology potency, more than for any other reason, that Rhodes instructed Jameson to make preparations for collecting an armed force on the borders of the Transvaal – at the nearest point to Johannesburg which he could find without actually setting foot in the republic.

Rhodes knew exactly what he had to do himself. He must manipulate the political situation so that he could be sure of the support of the Cape Parliament and of most of the Cape Dutch in any clash with their brethren in the north, and condition the thinking of the British Government so that they would not intervene, diplomatically or physically, until he wanted them to – but also that they *would* then intervene...

Nor was Rhodes oblivious of his own financial interests. His Gold Fields Company was about to launch itself wholeheartedly into deep-level mining. He was no less concerned than any of the other Rand magnates with a suitable return on investment. His final instructions were reserved for Hays Hammond, who was about to put into effect the secret plans they had made to buy up the remaining South Dip claims. In one of those scribbled injunctions which Rhodes scattered so cryptically along his trail he advised Hammond:

'Do not buy deeps with poor parents. Drunkards' children are no good. Go always into good things, not doubtful, unless they cost you nothing. Remember poor ground costs as much to work as rich ground. The only difference is the first cost.'

Johannesburg was being prepared for whatever role Rhodes wanted it to play. It was both the means and an end in itself. The cast had been chosen and their lines given them. Now Rhodes and Jameson, accompanied by Dr Rutherfoord Harris – another Kimberley medico whom Rhodes had enlisted in the services of the Chartered Company – set off for London.

Their announced intention was to address the annual meeting of shareholders, but the real purpose was the preparation of political and public opinion in England for the addition of yet another piece of Africa to what was coming to be regarded as Cecil Rhodes' personal empire.

CHAPTER NINETEEN

When Cecil Rhodes managed to secure the reappointment of Sir Hercules Robinson as High Commissioner, the tide of events and history was being made to conform to his pattern. Robinson was a Rhodes man. He had been High Commissioner and Governor of the Cape from 1881 to 1889, and on relinquishing those posts he had become a director of De Beers and a shareholder in the Chartered Company. Now Rhodes and Robinson were able to co-operate energetically in pursuit of common objectives, with only a token resistance from Whitehall's fading Liberalism.

When the Liberals were defeated in the 1895 British elections, Lord Salisbury became Prime Minister of a Conservative Government. The man of the hour in English politics – Joseph Chamberlain – chose for himself the Cabinet post of Colonial Secretary. The direction of affairs in South Africa was now in the hands of a man who had been deeply involved in the Ulster Movement – formed to carry resistance to Irish Home Rule to the point of armed rebellion – and who had been the strongest influence in the Cabinet decision to bombard Alexandria, which led to the occupation of Egypt in 1882.

There can be little doubt that foremost in Chamberlain's thoughts when he became Colonial Secretary was the South African Republic and Johannesburg, or that his solution of the problem implied the establishment of Britain as the sovereign power in Southern Africa; with a bit of luck and good management, the sole power.

But his idea of who should wield that power coincided with Loch's interpretation, not Rhodes'. As early as 1888 he was writing to tell his future American wife that he intended to be the Colonial Minister.

'I am inclined to advocate a bold policy in South Africa,' he wrote, 'fully recognizing Imperial responsibilities and duty. But then I intend it should be the policy of the Imperial and not the Cape Government and should be carried out by officials taking their instructions from the former.'

This was the antithesis of the Rhodes conception of Imperialism and in direct contrast to Sir Hercules Robinson's declaration at the end of his first term in Cape Town that government from Whitehall ought to be a diminishing factor in South Africa.

But British public opinion was lining itself up enthusiastically behind Rhodes and Jameson. They were lionized wherever they went on their visit to England (the Chartered Company territories were named Rhodesia for the first time) and they made the most of this popular adoration in the secret machinations, with Cabinet Ministers and Civil Service heads, which went on all the time they were in London.

From this welter of intrigue and confusion of aims and ambitions it became impossible to distinguish between truth and implication, between fact and distortion. What can be said is that when Rhodes and Jameson returned to South Africa in March they were themselves quite sure that the British Government knew all about their intentions in the Transvaal and would not discourage their fulfilment: provided intervention followed a popular uprising of the Uitlanders, and did not precede it.

Dr Jameson knew exactly what had to be done, and never for one moment during the whole of 1895 deviated from the course which Rhodes had set him. As far as he was concerned there were only two essentials – a sufficient number of armed men, and a place to start from.

Rhodes had deceived the directors of the Chartered Company into authorizing what must have seemed a startling increase in the strength of the British South Africa Police in Rhodesia, and the purchase of arms and equipment. Jameson and his swashbuckling aides, Sir John Willoughby and Bobby White, had completed the first orders of arms as early as January. These were ear-marked for the B.S.A.P. and his new force of Rhodesian Volunteers. They then proceeded to buy an extra 4,000 Lee-Metford rifles, three Maxim guns, and 300,000 rounds of ammunition, to be consigned to the Company's agents in Cape Town.

Now Rhodes and Jameson prepared a greater and far more devious deception. They had to have a jumping-off place for their invasion of the Republic, and it had to be as near to Johannesburg as possible. Together they looked at the maps of the area. Jameson put his finger on a small dot on the Bechuanaland chart, marked Gaberones. It was two miles outside the Transvaal border and about 200 miles west of Johannesburg.

'That's the place!' he said.

It was up to Rhodes to arrange with the Colonial Office for the transfer to the Company of a part of the Bechuanaland Protectorate which would include Gaberones. But Parliament was – and still is – extremely sensitive to any infringement of the rights and property of native races placed under the protection of the Crown. The request for transfer of a large slice of protected territory had little hope of success.

There was another way. Rhodes was anxious to proceed with the construction of a railway line from Mafeking to Bulawayo, skirting the Transvaal boundary. He applied for a strip of land two miles wide – with a block of twenty square miles at Gaberones for the establishment of a township. And at Gaberones he also sought permission to post a detachment of the B.S.A.P. to undertake duties in protection of the railway and its installations which would be beyond the strained resources of the Bechuanaland Border Police.

That was the position when Jameson passed through Johannesburg or his way to organize his forces in Rhodesia. He was gratified to discover that Hays Hammond had been right and that dissatisfaction and antagonism against the Pretoria régime were mounting daily. The National Union were organizing a monster petition as a final attempt to persuade Kruger and the Volksraad, by constitutional means, to give them what they considered to be their rights.

Rhodes himself, still reluctant to provoke a physical clash and always a great believer in the power of money, was more than willing to try bribery to achieve his ends in the Volksraad – not for the first time. He enlisted the support of Alfred Beit and Lionel Phillips, both of whom maintained their unwillingness to risk their great financial structure in any reckless adventure against the State.

The National Union displayed a temporary spirit of co-operation in this attitude when Leonard announced that his committee had decided to raise a fund which would assist progressive candidates in future elections to the Volksraad. This progressive movement was not inconsiderable, as was demonstrated in the elections held early in 1895 when the anti-Kruger party had several unexpected successes.

But the great majority of the Volksraad, though not always unsusceptible to the sort of inducement which Rhodes and Beit contemplated, could not muster sufficient enthusiasm for liberal reform to bring about any change in their outlook or legislation. When Phillips reported this failure to Rhodes, Jameson was given the go-ahead.

Jameson himself had been fretting and fuming up in Bulawayo. In his own mind he looked on the conquest of the South African Republic in the same way as he had regarded the conquest of Matabeleland. He foresaw Paul Kruger fleeing before him across the borders of the Transvaal into Portuguese East in the same way as he had seen Lobengula in flight across the Zambesi. While he awaited the next Rhodes summons, he read the biography of Robert Clive in Government House, and envied the freedom from restraint with which that other chartered company had been allowed to add the whole of India to the Empire. Discussing this with a group of friends one afternoon, he suddenly exclaimed:

'I've a jolly good mind to march straight down off the plateau with the men I have here, and settle this Transvaal business out of hand! The idea of the British and the rest of South Africa being trodden on in this way by that Pretoria gang is absurd. Bobby White has reconnoitred the approaches to Pretoria from the north. I've a good mind to get the fellows together and start tomorrow, through Tati.'

When some of the difficulties were pointed out to him, both military and political, Jameson slammed his book down on the table.

'You may say what you like,' he told them emphatically; 'but Clive would have done it!'

It was at this time that Joseph Chamberlain took over the Colonial Office. Like Rhodes he believed fanatically in the expansion of the British Empire. As a statesman he saw the extension of British power and protection – the *pax Britannica* – as beneficial for the whole world. As a Birmingham businessman he saw how it would also extend the market for British manufactures.

Although their objectives were similar, Rhodes regarded Chamberlain as an opponent rather than an ally, and he was confirmed in the impression by the difficulties the Colonial Office put in the way of the transfer of the Bechuanaland railway strip.

Another fear began to worry the conspirators. There was growing evidence that the more cosmopolitan and republican element among the Uitlanders, including financiers like Barnato, J. B. Robinson and Albu – and, of course, the concessionaires – would not be averse to an alliance with the progressive party in the Volksraad, to oust Kruger and his administration and set up a more liberal and conventionally democratic form of government, which might have satisfied the majority of the Johannesburg dissidents.

Rhodes could see that this would have destroyed his federal plans far more effectively than Kruger's continuing intransigence and enmity. He did not give a damn about the political rights of the Uitlanders. It was now essential to his whole vision that there should be an uprising in the Transvaal and that Kruger should attempt to crush it. Apart from anything else, it was the only excuse for intervention which the curious conscience of British public opinion would tolerate.

Rhodes realized the time had come to force the issue and step up the pressure. And he had to complete his arrangements for an alternative base for Jameson's force if the Gaberones plan did not materialize. His brother, Colonel Frank Rhodes, and Alfred Beit were chosen to set the new phase in motion, while Jameson's brother Sam maintained a personal liaison with the Johannesburgers. Neither Cecil Rhodes nor Dr Jameson was yet prepared to reveal the full scope of their scheme or its details, but it is certain that by the middle of 1895 both Lionel Phillips and Charles Leonard knew that the Cape Prime Minister had committed himself to a sponsored revolt in the Transvaal, to be followed by the High Commissioner's intervention.

Johannesburg was not yet ripe for revolt. There was the matter of the great petition which was being signed by thousands all along the Rand; and they had pressing domestic problems of their own which made all Rhodes' dreams and schemes seem pretty intangible stuff by comparison.

To start with, the Stock Exchange and the property market, after a considerable boom at the beginning of the year inspired by the mining industry's astonishing output figures, had collapsed in the face of mounting tension and startling rumours which swept not only through South Africa but through every chancellory in Europe.

Then there was the drought. The community, in spite of Kruger's warning, had profited little by the experiences of the great drought of 1889. The reservoir had been completed, but its resources were inadequate for the town and its expanding requirements. There was a constant tripartite feud between the citizen representatives, the Government and the Waterworks Company over the question of water supply. The failure of the summer rains at the beginning of 1895 made it a virtual certainty that the high-veld would be without rain until the following spring. Would the reservoir hold out? Not until the water supply was rationed to one hour's trickle through the taps in the morning and one hour in the evening did the townsfolk give it much of a thought. By then, like everything else, it was one more reason for getting rid of Kruger and his Boers.

In the meantime, members of the National Union were scouring the Witwatersrand collecting signatures for their petition to the Volksraad. The Union concentrated their demands on an extension of the franchise, for although only a minority of Uitlanders were deeply interested in such technicalities, the organizers realized that once they had the franchise they could have everything else. They based their case on the fact that they were governed by a minority who paid less than one tenth of the taxes, in defiance of the principle of equality enshrined in the republican constitution.

Naturally it was not possible to keep such a wide and energetic canvass secret, and it was not long before counter-memorials were being drawn up and signed in all parts of the Transvaal. Nevertheless a surprising number of full burghers showed that they were anxious for the franchise rights to be modified and extended.

When the National Union finally sent their petition to Pretoria, in time for the August session of the Raad, it had been signed by 35,483 persons of whom 32,479 were resident in Johannesburg. An additional memorial from Johannesburg demanded that the Raad accept the principle of one-man-one-vote before altering the franchise law. This secured 5,152 signatures.

The great Franchise Debate took place in the Volksraad in the second week in August. The Memorial Committee,

214

which passed judgment on all petitions, recommended that no alteration in the law should take place – only petitions signed by full burghers of the republic could be legally considered, and these were overwhelmingly against any extension of the franchise.

The opening debate was remarkable for a declaration by Lucas Meyer, chairman of the Memorial Committee and later to be among the most prominent of the republican generals in the Boer War, that he could not agree with his fellow-members.

'There is not a single man in this Raad,' he told them, 'who will use his powers more towards maintaining the independence of our land than myself. But I am convinced that it is the duty of this assembly to propose an alteration to last year's law which denies the right to vote to the Uitlander. Sooner or later some change will have to take place; slowly perhaps, but it will come. Even in the Committee this was recognized. To fulfil your duty then, you must put this proposal before the country. If the majority of burghers are against it, you stand or fall by that decision – but at any rate you will then be acting according to the will of the country and cannot yourself be blamed for the consequences.'

He paused as the murmured dissent came up to him from the crowded hall. In a few places, among the vigorous head-shaking, two or three beards would converge in a muttered conversation and part nodding in approval of Meyer's proposition. The speaker went on:

'Recently, the President has said that something must be done to admit a portion of the people behind the wall of the dam before the stream becomes so strong that the walls will be washed away and the country flooded. That is what will happen if you do not allow the water to flow, for the walls of this dam we have built here are not strong enough to hold so much water.'

Carl Jeppe, the new member for Johannesburg, was chafing as though he had a bit between his teeth as one after another Boer and burgher, with curious logic sustaining their unyielding obstinacy, declared against the extension of the franchise. At last the chairman motioned him to speak. Jeppe plunged straight in – forgetting, in his eagerness, the formalities of procedure.

'Who are the people,' he asked, 'who now demand from us a reasonable extension of the franchise? They are there for all to see in the petitions. There are to begin with almost a thousand old burghers who consent to such extension. There are eight hundred and ninety, also old burghers, who complain that the franchise has been narrowed too much by recent legislation. There are over five thousand who ask for extension subject to universally accepted principles of the ballot, and there is a monster petition, bearing thirty-five thousands and more names from the Rand gold-fields. And, in passing, may I add that I have convinced myself that those signatures, with a few exceptions, are undoubtedly genuine.'

Ignoring the laughter and the ribald comments Jeppe paused only to take a deep breath.

'There are not three hundred Rand people who can write whose names are not on that list. It contains the name of the millionaire capitalist on the same page as that of the humblest carrier or miner, that of the owner of half a district next to that of a clerk, and the signature of the merchant who possesses stores in more than one town of the republic next to that of the official. It embraces all nationalities: the German merchant, the doctor from Cape Town, the English director, the teacher from France, the Italian waiter, the American industrialist – all have signed it. So have, and this is significant, old burghers from the Free State whose fathers with yours founded this country. And it bears, too, the signatures of some who have been born in this country, who know no other fatherland than the Republic but whom the law regards as strangers. Then there are the newcomers. What about them?'

Jeppe paused as though waiting for interruptions. But the Raad was silent, caught up in his eloquence and sincerity.

'They have settled in this land for good. They have built Johannesburg, one of the wonders of the age, now valued at many millions sterling and which, in a few short years, will contain from a hundred to a hundred and fifty thousand souls. They own half the soil; they pay nearly all the taxes. Nor are they people who belong to a subservient race. They come from countries where they freely exercised political rights which can never long be denied to free-born men. All these persons are now gathered together, thanks to our electoral law, into one camp in antagonism to us. What will we do with them? Shall we convert them into friends or shall we send them away empty, dissatisfied, embittered? What will our answer be? Dare we refer them only to the present law which first compels them to wait fourteen years and then pledges them nothing except a Volksraad decision in 1905? Which one of you can say that you will be here in 1905 – or even that this Volksraad will be here?'

As he challenged them, half a dozen members leapt to their feet, shouting. The chairman called for order and waved them to sit down. Jeppe nodded his thanks to the Chair before he went on.

'Well, if we resolve now to refuse this request what will we do when, as we know must happen, it is repeated by two hundred thousand one day? You will all admit the doors must be opened. What will become of us or our children on that day when we shall find ourselves in a minority of one in twenty without a single friend among the other nineteen – among those who will tell us that they wished to be brothers but that we, by our own act, had made them strangers and enemies? Shall we say, as a French king did, that things will last our time and after that we reck not the deluge?'

He sat down abruptly, leaving the sudden silence like a dark blanket over the Raad. Before the arguments could start among the crowded seats Paul Kruger stood above them, his deep voice stilling the first rumbles of discord.

'I would like to say a few words on this subject, Mr Chairman, and the first thing I have to say is that those persons who signed this monster petition are unfaithful and not law-abiding—'

Jeppe leapt to his feet: 'I deny that!'

'Yes,' Kruger growled, glaring at him, 'I repeat, unfaithful.'

'I say they are not!' Jeppe shouted back at him, so that the chairman banged his gavel and ordered the Member for Johannesburg to be seated. Kruger went on:

'I say these people are disrespectful and disobedient to the law because they are not citizens, they are not naturalized. Now, can anybody contradict that? No you cannot, for the law says that you must be a burgher of the Republic before you can petition this Raad, and these people are not burghers.'

He looked round triumphantly. Jeppe could only shake his head impotently against such impenetrable logic.

'I am against granting any extension,' he heard Kruger

217

say, 'except in cases like that I mentioned the other day. Those who go on commando are entitled to it, but no others. Those who show they love the country by making sacrifices for it are entitled to the franchise, and they will get it. These memorials are being sent in year by year, and yearly threats are made to us if we do not open the floodgates. If the dam is filled, before the walls are washed away a certain portion of the water has to be drained off. Well, this has been done in the case of the commando men. They are the clean water which has been drained off and taken into the inner dam of pure water. But I do not wish to take in dirty water also. No, that has to stay in the outer dam until it is cleaned and purified. The Raad might just as well give away the independence of the country as give all the newcomers, these unfaithful, disobedient persons, the franchise.'

In mounting excitement it was pointed out by Mr Jan Meyer, as one who had once represented Johannesburg and knew how things were worked there, that it was not possible to obtain 37,000 signatures from a total population of 40,000. The petition was obviously a fraud. Mr C. B. Otto, the patriarch of Otto's Hoop in the Western Transvaal, shouted above the din:

'Look at that wonderful book on the table. As fat as a Rand millionaire with Uitlander names! Every one of them a lawbreaker. Yes, they have broken the law in signing that book and sending it here. We should have nothing to do with it. How many times has the Raad heard that if the franchise was not extended there will be trouble? I am tired of all these threats. I say, "Come on and fight, if you want a fight. *Come on!*"'

Pandemonium broke out in the assembly as the chairman vainly tried to restore order. Mr Otto was not to be silenced. Standing up on his chair he shouted again:

'I say to them, "Come on and have it out; and the sooner the better!" I cannot help it, Mr Chairman, I must speak out. I say I am prepared to fight them, and I think every burgher of the South African Republic is with me.'

'Order, order!' called the chairman, thumping the table violently while hubbub filled the hall, though whether it was for or against the speaker it was not possible to tell. Only Kruger sat grimly silent, his eyes flicking to and fro in their frames of puffed flesh. He made no effort to intervene as Otto swept on:

'Yes, this poor republic which they say they own three-quarters of: they took it from us once, and we fought for it and got it back! They called us rebels then. I say *they* are rebels! I will say it again! Those people who signed the memorials in that book are rebels and should be treated the way we always treat rebels!'

When he finally managed to make himself heard the chairman addressed himself directly to Otto.

'Will you keep order? You have no right to say such things. We are not considering the question of powers, but the peaceful question of the extension of the franchise. You must keep to the point, otherwise I cannot allow you to continue.'

'Very well, I will keep quiet,' said the old Boer. 'But I call the whole country to witness that you silenced me and would not allow me to speak out my mind.'

The debate went rumbling and roaring on for two days and through the morning of the third day. At last Kruger rose for the fourth time.

'We have talked this question out,' he told them. 'There is nothing new to be said about it. My counsel to the Raad is that you do not consent to Mr Lucas Meyer's proposal. I do not want it put to the country. This business is repeated from year to year until I am tired of it. There is no uncertainty about it. The mind and will of the burghers is well known. The way is open for Uitlanders to become burghers. Let them follow that road and not to try to jump over the wall. I have been told by these people that if I take them on the same cart as ourselves then they cannot overturn the cart without hurting themselves. That may be true, but they can also pull away the reins and drive the cart along a different road. Let Mr Jeppe go back to Johannesburg and tell his people that if they are obedient to the law and become naturalized they will not regret it.'

Kruger blew his nose loudly as he finished, turned his back on the Raad and slumped off the platform. It was left to Mr Otto to move that they accept the report of the Memorials Committee, refuse the request of the petitioners and refer them to the existing laws. Sixteen members voted in favour, eight against.

It was the last genuine attempt to find a constitutional

solution to a situation in which men and events were moving at ever-increasing speed towards a climax of violence – even as the railway lines from the coast were beginning to converge on Johannesburg from four directions.

When the Delagoa Bay line reached Pretoria at the end of 1894, Kruger and his Hollander associates began immediately to deploy the weapons it gave them against the forces encircling the Republic.

What irked the Uitlanders was that the high monopoly rates and preferential tariffs they were compelled to pay were going chiefly to the Netherlands Company and not for the benefit of the country as a whole, least of all themselves. What irked the mining industry was that the inefficiency of operation on the railways, added to high customs and mileage charges, was not only severely limiting their profits but making vast tonnages of low-grade ore unprofitable to work, thus restricting development of existing mines and making it impractical to open new ones which would otherwise have been payable propositions.

If Kruger was prepared to use his railways as a weapon, Rhodes was determined that he would find it a double-edged one. The Cape Government introduced new tariffs on their line as far as the Transvaal border, undercutting the rates on the Delagoa Bay route.

The Pretoria executive retaliated with a drastic increase in charges on that section of the Cape Railway which ran through the Republic between the Vaal and the Witwatersrand. The provocative hand of Rhodes showed again in the next move, when the Cape authorities decided to unload their goods at the Vaal River drifts and carry them on to Johannesburg by ox-wagon at the usual rates; whereupon Kruger issued a proclamation on August 28 closing the drifts as ports of entry to goods of overseas origin. It was to become effective on October 1.

The lengthy interval was stipulated in the hope that the Cape would change its mind, and to give shippers an opportunity of re-routing their Johannesburg cargoes through Delagoa Bay. Instead the Cape Government declared that the closure was a breach of the London Convention of 1884, and sent a formal protest to Kruger through the High Commissioner. The protest was not acknowledged.

October 1 became a new deadline for Rhodes. And a new opportunity. He had better get ready to meet it. The first priority was the base on the Transvaal border. He had given up hope of getting Gaberones in time; there was another way.

He consulted the High Commissioner, and with Robinson's approval sent his brother Frank and the Bechuanaland Administrator, Sir Sidney Shippard, to see two minor chiefs who ruled over about fifty square miles of territory around the village of Pitsani, just north of Mafeking. They had no great difficulty in persuading the bewildered but compliant chieftains to transfer administrative rights to the Chartered Company. With almost indecent haste the transaction was confirmed by Robinson and the Colonial Office, who found the consent of the chiefs concerned sufficient absolution for their official consciences.

Rhodes and Jameson had their base.

Jameson came to Johannesburg to see the leaders of the new Reform Movement. They met in Hays Hammond's office in the Consolidated Gold Fields building ... Jameson, Hammond, Frank Rhodes, Lionel Phillips, Leonard, Bailey and Percy FitzPatrick.

They had just taken lunch together at the Rand Club and the Doctor was still glowing from the warm hospitality, the excellent wine and the open admiration of members who obviously regarded him as holding the solution to all their difficulties with Kruger and the Volksraad. In the middle of Hammond's desk, on a square of blotting-paper, stood a decanter of port, and in front of each man was a small crystal glass which they refilled periodically in conventional clock-wise circuits. A rolled-up map lay in front of Jameson.

'There's no need to worry about a starting-point,' he was telling them in reply to a query from Hammond; 'Frank here has fixed all that up. Gaberones is out. The Colonial Office is too slow-moving. We've made a deal with Montsioa and Ikaning, and we've got Pitsani.'

He unfurled the map and put a heavy ink ring around the name.

'There! That's the place. That's where our force will be stationed. I'm going up to Bulawayo tomorrow to begin the movement south. But first of all, what are the plans at this end, Frank?'

Colonel Rhodes looked round at the others, who all

nodded their heads.

'Well, Jim, let's skip the preliminaries and the details. In the event of an uprising in Johannesburg the first objective will be the fort and magazines in Pretoria.'

Jameson looked a little startled.

'It'll be like a tea-party,' Bailey chipped in. 'Look, there are never more than one hundred men stationed there, and all except a dozen or so are asleep every night by ten o'clock. I've seen 'em. Fifty good men, well armed, could take the lot.'

'To make it easier,' FitzPatrick added, 'one complete wall of the fort has been knocked down for repairs and additions. We wouldn't even have to open a gate!'

'We know,' Rhodes went on, 'that there are ten thousand rifles, twelve million rounds of ammunition and fifteen pieces of field artillery in the arsenal. I've no doubt you know, Jim, what happens when there's a Boer mobilization. The outlying farmers, of course, have all got their own guns; but the rest just ride up to the fort, collect a rifle and ammunition and they're more or less ready for war. If we can grab that fort we've beaten them before they can start.'

Jameson nodded vigorous approval: 'Splendid. Splendid. I've only one criticism. Once you've got the fort you're going to have a counter-attack made against you pretty smartly. Can you hold out, say, until a relieving force arrives?'

'We're not planning to wait that long,' Frank Rhodes said. He looked across at Hammond. 'But this is where you come in, John. You tell him.'

'Well, it's fairly straightforward, Doc.' Hammond picked up the briefing. 'While one party's seizing the fort another force will take over the railway station and its approaches. Small groups will occupy every signal box and telegraph office along the line. Then we'll run in a goods train full of armed men who can act as reinforcements if necessary and supply the manual labour to load the trucks with the captured arms and ammunition. The field pieces will be blown up.'

'Then we'll all come back to Johannesburg by train!' Bailey grinned, unable to keep out of the discussion. 'Not first-class, perhaps, but free! And that's not all. While Hammond's outfit is raiding the arsenal, another bunch will be heading for West Church Street and Kruger's house.'

Jameson looked alarmed.

'You're not thinking of killing —'

' 'Course not, man! We're going to kidnap him. Bring him back to Johannesburg with us.'

'We thought,' Leonard added judicially, 'it would assist us to gain our demands in any subsequent negotiations with the Boer Government.'

Jameson stood up, and raised his glass to each in turn.

'Gentlemen, I congratulate you. Audacity and simplicity and courage. The three essentials to success in war.'

'And arms and ammunition,' Hammond said dryly. 'We're relying on you and Cecil Rhodes for those.'

'I was coming to that. But first of all, what arms have you got in Johannesburg at present?'

They all turned to FitzPatrick, who had taken on the job of secretary to the conspirators. He consulted a small note-book.

'Including the nearby mines, there are just over one thousand rifles privately owned, and an unspecified number of revolvers. There's probably enough ammunition for twenty rounds apiece – not more.'

'Well, that's not too bad for a start,' Jameson said. 'As you probably know by now, we were able to buy considerable quantities of arms and ammunition for the Chartered Company in England. But Frank here is more in touch with that side of the business than I am.'

Colonel Rhodes consulted a list of figures.

'At the present moment in Cape Town we have five thousand rifles, three Maxim guns and a million rounds of ammunition. They're being railed at this moment consigned to Gardner Williams, general manager of De Beers in Kimberley. He's had some very ingenious oil tankers constructed. Open the hatches at the top and they look full of oil. Turn the taps at the bottom, and what comes out? Oil! False bottoms; false tops. In between, each truck has space for about a thousand rifles and a dozen or so boxes of "ammo". From Kimberley these trucks will be railed to Pickering and Co. of Port Elizabeth, who will re-route them on to Consolidated Gold Fields here. The idea is that each truck will be sent to a different mine, where the arms can be unloaded and stored underground. At the right time your men – *our* men – will call at the appointed place, and each one will collect a rifle and a hundred rounds of ammunition.'

They were all getting a bit excited by this time. The decanter was still going round, and Hammond had to go to his cupboard for another bottle. They didn't see how they could fail. Especially with Dr Jim coming in with his force at the decisive moment.

But Lionel Phillips could not bring himself to share their schoolboy enthusiasm for an adventure which might bring ruin to the great financial enterprises for which he was responsible. He held up his hand to still the excited chatter round the table.

'Just a minute now – before we all go rushing off to Pretoria with six-shooters blazing! It seems to me there's a good chance of our getting away with a surprise raid on the fort. And even, maybe, with kidnapping Kruger. But after that, what? We'll have about twenty thousand well-armed and furious Boers encircling Johannesburg within two days. How are we going to deal with that? And how are we going to keep the mines working with the natives heading for their kraals as fast as they can go, and all the coal traffic stopped? How are we going to keep the pumps going, if nothing else? Every deep-level will be flooded in twenty-four hours.'

'That's where Rhodes and I come in,' said Jameson; he added with a broad smile, 'Not Frank – his little brother Cecil. As soon as the signal for revolt is given here you must send a telegram to Rhodes and the High Commissioner in Cape Town. That'll be the only justification Robinson needs for intervention on behalf of the British Government. And he'll be supported by Rhodes on behalf of the Cape. You'll also inform me at the same time, and I'll set off from Pitsani. What's known as protecting British lives and property.'

They all smiled, though not altogether happily. Hammond looked a little uneasy, but said nothing. Abe Bailey asked what sort of force Jameson would have at Pitsani.

'By December I should have some 1,500 mounted men, fully armed and equipped, at least half-a-dozen Maxims and a troop of field artillery. I will also be able to bring with me an additional fifteen hundred rifles plus ammunition for distribution to your men. Even if we ignore what you may get from the Pretoria fort, I estimate that our combined forces will total some 9,000 armed men with an adequate amount of Maxims and artillery. That, I fancy, should be enough for Kruger. Especially if you have him here in Johannesburg.'

'That's the part of it I like least,' Phillips said earnestly. 'Listen. Whatever the initial success of the military adventure, the whole scheme will stand or fall on intervention by the British Government and a negotiated settlement. If my anticipation of events is correct, the High Commissioner will come up here as an arbitrator and arrange terms which both Whitehall and Pretoria will accept. Presumably these will be the terms required by Johannesburg. Only one man can carry out those negotiations on the Boer side, and that's Paul Kruger. He'll never agree to negotiate as long as he's a prisoner. Nor will he or any of his burghers accept conditions to which he's been forced to agree while in captivity. I think you ought to drop the kidnapping plan.'

The men around the table were obviously impressed by the strength of this argument, and murmured among themselves as they thought it over.

'Well, gentlemen,' Jameson interrupted, 'there may be something in what Phillips says. But there's no need to make a decision now. We can leave that till later. The position now, I think, is that your weapons will be arriving soon and you must concentrate on getting yourselves organized so that if this railway crisis develops we can take full advantage of it. If, for instance, Kruger goes ahead with his fool plan to close the drifts. For my part, I leave this evening for Bulawayo. If we're to have the troops at Pitsani on time, there's a great deal to be done.'

Jameson stood up, threw back the inch of port still in his glass and looked deliberately round the circle of faces.

'I think that's all for the time being, gentlemen. I'll keep you informed of all developments and I'll be visiting you from time to time so that our intentions are fully understood and co-ordinated. I do not have to impress on you the need for absolute secrecy. If Kruger suspects for one moment why that force is gathering at Pitsani, our whole plan will be ruined. I bid you good-day, gentlemen, and good luck.'

The meeting did not break up when Jameson left. Lionel Phillips voiced the disquiet which had now affected the hard-headed businessmen at the table.

'We've got to find out exactly where Cecil Rhodes stands on this. We can't afford any sort of misunderstanding.'

'I agree,' said Charles Leonard. 'And what's more, we've got to make sure that our objectives and his are the same. I think somebody ought to go and see him.'

'That makes sense to me,' Bailey said. 'Why don't you and Lionel go to Cape Town and find out?'

There was a chorus of assent at this. Leonard nodded agreement.

'All right, then. But I think we ought to take Hays Hammond and Frank with us. It'll sort of demonstrate a wider unanimity.'

It seemed a good idea.

'One other thing,' Leonard went on. 'I think we ought to prepare some sort of statement – a declaration of rights, if you like – which we can all accept and sign on behalf of the Uitlander population.'

'Just the thing, Charles!' Hammond agreed. 'Why don't you and Percy draw that up and take it down to Rhodes for his agreement? Then we'll all know where we are.'

Leonard and FitzPatrick spent a week drafting their declaration of rights which, in its final form, was to be published as a full page in *The Star* of December 28 – the famous Uitlander Manifesto.

Jameson, meanwhile, had a more difficult problem on his hands. The base in Bechuanaland had been secured, but how was he to move his force into it? It could not be done without the British Government's sanction – to put it another way, without the Government's lack of opposition. It was not so easy to think up a sufficient excuse. Paul Kruger, once again the plaything of what must have seemed to him an incomprehensible destiny, came to Jameson's aid.

On October 1, before Leonard and his associates could set off for Cape Town, seven wagon-loads of goods for Johannesburg were stopped at the Vaal River by the Republic's customs officials and sent back to the Orange Free State bank. Rhodes and Jameson, who had never believed that Kruger would actually carry out his threat, could hardly credit their luck.

The Cape Government made an immediate appeal to the Colonial Office against the closure. Joseph Chamberlain sent a strong protest to Pretoria. Rhodes found it an opportune moment to reveal – to the Colonial Secretary and the High Commissioner – his plans to move a precautionary force from Bulawayo to Pitsani. He was not discouraged by either. He sent a telegram to Jameson, who immediately began the move into Bechuanaland.

CHAPTER TWENTY

The manager of the Grand National Hotel was half-demented with rage and frustration. Revolution was the least of his troubles. The daughter of the British Agent in Pretoria had been staying in the hotel for a day or two, on a sight-seeing tour of the mines. Coming back hot and dusty in the afternoon from a visit to Langlaagte, she had gone to the bathroom and turned both taps on. Nothing happened. Then she saw the Waterworks Company notice informing residents that owing to the prolonged drought no water would be available in the taps except between 6.30 and 7.30 in the morning and from 4.30 to 5.30 in the evenings.

The young lady was about to go and raise hell with the management when, on passing another bathroom further along the corridor, she noticed that the bath was full of clear water. Unable to resist its cool invitation, she was soon splashing happily as the lather flowed off her. A violent banging on the door reminded her that she had probably stolen somebody else's bathtub. Feeling a little guilty, she called out gaily, 'Won't be a minute!,' and dried and dressed hurriedly. The banging continued, and an irate voice shouted, 'For God's sake don't let the water out; it's all we've got!'

Feeling much refreshed, the girl opened the door and was surprised when the manager pushed past her, glaring. He took one look at the bath and groaned: 'No! Oh, no! My God!' Then he turned to face the bewildered guest. 'D'you know what you've done? You've used the only drinking-water in the hotel!'

In the bars men ordered whisky and soda, drank the whisky neat and took the bottles of soda home for their washing and shaving. Since most of the machinery in the town was steam-driven, it was not long before candles began to replace electric light as the sources of power gasped to a

228

standstill. Buckets of water, brought into town from out-lying streams and dams, were sold at a shilling a bucket; barrels fetched £1. A small dam near the Gas Works, used to irrigate an Indian market-garden, was raided by the townsfolk and within an hour every drop had been bucketed away, leaving only a damp, debris-filled depression. They even took water from the dam at the Robinson Mine – and survived its cyanide content. Then they turned their attention to the wash-holes just outside the township, where the population's weekly laundering was performed by an exclusive society of washerwomen. There were at least fifty of these wash-holes, fed by a reluctant stream, and within twenty-four hours they were dry and the stream had ceased to flow.

'Even decent men,' said a *Star* report, 'have not had a bath for days . . .'

Right through that October the Waterworks Company and its directors replaced the Volksraad and Kruger as the objects of Uitlander scorn and anger. It was not a situation Barney Barnato enjoyed. He consulted his newest co-director, Solly Joel, whose financial genius was rapidly establishing him in the higher strata of the Rand's aristocracy of wealth.

'What the hell can we do about this, Solly? If it doesn't rain soon, the mob'll lynch us. You ever been lynched?'

'So you should worry. They're not thirsty, are they? They're not drinking any less than usual, are they? When the beer and the whisky and the gin runs out, *then* you can talk about lynching. Water? What do *they* know about water?'

'Listen, Solly, the Waterworks Company said that supply will always be in excess of demand. We guaranteed it. It's in the prospectus!'

'How did you know Johannesburg was going to grow like this? Thousands more people every week. You can't guarantee it's going to rain, can you? It hasn't rained for ten months. Is that the fault of the Waterworks Company?'

'Wait a minute, Solly; wait a minute. You've given me an idea. You can't guarantee rain, you said. But *can't* we? You know those two Americans at the Wanderers? Norris and Graham? They're putting on that fireworks display next Wednesday night. Well, I hear one of them has been using rockets to burst clouds in the United States. Why shouldn't he try it here?'

'Why not?' shrugged Solly, and they set off straight away down Eloff Street to the Wanderers. There, in a distant corner of the ground, they found a little tin hut with a sign on the roof which read 'Pain's Firework Factory'. Inside it, in a confusion of Catherine wheels, wire frames, fragments of set pieces and gaily coloured posters, an elderly man was hard at work. He did not look round, and the two men watched him in silence for a few moments.

'Good morning,' Barnato said finally. 'Mr Norris, is it? Or Mr Graham?'

The man said briefly: 'Norris is the name.' He went on working.

'My name's Barnato. Barney Barnato.'

The man got to his feet and turned towards them with outstretched hand.

'Why sure, Mr Barnato. I'm glad to know you. Heard a lot about you.'

'Glad to meet you, Norris. This is Mr Solly Joel. He's my partner in the Waterworks Company.'

Barnato went on talking as the other two shook hands.

'I hear you've had some experience in rainmaking in the States, Norris. That right?'

'That's right, Mr Barnato. Spent all my life in the study and practice of pyrotechnics. Reckon I know just what they can do and what they can't do. And they sure can make clouds part with their raindrops, Mr Barnato. Yes, sir. I remember once in Arizona where Mr Pain was putting on a display at Tucson. There was a drought there just like you got here – only worse, 'cause there wasn't any gold with it, see?'

He paused while they all laughed – Barnato and Joel impatient to get down to brass tacks.

'Then you'll do it for us, Norris?' Joel asked. 'You'll blow up a cloud for us? God knows there's no shortage of clouds. They come over every afternoon, and just disappear over the horizon. I'd like to get my hands on one, I tell you, and wring its bloody neck.'

This set the old American off again into a long chuckling laugh.

'I can just imagine how you feel,' he said finally. 'But it's not all that easy. There are what you could call local pecu-liarities. F'rinstance, these here Transvaal clouds fly mighty

230

high. See this?'

He picked up a rocket and held it towards them. 'That's the biggest rocket I can make with what I got here. It's only about ten inches long. A Yankee rainmaking rocket's about three foot long – them's the kind'll go a clear two-and-a-half mile. I reckon this'n 'll be lucky to reach one thousand feet. It's gotta have a percussion charge on top, see. That's extra weight to push. Then there's the cloud: no use *any* old cloud. Got to be one of them tall ones, black as night at the bottom with whipped cream on top, and so dense you could lie on it. Ain't many clouds like that coming over. But soon as one does, Mr Barnato, you can bet I'll take a shot at it.'

'This afternoon? Tomorrow?'

'Now just a minute, Mr Barnato. I'm sure not going to wreck my own show! See what it says on that poster? Grand Firework Display – Wednesday Night. I'm not aiming to make any rain before Wednesday night.'

'But for God's sake, man – we need rain badly! The whole country needs it!'

'Not before Wednesday night, Mr Barnato. You come along Thursday afternoon – and bring a big cloud with you!'

He was still laughing as they said good-bye. After ten yards Barnato stopped and went back to the hut. He put his head round the door.

'Four o'clock on Thursday, Norris. There's a hundred quid for you if you make it rain, on Johannesburg. And one other thing,' Barnato said. 'Keep this to yourself. We don't want a crowd round here. If you don't make any rain they're liable to bust up your premises – and you too!'

When Barnato and Joel arrived at the Wanderers ground on Thursday they found Norris and his friend Graham setting up their equipment on the cycle track. A curious group of athletes, their training interrupted, had gathered round, but otherwise the secret of the attempt had been well kept.

'Well, Norris,' Barnato greeted them, 'you can't say we didn't bring a cloud with us. *Look* at them!'

The heavy nimbus were cruising across the sky like galleons of doom with all sails set – their bases black and heavy laden, the cumulus mass above soaring in dense, white turbulence thousands of feet into the upper air. The American nodded.

231

'Sure are good clouds, Mr Barnato. With one of them Yankee rockets, reckon we could bust that wide open.' He turned to Graham. 'You ready, Fred? Reckon that one drifting up now's good as any we'll get.'

Norris crouched behind the contraption on which the rocket was mounted, and took careful aim at the heart of the dark accumulation which was now directly above the town. Graham stood alongside the rocket, a lighted match in his hands hovering below a small length of fuse attached to a charge on the head of the missile. Norris struck a match, nodded to Graham and two flames touched two fuses simultaneously. A brief spluttering and hissing was drowned in the swift roar of propulsion as the device took off. Barnato and Joel looked up open-mouthed as the rocket soared upwards, trailing its tail of smoke and sparks glowing red against the black of the cloud. Then it suddenly disappeared. For three seconds of complete silence nothing happened. Then a muffled detonation mingled with the rumble of distant thunder, and the first large drops came plopping down into the dry earth of the cricket field, pocking it with small damp craters while the exquisite smell of rain and dust filled the nostrils of the onlookers.

In the town and suburbs men and women rushed into streets and gardens with unbelieving, upturned faces; shouted delightedly to each other, stood open-armed to welcome the downpour as it soaked shirt and blouse and skin.

At the Wanderers the cheers of the small group around the rocket machine were drowned in the swelling tattoo on the tin roof of the grand-stand. The athletes cavorted gaily about while Barnato and Joel – more careful of their frock-coats and fine linen – headed for the shelter of the nearby band-stand. There they were joined by Norris and Graham, lugging their precious pyrotechnics into the dry circle.

'Give him his hundred quid, Solly,' Barnato said, adding when Joel looked quickly at him, 'sign it for the Water-works Co. They're the ones who'll benefit most.'

Joel wrote out a cheque, signed it and then insisted on Barney signing it, too. They handed it over to Norris, who grinned happily. As he began to thank them, the downpour ceased abruptly, leaving only the rumble of its progress as it moved away to the east.

'Don't worry, gentlemen,' Norris said, 'we'll get some

232

more for you; and I've written to the States for the stuff to make bigger rockets.'

'If it doesn't rain by the time they've reached here we might just as well all pack up and go home!' Solly Joel muttered. 'But you keep on trying, Norris; there's an extra bonus for you with every foot of water we get in the reservoir.'

'As a result of your rockets, of course,' Barney added quickly. 'You understand that?'

Experiments were continued for the next two afternoons, but on each occasion the rockets failed to reach the clouds. The resultant explosions, though they produced no rain, reverberated round the republic and echoed in the debating chamber of the Volksraad in Pretoria. Unfortunately the rainmaking experiments coincided with the appearance in the newspapers of a communication from Captain von Brandis:

'A proclamation will appear in the *Staatscourant* of October 30 stating that Sunday, the 2nd prox., has been fixed by His Honour the President, with the advice and consent of the Executive Council, as a day for the people to humiliate themselves under the chastening hand of God, on account of the numerous plagues such as locusts, sickness among human beings and cattle, and diseases in the crops, and the prolonged drought in various places, etc.; and to pray Him to mercifully avert the plagues and sickness from our people. Ministers and leaders of the various denominations are requested to place the matter before their congregations and the Government requests you, as far as your jurisdiction extends, to draw the attention of the public to the proclamation.'

To the Boers, preparing themselves for their day of humble supplication, the rainmaking rockets were an abominable blasphemy. Hundreds of protests poured in to the President from horrified burghers. In the Volksraad a petition from Krugersdorp was read praying that the Raad would pass a law to prohibit 'the sending up of bombs into the clouds to release rain as it is a defiance of God and will surely bring down a visitation from the Almighty'.

The Memorial Committee reported that they disapproved of such activities, but did not think they could make a law on the subject. That started it.

Mr A. D. Wolmarans, member for Pretoria and of the

Executive Committee, jumped to his feet.

'I am astonished at such advice!' he cried angrily. 'We expect better than that from the Memorial Committee. If one of our children fired towards the clouds with a revolver to try and make rain we would thrash him with a *sjambok*. Why should we permit people to mock at the Almighty in this manner? It is too terrible to think about. I strongly urge the Raad to take steps to prevent such things happening.'

The Chairman, who was also a member of the Memorial Committee, interposed mildly to suggest that the rocket attempts were only made to settle wagers. They knew how the Uitlanders settled everything by wagers.

This was indignantly repudiated by Mr Erasmus, another Pretoria Member, who insisted that the experiments were carried out in real earnest and some of the men concerned had actually been paid 'by rich Jews' to do them.

'It is the truth, Your Honour!' a Member shouted. 'How much longer are these Godless Uitlanders to be allowed to continue this outrage? Every time they send up one of these dynamite rockets they are poking their fingers in the eyes of God!'

After considerable discussion Mr Wolmarans finally moved: 'That this Raad, considering the Memorial now on the Order Paper, resolves to agree with same and instructs the Government to take the necessary steps to prevent a repetition of the occurrences referred to.'

This was agreed to without dissent and the Raad passed on to a motion which attempted, unsuccessfully, to abolish barmaids.

Within the week the drought had broken and heavy rains fell throughout the territory. Whether this was due to the intercession of Providence, or to Messrs Norris and Graham, was a matter of opinion.

CHAPTER TWENTY-ONE

The Johannesburg delegation came back from Cape Town at the end of the month with Cecil Rhodes' approval of their schemes and of the Manifesto. He assured them that he would keep Jameson's force at Pitsani as long as it was necessary for moral support, and to come to their assistance if they wanted it.

As a result of that visit Lionel Phillips was able to shed his restraint, if not his fears. His speech at the opening of the new Chamber of Mines building in the first week in November was a deliberate warning to Kruger that the mining industry and the big financiers were now allied to the proletarian National Union. For Phillips – spokesman of the Randlords – it was a moment of renunciation, the end of his and their hopes that reconciliation was possible at some half-way point between Boer and Uitlander. There was no way of meeting Kruger's inflexible will to maintain the integrity of the Republic except by going all the way towards him.

Jameson arrived in Johannesburg on November 19. He had spent the previous week with Rhodes in Cape Town, and although he let it be known that he was coming to the Rand to see his sick brother Sam, it was realized by the conspirators that this would be the final briefing, a time for revolutionary decision.

They met once again in Hammond's office at the Consolidated Gold Fields. There were present, in addition to Jameson, Charles Leonard, Frank Rhodes, Lionel Phillips and John Hays Hammond – the very core of the revolutionary movement. Jameson, as usual, sat in the centre of the group gathered round the office desk. Spread out in front of them were several maps. Jameson drew three rings at regular intervals between Johannesburg and the border.

'Well, Frank,' he said. 'If you can arrange replenishments

235

of food and water for horses and men at those three points, I think you can leave the rest to me. Will you be able to do it?'

'It's all in hand, Jim. You remember Henry Wolff, that American doctor who used to be in Kimberley?'

Jameson nodded.

'He's our sort of Secret Service,' Rhodes went on. 'He's invented a company called "The Rand Produce and Trading Syndicate", which deals in maize and fodder. He's also arranged to buy a couple of hundred horses in case you need any remounts. He's let it be known that he's starting a coaching service between Mafeking and Johannesburg.'

Rhodes' finger found a place on the map.

'That's where they'll be waiting. About half-way. It's a farm belonging to a man called Malan, who's agreed to look after them. Incidentally, he's a member of the Volksraad.'

'Well I'm blowed!' Jameson laughed like a delighted schoolboy. 'Tell Wolff I think he's done splendidly. Now we've got to decide on a date.... Is something worrying you, Lionel? D'you want to say something?'

Phillips had been whispering to Leonard. Now he looked at Jameson.

'Well, Doctor. There is this one thing. Suppose everything goes off at this end according to plan and you and your men reach Johannesburg, what's the reaction going to be in London? We know we can be sure of you, and we're sure of Cecil Rhodes; but what about the High Commissioner? And what about Chamberlain and the home government?'

'I think I can set your mind at rest on that score,' Jameson said casually. 'As you know, I'm Sir Hercules Robinson's physician. Whenever I see him in my professional capacity I keep him informed of the latest developments. You should see what it does to his blood pressure! But you can take it that he knows every detail of the arrangements. In fact the last time I saw him, less than a week ago, he told me that he was going to have a special train standing by at Cape Town to rush him up to the Rand when the time came.'

'And Chamberlain?' Leonard interjected.

'His position is not an easy one, as you can imagine. He knows what's going on, of course, and approves of it, but

236

he'll not be able to give anything his official support until your rising has been successful and he thinks the time ripe for the Government to intervene. But you can leave all that side of it to Robinson. As for Chamberlain, I think you can say that Joe knows all about it, but the Colonial Secretary knows nothing.'

They all laughed; Jameson looked inquiringly at Phillips.

'All right, Lionel? ... Good. Now we've got to get a date settled. I'll need another fortnight to complete my arrangements. I've not yet got enough troops at Pitsani, and I've got to see Cecil Rhodes again. Some time in the last week of December, I suggest. Say between Christmas and New Year. How about December the twenty-eighth?'

Leonard looked quickly at the others, who each nodded assent. He turned to Jameson.

'December 28th will do provisionally. What I think we'd better do is call a public meeting for the 28th at which we'll announce our Manifesto. That'll be the ultimatum to Kruger and the signal for you to start. But there's one thing we feel we must make quite clear. Whether you start from Pitsani just before or just after the rising in Johannesburg, under no circumstances are you to cross the border until you get the word from us. That must be clearly understood.'

Jameson hesitated before replying.

'I think that what we must aim at,' he said, doodling on the map before him, 'is a simultaneous movement here in Johannesburg and at my end; the signal to be given by you, of course. In the meantime I'll carry on on the assumption that December the twenty-eighth is the day; but for heaven's sake remember that if the Transvaal Government get word of this and start moving troops towards the border I might have to jump the gun.'

This seemed to satisfy everyone. Jameson went on, 'I'll need a letter of sorts from you people. I mentioned this to Lionel Phillips last time I saw him. Have you told them, Lionel?'

Phillips nodded and said: 'I've discussed it with Leonard and we've drafted a letter addressed to you. Like to read it, Charlie?'

Leonard pulled out a long envelope from his jacket pocket. Taking out three sheets of neatly written paper, he looked up at Jameson.

'I'm not altogether happy about this, but I appreciate

you'll need something to show the Chartered Company directors at a later stage – if only for their minutes covering the use of company troops and equipment.'

'And to read to my troops at the appropriate moment,' Jameson interrupted. 'I think it very necessary that they should know they're coming in at the invitation of Johannesburg and to rescue their countrymen from a situation of grave danger. I'm sure you understand?'

Leonard smoothed the letter on the table. 'Very well, then. I think you'll find this will meet your requirements. If you'll allow me to read it right through we can deal with any objections after I've finished.'

Frank Rhodes lit his pipe noisily in the silence which waited for Leonard's voice.

'It's addressed to Dr Jameson from Johannesburg,' Leonard began, and started to read:

' "Dear Sir, The position of matters in this State has become so critical that we are assured that at no distant period there will be a conflict between the Government and the Uitlander population. It is scarcely necessary for us to recapitulate what is now a matter of history; suffice it to say that the position of thousands of Englishmen and others is rapidly becoming intolerable.

"Not satisfied with making the Uitlander population pay virtually the whole of the revenue of the country while denying them representation, the policy of the Government has been steadily to encroach upon the liberty of the subject and to undermine the security for property to such an extent as to cause a very deep-seated sense of discontent and danger. A foreign corporation of Hollanders is to a considerable extent controlling our destinies and in conjunction with the Boer leaders endeavouring to cast them in a mould which is wholly foreign to the genius of the people. Every public act betrays the most positive hostility not only to everything English but to the neighbouring States.

"Well, in short, the internal policy of the Government is such as to have aroused into antagonism to it not only practically the whole body of Uitlanders but a large number of the Boers; while its external policy has exasperated the neighbouring States, causing the possibility of great danger to the peace and independence of this Republic. Public feeling is in a condition of smouldering discontent. All the petitions of the people have been refused with a greater or lesser degree of contempt; and in the debate on the Franchise petition, signed by nearly 40,000 people, one member challenged the Uitlanders to fight for the rights they asked for, and not a single member spoke against him.

"Not to go into details, we may say that the Government has called into existence all the elements necessary for armed conflict. The one desire of the people here is for fair play, the maintenance of their independence, and the preservation of those public liberties without which life is not worth living. The Government denies these things and violates the national sense of Englishmen at every turn.

"What we have to consider is : What will be the condition of things here in the event of a conflict? Thousands of unarmed men, women and children of our race will be at the mercy of well-armed Boers, while property of enormous value will be in the greatest peril. We cannot contemplate the future without the gravest apprehensions. All feel that we are justified in taking any steps to prevent the shedding of blood, and to ensure the protection of our rights.

"It is under these circumstances that we feel constrained to call upon you to come to our aid should a disturbance arise here. The circumstances are so extreme that we cannot but believe that you and the men under you will not fail to come to the rescue of people who will be so situated. We guarantee any expense that may reasonably be incurred by you in helping us, and ask you to believe that nothing but the sternest necessity has prompted this appeal." '

There were a few seconds' silence as Leonard finished. Jameson was the first to speak.

'That'll do me very well. It explains the situation in a nutshell, if I may say so, Leonard. All it needs now is your signatures.'

It was clear that nobody else in the room was as happy about the letter as the Doctor. They sat there with concern showing plainly on their faces.

'What about the date, Charlie?' Hammond asked. 'As I recall, you didn't mention a date. The date on the letter, I mean.'

'Well, I've purposely omitted that. It's understood among us that this letter will be used for no other purpose than that already stated. And is not to be so used without instructions from us. At that time we can also inform Dr Jameson of the date to be put on the letter.'

239

'Well then, gentlemen,' Jameson said, obviously pleased, 'all that is now required is your signatures. Will you start, Leonard?'

Charles Leonard reached for the pen in the middle of Hammond's table. He looked once round the circle of faces, inviting their objections and comments. They stayed silent; with a sudden flourish, he scrawled: 'We are, yours faithfully,' and added his signature 'Chas. Leonard'.

He passed the letter round the table for the other three – Francis Rhodes, Lionel Phillips, John Hays Hammond.

'What about George Farrar?' Hammond suggested as he patted the blotting-paper. 'His name should be on this.'

'He's at the Cape on holiday,' Phillips told them.

'Then that's no problem,' nodded Jameson. 'I'll get his signature myself. I'm going straight down to Cape Town from here. Leave that to me.'

He took the letter from Hammond and the envelope from Leonard. Hastily, as though half-expecting them to change their minds, he folded the sheets of paper and slid them into the envelope. For a moment he paused as a sudden thought crossed his mind. Then he thrust the letter deep into an inside pocket – unsealed. Now he had everything he wanted except a revolution. And perhaps he could do without that, too! He turned to the conspirators, his infectious charm and confidence pouring over them. He could not fail to perceive their lingering doubts and disquiet.

'Thank you, gentlemen. I'm personally most grateful to you, and I think I can say that before long many thousands of others will be grateful, too. You need have no worries for the future. You play your part. I'll play mine.'

'Not before we tell you to,' Phillips interrupted. 'This is not to be an invasion. You come in by invitation only.'

'Like coming to a party?' Jameson sounded amused. 'I agree, and I accept ... Just one more thing. There'll probably be some need in these last few weeks to exchange information and instructions. We must, of course, conceal our intentions from the Boer Government. A simple code —'

'I'd thought of that,' Frank Rhodes said. 'We could use Stock Exchange language. We're all familiar with that. For instance, if you get a telegram saying "Company flotation fixed for next Saturday" you'll know perfectly well what's

The first outspan

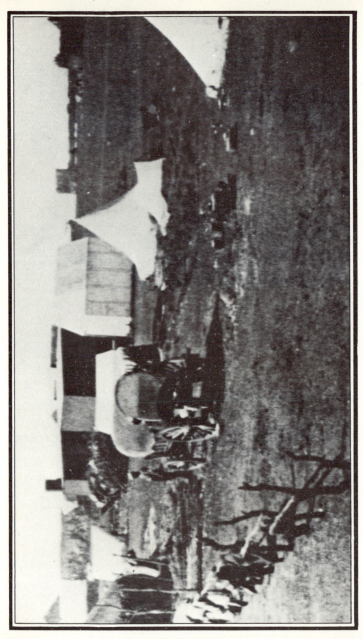

Ferreira's Camp: first organised community on the Witwatersrand

City and Suburban Mine, 1887

Commissioner Street, Johannesburg, 1887

The first chemist's shop

A view of Johannesburg in 1888

Bendoff comes up for the last round

President Kruger visits Johannesburg, 1887

C. J. Rhodes

J. B. Robinson

Abe Bailey

George Farrar

J. B. Taylor

Barney Barnato

Jameson Raid: At the Reform Office

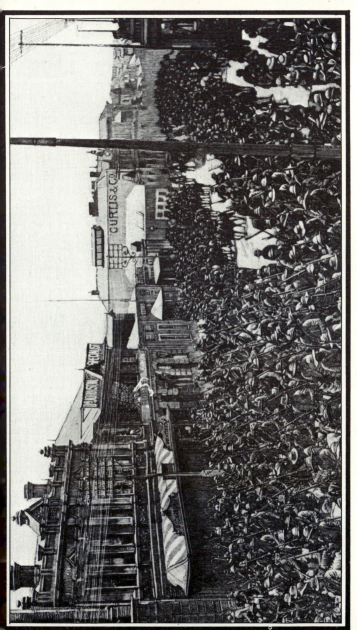

Boer Commando passing through Johannesburg

Surrender: taking down the South African Republican flag, 31st May 1900

meant.'

Jameson laughed. 'I hope it's the only message you ever have to send me.'

He stood up, shook hands warmly with each of them and moved over to the door, his hand involuntarily resting over the letter in his breast-pocket. They were all standing now, sharing the same query: when and how would they see Jameson again?

'Good-bye, gentlemen. When we meet again it will be to hoist the Union Jack over the Government Buildings in Pretoria.'

Then he was gone.

There were a few moments' blank silence in the room. Then Hays Hammond growled, 'What did he mean by that hoisting the Union Jack? If this is a rising on behalf of the British Empire, you can count me out!'

When Abe Bailey returned to Johannesburg from a visit to London in mid-December, he told the Reformers that he had seen Rhodes in Cape Town and that there was little doubt it was intended by both Rhodes and Chamberlain, and certainly by Jameson, that the rising should take place under the British flag. While this was undoubtedly very pleasing news to Abe Bailey, it was less enthusiastically received by the majority of his colleagues in Johannesburg.

The flag issue now became the critical factor in the whole revolutionary project. The Reformers were adamant that there could be no rising if it was to result in the transformation of the Republic into a British Colony. They were well aware of the feelings of the great majority of the Rand population. Financiers, miners, shopkeepers, businessmen – all were doing very nicely. They had come to Johannesburg to make money, and they were making it. The thought of Jameson pulling down the *Vierkleur* while Sir Hercules Robinson hoisted the Union Jack over Pretoria appealed to only a minority of the 130,000 British, American, German, French and Russian Uitlanders who had swarmed into the Transvaal – with 60,000 concentrated in Johannesburg. It seemed inevitable to most of them that 40,000 Boers must eventually give way without the necessity for resort to arms.

There was also the matter of the Summer Meeting of the Turf Club. Although it was no doubt true that a majority of the Witwatersrand population would far rather go to the races than start a revolution, this was not the real reason for Frank Rhodes' telegram to Jameson – which infuriated him – that 'the polo tournament' had been postponed until after the New Year to avoid clashing with race week. The point was that at the decisive time there would be an influx to Johannesburg of about 10,000 visitors whose behaviour, during a week of festivities, was unpredictable.

The worried leaders decided that somebody would have to go and see Rhodes to clear up the flag question before Jameson started. Their choice of an emissary fell on a recent arrival in the Transvaal – Captain Francis Younghusband, the special correspondent of the London *Times*.

The editor of *The Times* was directing the policy of the paper almost blatantly towards the promotion of revolution in the Transvaal and the establishment over the country, by force if necessary, of British sovereignty. Before his departure he had briefed Younghusband thoroughly in all the possibilities, and it was clear that the latter was to be a good deal more than a newspaper correspondent. In his luggage was a code book for transmitting secret messages, and he must have pondered deeply his editor's covering letter: 'Contact Rhodes as soon as you reach Cape Town. Find out all about the prospects of floating the new company before you see the Johannesburg directors. I want to impress upon Rhodes that we hope the new company will not commence business on a Saturday – because of Sunday papers.'

Younghusband, a first-class reporter, had not taken long to sum up the position in the Transvaal. No newspaperman could resist the sort of assignment the Reformers offered him. He left for Cape Town on December 19, and on December 22 he was at Groote Schuur explaining to Cecil Rhodes that there were really three groups of revolutionaries on the Witwatersrand. One group was intent only on reforming the Government, securing their rights and retaining the *Vierkleur*; some were all for driving out Kruger and his clique altogether and flying the Union Jack over the Transvaal; the third group – financiers interested chiefly in the exploitation of the natural wealth of the country – wanted an independent republic with laws and regulations designed to give greater assistance to their own objectives.

'The Reform Committee,' Younghusband told Rhodes, 'is

adamant that Jameson must not be allowed to make a move until this question of the flag is settled, and settled the way they want it.'

'And that, I take it,' Rhodes said surlily, 'means no Union Jack.'

'That is correct, sir.'

Rhodes' frustration and anger glowed in the normally ice-cold eyes; his fist thumped the arm of his chair, and his voice rose to the high pitch which always revealed his excitement.

'What do these Uitlanders expect? *They're* the ones who want a rebellion! What's a flag to them? They're only interested in making money! Now they suddenly *don't want* a rebellion. Tell me, young man, is there no one in Johannesburg who will risk being shot and will lead a revolt?'

'There is no one I can think of, sir, if their present mood continues.'

'Then won't *you* do it? D'you mind being shot at? Won't you lead them?'

'Me, Mr Rhodes? I'm a newspaperman. I've no interest in the revolution except as an observer. I wouldn't dream of leading it.'

For a full minute Rhodes gazed out across Table Bay and the wide expanse of the Cape Flats in silence. Then, with a sudden gesture, he heaved himself out of his chair and turned to his visitor.

'Well, if they won't, they won't. You can tell your Reformers that I shall wire Jameson to keep quiet.'

He held out his hand to the reporter, wished him a pleasant journey to Johannesburg, and asked him if he would like a carriage back to Cape Town.

'No thank you, sir. It's a beautiful afternoon. I'll walk through the woods.'

Rhodes nodded absently and went off into the big *voorkamer* of the house. Younghusband paused a while to look after him; then, with a quick shrug, walked off along the path that would take him over the shoulder of Devil's Peak down to the port and railway station. His mind worked over the message he would take back to Johannesburg and the effect it would have on the conspirators. What about the flag? Nothing very positive, to be sure. But in accepting the decision to tell Jameson to wait there was a concession on the flag, too. There was to be no insistence on the British flag. He was safe in telling the Committee that. Or was he? He heard quick footsteps behind him and turned to see one of Rhodes' agents hurrying after him. It was Rutherfoord Harris.

'Captain Younghusband,' Harris said, a trifle breathlessly, 'the Prime Minister has a message for you. He has sent me after you to say that, on reflection, he wants it to be clearly understood that when the proposed rising does take place, it should be under the British flag...'

Christmas Day, 1895. All along the Witwatersrand lights and candles glowed as Uitlander families recaptured in their Christmas trees, their bogus holly and mistletoe and other decorations, the homes they had left behind in Europe and America. Every church was full of dutiful Christians, absolving themselves of past absence, bethinking themselves in this annual hour of remembrance of the Man who had died in a supreme act of atonement for all the sins of all outlanders everywhere.

But there was something wrong with a Christmas in mid-summer. You needed snow on the window-panes, enough mist on them to scribble your name in, a roaring fire: not this full-bodied sun that was hot by the time you came out of early Communion. And you didn't want Christmas with a man like Jameson and 1,000 tough troopers sitting just across the border. If you were a member of the central conspiracy, how could you work up a Christmas spirit in Johannesburg on December 25, 1895?

Charles Leonard contemplated his eggs and bacon without appetite, swatted more viciously than usual at the flies which shared all meals with every household. He propped the morning paper up on the marmalade jar, and was just pouring himself out a cup of coffee when he heard knocking on the door and then his native servant's quick footsteps along the passage.

'Where's the baas?' (He recognized George Farrar's voice.) 'Having breakfast? Good – I'll have some coffee with him.'

Leonard went across to open the dining-room door. The two men shook hands.

'Merry Christmas, George.'

'And the same to you, Charlie. Though I don't know what's merry about it.'

'What's bothering you? Had breakfast?'

'Just a cup of coffee, thanks. Sorry to barge in on you like this, but I was talking to Lionel in the club last night – we'd had a few whiskies for Christmas Eve and it was a bit late – and he told me he was sure Jameson was going to come in under the Union Jack.'

He looked hard at Leonard, who said nothing. Farrar went on, 'I made up my mind I'd come round and see you first thing in the morning. Look here, Charlie, I haven't been in on all your meetings, but if Jameson's coming to hoist the Union Jack then I'll have no part of it. I've induced every man who's joined me and who's helping me in this business to go in on the basis that we want a reformed republic – but still a republic.'

Leonard filled two cups with coffee.

'How many sugars, George?'

'Two. Thank you.'

For a few moments they stirred their coffee in silence. Then Farrar took a sip, put his cup down on the table and leaned towards Leonard.

'Listen, Charles. This is the Boer's country. It would be absolutely morally wrong to think of doing anything that would change the republican status, and I will not go a yard further in the business unless I have the assurance of you and the others that that is the basis of the rising.'

'I can give you that assurance as far as *I'm* concerned, George. And I think I can speak for every member of the Reform Committee. But whether that's going to have any effect on Jameson is a different matter. Rhodes is the only man who can stop him now, I'm afraid. As a matter of fact Younghusband is due back from the Cape at noon today – if the train's on time. A meeting has been arranged at Frank Rhodes' house immediately after it gets in. You'll be there, of course?'

'You bet I will. But I want you to be quite clear on my position in this. There's to be no Union Jack!'

The Cape train was just over an hour late. The message summoning the Reformers interrupted their festive dinners. Leonard, a little annoyed at his inability to eat his meals in peace that day, decided to finish his Christmas pudding. But he reached the meeting-place, where there was a full gathering of all the ringleaders, in time to hear Younghusband's report on his interview with Cecil Rhodes and the conversa-

245

tion with Harris. Younghusband made it clear enough that they must not think that Rhodes was supporting the uprising in order to maintain a republic in the Transvaal.

It was obvious that this was completely unacceptable. Several men at the meeting refused emphatically to take any further part unless the original arrangement was adhered to.

'How can we adhere to the original arrangement?' Phillips demanded. 'The original arrangement was that Jameson would start on December the twenty-eighth. At all costs we've got to stop Jameson until this matter's settled. I move we postpone the whole thing until we can be more sure of what we're doing.'

'That would be very dangerous, gentlemen,' Frank Rhodes told them. 'I've already had messages from Jameson saying that the Pretoria Government are getting restless, and he understands they are calling up commandos in the Zeerust district on his line of march. He is most anxious, if he's to succeed, that he should leave in time.'

'We must have a week or two,' Leonard said. 'I suggest that a deputation goes immediately to Rhodes from us to get the flag question straightened out. And we're still short of arms. We need more time for that. I propose that we call a public meeting on January the fourth at which an ultimatum can be delivered to Kruger, that we seize the arsenal that night, and that Jameson be ordered to wait on the border until he receives instructions from us.'

Hays Hammond pointed out that it would be unwise to alert the Government before they raided Pretoria. He suggested that the public meeting be announced for January 6 so that the essential element of surprise would not be lost.

After several hours' discussion and argument it was finally agreed that Leonard and F. H. Hamilton, the new editor of *The Star*, should go immediately to Cecil Rhodes to tell him they would not have the British flag, that the meeting should be called for January 6 to deceive the Pretoria Government, and that Jameson must be informed of the new date and made to wait for it. It was also decided, in order to quell the alarming rumours circulating up and down the Witwatersrand, that *The Star* should publish the next day the full text of Leonard's Manifesto. Leonard spent the last hours of that Christmas Day reading his document to the plotters. They heard him through in silence as the controlled, experienced voice recapitulated the origin of the National Union movement, the grievances and the motives that inspired them. Finally he said:

'Now I come to the last heading in the Manifesto – "The Charter of the Union". This is what I've written: "We have now only two questions to consider. (a) What do we want? (b) How shall we get it? I have stated plainly what our grievances are and I shall answer with equal directness the question, *What do we want?* We want the establishment of this Republic as a true Republic; a Constitution which shall be framed by competent persons selected by representatives of the whole people and framed on lines laid down by them – a Constitution which shall be safeguarded against hasty alteration; an equitable franchise law and fair representation; equality of the Dutch and English languages; responsibility of the Legislature to the heads of the great departments; removal of religious disabilities; independence of the courts of justice with adequate and secured remuneration of the judges; liberal and comprehensive education; efficient civil service with adequate provision for pay and pension; free trade in South African products. That is what we want. There now remains the question which is to be put before you at the meeting of the sixth of January, viz., *How shall we get it?* To this question I shall expect an answer in plain terms according to your deliberate judgment." That's the lot, gentlemen. Have you any corrections or additions you'd like to make?'

Leonard looked around the small circle. Phillips, after a brief pause, said: 'That seems to say everything we need to say, Charles. I think I speak for the whole Committee when I express our thanks and congratulations on a splendid piece of work.'

'Then I take it,' Leonard ended, 'that Hamilton here can now arrange for the publication of the Manifesto in to-morrow's *Star*.'

With the full realization of what they were letting themselves in for if this technically alien force invaded the Republic, the conspirators began to reorganize their plans and objectives. They would continue to import arms and, if possible, trained soldiers in the guise of ordinary immigrants, and they decided that they would hold the public meeting on January 6 in the expectation that Kruger, confronted by

247

such a massive demonstration of purpose, would be prepared to negotiate and eventually to accede to the Uitlanders political demands. If he refused to negotiate and attacked Johannesburg, they were confident they could withstand the first assaults and gain time for the outside intervention which could not then be delayed, and which would then be Kruger's responsibility.

With the departure of Leonard and Hamilton to see Cecil Rhodes, a frantic series of telegrams began to pass between Johannesburg and Cape Town, Johannesburg and Pitsani, Pitsani and Cape Town. Sometimes the devious language of subterfuge failed altogether to make itself intelligible, while some of the pseudonyms adopted by various plotters defied identification.

Speeding ahead of Leonard went a telegram from Frank Rhodes to his brother that it was 'absolutely necessary to delay flotation'. Sam Jameson sent a similar one to his brother in Pitsani. These messages crossed a wire from Cape Town which informed the Committee that it was 'impossible give extension of refusal beyond December as Transvaal Boer opposition shareholders holding meeting near Pitsani'.

Jameson, too, had a long wire from Cape Town: 'Sicheliland concession shareholders meeting postponed until sixth day January meanwhile circular been publicly issued and opinion of all interested will then be taken and action decided upon stop Am beginning to see our shareholders in Matabeleland concession very different to those in Sicheliland matter so you must not move until you hear from us again stop Too awful very sorry.'

That one was signed Rutherfoord Harris, and Jameson could not have failed to realize that it represented Rhodes' opinion.

Nevertheless Jameson, the mantle of Clive about his shoulders, sent a small party of his police forward on the 27th to cut the telegraph wires to Pretoria so that news of his advance – which he still intended to make as planned – would not reach the Government until it was too late. He sent a telegram to Col. Rhodes informing him of this and of the difficulty of stopping the wire cutters. The telegram went on: 'We must carry into effect original plans stop. They have then two days for flotation stop If they do not will make our own flotation with help of letter which I will publish stop Guarantee on flag given therefore let J. Hays Hammond telegraph instantly all right.'

To this Hammond replied: 'Wire just received stop Experts decidedly adverse stop I absolutely condemn further developments at present.'

The Reformers were now convinced that if Jameson started, all their plans and they themselves would be ruined. *He had to be stopped.* But were telegrams enough? There could be delays, mistakes, even failure to deliver. They could not afford to take any chances. They summoned two of Jameson's own officers, Major Heany, an American from the Southern States who had been one of the doctor's closest companions in Rhodesia, and Holden, both of whom had been sent to Johannesburg to help in the military preparations and to supervise the smuggling and distribution of arms.

They were asked if they would go to Pitsani, by separate routes, to persuade Jameson not to start. Both agreed, reluctantly. For half an hour they discussed with the Reformers the best arguments for persuading Jameson to stay where he was. When, finally, they asked Heany what he thought Jameson would do, he told them bluntly, 'He'll come in as sure as Fate.' Then he added, 'But I can see you're not yet ready for a revolution. You can rely on me to do all I can to stop Jameson.'

Holden was sent across country on horseback, making for Pitsani along the route Wolff had prepared. Heany went the roundabout route by train through Bloemfontein, De Aar Junction and Kimberley. Before he left he wired Cecil Rhodes to arrange a special train at Kimberley to take him on to Mafeking. He ended the telegram: 'Stop Jameson until I come.'

There was nothing much more for them to do in Johannesburg except wait. Jameson could not possibly ignore all the orders, advice, pleadings not to start. The latest news from Pretoria was reassuring. There was a distant chance that they would get much of what they were demanding without a shot being fired – unless Jameson pulled the trigger . . .

CHAPTER TWENTY-TWO

The days of climax had been a week of wild rumour along the Witwatersrand and in Pretoria. Its details, incredibly, were still known only to the narrow circle of ringleaders; but the arrival of arms in Johannesburg and along the Reef was reported almost daily in the newspapers and it was impossible to conceal the presence of Jameson's men on the frontier. The Boer Government must have known what was going on, and their slow reaction was due chiefly to the fact that they felt quite sure of being able to deal with a disorganized, unsupported Uitlander revolt; they just did not believe that Jameson would invade the Transvaal with his troops.

A week before the raid, Paul Kruger was not even in Pretoria. He was on one of his annual tours of the republic, and he did not return to the capital until Saturday, December 28. The previous afternoon at Bronkhorstspruit, about twenty miles east of Pretoria, the burghers of the district had gathered to welcome him and talk things over, as was the custom on these presidential circuits. Old Hans Botha spoke up for his fellow Boers:

'Your Honour, is it true there may be a rebellion in Johannesburg? We hear much talk of it.'

'Truly, there is much talk of it, Oom Hans.'

'Now well, Your Honour; I have many bullets in me still from the War of Independence, but I can make a place for a few more if it is a question of fighting those red-necks again.'

'I do not think you will need to do that, Oom Hans. I have heard all the stories from Johannesburg, but I do not have to believe them. You do not have to believe every lion story you hear, not so? I cannot tell you what is going to happen, but remember this – if you want to kill a tortoise, you must first wait till it puts its head out of its shell!'

Publication of the National Union's Manifesto the previous Thursday had brought a certain amount of reason and cohesion into the speculative chaos. It did much to fuse the distinctive and often antagonistic groups along the Witwatersrand into a single community with a common objective. Even the German and French sections of the population, bitterly opposed to any suggestion of British intervention, found themselves with the rest of the new population in their acceptance of the Manifesto.

The independent Randlords – the big financiers who were not Rhodes' men – also found themselves drawing closer together and towards the Reformers by the end of the week.

J. B. Robinson, who aspired to a special position in his relations with Paul Kruger, sent an emissary to Pretoria on Saturday to try to persuade the President to concede some of the Uitlander demands in order to prevent more serious trouble. Robinson's man was treated with little courtesy, and was sent back to Johannesburg with this message: 'Either you shall be with me, or you shall be with the enemy. Choose which course you will adopt. Either call a meeting to repudiate the Manifesto, or there is a break between us that will not be healed.'

This was a rebuff which J. B. Robinson's sensitive ego could not accept. His sympathies were thereafter, and probably for the first time, transferred to the cause of the Uitlander movement.

Barney Barnato found himself in a strange and unreal world. In London throughout the time in which the crisis was building up he had done his best to sustain the market against what he thought was a purely financial attack. He was on terms of personal friendship with Paul Kruger. He recognized Johannesburg's case for local government powers, but was convinced that the town and the gold mines would get the concessions they wanted without violence. His political position had been made clear enough.

'Men do not come to the Transvaal to vote,' he said in Johannesburg and London. 'They come to earn money. The franchise would cost blood as well as money. It would not add a sixpence to anyone's wages, and even if it was granted not one Englishman in a thousand would give up his nationality to take an oath of allegiance to the Transvaal Republic. As for education, if the Uitlanders want education for their children in English, let them pay for it. You

251

can't expect an Afrikaner government to treat its own language as a foreign one.'

Barnato's fellow-financiers were his natural enemies. He was suspect politically and socially. The Reformers took considerable pleasure in leaving him out of the great conspiracy altogether.

Leonard's Manifesto erupted on Johannesburg as a full page in a late edition on the evening of Boxing Day. The crowds had just returned to town from the first day of the Turffontein races. A carnival and fête was in progress at the Wanderers Ground; the outstanding spectacle of the festivities was a torchlight procession by the bicycle clubs with 10,000 lamps and lanterns, climaxed by the release of an enormous magnesium balloon. But at the Standard Theatre that evening, where Leonard Rayne and Amy Coleridge were playing in *Othello*, and around the interval bars at the Empire Music Hall – where the Tilly Sisters were the toast of the town – the talk was all of crisis.

The unease of the populace was reflected in a hastily summoned meeting of the Mercantile Association. They were not privy to the plans and intentions of the ringleaders. They could see only the shutters going up on the shop windows, hear only the crackle of gunfire and the thunder of shells blowing their businesses and goods into republican dust. On their own initiative they decided to send a deputation to Kruger repudiating the revolutionary movement and affirming their loyalty to the constitution.

Nor could the plotters rely on the reaction of the considerable and influential American section, whose anti-British feelings had been stimulated by an ultimatum from President Cleveland to the Foreign Office over some obscure issue in Venezuela. This diversity of loyalties was further complicated by the existence of an explosive element of toughs and criminals such as every mining adventure attracts; and by the presence of 60,000 to 80,000 native mineworkers, who were controllable as long as they were working and contained in the mine compounds. It was necessary not only to start a revolution, but to make absolutely sure of the maintenance of law and order in Johannesburg while it was going on.

They gave the job of organizing a citizen police force to Andrew Trimble, a retired sergeant in the Inniskilling Dragoons who in clearing up the illicit diamond dealing at

252

Kimberley had acquired an unrivalled knowledge of South Africa's underworld. On December 18 he was interviewed in *The Star* offices by the four ringleaders, who explained the whole conspiracy to him.

Trimble asked for a little time. 'This is a hanging matter,' he told them. 'I must ask for a night to decide.'

The next morning he was back. 'Gentlemen,' he said briefly, 'I have decided to put my neck in the same noose with yours. If we are hanged we shall all be hanged together.' Whereupon he raised his right hand, and to the astonishment of the four men, swore an oath of obedience to Colonel Frank Rhodes.

By the week's end Kruger and the Commandant-General, Joubert, were back in Pretoria, and the thousands of Boers who had come into the capital for the religious ceremonies of *Nagmaal* at Christmas stayed camped on Church Square instead of returning to their farms. A raid on the fort and arsenal was now out of the question.

Publication in all South African newspapers on Saturday of a Reuter message revealing for the first time the imminence of an armed rising in Johannesburg started almost a panic rush from the Witwatersrand. From the outlying mines and villages refugees poured into the town, where special arrangements had to be made for feeding and housing. On the East Rand, Cornish mineworkers waited for their pay packets on Saturday and then walked out, compelling the mines to close down.

The exodus from Johannesburg began on the Saturday evening mail train to the Cape. Extra carriages were put on at Braamfontein, where there was a rush to board them several hours before it was due to leave. By the time the train reached Park Station a crowd of 5,000 had gathered on and around the platforms. When it was seen that the crowded carriages contained many men and there was no room for the women and children anxious to leave, there was an effort to make room for the latter by throwing out some of the former. Fortunately everybody kept their heads and their sense of humour, and it was finally accepted, after a good deal of pushing and shoving and multifarious advice, that the next train to Cape Town or Natal would do just as well. Police and railway officials, aided by co-operative members of the public who had their wives and families aboard, at last got the crowd away from the coaches and

253

track; the express moved off, an hour and a half late, in a hot cacophony of steam, whistles, cheers and tears. It was a scene that was to be repeated at Braamfontein and Park Station for each departing passenger train during the next three days.

In Pretoria, President Kruger gave one of his rare interviews to the Press. He told a representative of *De Volkstem* that although the position was grave he was confident that common sense would prevail and that the law-abiding members of the community, especially the English-speaking section, would support all measures for the preservation of law and order.

'I must tell you,' he said, 'that my efforts to get concessions for the Uitlander population have been spoiled by the Uitlanders themselves with all their foolish and threatening talk and actions. How can I persuade the Volksraad that such men would make good burghers of the Republic?'

He added: 'If people continue to be foolish, if they continue to set themselves up against the Government of the land, then let the storm rise and the wind thereof separate the chaff from the grain. The Government will give every opportunity for free speech and free ventilation of grievances, but it will put a stop immediately to any movement made for upsetting law and order.'

On the same day a deputation of Rand Americans visited Kruger. They were as keen as anybody else on the reforms demanded in the Manifesto, but they completely rejected the imperialist inspiration of Rhodes and Jameson, and had passed a resolution promising their support to the maintenance of the republic if some of their grievances were met. They were convinced they could make the President see reason when confronted with the alternatives.

Kruger greeted them civilly and listened quietly as the spokesmen, two mining engineers called Hennen Jennings and Perkins, presented the American case. Then he said abruptly: 'It is not a time for talking when danger is at hand. That is the time for action.'

'With your permission, Mr President,' said Jennings, 'there is no danger at hand unless the Government creates it. If Your Honour will deal with the people in a liberal manner and acknowledge the reforms that are sure necessary, there will not be anywhere in the world a more loyal community than in Johannesburg.'

Kruger was staring at his favourite spot above his visitors' heads, shaping the future of his country in the heavy tobacco smoke that drifted from his pipe.

He asked them slowly: 'If a crisis should come about, on which side shall I find the Americans?'

Jennings was ready for this one. 'On the side of liberty and good government, Mr President.'

'You are all alike,' Kruger said. 'All tarred with the same brush. You are British in your hearts.'

He waved his hands at them in dismissal, got up from his chair and strode into the house without another word.

While the Americans were absorbing the rebuff which put them solidly behind the Reformers, several hundred excited Australians held a meeting on Saturday evening in the dining-room of the Goldfields Hotel. The intention was to form a Red Cross Brigade 'for the sacred purpose of protecting the lives of defenceless women and children and the property of all regardless of nationality'; but it became clear at an early stage that a neutral and non-combatant role was not to the liking of many of those present. The resultant uproar was only quelled when a speaker pointed out that there were different ways of protecting life and property: it was a foregone conclusion that if it was necessary to fight to do so, the Australians would be in the front rank. Nobody was quite sure at the end of it all what exactly the role of the Australian Brigade would be. What they were all quite certain about was that it would be the most belligerent non-belligerent unit in the world.

On Sunday morning the congregation of St Mary's Church heard an unusual sermon from their rector.

'We have been praying day by day, and twice a day, that it would please God to bless, keep and guide the President. Now we should redouble our prayers when so tremendous a responsibility rests upon a single pair of shoulders; when a single reckless word or act might lead to a bloody conflict, to his eternal shame and disgrace. May he learn to rule an unfortunate tongue and temper, and talk no more of chopping off tortoises' heads. . . .'

None of the ringleaders was at church. Some had gravitated, after late breakfasts, from their various homes and hotels to Frank Rhodes' house in Doornfontein. An air of suppressed excitement and expectation hung over the town and was reflected in the anxious speculations of the conspirators. Heany or Holden must be at Pitsani by now. Why had nothing been heard? And what about Leonard and Hamilton? They must surely have seen Rhodes by now?

Shortly after ten o'clock there was a loud knocking on the front door; Colonel Rhodes went quickly down the passage. It was a messenger boy from the Post Office with two telegrams. One was addressed to Frank Rhodes, the other to Sam Jameson. The flimsy paper crackled in the silence as his friends crowded round.

'It's from Leonard,' Rhodes said. 'Some of it's in code. Won't be a minute.'

'Mine's from Jim,' said Sam Jameson. 'In the Bedford–McNeil Code. Will you decipher this one too, Frank?'

The men sat around the room in silence, or paced nervously up and down as Colonel Rhodes worked through the code-book. Every now and again one of them would walk out on to the stoep and stare across the corrugated iron roofs and brash towers of the township – westward, where Jameson lay waiting at Pitsani...

Frank Rhodes closed the code-book with a slam, stood up with the scrawled sheets in his hand.

'Well, it's all right at Cape Town, thank God!' he told them. 'This is what the telegram says: "We have received perfectly satisfactory assurance from Cecil Rhodes but a misunderstanding undoubtedly exists elsewhere. In our opinion continue preparations but carefully and without any sort of hurry as entirely fresh departure will be necessary. In view of changed condition Jameson has been advised accordingly." That's from Leonard, and I think you'll agree it means that my brother has ordered Jameson to wait.'

Relief flooded into the room. It was going to be all right. Jameson would listen to nobody but Rhodes; and Rhodes had stopped him. Now they could go ahead with their plans for getting what they wanted by negotiation. Kruger could see now that they were in deadly earnest, prepared to fight for their rights. There could be no more procrastination, no more broken promises...

'What about the Doctor?' Hammond asked. 'What does he say?'

'I can't quite make it out. Seems a bit muddled to me. Here, Sam – you may know what it means. You read it.'

Sam Jameson took the decoded message and glanced through it quickly. A puzzled frown creased his brow.

'Well, I dunno. Most of it's gibberish. Must have got mixed up in the telegraph office. But this is clear enough. "Inform Dr Wolff distant cutting. He will understand. I shall start, without fail, tomorrow night."'

They all looked at Dr Wolff, who had been at Pitsani the previous week. For a moment or two the doctor hesitated. He knew what it meant, all right. He was to cut the telegraph wire between Zeerust and Pretoria. He had also arranged a rendezvous with Jameson west of Krugersdorp to tell him whether to march on Pretoria or go straight through to Johannesburg. But was it necessary to tell them this now? Jameson was going to be stopped anyway.

'I don't understand any more than you do,' he told them. 'Maybe the rest of the telegram would help us, if we could get it straightened out.'

Hammond asked anxiously: 'What time was it sent?'

'At 2.30 yesterday afternoon,' Sam Jameson said.

'Then it doesn't really matter, does it? The Doctor must have sent that before he had seen either Heany or Holden, and before he could have heard from Cape Town after Leonard had seen Rhodes.'

'You're right, Hammond,' Lionel Phillips agreed. 'Whatever he had in mind yesterday afternoon, Jameson could not possibly start in defiance of our wishes and against the orders of Cecil Rhodes. But what a good thing we made sure! That brother of yours, Sam, takes some holding!'

'Phew!' Abe Bailey mopped his forehead. 'I feel like a drink. Who's coming to the Club?'

'You watch out over there, Abe,' Phillips told him. 'The town's like a powder keg. We don't want any alarming rumours to start flying.'

The gathering broke up; Phillips, Farrar, Dr Sauer, Fitz-Patrick and Bailey headed for the Rand Club; Hammond went home for lunch with his family; Sam Jameson and two others stayed behind with Frank Rhodes.

Hays Hammond confided to his wife that they had as near as dammit started a revolution, but that he was sure they could now get what they wanted without fighting.

'That Jameson!' he added. 'It's like trying to stop a hard-pulling horse heading for the stables. He's had all of us tugging on the reins. But I guess we stopped him all right.'

Down in Cape Town, Rhodes sent for Sir Graham Bower, the Imperial Secretary.

'The uprising in Johannesburg has fizzled out like a damp squib,' he told him. 'We've stopped Jameson – I hope – but I think you'd better let the Governor know it's all over for the time being.'

'Are you sure about Jameson? Can he control those hot-headed young officers of his?'

'Jameson's all right. He'll sit still there for years if necessary. But I'll need him now in Matabeleland. The troop can stay at Pitsani. They'll serve a useful purpose as long as Kruger continues his present policies. This Johannesburg business has cost me a lot of money; but there's plenty left and it must now be used for the development of the North. Johannesburg will have to make its own arrangements.'

Late in the afternoon Sir Hercules Robinson cabled Joseph Chamberlain: 'I learn on good authority movement at Johannesburg has collapsed. Support of the British flag by two capitalists financing venture has led to complete collapse of movement and leaders of National Union will now probably make the best terms they can with President Kruger.'

In the desolation of Bechuanaland, where Pitsani secured recognition on the map by the existence of a single tumble-down store in the unending expanse of sand and thornbush, Dr Jameson ended the hot somnolence of Sunday afternoon with an order for a dismounted parade of all ranks. That morning he had talked to Heany and Holden. For twenty minutes after, he had paced the sandy level in front of his tent. Then he had gone to the telegraph office and sent two telegrams – one to Rhodes in Cape Town and one to Dr Wolff in Johannesburg.

In those twenty minutes he had found the excuse he needed for the justification for his invasion. At that moment he was more certain of his destiny than he had ever been. He was the chosen instrument of history. The fact that the Johannesburg reformers did not have the guts to go ahead with their plans did not affect his own. Once he got there, or to Pretoria, they would all swing round behind him. But the justification – he must have that off pat! Not only because of Rhodes and the British Government, but to convince his men that they were doing the right thing.

There was that letter, of course. And the Reuter message which had only reached Pitsani that morning. That was it! British lives were in danger: women and children were fleeing from the advancing Boers. How could they sit still and watch it happen under their noses?

The troops formed a square: 372 men of the Mashonaland Mounted Police, the Maxim gun teams and a detachment manning the 12½-pounder field-piece. In the hard, hot light of midsummer, faces were dark ovals of shadow under helmets. The muttered grumbling of soldiers called to parade on a Sunday afternoon-off was stilled as Dr Jameson came from his tent; an N.C.O. bellowed them to attention.

Around them only the song of the Christmas beetles disturbed the siesta of the Bechuanaland bush. To the westward there was nothing between them and the Atlantic except yellow grass, thorn and sand and the Great Thirst of the Kalahari. Eastward the land sloped up unbroken to the vast plateau of the Transvaal high-veld and the long Ridge of White Waters. There, too, was Johannesburg with its bright lights, bars, music-halls and women. They were sick to death of Bechuanaland and bush.

Jameson walked into the middle of the square – small, slightly bow-legged in his riding breeches, the sallow face dominated by a moustache which hid all his mouth except the obstinate lower lip. He stood bareheaded, surrounded by his men. In his hand was a sheet of paper.

'Stand them easy,' he murmured to Sir John Willoughby. Jameson looked slowly round the square of troops, giving each man a feeling of personal contact with the leader and with what he was about to say.

'Well, men,' the brisk voice began. 'You've had a long wait, and now the waiting's over. Most of you will have seen the Reuter message from Johannesburg. What many of us feared would happen, has happened. Your countrymen have been placed in great peril through insisting on rights and reforms which are the birthright of all Britons. We know now that women and children are fleeing from the danger which surrounds them as Boer forces begin their encirclement of the town. Perhaps, even as I am talking to you, the first shots are being fired and British blood is flowing on the streets of Johannesburg. We can delay no longer.'

He waved the paper in his hand.

'I have here a letter from the leaders of the reform movement. This is what it says.'

Jameson read slowly through the letter he had been given at the November meeting in Johannesburg. Every man who heard it was under the impression that it was an urgent call for help and that it had just arrived – and there is no doubt that was the impression Jameson wanted to create. There was a restless movement in the ranks, a growl of comment as they heard the words: 'Thousands of unarmed men, women and children of our race will be at the mercy of well-armed Boers.'

At the last paragraph Jameson paused for a long three seconds. Then very deliberately he read out: 'It is under these circumstances that we feel constrained to call upon you to come to our aid.'

He stopped abruptly, folded the letter and put it in his breast pocket. Only Willoughby, who had seen the original, was aware that Jameson had left out five vital words at the end of that sentence – 'should a disturbance arise here'. But these troopers didn't have to know everything: just enough to get them started and keep them going. Jameson went on:

'The critical moment for Johannesburg has arrived. I do not believe that the Boers are aware of our plans. All the telegraph wires from this area to Pretoria have already been cut. If we move fast I believe we can reach Johannesburg or Krugersdorp without a shot being fired. I want to impress on you that this is not an attack on the Boers or the Transvaal Republic. We are going to the relief of our countrymen in peril. No red blood need be spilt unless we are attacked on the march – when, of course, we will defend ourselves.'

Jameson smiled as he said this, and again there was a murmur round the ranks. Somebody laughed gaily.

'All preparations have been made. Remounts, rations and forage have been provided all along the route we intend to take. The Bechuanaland Police will start simultaneously from Mafeking, and an armed force will move out from Johannesburg to meet us and guide us in. Should the worst come to the worst I think I can tell you that other troops are available in the Cape and Natal. But I do not expect for one moment they will be necessary.'

Jameson stopped, and once again turned full circle scanning his men, including them all within the influence of his personality. Then he said almost off-handedly:

'There is no compulsion on anybody to come with us, but I am confident all will respond to this call from your countrymen. I have asked your commanding officer, Sir John Willoughby, to reassemble the parade at sundown – mounted and in full marching order. I hope you have a pleasant ride.'

Somebody shouted, 'Three cheers for Doctor Jim!' While the surrounding bush still echoed to this rousing yell, so that even the Christmas beetles were frightened into silence, the whole parade came spontaneously to attention and sang 'God Save the Queen'.

In Mafeking, where the need for secrecy was greater, the police force was not paraded until half-past seven in the evening. Not all of them had accepted the offer to transfer to the service of the Chartered Company, and these fell-in separately, to the rear of the main body. There Captain Coventry spoke to them.

'It's no good keeping it from you any longer. We're going to Johannesburg. We've got to get through in fifty hours and I want you all to come along with us. Those who wish to may now join the other parade.'

Nobody moved. Captain Coventry asked them crossly:

'What's the matter with you men? Why won't you come with us?'

'Well, sir,' one of them spoke up; 'what we want to know is whether we're going to fight for the Queen, or what?'

'No,' Coventry replied. 'You are not actually going to fight for the Queen, but you are going to fight for the supremacy of the British flag in South Africa.'

This seemed to satisfy them; when, an hour later, the column moved off into the night for their rendezvous with Jameson, only a handful of officers and men remained behind.

CHAPTER TWENTY-THREE

Late risers in Johannesburg on Monday morning had barely finished their breakfasts when the news came from Pretoria that the Mercantile Association had been very well received by the President and the Executive Council. Overnight a proclamation had been drawn up calling on the people of Johannesburg to obey the law and assuring them that grievances presented in a legitimate manner would receive immediate consideration. Now Kruger himself had the proclamation altered to announce withdrawal of the special duties on foodstuffs, consideration of proposals to grant equal subsidies to Dutch and English-medium schools, and a reduction in railway tariffs. The proclamation culminated in a Presidential promise to give the full franchise to all Outlanders who had demonstrated their support of the Government and the Republic during the crisis.

Reaction in Johannesburg was one of relief and jubilation. Old Kruger had got the wind-up! They were going to get what they wanted without having to fight for it – as long as they showed the Boers that they were *ready* to fight for it. This was not a time to relax or to end their preparations; they had heard these promises before. But this time it was different.

The leaders of the reform movement had concentrated at Hays Hammond's office at an early hour to discuss their plans and the latest developments. They were much relieved at the trend of events in Pretoria, and their new optimism was only slightly damped when Sam Jameson hobbled along to the Goldfields building with another telegram from Dr Jim. It had been addressed to Wolff, but the latter, thinking the crisis was over for the time being, had gone off into the district to resume his neglected rounds; Sam had decoded the message himself. It repeated the injunction to Wolff to meet Jameson as planned and to make the cutting. When

262

Hammond saw that it had been sent from Pitsani the previous morning at five-past nine, he pointed out with a grim smile what a near thing it had been; how wise they'd been in dispatching Heany and Holden and making sure that Cecil Rhodes would order Jameson not to move!

'If we'd left it for another twelve hours,' Hammond told them, 'that man would have been half-way to Johannesburg by now.'

A sigh of relief breathed through the township, causing shopkeepers and merchants to open their doors and take down protective boarding. That wasn't the only thing they had put up: the prices of nearly every commodity in the stores were raised overnight by amounts varying between fifty and one hundred per cent. The price of bread was doubled; between morning and afternoon flour rose from 50s. to 80s. a sack, and later shot up to 100s. Paraffin prices doubled from 10s. to 20s. a tin, and forage went up, even as men were giving their horses the first feed, from 65s. to £5.

This drastic rise in the cost of living was more a natural expression of the opportunism and keen business sense of Johannesburg's traders than a result of any shortage of supplies. For months vital foodstuffs and other commodities had been secretly stored in preparation for emergency. A siege had been anticipated rather than any decisive battle, and supplies were adequate to cope with a long encirclement.

What annoyed the inhabitants most of all was that the careful merchants insisted on cash terms – an unheard-of imposition.

The sudden rise in the cost of necessities caused considerable hardship among the poorer classes, and it was a typical Johannesburg reaction that within a few hours the Committee of the National Union was able to announce the subscription of £5,000 to a fund for the relief of distress in the town due to high prices.

As noon struck on the Post Office clock a telegraph boy was seen speeding down Simmonds Street on his bicycle. He stopped outside Abe Bailey's office, selected a pink envelope from the bundle in his satchel and went inside. Within a minute Bailey, hatless and coatless, came tearing out and ran all the way to the Goldfields offices. He burst in on Hammond and three or four of the other ringleaders, waving the telegram at them.

'Who the hell is Godolphin?' he shouted. 'Have we got a man in Cape Town called Godolphin? Is it a code name?'

'Just a minute, Abe,' Hammond said suavely. 'What's all this? First of all, what's in that telegram?'

'You may well ask! Just listen to this. It's addressed to me from Cape Town; dispatched at seven-thirty this morning. Seven-thirty this morning, remember that. "The veterinary surgeon says the horses are now all right stop He started with them last night will reach you on Wednesday stop He says he can back himself for 700 Godolphin." *What the hell d'you think of that?*'

Hammond had risen to his feet as Bailey read. 'You're quite sure about the time, Abe?'

'See for yourself. There's no mistaking it. Half-past seven this morning. We know who the veterinary surgeon is; we *don't* know who Godolphin is. But whoever he is, what this telegram means is that Jameson left Pitsani last night with seven hundred men.'

'Unless it's a very bad joke,' Hammond growled.

The others in the room were too flabbergasted to speak. They stared at each other in dismay. Hammond turned to Sam Jameson.

'Sam, can you make it to Frank's house? I think we'd better stay together now, until we have more definite news. Tell him to get word to Lionel Phillips and George Farrar. We must be ready to act. And Sam —' Hammond added, 'Don't say anything to anybody; we don't want to start a panic, or a riot!'

With no further news by four o'clock and not a word of any untoward developments in Pretoria, the conspiracy of reformers in Johannesburg grouped around Hammond's desk had come to persuade themselves that it was a false alarm.

'It's all too preposterous,' Phillips repeated over and over again. 'Jameson can't be *that* mad. Especially now that we're getting concessions from Kruger.'

'Jameson wouldn't know about that,' Farrar said. 'But I agree with you, Lionel – it's just so unbelievable it can't be true. Rhodes would have stopped him, even if we couldn't. What d'you think, Hmmond?'

'I think it's a leg-pull, myself. There are lots of people on the Witwatersrand with a curious sense of humour; and lots

264

of people who aren't particularly well-disposed towards us. Still, I don't think we ought to take any risks; we oughtn't to be unprepared.'

Hammond turned to Frank Rhodes. 'Frank, I think we should start getting things organized. Don't you think we ought to get Trimble here?'

But there was no need to send for Trimble. He was coming up the front steps of the entrance two at a time. Such was the urgency of his appearance as he burst among them that they all rose to meet him.

'We've just intercepted an official telegram,' Trimble told them breathlessly, 'from the Commandant-General in Pretoria to the Heidelberg commando. It orders them to ride through Johannesburg shooting right and left indiscriminately so that any idea of a revolution can be crushed before it starts!'

'The bloody fools!' Bailey exploded. 'If they want to start a war they couldn't choose a better way of doing it. Lionel – you must wire Rhodes and the High Commissioner immediately. This is an Imperial Government matter now. We can't have Englishmen shot down in the streets like dogs!'

'May I suggest, Abe,' Hammond said dryly, 'that it's not only Englishmen involved here. I think this is a time for calmness. If we panic, everybody'll panic. We've got to keep control of the town whatever else happens. Some of us,' he added, 'have our wives and children to think of.'

'Hammond's right,' Phillips nodded. 'That message that Trimble intercepted shows what a state the Government's in. If we play our cards right we can still come out on top. I don't believe Kruger would do such a damn-fool thing, and we still have no positive proof that Jameson has actually crossed the border. We've only got a crazy telegram sent by somebody called Godolphin. And God only knows who Godolphin is!'

'All the same,' Frank Rhodes said, 'I'm going out to put the first part of our plans in motion. I've ordered all brigade commanders to report at my house at five o'clock. If anything new turns up, let me know there.'

On his way out he saw Arthur Lawley, a railway contractor who was one of the inner circle of conspirators, and another man, approaching the Goldfields office at a trot.

'Don't go, Frank!' Lawley panted, waving another telegraph form. 'I've got something that'll interest you. But first of all get Trimble out. This chap's got something urgent for him. Won't tell me what it is.'

Frank Rhodes yelled through the passageway for Trimble, who came out as soon as he saw the man at the entrance.

Lawley strode into Hammond's office. 'It's all up, boys. He's started in spite of everything. Read this.'

He threw the telegram down on the table in front of Hammond, who picked it up and read aloud.

'The contractor has started on the earthworks with seven hundred boys stop Hopes to reach terminus on Wednesday Jenkins.'

Hammond looked up.

'I see this one's from Mafeking. Timed at noon. Who's Jenkins, Arthur?'

'One of my men at Mafeking. Absolutely reliable.'

'Well, gentlemen,' Phillips said quietly, 'that's that. Jameson and his troops have been riding for nearly twenty-four hours. We can't stop them now. But can we stop a war? That's the next problem. What's Trimble got hold of?'

Trimble came back into the office looking considerably relieved.

'Joubert has cancelled that order. Instead, I think they're planning to withdraw the "Zarps" from Johannesburg. They'll have to, won't they, if anything starts? That's sensible.'

Outside in the street they heard the sudden rush of newsboys and their shrieks of 'Extra! Extra! Jameson Crosses Border!'

Trimble ran out of the building and came back with half a dozen copies of the pink edition of *The Star*. They turned the pages feverishly to the main news columns in the middle, where the headlines screamed:

CROSSED THE BORDER
CONFLICT LAMENTABLY IMMINENT
SUSPENSE AT AN END
IMMEASURABLE GRAVITY OF THE SITUATION

For two minutes they read in silence. Then Hammond muttered softly, '*The goddamn fool!*'

At nine o'clock that Monday morning the Chief Justice

of the Republic, Judge Kotze, was about to enter his chambers in the Government building in Pretoria when he met a flustered and dishevelled British Agent coming out.

'Good morning, Sir Jacobus,' Kotze greeted him. 'Hot day by the look —'

'The fat's in the fire, Judge. Dr Jameson's crossed the border with a force of eight hundred armed men, probably marching towards Johannesburg. The President's waiting for you.'

In Kruger's office the Chief Justice found a surprising atmosphere of calm and deliberation. The tortoise had stuck out its head and now the President was about to chop it off. Jameson's men had failed to carry out their orders to cut all the telegraph wires from the west, and since dawn news of the invasion had been trickling into Pretoria. Telegrams had gone back to the townships they had passed in the night, rousing the commandos, while other orders summoned Boers and burghers from all corners of the republic; streams of mounted men poured through Pretoria towards Krugersdorp to stop Jameson's further progress, while other slouch-hatted groups – each man carrying only his gun and ammunition and enough biltong rations to see him through a week – concentrated and closed in behind him. Other Boer forces took up positions on the perimeter of Johannesburg.

In the town the first shock of the news had been absorbed in the realization that by starting before he was summoned Jameson had knocked the bottom out of the whole plan of the Reformers to capture the Pretoria arsenal.

In Hammond's office the ringleaders argued desperately over Jameson's action. He and Cecil Rhodes were both denounced as traitors to the Uitlander cause in pursuing their own ambitions; but when reaction and frustration had expressed themselves, reason prompted a calmer assessment.

It was assumed that the telegrams had not reached him in time and that neither Heany nor Holden had managed to get through; or, if they had, that they had failed to dispel Jameson's fears that the Boers were preparing to act against Johannesburg.

They were prepared to give Jameson the benefit of the doubt; but whatever his motives, his action had created a situation which they had not anticipated and which had to be dealt with immediately. If the ringleaders were perplexed, the rest of the community – in complete ignorance of the situation – was seething with rumour and speculation, and on the verge of panic.

With Leonard still in Cape Town, Lionel Phillips took over the leadership, by virtue of his special position as Beit's representative and as president of the Chamber of Mines.

'What we've got to do,' he told the group gathered round the table, 'is form a committee of action – a Reform Committee – on which all sections of the community can be represented.'

He turned to Percy FitzPatrick.

'Percy, I want you to take on the job of secretary – co-ordinate things, get things moving, keep a record of proceedings and events.'

FitzPatrick nodded, and moved his chair nearer the table, where Hammond provided him with paper and pens. Phillips went on, 'The first thing we've got to do is summon a meeting of all the prominent men who've already demonstrated their support of the movement. You'd better get word straight away to Frank Rhodes to that effect, Percy. Tell him we'll be using his office here as our headquarters and he'd better be there as much as possible. When we're all together we can decide exactly what we're going to do. Now we haven't got much time. Shall we say in half an hour in Frank's office?'

The others nodded their agreement and the meeting broke up, each hurrying off on his urgent task. Hays Hammond scribbled a note on a piece of paper, put it in an envelope and called for his native coachman.

'Take that out to the missis right away, David. It's important.'

David's eyes grew round and white at the sense of urgency in his employers manner. The Africans in the township knew all about the rumours, and had embellished them with their own colourful fantasy. 'Yes, baas!' David hissed, saluting with his whip stock, and hurried out of the room with the envelope clenched in his hand as though it was an ultimatum to the President. Ten minutes later he was handing it to Mrs Hammond.

'Jameson has crossed the border. Things are very uncertain. I have arranged four rooms for you and the family at Heath's Hotel. I think it wise for you to move in immediately. See you there for dinner tonight.'

Mrs Hammond gathered the household in the drawing-room and explained the situation to them – offering them the choice of staying at Doornfontein or moving into the town. The four white servants elected to remain where they were, but each of the Africans found good reason for going.

'I go fetch my wife from Pretoria, missis; those Boers kill her!'

'Me go home Zululand. See my mother. Tell her we all right.'

'If white men fight, time for black men go home!'

At the Pass Office in Marshall Square, where each immigrant native in search of work in the mines or in the township was given his registration card or 'pass', about 1,200 mine-boys, mostly Zulus, besieged Mr Marwick, the representative of the Natal Department of Native Affairs, clamouring for the written permission and the official stamp that would permit them, legally, to return to their homes or move from one place to another.

Mr Marwick tried to reason with the two or three spokesmen who had come into his office. To him it was an inexplicably sudden and unanimous decision. He was less well-informed than these alien Africans who had, and still have, in their manifold contacts with the white people at all levels thousands of listening posts and an astonishing system of secret, intimate intercommunication – the 'bush telegraph' brought to town. They told him the white men were going to fight among themselves and that they did not want to take part on either side. They wanted to go home. Mr Marwick knew enough about Africans to realize that on simple issues ten thousand of them can be as single-minded as a flock of sheep. He began to stamp their passes.

Half-an-hour after getting the message, Mrs Hammond drove to Heath's Hotel through a town that was as still and quiet as a charge of dynamite with the fuse faintly hissing. Only at Park Station the undercurrent of emotion and fear translated itself in the crowd that had gathered, with suitcases and bundles of rugs and babies, to try to find a few square feet of space on the evening mail train to the Cape. It was essentially a women-and-children-first exodus, and already the more circumspect males were being presented with white feathers as they sat embarrassed but determined on their small squares of masculine reservation in a damp female world of flight, farewells and nappies.

All the nervous energy of the evening concentrated on

the Goldfields building. There the prominent men of the town who wished to be identified with the revolutionary movement had gathered together in response to Frank Rhodes' summons.

By eight o'clock some sixty of the town's leading citizens were squeezed into the company boardroom, where they were briefly addressed by Lionel Phillips standing on a table at the end of the room and flanked by Hammond and Farrar.

'Well, gentlemen,' Phillips began, in his brisk, precise manner; 'as you all know by now, Dr Jameson has left Bechuanaland and is marching with seven hundred men towards Johannesburg. He has done this without our invitation and against our expressed wish. However, we're now concerned with the fact of this move and what we're going to do about it. In the circumstances, and in view of the unpreparedness of Johannesburg and the shortage of arms available for distribution, there's no doubt that the logical, cold-blooded course would be to repudiate Jameson and let him resolve the situation he has created on his own.'

There was an instant murmur of disapproval round the crowded room, one or two loud shouts of 'No! No!' and 'Shame!' Phillips and Hammond both held up their hands for silence.

'That's just what I thought you'd say,' Phillips went on. 'We're all aware that Jameson wouldn't have been on the border at all if it had not been to help us if the need arose; and he might well have come to the conclusion, as a result of recent reports and rumours, that that moment had now arrived. Thirdly, it's not likely that the Boer Government – who must know something of our plans and the arms that have been smuggled in – would dissociate Jameson from the reform movement in Johannesburg or that they'd believe us if we said we had nothing to do with his latest activities. Finally, I believe I'm right in saying that the people of the town would not accept a repudiation of Jameson – even if there could be found among us anyone who'd be prepared to do so.'

The general chorus of 'Hear, Hear!' which greeted this showed the temper of the meeting.

'As the originators of the reform movement, my colleagues and I have come to the conclusion that our main responsibility is to the unarmed population of Johannesburg and other Reef communities. It's with the object of fulfilling that obligation that we've decided to arm as many men as possible and to fortify as far as possible the perimeter of the town. Our sole purpose is the defence of the town and its inhabitants in the event of a Boer attack on us. We're not equipped for any aggressive action, and our intentions are limited to holding Johannesburg until help arrives – either from Jameson or from other outside sources.'

Cheers drowned the rest of his words and flowed out into the street, where they were caught up spontaneously by the small crowd of the curious, the anxious and the eager who had been gathering there.

That night the Reform Committee was born. The movement threw off all disguise and set about putting into effect the plans and preparations that had been drawn up for the emergency which, in an unexpected form, was now upon them.

Half a dozen sub-committees were formed, each with one of the inner circle at its head, to organize the town on a defensive military basis. Priority was given to the arming of the citizens and their allocation to various roles already determined, and to the maintenance of public order.

The ever-ready Trimble was told to get his police on duty.

Frank Rhodes assumed immediately his intended post of military commander, and that night set about the job of issuing arms. Other committees were appointed to deal with the formidable influx of people, especially women and children, from outlying mines and communities of Uitlanders as the news of the raid spread along the Witwatersrand; and with the control and maintenance of the vast throngs of natives thrown out of work and discipline as the mines closed down.

This preliminary work completed, Hammond, Phillips and FitzPatrick sat down to draft the Reform Committee's first public announcement; it appeared in all Johannesburg newspapers the next day, and urged the people not to take any action which could be considered 'an overt act of hostility against the Government'.

'There's one more thing, John,' Phillips said, turning to Hammond. 'With your agreement, I propose to send telegrams to the High Commissioner and to Cecil Rhodes – in his capacity of Prime Minister – informing him of our position here.'

271

'We must be very careful about this, Lionel. If any rumours get about that the High Commissioner's on his way to run up the Union Jack, you'll have to count me out – and every other American, German and Frenchman in the town. Now if Sir Hercules was invited here as a mediator, to prevent bloodshed – that'd be different.'

'Of course, of course. Percy – get this telegram to the High Commissioner at Cape Town, with a copy to Rhodes. "Owing premature start Jameson with armed force into Transvaal Johannesburg placed in position of extreme peril which completely unprepared to meet stop Urge High Commissioner proceed immediately Johannesburg or Pretoria to negotiate peaceful settlement and prevent civil war stop." Better sign that "Lionel Phillips, for Reform Committee" so that he doesn't think I'm acting on my own initiative. Put it in code, Percy.'

Johannesburg passed an uneasy night of almost unnatural calm. In the sultry air of an imminent thunderstorm many of the inhabitants sought relief from restlessness on cool verandas or at open windows. Even the hotel bars were strangely deserted as men made final arrangements for the protection of their families or, free of this sort of responsibility, began to assemble at designated points in response to orders that were even then percolating through the populace. At midnight a horseman galloped wildly down the street towards the Goldfields office, shouting: 'A dispatch, men, a dispatch! We've licked the Dutchmen!'

But the townsfolk, inured to exhibitionism and still uninformed and bewildered, were not ready to react blindly to this sort of stimulant. The horseman was allowed to clatter, noisy and anonymous, in and out of the history of the first night of Jameson's Raid.

Tuesday morning was an anti-climax. The Government had cut the town's communications with the outside world; the Reform Committee's announcement appeared in the morning papers, alongside editorials which deplored the action of the Bechuanaland force in entering the Transvaal; later in the morning the first edition of *The Star*, mouthpiece of the Reform Committee, further dampened excessive enthusiasm by hoping that 'a tumult would be avoided and a national compromise adjusted'.

Shops and banks opened – a little cautiously perhaps,

certainly optimistically. But as the intentions and organization of the leaders became revealed, the tempo of events changed rapidly. If there was a decisive moment of such change, it was when Hays Hammond stood on the roof of the Goldfields building and hauled a large *Vierkleur* to the top of the flag-staff. That morning, more concerned than most of his British associates with the character of their revolution, he had taken the flag along to the Reformers' headquarters. There, in a moment of slightly incongruous solemnity, the assembled group of leaders – each with one hand raised in the approved manner and the other resting on the outspread bunting – swore allegiance to the banner of republicanism which Jameson and Rhodes and Chamberlain were so bent on tearing down.

The subtle, baffling alchemy of those four broad colours floating over Johannesburg transformed the atmosphere from civilian inertia to warlike ardour. Streams of men concentrated at the Goldfields building and at other points, demanding arms and horses. Trimble's police stepped unobtrusively into the place of the 'Zarps', who had withdrawn to the gaol on top of the hill overlooking the town. Enthusiasm mounted as it became known that during the night parties of men had been digging trenches and earthworks on the outskirts and that machine-gun detachments had been in position since dawn guarding the northern approaches from Pretoria.

Frank Rhodes was determined to conceal from the Uitlanders as well as the Boers that he only had 3,000 rifles to distribute among the 20,000 men who, during Tuesday and Wednesday, clamoured outside his headquarters for arms. He overcame their impatience and growing annoyance by organizing them into small and highly personalized 'brigade groups' and apportioning them to various sectors of the town's perimeter, where they drilled and performed tactical manoeuvres under experienced officers and ex-servicemen.

By sunset on Tuesday eight 'brigades' had been formed – Australian, Scots, Afrikaner, Colonial, Natal, Irish, Northumbrian and Cornish. It was a convenient concentration of interests and did much to prevent the revolution developing into internecine strife among the revolutionaries. In addition, Colonel Bettington was given command of a regiment of mounted men known as Bettington's Horse, and all the medical men in the town came forward to organize and equip an Ambulance Corps, which was fully functional by nightfall. The Americans held another meeting in the afternoon and, with only five dissenting voices, voted to support the Manifesto and the Reform Committee: the George Washington Corps enrolled 150 men immediately.

All day long the work of organization continued, while merchants and shopkeepers barricaded their doors and boarded up their windows. Groups of miners, Cornishmen mostly, marched into town through crowded, cheering pavements. Clusters of horses were brought into the town centre and marshalled in front of the Reform headquarters. There 'they were surrounded by citizens eager to change their walking-sticks and canes for Lee-Metford rifles, their top-hats and bowlers for the wide-brimmed felt hats turned up on one side.

The mounted units were paraded there in the middle of the street, issued with brand-new saddles and bridles and then sent straight out on their patrols.

Nothing was more remarkable than the unobtrusive manner in which authority passed from the Government into the hands of the Reform Committee. Overnight the 'Zarps' disappeared off the streets, to be replaced by Trimble's men who, throughout the days and nights of high excitement and uncertainty, maintained an order and discipline such as the township had never before experienced.

They were greatly assisted in their efforts by the prompt action of the Committee in closing the canteens. Fearful of what would happen of 80,000 workless mine-boys got among the liquor stores and shebeens, the Committee gave a high priority to this problem. With incongruous propriety and respect for the authority which they were supplanting, a deputation called in the Landdrost, head of the Licensing Board, and requested the co-operation of the Government in closing the canteens. This was gladly given, and Committee-appointed officials visited all the liquor houses along the line of mines ordering the owners to close until further notice – with the threat of confiscation of stocks if the order was not obeyed. In some of the lower dives, where no sort of authority was ever recognized, it was necessary for patrols to arrest the owners, seize the liquor and destroy it – with agreed compensation.

It can be said with some certainty that there were fewer cases of drunkenness in Johannesburg during those days of crisis than during any other fortnight before or since.

Summary courts were established to deal with civilian and military offenders. The Reform Committee was in complete control of Johannesburg – with the consent of the Government.

The most complicated task was that of the commissariat department. They not only had to ensure rations for the brigades, patrols and guard-posts, but had to provide shelter and food for thousands of refugees who had poured into the town as soon as the news of Jameson's advance spread. By Tuesday night more than 2,000 women and children had been provided with beds and meals in commandeered offices and halls. The Wanderers Club was converted into a refugee hostel for nearly 500. The ballroom was the dormitory, the supper-room the sick bay and the roller-skating rink a maternity ward – for not the least remarkable manifestation of the stresses and excitements of the week was the number of premature births that were brought on.

The extent of this civilian invasion from the surrounding districts had not been foreseen, but a Relief Committee was soon functioning and a fund opened to support it; within a few minutes of the lists being opened, more than £80,000 had been subscribed.

A marked change in atmosphere had come over the town. A sense of purpose and unity had replaced the uncertainty, fear and apathy of the preceding days. By Tuesday afternoon, Johannesburg was united against Pretoria. British, American, French, Russian, German, Greek and Italian – even Dutch from the Cape Colony – then had submerged their national identities, and stood together as one community of Uitlanders.

Over in the capital the liberals among the Boers were a good deal more concerned than Kruger at the sudden change in tempo and temper of event. Prominent among them was Mr Eugene Marais, editor of the leading Dutch newspaper *Land and Volk*. On his own initiative, but with the approval of General Joubert, he had visited Johannesburg on Monday morning and met Abe Bailey and one or two other Reformers at the Rand Club. The conversation was straightforward, between men who knew, liked and respected each other. Bailey was emphatic that the responsibility for the present situation rested squarely on the shoulders of Kruger and the Volksraad.

'Now let them take what's coming to them!' he told his visitors.

'I cannot believe, gentlemen,' Marais said urgently, 'that even at this stage things are so bad that any thought to provoke a civil war would be justified. I believe that the latest developments and the prevailing excitement will convince the Government that they have gone too far in denying the Uitlanders their rights ... if the people of Johannesburg are serious in what they profess, and really desire reform and not revolution, they will, even at this eleventh hour, be willing to meet the Government.'

'Of course that's what we desire!' Bailey told him. 'If we do have a revolution it'll only be to get reforms that the Government won't give us ... We don't want bloodshed. We've always offered the olive branch and tried to live in harmony with your Boers. But we can't go on indefinitely in that manner ... getting nowhere. If the Government are in earnest, let them now take the first steps!'

This was the message that Eugene Marais took back to a fully-attended meeting of the Executive Council at Pretoria. Whatever Kruger's feelings may have been during a week-end of mounting crisis, Monday morning's telegrams announcing the armed invasion from Bechuanaland turned him at once into the man of action; relieved him, too, of all the moral doubts with which the Uitlanders had loaded his conscience.

The situation could now be reduced to its simplicities. The Republic was confronted with two enemies; if they could be kept apart, their defeat separately would be an easy matter. There were thus two tactical battles to be fought – first against Jameson and later against Johannesburg. If he won the first it was unlikely that he would have to fight the second. Now that Jameson had deliberately violated the frontier – and, with it, every treaty which existed between Great Britain and the Republic – there could be no armed intervention by the British; world opinion would not tolerate that, and Queen Victoria, he was sure, would not allow it to happen in her name. So Johannesburg could be contained with the weapons of words and gestures and a few commandos trotting around the outskirts – while he rubbed out Jameson.

It was with these thoughts in his mind that the President attended the Executive meeting at which Eugene Marais reported on his Johannesburg discussions. . . .

'So there it is, Your Honour and gentlemen. The Uit-landers say it is they who have always offered the olive branch, and you who have rejected it. Now it is —'

Kruger leaned across to one of his colleagues: 'Olive branch? Olive branch? What is this about an olive branch?'

'Your honour,' Marais explained, 'in ancient Greece the olive tree was the symbol of peace. Thus, to hold out the olive branch to an enemy is to make overtures for peace. It is an act of friendship.'

'Good!' Kruger nodded his top-hat emphatically. 'Let us exchange olive branches by all means.'

Another erudite member of the Council pointed out that the olive branch was also a symbol of fertility and that its leaves were worn as a headdress by brides in the hope that the marriage would be blessed with many children.

'*Magtig!*' Kruger ejaculated. 'That is *another* matter. There are too many Uitlanders already!'

Mr Wolmarans interrupted the general laughter to tell Marias: 'Go back to the Johannesburg people and tell them that we have already offered the olive branch, as they call it, by withdrawing our police from the town in order to avoid conflict. It is for them to say whether they will accept it.'

'Yes, that is what you can do, Mynheer Marais,' Kruger added. 'Let Mr Wolmarans arrange a commission here which can receive a deputation from Johannesburg. You can go and tell them that. But just be careful which olive branch you take with you!'

The meeting between the Reform Committee and Marais was arranged for nine o'clock on Tuesday evening in the Goldfields building. Marais was accompanied by Abraham Malan, son-in-law of General Joubert.

Both men addressed the meeting, outlining the recent course of events and the Government's attitude to the Uit-landers and their grievances. They gave a full account of the talks with the Pretoria Executive.

'We are sent here tonight,' Marais told them, 'to invite you to send a deputation to Pretoria in order that your grievances and your suggestions can be put before a special Commission which has this very day been appointed under the chairmanship of the Chief Justice. I can assure you that the Government are willing to give the most sympathetic consideration to your case and are anxious, above all else, to avoid a civil war. We come, in fact, to offer you the olive branch of peace. It is for you to say if you will take it. If you are sincere in your profession of loyalty, you will.'

When Marais sat down arguments flared up like small fires around the room as individual debated with individual, and group with group. Finally Charles Leonard's brother, also a barrister, got to his feet, and Phillips, in the Chair, called for silence.

'I think I speak for all here tonight,' he began, 'when I say that we have the greatest respect and the fullest confidence in the two gentlemen who have come here as representatives of the Government.'

The unanimous chorus of approval was resumed when Leonard added: 'But we have no such confidence in the Government. We mistrust the motives which inspired them to send you here.'

He paused to let the noise around him die down. Then he went on:

'Whenever the Government are earnestly intent upon deceiving us they select emissaries in whose character and good faith we have complete trust and, by deceiving them, ensure that *we* shall be deceived.'

In the applause which followed Marais stood up again to assure them that whatever the Government's attitude had been in the past, they were now genuinely anxious to remove the causes of discontent which had so obviously become a threat to the continued existence of the republic.

'Moreover,' he added, 'I believe I can say to you now that you will get practically all you ask for in your Manifesto.'

'What d'you mean by *practically* all?' they shouted back at him.

'Well now, you cannot expect the Government to come all the way along the road from Pretoria to meet you here in Johannesburg. You must go part of the way to meet them, not so? It is a matter of compromise, and there are one or two points on which you may have to give way.'

It was George Farrar who asked if the points he had in mind were the franchise and religious difficulties.

'Everybody knows,' Marais replied, 'that there are these difficulties, and I myself deplore them. As you know I have always advocated an extension of burgher rights to the new population. But I am certain the Government is open to

278

discussion on these and other matters and that understanding can be reached on even the most difficult questions.'

Abe Bailey wanted to know if the Government's change of heart and this sudden reasonableness was not due to the fact that Dr Jameson was on his way to Johannesburg with a well-trained and well-equipped force. Not quite everybody joined in the cheers which greeted this suggestion. There was nobody in the town who doubted that Jameson would reach them. Marais and Malan held a brief conversation, and then the former rose to his feet.

'Gentlemen, you are probably unaware at this stage that the High Commissioner in Cape Town has issued a proclamation denouncing Dr Jameson's adventure and calling on him to return to British territory at once. This proclamation has been dispatched to Jameson, wherever he may be, and it is expected that he will get it some time in the morning. There seems little doubt that he will be compelled to turn back.'

There was complete uproar at this; Marais remained standing, with Phillips alongside him, trying to quell the noise. Somebody at the back shouted: 'How can we believe you? How do we know this is not all just a trick of the Government's to gain time so that we can't join forces with Jameson?'

'Answer! Answer!'

Phillips climbed on the table top to quieten them.

'Mr Marais is perfectly prepared to answer you, if you will allow him to. I think we should remember this is a committee meeting, not a political gathering. Let us hear what our visitors have to say. No more demonstrations, please!'

He turned to Marais, nodded and clambered off the table. Marais waited for the last echoes to disappear.

'You do not seem to have appreciated, gentlemen, that my personal reputation is involved here. I come in good faith and I believe I am honestly interpreting the feelings of the Government at this moment. The proclamation has been made and is on its way to Jameson. It is being communicated to you by Sir Jacob de Wet, the British Agent in Pretoria. For all I know it is in the telegraph office waiting for you now.'

He held up his hand to keep them patient.

'There is something else I must tell you. If Dr Jameson

fails to obey the High Commissioner's order to return, both Mr Malan and myself will be in the commandos that ride against him. We and our friends in Pretoria are making every effort to avoid a civil conflict, but if it comes to a clash between the Government and a revolutionary force from Johannesburg you need have no doubts that all of us will be alongside our countrymen.'

Marais and Malan then left the meeting and at midnight, after much argument and some polemics, were presented with a unanimous resolution accepting the Government's invitation and informing them of a decision to send a deputation, consisting of Lionel Phillips, Abe Bailey and two others, to Pretoria first thing on Wednesday morning.

Wearily Hays Hammond climbed the stairs to the first floor of Heath's Hotel. His wife, like many other Johannesburg wives that night, sat alone on the stoep outside her room overlooking the street.

'I've just come to see if you're all right. Then I must go back. There's a lot to be done before morning.'

'We've heard all sorts of stories. Is the news about Jameson really true? That he's won a battle and is heading for Johannesburg?'

'I've heard only the same rumours as you, my dear. We don't know *where* Jameson is.'

The road below rumbled with the passing of a heavy-laden wagon, while the pavements clattered with hoof-beats. Mrs Hammond looked down curiously.

'Why, John! There's a gun on that wagon! A big gun. I didn't know we had —'

'It's just a bluff, my dear. The Boers get told everything that happens here. We're hoping that by tomorrow they'll have heard we're moving big guns to the northern outskirts. Actually it's a drain-pipe.'

CHAPTER TWENTY-FOUR

It was a short, short night for Johannesburg. Those who had gone to bed rose before dawn to join the rooftop sentinels or clamber up the high ridges behind the town, whence they searched the western horizon and the converging tracks. A few, unable to restrain their anxiety or impatience, rode out towards Krugersdorp.

The name of Jameson was on everybody's lips. They were ready that morning to give him a hero's welcome when he came in at the head of his gallant column. The previous day's reports of fighting had burgeoned with repetition during the night until fifty of Jameson's men had been killed, and more than three hundred Boers. The absence of any noise of conflict or any other evidence of encounter merely confirmed the rumours that Jameson had won his battle and was now on his way to Johannesburg unmolested. Enthusiastic property-owners began to festoon their buildings with streamers of patriotic bunting.

On the edge of the town, where the road from Krugersdorp came in, the Robinson Mine was being held against possible Boer attack by the Australian brigade under 'Karri' Davies, a timber importer. On Tuesday afternoon they had received orders from the Committee to have food and drink ready for Jameson's men. By Wednesday morning the long trestle tables were laid under the blue-gum trees with joints of meat, loaves of bread and crates of beer. A look-out was stationed in the tall headgear of the mine to give early notice of the column's approach.

No need that morning for the paperboys to pursue customers as they shrilled into the streets with their dawn bundles. The population was waiting for them at every corner and in every doorway. Where was Jameson? That was the one question everybody expected the unfolding pages to answer. And then the town caught its breath at the black, sad headlines announcing the disaster to the Natal train, filled with refugees fleeing to the sanctuary of Durban. Forty people had been killed, whole families wiped out. Scores more had been seriously injured as the carriages, overcrowded to a state of top-heaviness, slewed off the track at a sharp curve.

The shock of the news penetrated to the inner sanctum of the Reform Committee, where the deputation to Pretoria was ready to leave for the station. In the last hour of the night they had decided to send a word of good cheer to Jameson by means of a dispatch rider from the Bicycle Brigade. Frank Rhodes had scribbled a letter on a sheet torn from a telegraph pad in front of him:

'Dear Dr, The rumour of massacre in Johannesburg that started you to our relief was not true. We are all right, feeling intense. We have armed a lot of men. Shall be very glad to see you. We are not in possession of the town. We will send out some men to meet you. You are a fine fellow.
Yours ever,
F.R.'

Lionel Phillips was waiting at the door when Rhodes asked him:

'Would you like to add any message, Lionel?'

Phillips nodded, came across to the table, picked up a pen and scrawled across the page: 'We will all drink a glass along o' you. L.P.'

Then, with Bailey and the other two members of the deputation, he walked from the room. Frank Rhodes read through his letter and handed it to Farrar and Sam Jameson who, with Percy FitzPatrick, were the only ones left in the room. They glanced casually at the hurried words, and FitzPatrick asked Rhodes if he should bring in the dispatch rider. Rhodes nodded and then, as FitzPatrick went to the door, he said suddenly, 'Just a minute, Percy. I think we'd better have two men.'

FitzPatrick left the room and Rhodes took another sheet of paper. On this he wrote: 'Kruger has asked for some of us to go over and treat; armistice for twenty-four hours agreed to. My view is that they are in a funk at Pretoria, and they were wrong to agree from here. F.R.'

He put Dr Jameson's name in the bottom left-hand corner, and then folded both letters and sealed them in two separate envelopes just as the two dispatch riders came through the doorway. Each bicycle had been prepared so that letters could be hidden in the hollow, tubular frame. As the sun rose they set off on their strange ride.

Shortly after 10 o'clock Jameson was startled to see two cyclists approaching his headquarters from the direction of the Boer lines between him and Krugersdorp. The messages and the conversation he had with the two riders brought a great deal of much-needed encouragement to the doctor and his men, who were exhausted by lack of sleep and lack of food; they had been surrounded on every yard of their march by distant evidence of Boer forces massing on all sides.

Now he summoned Colonel White from where he had been watching the failure of an assault on one of the Boer positions ahead of them.

'Good news from Johannesburg, Bobbie!' he said, handing him the two notes. 'How d'you think we should answer them?'

White read them through quickly.

'Well, doctor. We could certainly use some of those men. In fact, unless we —'

Jameson motioned him to abrupt silence.

'I think we can best do it this way. Write an answer telling them that we're very pleased by their letter. Mention the fighting we've had already, and then say that we hope to reach Johannesburg tonight, depending, of course, on the amount of fighting we have.'

White was writing fast in his field dispatch book. Jameson paused while the pencil caught up with the words, then he went on:

'Now put this – just as I say it. "Of course we shall be pleased to have 200 men meet us at Krugersdorp as it will greatly encourage the men, who are in great heart although a bit tired." '

White passed the paper over to Jameson for signature. The latter added the line 'Love to Sam, Phillips and rest. L.S.J.' before folding up the letter and handing it to the messengers.

The message never reached the Reform Committee. Intercepted by Boer outposts, the cyclists abandoned their machines; it was only months afterwards that a mechanic, dismantling the bicycles for spare parts, came across the tube of paper.

Sir Jacobus de Wet in Pretoria had received the High Commissioner's proclamation from Cape Town. He immediately telegraphed it to the Reform Committee in Johannesburg. Shorn of its preamble and formality it commanded Dr Jameson to retire forthwith from the territory of the South African Republic, and called on all British subjects in the republic 'to abstain from giving the said Dr Jameson any countenance or assistance in his armed violation of the territory of a friendly state'.

It can be said that up to this moment the Committee had never lost hope that some sort of Imperial intervention might occur that would compel Kruger to grant all their demands, whatever the outcome of the mission to Pretoria. Now they were going to be saddled with an invading force which had been virtually outlawed by the British Government but which they had a moral obligation to continue to support. It was quite imperative to prevent Jameson reaching Johannesburg.

Accordingly the remaining Reformers sent a reply to the British Agent telling him that they were unaware of the reasons which had impelled Jameson's action, but as they presumed he was coming to their assistance in good faith they felt morally bound to provide for him. They therefore urged Sir Jacobus to make sure Jameson got a copy of the proclamation before any serious fighting should begin. They even offered to deliver the proclamation themselves if they were given safe conduct through the Boer lines.

Along with this message to the British Agent the Committee sent a telegram to their representatives arguing away in Pretoria:

'Meeting has been held since you started to consider telegram from British Agent, and it was unanimously resolved to authorize you to make following offer to Government. Begins – In Order to avert bloodshed on grounds of Dr Jameson's action, if Government will allow Dr Jameson to come in unmolested the Committee will guarantee with their persons if necessary that he shall leave again peacefully with as little delay as possible.'

Andrew Trimble, the one-time corporal in the Inniskilling Dragoons who was now solely responsible for public order in the town, had a force of 500 picked men at his command. His military instinct told him that the Uitlanders and their allies were about to be defeated in detail and that the tactical necessity was to attack the Boer forces in the rear while they confronted Jameson. He went to Colonel Rhodes with his plan – to strike at Krugersdorp with 500 men.

'One successful blow like that, Colonel Frank, and Jameson could come straight in to Johannesburg and we could get what terms we liked from the Boers.'

Rhodes refilled the two whisky glasses generously.

'I think you're right, Trimble. In fact I'm sure of it! But we've agreed to an armistice for twenty-four hours. I can't countermand the instructions of the Reform Committee – much as I disapprove of them. Besides, what'll happen to discipline in this town if your excellent force removes itself?'

'Then let me take two hundred and fifty men, sir. That'll leave enough to keep order in the town, and give me enough to lick the Boers.'

'No, Trimble, I can't do it. We must respect the armistice. You know that.'

'Very well then, sir; within the terms of the armistice, let me pay a visit to Dr Jameson's headquarters with twenty-five of my men. We could then invite him and his friends to visit your headquarters – for tea or dinner, you understand. If the Boers tried to stop us, *they'd* be breaking the armistice, not us; and the rest of my men could then come out to help us in.'

'A very fine plan, Trimble. But I would have some difficulty in explaining the ethics of it, as distinct from the tactics of it, to the Reform Committee. I'm sorry Trimble, but my hands are tied.'

In Pretoria things had not been going quite as the Uitlander deputation expected. They met the Government Commission under the chairmanship of Chief Justice Kotze at noon, and were taken aback by the immediate explanation that Marais and Malan had not been authorized to treat with the Reform Committee but had acted on their own initiative although with the President's knowledge and approval. The Government, said Judge Kotze, maintained its attitude that any representations submitted in a constitutional manner would be considered.

The four Reformers held a quick, whispered consultation. Then, with Bailey and the others nodding their heads in approval, Lionel Phillips stated the case for Johannesburg.

'Your Lordship —' he began, when Kotze cut him short.

'We have no lordship in this republic, Mr Phillips. I have no objection to the title of Judge, or plain Mister, or in this case Mr Chairman – since I am here as chairman and not as a judge.'

'Thank you, Mr Chairman. I was about to say that it is an impression shared by all members of the Reform Committee who heard Mr Marais last night that he and his colleague were in fact representing the President and Executive, on whose behalf the invitation to meet the Commission was extended.'

Judge Kotze and the two other Commissioners shook their heads emphatically.

'I must emphasize, Mr Phillips,' said Kotze, 'that my colleagues and I are appointed to hear your representations and grievances. Our sole intent is to report to the Government on what you tell us. We ourselves can decide nothing, nor commit the Government to any course of action.'

'Very well, then,' Phillips replied. 'There's no point in pursuing that aspect of the matter any further. I propose to deal with the grievances of Johannesburg and the Government's aggravating attitude to what we consider our just claims.'

Phillips detailed at considerable length the state of affairs in Johannesburg leading up to the crisis, and took the Commissioners carefully through the grievances listed in the Leonard Manifesto.

'The Government,' he told them, 'acts as if it doubts the genuineness of the Manifesto or that it represents the real feelings of the majority of the Rand inhabitants. We are here today to vouch for the unanimity of the new population behind the Manifesto, and to impress on you the extreme gravity of the position in Johannesburg. We recognize, however, that it may not be possible to obtain redress of all our grievances in one act of legislation – even if the Volksraad were willing – but we are prepared to accept what I may describe as a reasonable instalment of redress.'

He paused for a moment while Judge Kotze leaned in turn towards the man on each side of him and exchanged a few words. Then he turned to Phillips.

'We are wondering, Mr Phillips, what part Dr Jameson plays in your attempt to secure redress of these alleged grievances.'

'I am coming to that, Mr Chairman. Because we felt unable to make any progress with the Pretoria Government by conventional methods, and because even the constitutional approach was denied us – yes, that is perfectly true, Mr Kotze, as you will discover from reports of the last franchise debate! – because of these difficulties, we in Johannesburg decided that the best way of convincing the Government and the burghers of the seriousness and earnestness of the Uitlanders was to start a local movement and agitation among ourselves. We did this, let me say, in preference to appealing to Great Britain or other outside Power, as we do not consider the Republic our enemy and would not wish for any outside interference that might endanger the existence of the Republic.'

Judge Kotze interposed mildly: 'That is, no doubt, a satisfactory explanation of the *Vierkleur* which, I am told, is flying above the headquarters of your Reform Committee; but it hardly explains Dr Jameson's present position on the approaches to Krugersdorp.'

'Nevertheless, Mr Kotze, it explains our need for communication with Dr Jameson, who was at Pitsani with an armed force, to give direction and discipline to an unorganized body of citizens. It was also necessary to have some effective military force available in an extreme situation when Johannesburg might require assistance. Far from sending any invitation, the Committee has exerted every effort to stop him entering the Transvaal, and is even now engaged in trying to persuade him to turn back. I might add, Mr Chairman, that we have had not one single communication from Dr Jameson since he left Pitsani, and have no knowledge whatever of his present position or intentions.'

'I think it can be said, gentlemen,' Kotze said dryly, 'that the Government is perhaps better informed of Dr Jameson's movements than you are. As to his intentions, I believe it can also be said that they have no hope of being realized.'

'I bow to your superior knowledge, Mr Chairman. At the same time it is possible that Dr Jameson paid more attention than was prudent to the wild rumours that have been current in South Africa during the past weeks, and that he set off in good faith to come to our assistance. Since we are all under the impression that he is certain to reach Johannesburg, the unanimous feeling in the town and in the Reform Committee is that we must stand by him. I, and my friends here, accept that responsibility.'

Phillips looked for confirmation to his colleagues who nodded their emphatic assent; Bailey half rose to say something, but he was motioned to silence by one of the commissioners.

'You are aware, Mr Phillips, that since you have taken up arms and erected fortifications against the Government – and even, so I am told, sent big guns out on the Pretoria road – you are nothing but rebels?'

'You can call us rebels if you like,' Phillips replied. 'All we want is justice, decent treatment and honest government. That is what we have come to ask you.'

'You and your deputation,' went on the second commissioner, 'speak as though you represent the whole of Johannesburg, whereas for all we know your Committee may be nothing more than a small group of prominent individuals without popular support. You appreciate we must be quite sure who we are dealing with.'

Phillips and his associates walked right into the trap. They gave the Commissioner a number of names from memory, and promised to telegraph the rest.

'It will prove to you,' Phillips said, 'that the Reform Committee is representative of the whole Johannesburg community and has the full support of the public.'

The telegram with sixty-six names was duly delivered to the Executive, providing indisputable evidence of participation and conspiracy.

When Phillips had finished, the Chief Justice probed him gently on more specific points.

'Will the people of Johannesburg consent to lay down their arms if the Government grants most of what you ask?'

'Yes, certainly,' Phillips told him. 'I think I can say that after enfranchisement most of the new population will consider it a privilege to take up arms again as burghers of the

288

republic should the need arise.'

'On what lines does the Reform Committee propose the franchise should be granted?'

'We would be content, as a first step, if the Government would accept the principle. The details could possibly be left to a Commission of three – one representative of each side and the third to be mutually agreed upon.'

The Chief Justice nodded gravely, and made a few notes on the pad in front of him. 'It seems to me, gentlemen,' he said, 'this would be a convenient point at which to break off this meeting so that we may report to the President and Executive Council. We will adjourn, therefore, until four o'clock this afternoon.... Yes, Mr Phillips?'

'Before we adjourn, Mr Chairman, I would like you to take the following request to the President: that Dr Jameson should be allowed to enter Johannesburg peaceably with his men and then retire to Bechuanaland. We, as members of the Reform Committee, pledge our lives as hostages that he will do so.'

When this was reported to Kruger in the afternoon he was greatly amused. The Pitsani tortoise had stuck its head out so far that it was only necessary to let the axe fall in order to cut it off. In the meantime the Pretoria cat would continue to play prettily with the Johannesburg mouse. Jameson and the Reform Committee were no longer significant in the brief drama. They were still on stage, but as puppets dangling on strings held firmly in the hands of Paul Kruger and, less firmly, of the British Colonial Secretary through his deputy the High Commissioner. Cecil Rhodes, producer and director of the whole performance, had skulked off into the gloomy twilight of the wings.

When Jameson marched, Rhodes' last remaining hope was Sir Hercules Robinson and direct intervention by the British Government. With Jameson's repudiation by Chamberlain, this hope vanished. The High Commissioner was now under positive instructions from Whitehall to dissociate the British Government from Jameson's actions and to use all his efforts to prevent an inevitable conflict between the invaders and the Boer forces from spreading to Johannesburg. The proclamation denouncing Jameson was thus followed up by Robinson's offer to Kruger to come to Pretoria as a mediator in the crisis.

The offer arrived in Pretoria on Wednesday morning.

When Kotze met the Johannesburgers again at four o'clock he gave the Government's answer in the form of an Executive resolution which he handed to Phillips.

'Perhaps you would care to read that out aloud for the benefit of your colleagues, Mr Phillips. I think it is self-explanatory, and represents the Government's attitude to Johannesburg at this moment.'

Lionel Phillips glanced down at the sheet of paper placed in his hands. Then he read slowly

'The High Commissioner has offered his services with a view to a peaceful settlement. The Government of the South African Republic have accepted this offer. Pending his arrival, no hostile step will be taken against Johannesburg provided Johannesburg takes no hostile step against the Government. In terms of a certain proclamation recently issued by the State President the grievances will be earnestly considered.'

Phillips stopped reading and looked at the expressionless faces of his three companions. They did not know whether to be relieved or anxious, happy or angry. On balance it was a satisfactory situation. The main thing was that the High Commissioner was on his way and that Johannesburg would not be attacked. Provided Johannesburg takes no hostile step ... then their bluff had worked! The Government was frightened of an armed assault on Pretoria! Abe Bailey leaned across to murmur in Phillips' ear. The latter nodded, and asked Kotze:

'Mr Chairman, may I inquire whether this offer of the Government's – the offer to avoid hostile action, that is – is intended to include Dr Jameson and his troop?'

'Dr Jameson is in a different category,' the Chief Justice said briefly. 'He is a foreign invader, and will be driven out of the country. The Government cannot treat with him except on terms of unconditional surrender.'

'It seems to me, Judge Kotze,' Phillips said, 'that we are both anxious to see Dr Jameson return to Bechuanaland. On our side we have no wish to destroy the independence of the State. But this deputation is not empowered to accept terms which do not explicitly include Jameson. It is something which will have to be discussed with the Reform Committee and a reply sent to you as soon as possible.'

'I think you gentlemen are under some misapprehension,' Kotze said politely. 'The Executive's resolution does not require an answer. It is, in fact, their answer to the proposition you have so ably put before them. If the people of Johannesburg observe the conditions, there will I hope be no further trouble; but if they disregard them they must bear full responsibility for all the consequences. And now, gentlemen, I am sure you will appreciate that there are many urgent matters to be dealt with here....'

The deputation returned to a dumbfounded Johannesburg. A horseman had just been through the streets distributing copies of the High Commissioner's proclamation. What was all this? The Queen's representative ordering them to abstain from giving any assistance to Dr Jim? Armed violation of a friendly State? It didn't make sense.

The sixth edition of *The Star* came on the streets with a report that Jameson was only fifteen miles away and had fought another battle with the Boers. *That* was more like it. To hell with the proclamation! To hell with the High Commissioner! Jameson was their man: they'd go and fetch him in. What was the Reform Committee doing?

Rejoined by Phillips and Bailey in the comparative sanctuary of Hammond's office they were, in fact, preparing a notice that was to have an even more disheartening effect on Johannesburg than the afternoon's proclamation. It informed the people of the result of the deputation to the President and then added, rather cunningly: 'Desirous as the committee has always been to obtain its objectives without the shedding of blood and incurring the horrors of civil war, the opportunity of achieving its aims is welcome. The Reform Committee desires that the public will aid them with the loyalty and enthusiasm which they have shown so far in the maintenance of its organization, and will stand firm in the cause of law and order and the establishment of their right.'

While they were arranging for this to appear in the final edition of *The Star* and for its distribution as a pamphlet, a messenger from the British Agent arrived with the High Commissioner's proclamation en route to Jameson. He applied for a safe-conduct through the town's defences.

Whatever the populace wanted, the Committee by this time had only one thought in mind – to stop Jameson and get him out of the Transvaal as quickly as possible. They could see that if Jameson reached Johannesburg the reckless enthusiasm of the crowd would sweep the Committee's restraint and discipline aside.

Now they decided to send a member of the Committee along with the Agent's messenger to explain the situation in Johannesburg and make a final effort to persuade Jameson to go back. They were sustained in their attitude by the revelation that Jameson and Rhodes had caused to be published the letter of invitation given to the Doctor in November, and had made it appear, by having the date December 20 inserted, that the invasion had taken place as a result of a desperate appeal by the leaders of the Uitlanders.

They realized, too late, the motives that were inspiring Jameson, and that he had moved without thought for the consequences on Johannesburg and its inhabitants. They also realized that it would have been impossible and even dangerous to try to persuade the restless crowds that Jameson had let them down.

Mr J. Dale Lace volunteered to accompany the Agent's messenger, and they set off to ride through the night under the safe-conduct of both sides. Outside the Committee's headquarters the crowd was increasing as rumour piled on rumour and the reports of Jameson's progress multiplied. They were demanding action from their leaders; while some shouted for information, others called for arms and aid for Jameson.

At 11 p.m. Lionel Phillips came to the entrance of the Goldfields Building and was given a great ovation by the crowd. Now they were going to get action, they thought; no more playing about in sham fights with dummy rifles. Together with Jameson they were going out to smash Kruger . . .

Phillips' task was a delicate one. It was not difficult to sense the temper of the crowd or their need for decisive action. Every man believed that Jameson's triumphant entry was imminent. All of them looked on that event as the ultimate victory that would mean an end to Boer oppression and the beginning of a new and glorious era for Johannesburg. Very few outside the Reform Committee could see that Jameson's entry would mean an end to everything they had so carefully constructed; that in all the world there would be not one hand stretched out to help them – though there would be many hands stretched out to help themselves to the tumbled fragments of the golden structure they had created. Who would be the new Randlords? Not Rhodes, nor Beit, Phillips, Farrar, Bailey; Solly Joel, as a member of the Committee, had compromised the Barnato Group, and J. B. Robinson was out of favour with Kruger. No, the new Randlords would be Germans and Dutchmen and Frenchmen. Not even the Americans would be forgiven . . .

As Phillips came out to talk to the crowds he knew he had to destroy their illusions without destroying their hopes, and he had to maintain their confidence and the authority of the Committee. He could only do this by playing it down for all he was worth. He bored them stiff with his recital of the day's events in Pretoria: the courtesy with which the deputation had been received, the good impression they had obviously made on the Government commissioners, the earnest consideration which would be given to their proposals and the determination of the Reform Committee to stand by the Manifesto.

'What about Jameson?' someone yelled, and soon they were shouting Jameson from every section of the crowd. Lionel Phillips held up both hands to quieten the shouting.

'I'll tell you about Jameson, if you give me a chance!' he shouted back at them. And because they wanted to hear this, they gave him the chance with their silence.

'The leaders of the Reform Committee arranged with Jameson to come to our assistance when it was required. Unfortunately he has come in *before* he was required.'

He held up his hands again before the murmurs of disapproval could become a roar, and went on quickly.

'He has obviously acted on some false report that here in Johannesburg we were in danger, that the Boers were in the town killing and looting, and that he must rush to help us. For that we must honour him. But, of course, no such things were happening or, so far as we know, are likely to happen. The reason why we're now surrounded by armed commandos – and why we've been repudiated by the British Government – is because Jameson has committed this act of war on a friendly state.'

'Friendly to who?' yelled a voice, and again the street echoed to the shouting. Phillips waited till it died down.

'Don't let's forget,' he told them, 'that we are all in this together. We're all on the same side. Including Dr Jameson. We in the Committee may regret his too-hasty action in coming in before we'd sent for him. But we're not going to let him down now. We're going to stand by him!'

Now the air filled with cheers for Jameson and the Reform Committee. Phillips breathed a small prayer of thanks and a great sigh of relief.

'It is as a result of our efforts that the Government has been persuaded to accept the offer of Her Majesty's High Commissioner to come to Pretoria to try and settle differences and avert bloodshed. An armistice has been agreed between us pending the arrival of Sir Hercules. This is expected on Saturday. Now, you all know what an armistice means. It is an honourable undertaking on both sides not to indulge in any act of war for as long as the armistice lasts. It is an undertaking which all of us are in honour bound to carry out.'

Again the shouting started: 'What about Jameson?'

'Naturally, I cannot answer for Jameson. But I know that the High Commissioner's proclamation – the same one you had here this afternoon – is on its way to him at this moment. You know the terms of it. It is an order he cannot fail to obey without declaring himself against the British Government and his Sovereign as well as the Pretoria Government and the President. But I am instructed by the Reform Committee to tell you positively, as I have done the Government in Pretoria, that we intend to stand by Jameson. Gentlemen, I now call upon you to give three cheers for Dr Jameson!'

At 5.30 on Thursday morning, before it was light enough for good shooting, the Boers passed the dispatch rider and Dale Lace through their lines under escort so that they could deliver the messages to Jameson in person. The little group, white flag fluttering, was halted by a Bechuanaland Police patrol. One of these rode in to headquarters with a report that a Mr Leyds and a dispatch rider from the British Agent in Pretoria had arrived.

Willoughby, the gloom lifting from his face, remarked to Jameson that if the Boers thought it advisable to send their State Secretary to negotiate, things must be in a pretty bad way in Pretoria. It was a short-lived relief from the tensions of the morning and the grim outlook for the day ahead.

Jameson's force was completely surrounded. Behind them lay the long, empty trail to Pitsani with all food and provender consumed and every pass and ford occupied by the enemy. The koppies and dongas on each side were full of Boers waiting for the sun on their gun-sights. Between the invaders and Johannesburg lay the main forces of the Republic – invisible behind the rocks and boulders of the Witwatersrand but, as probing patrols had discovered the previous evening, ready with an impenetrable barrier of well-directed lead to deny every other yard of Transvaal soil to the raiders.

Well then, what news did these two men bring? Jameson read quickly through the High Commissioner's proclamation. He paused in silence for a long ten seconds when he had finished; then he turned to the messenger. 'Tell Sir Jacobus de Wet that I have received his dispatch; and that I shall see him in Pretoria tomorrow. Now Mr Lace, what news do you bring?'

With the Boer escort urging him to be quick, Lace told Jameson, concisely and faithfully, the situation in Johannesburg as the Reform Committee saw it; and he delivered their urgent request that he should go back immediately to Pitsani.

'It's too late now to go back,' said Jameson. Then, thinking of the letter from Frank Rhodes with its promise of men, he asked Lace, 'Where are the troops?'

'What troops d'you mean?' Lace asked, completely bewildered. 'We know nothing about troops.'

The gruff voice of the escort commander interrupted them.

'That is enough! You have delivered your messages: now must we go.'

At the same time as Dale Lace was having his brief interview, Bugler Vallé rode into Johannesburg with a message for the Committee from Dr Jameson. He was taken straight to the Goldfields building where the weary and dispirited leaders awaited a climax they knew was inevitable. Coffee and sandwiches were sent for while Vallé told them of the previous evening's battle at Doornkop, just the other side of Krugersdorp.

'We had a bit of a time there, I can tell you. Boers everywhere, potting away at us, and hardly a sign of them to shoot back at. We were driven off the position we'd taken up and I don't mind telling you I was glad of the chance of getting out of there. Y'see, the Doctor sends for me round about midnight and says: "Vallé, I'm going to give you the best horse in the troop and I want you to ride as hard as you can to Johannesburg with this message for Colonel Frank Rhodes." That's what he says to me; and here I am!'

Frank Rhodes came round the table and patted the bugler on the shoulder.

'You've done very well, lad. I'm Colonel Rhodes. What was Dr Jameson's message?'

'The Doctor says: "Tell him I am getting along all right but they must send out to meet me." That's what he said.'

'What exactly does he mean by "send out to meet me"? Does he want us to send out an armed force?'

'No, sir. The Doctor says he's getting along all right, but you must send out to meet him.'

That was all they could get out of Bugler Vallé. They showed him into another room where a breakfast was ready for him, and then the conspirators had their first serious and bitter disagreement.

Frank Rhodes was the unhappiest man in Johannesburg. The strong natural bonds of brotherhood with Cecil had been cemented by admiration for his achievements and ambitions; Frank had placed himself wholeheartedly and obediently at the disposal of the Reform Committee, but now that superior loyalty directed his thoughts and actions. As soon as the door closed on Vallé, Rhodes said vigorously:

'Well, what are you going to do about it? You know what that man's message means?'

'As far as I can see,' George Farrar replied, 'it means that Jameson is all right and is, unfortunately, pressing on to Johannesburg at this moment – unless the High Commissioner's proclamation has stopped him.'

'He sure can't ignore *that*!' Hammond observed. 'Dammit, the man's been made an outlaw by his own Government! We've told him to go back, Cecil Rhodes has told him to go back, even your Queen has told him to go back. Why the blazes is he coming on?'

'I'll tell you why he's coming on,' Rhodes said bitterly. 'Because there's no other way he can go. How do we know what instructions he's received? Or that he's had any at all? I tell you Jameson's now faced with a purely military situation requiring a purely military decision and a military solution. You know what Vallé's message means? It means Doctor Jim wants help badly, but is ashamed or too proud to say so. I'm going to see that he gets it.'

'You can't do that, Frank,' Lionel Phillips told him. 'We all know how you must feel about this. And believe me, we share your feelings. But don't you see, it's now a question of Jameson or Johannesburg. We can no longer expect any outside help. Without sufficient arms we can't hope to resist the full strength of the Boer forces. We've done all we could to secure the lives and liberty of Jameson and his men. The responsibility for his actions is now his alone. He acts without the authority of the Reform Committee – as, indeed, he has done since the beginning. We could easily denounce him, but we've decided to stand by him as far as lies within our powers. Be reasonable, Frank!'

Rhodes shook his head.

'I cannot accept your appreciation of the situation, gentlemen. I believe it is our duty to help bring Jameson's force into Johannesburg. I believe that once he's here the situation could change dramatically in our favour. It is, of course, a matter of opinion; but as the military commander in Johannesburg it is my opinion that counts in this matter, and it is *my* opinion that I propose to act on now.'

He stood up while the urgent pleadings beat against him. Hammond came up to put a restraining hand on his arm.

'Listen, Frank. There's another military situation to consider. As you know, the Boers are massing on the north-west outskirts of the town. We think an attack on us is imminent. We can't spare a single man with a rifle. You know that.'

'The military answer to that John,' Rhodes said brusquely, 'is that we need Jameson's well-trained and well-equipped force in this town more than we need anything else. I regard it as my duty to see that we get him here.'

He strode from the room, leaving behind him looks of dismay and anger, and sudden, agitated discussion. Outside his own office he sent a dispatch rider for Colonel Bettington. There was no delay. Bettington was waiting on the front steps. He burst into Rhodes' room.

'Frank! There's heavy firing coming from the direction of Krugersdorp. This is the moment: if we can attack the rear of the Boer positions while Jameson's attacking the front, he'll be through.'

'That's just why I sent for you,' Rhodes said. 'How many men have you got, mounted and armed?'

'Just over a hundred.'

'Right. Take them out on the Krugersdorp road until you encounter the Boer positions. After that act on your own initiative. The objective is to secure the entry of Jameson to Johannesburg.'

Bettington completely forgot to salute. He ran, jubilant, out of the building.

Half an hour later Bettington was riding at the head of his hundred men through the little village of Maraisburg on the way to Krugersdorp. They were puzzled by a number of starshells that were bursting in the sky above the ridges ahead of them. An officer touched Bettington on the shoulder.

'There's somebody galloping after us, sir.'

Bettington took a quick look through his binoculars.

'That's Sandilands, the Committee's chief-of-staff. Ten to one he's been sent to stop us.'

'Shall I shoot his bloody horse, sir?'

'That's an idea! But – better not. Let's hear what he has to say.'

Sandilands rode up full-tilt and reared to a stop in a cloud of dust alongside Bettington.

'A dispatch from the Committee,' he said abruptly, and handed over an envelope.

A few scribbled lines informed Bettington that a Boer attack was expected from the north-west; he was to take his men and patrol the area immediately.

Bettington hesitated for so long that Sandilands reminded him he was under the orders of the Reform Committee – there could be no question of disobeying them. In a gesture of anger and disgust Bettington crumpled the letter into a small ball, threw it into the dust and spat on it. Then he waved his arm to the quadruple rows behind him and they trotted off at right-angles to the road to Krugersdorp.

In doing this he not only saved the lives of Jameson and his men, who would certainly have been either all killed in battle or hanged later, but the future of Johannesburg and its inhabitants. The Reform Committee, too, were not altogether unaffected by the thought of a rope around their necks. For by this time, Jameson was past helping.

Back in Johannesburg, where the sound of firing was

interpreted in the crowded streets only as the prelude to Jameson's victorious entry, a vague uneasiness spread as a half-formed rumour that things were not going well gathered momentum. Instinctively there was a movement towards the western perimeter, and the clusters of men and women wandered haphazardly in the direction of Krugersdorp.

Francis Younghusband rode forward to where desultory shooting had replaced the noisy volleys of the earlier part of the morning. Below the ridge leading up to Krugersdorp he came across the first of the Boer patrols, then in process of occupying all the villages on the outskirts of Johannesburg. By skirting these he was able to reach the top of the crest unchallenged. Directly beneath him the battle-field was spread out. He saw two large bodies of men confronting each other, giving every indication of being about to launch an attack. Then, to his surprise, the one group turned their horses about, and slowly left the field. By the regularity of its formations and movements Younghusband knew at once that it could only be Jameson's force, though the full realization of what was happening did not occur to him until he approached a Boer officer.

'Well!' said the officer. 'Your great Jameson has surrendered. It's the finish for all you Johannesburg people.'

'Surrendered? I can't believe it!'

'Then why don't you go and find out for yourself? Go on now, the fighting's over.'

The reporter rode on, and it was only as he drew near the moving ranks of Jameson's troopers that he saw they were riding, disarmed, between escorting files of mounted Boers.

Ten minutes before, caught in the trap which the enemy had led them into among the koppies and kloofs of the farm Doornkop, completely surrounded by invisible marksmen and confined to a pocket of ground where they were at the mercy of increasingly heavy shell-fire, somebody had run up a white flag – and Jameson's Raid was over. It was 9.15 a.m. on Thursday, January 2, and within fourteen miles of Johannesburg.

Nobody knew who performed that final act in the drama. It was not Jameson. But it was not a matter for remonstrance or dispute. The end was inevitable. If they had not surrendered they would have been picked off one by one until not a man was left. The horses would have been spared – because the Boers liked horses.

They did not look like a defeated company to Young-husband. They were still hard and determined; they had yielded the battle but not their spirit. There was no fear in them, no sense of subjection. But they were tired and hungry. They had been in the saddle almost constantly for ninety hours. They had ridden 180 miles in a straight line from Pitsani, and many more miles than that in patrolling, scouting and skirmishing. They had had no sleep and no food since the morning of New Year's Day, and for twenty-four hours they had been in a running fight with the encircling Boers. In the few hours of daylight on that Thursday morning they had lost sixteen killed and nineteen wounded; twenty-five others had just disappeared.

Sir John Willoughby sent a note to Commandant Piet Cronje, an old antagonist of the British, offering to surrender provided there was a guarantee of safe conduct out of the country to every member of the force. In the circumstances it was an odd request. It was asking the Boers to allow them to do what Rhodes, Robinson and the Reform Committee had been begging and commanding them to do for nearly a week. The forbearance of Cronje's reply, after half an hour's discussion with his colleagues, was no doubt influenced by his awareness of 20,000 armed and angry Johannesburgers behind his back. He wrote to Willoughby:

'I acknowledge your letter. The answer is that if you will undertake to pay the expense which you have caused the South African Republic, and if you will surrender with your arms, then I shall spare the lives of you and yours.'

It was a magnanimous message. The Boers did not try to conceal their admiration for the physical bravery of Jameson and his men, but they were incensed by the action, by the attack without provocation and without even a quarrel.

Willoughby had a brief conversation with his now dejected and morose chief, and then sent a reply back to Cronje:

'I accept the terms on the guarantee that the lives of all will be spared. I now await your instructions as to how and where we lay down our arms. At the same time I would ask you to remember that my men have been without food for the last twenty-four hours.'

Even in the ignominy of defeat Willoughby contrived to give an impression of condescension.

300

By lunch-time word of the surrender of Jameson and his force had reached Pretoria, where Kruger received it with the calmness of certainty. In the afternoon the news burst on Johannesburg like a thunderclap.

At first the brief report was greeted derisively as another Boer-inspired rumour. Why, Jameson was about to enter Johannesburg: they were waiting to greet him at the Robinson Deep. Then confirmation of the news and rumours swelled to an anguished 'Jameson has surrendered!' which swept through the streets and buildings with the force of a tornado – leaving in its wake the shattered dreams and hopes of 60,000 Uitlanders.

Derision gave way to dismay and bewilderment, dismay gave way to all the anger of despair and frustration. Only the most coldly analytical citizens recalled the report (taken from the Government newspaper in Pretoria) published in *The Diggers' News* on Wednesday morning, that the Boer commander had stated publicly his intention to stop the invaders at Doornkop. It was regarded at the time as just another rumour, another example of heavy Afrikaner humour.

It was the failure of the infallible that shocked Johannesburg most. Not one person in a thousand had doubted that Jameson would reach the town. In the first place, they did not appreciate the Boer facility for overnight mobilization; secondly, they fully believed that 800 well-trained and well-equipped Britishers would not be stopped even by 5,000 Boers. And there was Jameson – to whom, surely, all things were possible.

There could only be one reason for the ignominious ending to such a great adventure. Jameson had been let down by those who had promised support. This suspicion roared to furious certainty when the Pretoria Government made it known that among the documents captured with the raiders was the letter of invitation signed by Charles Leonard, Phillips, Frank Rhodes, Hammond and Farrar. News of this was telegraphed to Johannesburg in the afternoon.

The first reaction was a deputation to the Reform Committee from the Scottish section of the community, who said they had a thousand men armed and ready to go immediately to rescue their countryman, Jameson. It was a serious intention, and the Scots desisted only when it was pointed out to them that their task was militarily impossible and that it would almost certainly endanger the lives of Jameson and all his men and bring about the bombardment of Johannesburg.

By nightfall the frustration and anger of the crowds had concentrated itself against the Reform Committee, and fresh horror was added to their desperation when it was rumoured that the Doctor and his senior officers were about to be shot. They swarmed around the Goldfields building, hurling abuse at individual Committee members, shouting for Jameson and demanding arms with which to go to his rescue. Trimble, with his usual foresight, had stationed a solid phalanx of his best men at the entrance to the building, and now one of them came agitated to Hammond's office where the ringleaders, exhausted from lack of sleep and pale with anxiety, held permanent session. He reported to Trimble:

'Sir, there are a number of men in the front of that crowd planning to blow up this building. We can hear them quite plainly. They've already sent off to fetch cases of dynamite.'

In the despairing silence which followed, Phillips covered his face with his hands and Trimble nodded a brief dismissal to his policeman: 'Thanks, Johnson. Keep us informed of any development.'

'Well now, gentlemen,' he said, when the man had gone. 'It's no use asking my chaps to take on that lot outside. We've got to use reason, not force. If that crowd gets out of hand they'll tear the town apart and us with it.'

'What do you suggest then, Trimble?' Phillips asked wearily.

'You'd better try a little speech-making, for a start. From the window.'

'Good idea!' said Farrar. 'I know those men out there, and they know me. I'll have a go.'

He went across to the big Georgian window of Hammond's office and opened it on the night and the noise. It poured into the room like a cataract. When the crowd saw Farrar standing there, they redoubled the volume of abuse and hysteria. Farrar tried to roar back at them, but even the men in the room behind him could not hear his words.

He stepped back angry and breathless, a trickle of spit running from the corner of his mouth.

Quickly, Lionel Phillips stepped to the open window. But the crowd, sensing that here was the real responsibility, linking him with Beit and Rhodes and all the other invisible influences to whom men's lives were less important than their own vast schemes and ambitions, gave him a much worse time than they had Farrar.

Somebody yelled, 'We want Jameson!' and soon the mob had taken it up like a battle-cry, chanting 'We want Jameson! We want Jameson!' in unison and in such overwhelming volume and insistence that the men in the Committee room put their hands over their ears not to stop the noise, which was impossible, but to protect the very substance of their brains.

On a sudden impulse Trimble went to the window and, leaning far out, began applauding the crowd and waving to the hundreds of familiar faces he could see – flickering, mobile, ugly – in the close-packed street. He caught them unawares. Besides, Trimble was not a financier. He was one of them. And he had kept the peace in Johannnesburg during a week in which anything could have happened. He was on their side and they were on his. Soon cries of 'Good old Trimble!' were mingling with the Jameson rhetoric, and in a few minutes they were ready to obey his gesticulations to keep quiet. When he had got them silent and waiting, he shouted down to them.

'I can't give you Dr Jim. I wish to God I could. But I can give you the next best thing.'

He looked quickly over his shoulder. 'Come on, Sam. It's up to you. Say something to them.'

Sam Jameson looked startled for a moment, then nodded his head and moved across to the window as Trimble's voice went echoing down the street again:

'Here he is ... *Sam* Jameson!'

When they saw Sam's familiar face and figure framed in the lighted window, the mob roared its applause. It wasn't exactly what they wanted, but it was the same flesh and blood. He gestured for silence, got it; then spoke to them quietly, the acoustics of the concrete that enclosed the street carrying his words over the sudden stillness.

'Gentlemen, I beg you, for my brother's sake, to maintain a spirit of calmness and restraint. I assure you, as his brother, that we in the Reform Committee have done everything in our power for him – as will be recognized when all the facts are known. We have used our best judgment on his behalf and your behalf. The circumstances were far more complicated than any of you could possibly appreciate now. I believe the course we have chosen is the right one, and that no other course could have been followed that would not have led to an even greater tragedy than has already occurred. It is possible that my brother's life may be in grave danger; by your actions tonight and in the days to come you may decide his future and the future of all the brave men who followed him from Pitsani.'

He spoke with obvious sincerity and with a controlled emotion which had an immediate effect on the crowd. There was no more shouting, just a subdued murmur of conversation as comment and agreement passed from lip to lip. One voice was raised to call out:

'All right, Sam. You leave it to us!' In a chorus of 'hear, hears', the mob began to splinter and disintegrate.

CHAPTER TWENTY-FIVE

Doctor Jameson and his men arrived in Pretoria at noon on Friday. There they were marched twice around the Market Square amid the hoots and jeers of the townsfolk and impromptu speeches demanding their immediate execution. It was a relief for them to be finally locked up in hastily-prepared and inadequate prison accommodation.

Kruger and his Executive pondered how they could best turn the event to the advantage of the Republic, how they could relate it to the vast, unresolved problem of Johannesburg with its 20,000 rifles, big guns and organized defence.

'They may not have twenty thousand rifles,' Kruger rumbled. 'But it is not worth a single burgher life to find out all the lies those Uitlanders tell! The Lord will show us another way.'

The Lord obliged in the form of a little black dispatch box found among the raiders' baggage. It not only contained most of the messages transmitted and received by Jameson and his associates, and the code to go with them, but the letter from the Reform Committee to Jameson urging him to come to their assistance.

There it was; signed by Charles Leonard, Lionel Phillips, Francis Rhodes, John Hays Hammond, George Farrar. And what was this? Dated December 20? Less than two weeks before Jameson rode across the border!

The anger of the Boers switched dramatically from the raiders to the Reform Committee. *They* were the traitors, the archconspirators, the real enemy! All that talk, all those protestations of loyalty to the Republic! They had denied Jameson even more emphatically than Peter had denied Christ – not three times, but a dozen times they had told Kruger that all their pleas and urgings to Jameson had been to stay in Pitsani, and that then, when all these had failed, they had tried to persuade him to go back. Now here was

305

the proof that Jameson had come at their express invitation. And not only that – the whole letter was a pack of lies. Not a single woman or child was in any danger at all – except from their own cut-throat, Uitlander rabble! As for the thousands of unarmed men...!

When the news of this letter was released in Pretoria, the burgher forces now largely concentrated in the capital and its outskirts became concerned. Their leaders urged Kruger to demand the immediate and unconditional surrender of Johannesburg with all its arms, the imprisonment and trial of the members of the Reform Committee, and the repudiation of the London Convention. The more hot-headed groups – and they were all a little flushed with their one-sided victory – wanted to attack Johannesburg forthwith, and made no secret of their intention of lining up the five ringleaders and 'drilling a hole through each one of them'.

Johannesburg got confirmation of the ugly rumours on Monday morning, when the pro-Government *Diggers News* published the letter in full – with a few appropriate comments and a description of its finding in a dispatch box at Jameson's headquarters. To the four signatories who read the report each sentence must have sounded like the beginning of a death sentence. Poor Mrs Hammond, distraught with fears for her husband's life, but determined not to let any emotion die unrecorded, rushed to her diary and put down her reaction to the discovery of the letter among Jameson's papers:

'Why in the name of all that is discreet and honourable,' she wrote, 'didn't he eat it?'

Now the Reformers had something far more intimate and personal to fear. Not only was the future of Johannesburg and its great gold-mining industry at stake, but the lives of all of them were imperilled. Everything depended on the High Commissioner and Cecil Rhodes. They had such vast resources at their disposal that it was ridiculous to think a little tin-pot Government in Pretoria could triumph over them.

The first disillusionment came from Hamilton, the editor of *The Star*, who returned from Cape Town, without Leonard, to tell them of the complete collapse of Rhodes and his power to intervene.

'He's a broken man,' said Hamilton to the depressed

circle who had gathered in the Goldfields to hear his report.

'I'll never forget last Monday morning. I called on him about midday. He was in a pretty desperate condition. He began to tell me what Jameson had done, and I must confess that I could hardly believe it myself. But he made it quite clear to me that Jameson had moved contrary to his orders...'

'But what about *us*?' Phillips interrupted. 'What's he doing to help us?'

'He can do nothing to help you, I'm afraid, gentlemen. He's been repudiated by the Colonial Secretary and the High Commissioner. He is, for the time being, a broken man. He's tendered his resignation, but Robinson has persuaded him to stay in office at least until he himself returns from Pretoria.'

Kruger, having identified the real enemy, laid his plans accordingly. He had isolated Jameson and Johannesburg from each other so that he could deal with Jameson's force piecemeal. Now he would use Jameson to subdue Johannesburg. He did not want a fight with the Uitlanders. Apart from the international reaction, how did you attack a big town like Johannesburg with its 20,000 armed citizens? No, there was an easier way to bring Johannesburg to submission...

Both sides saw in Sir Hercules Robinson the answer to the situation created by Jameson. Kruger, after initial hesitation, recognized the opportunity for imposing a Republican solution on Johannesburg with Imperial authority; to the hard-pressed and anxious Reformers, Robinson was the straw at which their hands clasped desperately as they saw themselves being swept away. And a man of straw he turned out to be, so far as the Uitlanders were concerned.

Poor Sir Hercules – old, sick and unwilling; ensnared by Rhodes in the web of his grandiose dreams; seeing clearly that whichever decision he made was going to alter history in a way that would make him unpopular somewhere. He had had enough of Rhodes and Jameson and the whole tribe of Uitlanders: their biggest failure was that they had failed. How different it would have been if Kruger had invited him to Pretoria to intercede on behalf of the Boers with the victorious Johannesburgers!

307

Robinson arrived at the Transvaal border late on Saturday to be met by the Chief Justice, Kotze, and an escort of the Staats Artillerie under the President's nephew, Lieutenant Tjart Kruger. They did not reach Pretoria till 9 p.m. There was no official reception, but a large crowd, four rows deep, lined the road from the station – silent and hostile in the darkness.

It was not an impressive arrival for Her Majesty's representative. The burden of his seventy years was increased by the weight of this new disaster and the collapse of the colossus at Groote Schuur. The dropsy from which he suffered was causing him great discomfort, and he stepped gingerly down on to the platform on the arm of a nurse. Behind him, expressionless, came the Imperial Secretary, Sir Graham Bower.

Making his way to the coach, he could not but contrast the silent enmity which surrounded him with the fervour of his predecessor's visit. Not a Union Jack in sight! If there were friendly figures in that mass on the pavements, they gave no sign of their presence. The horses' hooves clattered loudly as they trotted down the hill to the Market Square and the Transvaal Hotel.

'It's like a funeral procession,' Sir Hercules muttered to Judge Kotze alongside him. 'And perhaps it *is* one . . .'

The High Commissioner had only one request before he shambled off to the suite reserved for him and where, only eighteen months before, he had felt himself holding in his hands the destinies of two peoples. Now he was empty handed – and that infernal leg was giving him hell. As he bade good night to the Chief Justice he asked if there was a good doctor in the town. Kotze promised to send one round in the morning, and added, 'Your Excellency will be expected to call formally on the President tomorrow at noon – after he has been to Church. You will not be required to mention the purpose of your visit as His Honour makes a firm rule of never discussing matters of State, or any other business, on the Sabbath Day. But you will enjoy the coffee – there is plenty of that.'

A Sunday of intense frustration passed interminably for the ageing Robinson. For an hour he and Kruger talked about the weather in the Transvaal (they still needed more rain if the mealie crop was to be any good), while the room filled with pipe-smoke and the bottom of a waste-paper tin grew liquid with accurate Presidential expectoration.

When he got back to the hotel he found Bower had made himself familiar with both sides of the political situation. A delegate from the Reform Committee had explained the rather precarious armistice that had been arranged between Johannesburg and Pretoria, and Kruger had made certain that the British representatives did not lack enlightenment on the attitude of burghers and Government.

'There is no doubt, Sir Hercules,' Bower said gravely, 'that the lives of Jameson and his officers are in danger. I do not believe it is the intention of the President or any responsible member of his government to have them shot but it has been made abundantly clear to me that if the Johannesburg people take any offensive action, and fighting breaks out, the President will not be able to restrain what he considers would be the just anger of his burghers against their prisoners.'

'You can't really blame them, can you, Bower? In the circumstances. So what we've got to do is get Johannesburg to lay down its arms, not so?'

'Precisely, Your Excellency.'

'It's not going to be easy. I think the Reform Committee will see reason, but will the people obey their orders? That's the question.'

'We must persuade the people first that Jameson's life is in their hands. They still think of him as a hero. We must create the impression that only the people of Johannesburg can save him. Then, when they've had the night to think it over, you can send your official instructions tomorrow morning.'

'Very good, Bower. Then there's no time to lose. You'd better get that man from the Reform Committee off with the necessary messages. Tell him —'

'If you will forgive the interruption, Sir Hercules, I have already done so. He left Pretoria about half an hour ago.'

'Oh, you have. Hm-m-m. Very good, very good. Now there's only one thing to be done. We must draft a cable to the Colonial Secretary. Take this down . . .'

In London, first reaction to the news of Jameson's surrender had been one of deepest gloom mixed with condemnation of the attack. It had been such a blatantly offensive military action, without any provocation, that those who

309

escaped the nagging of a guilty conscience deplored the stupidity of it. The balance of public opinion was on the side of Kruger. Only the twenty-one-year-old Winston Churchill was critical of what he called 'the Government's timid handling of the crisis'. He felt that Jameson and his men had set out very properly to avenge Majuba.

Chamberlain's repudiation of Rhodes and Jameson was tainted with a bitter disappointment at the failure of his own intentions to extend the Queen's dominion over the whole of Southern Africa. He could not forgive them for that. Then a few words in German on a cable form changed the mood of Britain.

In his palace in Berlin on the afternoon of January 3, the Kaiser Wilhelm contemplated, with a good deal of satisfaction, news he had just received from Bismarck. It informed him of the surrender of Jameson to the forces of the South African Republic, and their imprisonment in Pretoria. This was the opportunity he had been looking for to rub those Englanders' noses in the dust of Africa. With a bit of luck the Transvaal and its wealth would come to the Fatherland. The Kaiser thought earnestly about the message he was going to send to Kruger; then he picked up his pen and wrote:

'To the President of the South African Republic. I express to you my sincere congratulations that without calling on the aid of friendly Powers you and your people, by your own energy against the armed bands which have broken into your country as disturbers of the peace, have succeeded in re-establishing peace and defending the independence of the country from without. Wilhelm, I.R.'

It was calculated, diplomatically, to give the maximum support to Kruger and the maximum offence to Britain. It implied that if Kruger had appealed to Germany for assistance it would have been forthcoming, and in its emphasis of the Transvaal's independence it challenged the limited sovereignty of the Crown written into the London Convention.

In England, the effects were profound and far-reaching. Patriotic heat fused all shades of political opinion into enmity of Germany and an unspoken determination to wipe out, sometime or other, the memory of Majuba and the fiasco of Jameson's Raid. Queen Victoria, clearly, was not amused. She wrote to her errant grandson:

'My Dear Wilhelm,

I must now also touch upon a subject which causes me much pain and astonishment. It is the Telegram which is considered very unfriendly towards this country – not that you intended it as such I am sure; but I grieve to say it has made a most unfortunate impression here. The action of Dr Jameson was, of course, very wrong and unwarranted but I think it would have been far better to have said nothing...'

The Kaiser was quick to reply:

'Most Beloved Grandmamma,

Never was the Telegram intended as a step against England or your Government. I thought the raiders were a mixed mob of gold-diggers, the scum of all nations, never suspecting that there were real Englishmen or Officers among them ... I was standing up for law, order and obedience to a Sovereign whom I revere and adore.'

If the subtler nuances of this missive were lost on Victoria – who appears to have accepted the letter as an expression of contriteness – the final summing up of this episode was made by Cecil Rhodes nearly three years later. In a conversation with the Kaiser, he told him:

'You see, Your Highness, I was a naughty boy and you tried to cane me. Now, my people were quite ready to cane me for being a naughty boy, but directly *you* did it they said, "No; if this is anybody's business it's ours!" The result was that Your Majesty got yourself very much disliked by the English people, and I never got whipped at all!'

By that time, obviously, Rhodes had forgotten the agony of his ordeal, and there was no reason to tell the Kaiser that the other reason why he was not publicly caned was because so many others would have been caned with him.

Throughout this new Germanic diversion, which might have provided a lesser man with all kinds of opportunities, Kruger kept his head. He knew what Wilhelm was after, as well as Wilhelm knew it himself. His reply to the congratulatory telegram gave the Emperor nothing but the formality of thanks. He much preferred his alliance with God to any intervention by Wilhelm. At least God was not contemplating annexation of the Transvaal and its gold. What he thought privately of the situation between Queen Victoria and her grandson was expressed with customary simplicity to the German Consul in Pretoria:

'The old woman just sneezed,' said Kruger, 'and you ran away.'

The consequences of these events in Europe were not immediately noticeable in Johannesburg. There, activity was stimulated throughout the weekend by constant reports of Boer commando movements on the outskirts of the town. Johannesburg was visibly encircled by a hostile army. Irrespective of what the conclave of the Reform Committee might think, the rank and file and most of the officers were more than ready to deal with it. The problem was to restrain them rather than to encourage them.

In the uneasy peace which hung over the township during the weekend, drilling and skirmishing practice suddenly ceased being a joke. The streets were drained of men as the citizen soldiers went to their concentration points or were dispatched to allotted positions on the perimeter. Several of the units held church parades on Sunday – notably the George Washington Corps, whose commemoration of the message of peace and good will was punctuated by some particularly warlike hymns, and by a sermon from their volunteer padre which sent most of the congregation away itching to get their hands on 'those Dutchmen'.

The townsfolk not engaged in these military exercises took picnic lunches out to the topmost ridges from where they could see clear across to the pass above Pretoria and the Boer stronghold of Heidelberg. To the west the tin shacks of Krugersdorp, just visible, marked the end of the Witwatersrand and the end of the line for Jameson.

In Cape Town the Anglican Bishop, preaching in the Cathedral, implored all people to restrain themselves until the result of the High Commissioner's mediation was known. At the other end of the sub-continent a mass meeting at Salisbury telegraphed a unanimous resolution:

'From the people of Salisbury to Dr Jameson, care of the State Secretary, Pretoria. The people of Salisbury desire to convey to you an expression of their deepest and heartfelt regret at the position in which you and your comrades are placed through a most unfortunate misconception of the true circumstances of Transvaal politics. They desire to record their admiration of the magnificent courage and endurance displayed by yourself and force and their warm appreciation of the chivalrous and generous treatment which you have experienced at the hands of your brave opponents.'

In Johannesburg the Sabbath armistice was broken only by several raids by Trimble's amateur police on canteens whose owners had interpreted the calm as permission to re-open, and on gambling stands which had been brought out of their hiding-places and set up in the main streets. As the raiding parties were headed by a number of well-known pugilists, the forays were brief and bloody.

Shortly before noon on Monday the High Commissioner emerged from his hour-long session with Kruger and the Executive and went immediately to the Transvaal Hotel, where the British Agent and Bower were awaiting him.

'Chamberlain can wait, Bower,' Sir Hercules said. 'We've no time to lose if we're going to save Jameson and the other prisoners. Just let me get this damned leg comfortable and then we can proceed ... Now then, Sir Jacobus. Johannesburg is the key to the whole situation. This is what you must do. Send a telegram to the Reform Committee informing them that the Boer Government will not open negotiations or give any consideration to Uitlander grievances until Johannesburg surrenders its arms. You must make them understand that that is the first essential to any progress which I may be able to make, and the decisive factor in determining Jameson's fate.'

'Were you given any indication of what that fate will be?' Bower inquired.

'No decision has yet been made by Kruger. It will, as I have said, be determined by the attitude of the Johannes-burgers. But Kruger pointed out that he has had eight thousand of his burghers under arms for nearly a week and that they are impatient to finish off this business one way or another. It is just as likely to be by shooting the raiders and attacking Johannesburg as by any other means. The Reform Committee have got twenty-four hours, from four o'clock this afternoon, to make up their minds. You will inform them of that, Sir Jacobus, and add my earnest personal wish theat they accept these terms without further delay. If they do not, then I can do nothing for them. Now, you'd better draft that telegram and get it off right away.'

When the British Agent had gone, Bower probed the High Commissioner on the nature of his interview with the

President.

'Of course I had to apologize, Bower,' Sir Hercules answered, a little impatiently. 'I expressed Her Majesty's Government's sincere regret at the unwarrantable raid made by Jameson, and thanked the President for the moderation shown under trying circumstances. It created a good atmosphere for the rest of our talks – and dammit, it's true, isn't it?'

'I agree entirely, Your Excellency. But what impression did you get of the steps the President will take if and when Johannesburg lays down its arms?'

'I tried to get something out of them on that, but nothing doing. They told me politely but firmly that the Government of the South African Republic had nothing more to say on this subject other than what had already appeared in the President's original proclamation.'

'That's the one which promises to consider all grievances which are properly submitted, and to lay them before the legislature without delay?'

'Precisely. And let's face it, Bower, in the circumstances it's something the Uitlanders have forfeited the right to expect. The fact is that Kruger is complete master of the situation. We haven't got a move left ...'

The telegram from the British Agent was delivered to the Reform Committee as they gathered together after lunch. The indefatigable Phillips and Fitzpatrick had had lunch sent across from the Rand Club; Frank Rhodes and Trimble, keeping contact with their forces through a constant stream of dispatch riders, chewed sandwiches while they issued orders. Reports were frequent of provocative Boer demonstrations around the perimeter defences, and it was astonishing how the imposed discipline of restraint was maintained by so many undisciplined individuals.

The whole town was waiting for the message from the High Commissioner. They were waiting for more than a message. They were waiting for a miracle. When it came it contained only the news which the Committee had expected, but hoped not to receive. Phillips sent off a quick acknowledgment to Robinson with an assurance that the Boer demands would receive earnest and immediate consideration. Then he summoned all the members of the Committee to the Goldfields boardroom.

It was another bitter, disputatious debate. The leaders

314

knew there was no choice before them except to accept the terms of the ultimatum and lay down their arms. The majority of members, however, were convinced that once they had surrended their arms they would have surrendered their whole case. They did not believe the Boer Government would keep faith, and they did not think that Kruger and his associates had any intention of conceding their demands. They were all for making a fight of it, with the first priority the rescue of Dr Jameson and his fellow-prisoners.

Only the intervention of Sir Sidney Shippard, who had come up from Bechuanaland to see what he could do for Jameson, persuaded the meeting that any conflict of arms between Johannesburg and Pretoria could only end disastrously for Jameson and for all the Uitlander objectives.

They were still arguing late in the afternoon when another telegram arrived from Sir Jacobus de Wet, saying that he had been instructed by the High Commissioner to come in person to Johannesburg to meet the Reform Committee and explain the situation to them. Robinson, it was clear, had not expected any delay in Johannesburg's acceptance of the conditions; he was sending the British Agent over to get it.

The meeting took place early on Tuesday morning. Sir Jacobus lost no time in producing a telegram he had just received from the High Commissioner.

'I had this from Sir Hercules not ten minutes ago. It's marked "Most Urgent". Let me read it to you.'

Sir Jacobus adjusted his glasses carefully to get the full effect of the silence, then read from the telegram:

'You should inform the Johannesburg people that I consider that if they lay down their arms they will be acting loyally and honourably, and that if they do not comply with my request they forfeit all claim to sympathy from Her Majesty's Government and from British subjects throughout the world as the lives of Jameson and the prisoners are now practically in their hands.'

He put the telegram flat on the table in front of him and looked slowly round the room.

'I have only one thing to add to that, gentlemen. Before I left Pretoria the High Commissioner told me that he had been assured by President Kruger that once your arms have been surrendered Jameson and his men will be handed over

315

to the British Government for trial.'

This caused an excited buzz of conversation. In the front row of seats Phillips leaned across to Hammond, and the two ringleaders spoke earnestly for some seconds. Then he turned to Farrar and got an emphatic nod of acquiescence. He began to write busily on a sheet of paper. At the end of the row of chairs Abe Bailey and Frank Rhodes looked morose and dubious. From the back of the boardroom someone said loudly: 'What about our grievances? Do we get them put right?'

'To be quite frank, gentlemen', Sir Jacobus said a little frostily, 'I do not think you are in a position to demand conditions. In the circumstances in which you now find yourselves I do not think you can expect anything more favourable than the discussion and consideration of your grievances which the President has promised the High Commissioner. I would add that if there is any spirit of reason left in the community at all, you will be content to leave your case in the hands of an experienced statesman like Sir Hercules, a man whose every instinct and training is towards fair and decent government.'

'That's all very well!' Bailey could restrain himself no longer. 'But how do you know what the Boer Government 'll do once Johannesburg has surrendered its arms? How do we know they won't turn on us in here as soon as they're sure we can no longer resist them?'

There were loud murmurs of approval at this. It was a thought that had been worrying every member of the Reform Committee ever since Jameson crossed the border. The British Agent addressed himself directly to Bailey.

'I think I can assure you that once you comply with the terms of the ultimatum – and I must remind you that it expires at four o'clock this afternoon – not a hair of the head of any man in Johannesburg will be touched.'

Lionel Phillips asked: 'Will this immunity be extended to the leaders? For instance, will it be extended to those who signed the letter to Jameson?'

'Yes, I can give you that assurance. Not one among you will lose his personal liberty for a single hour. John Bull would never allow it.'

'Forgive me, as a foreigner, from interrupting what has become an exclusively British argument,' Hays Hammond said dryly. 'But I think I can claim to be in the same boat as the rest of you, whatever flag's at the mast-head. It seems to me John Bull has had to put up with a good deal in this country. What exactly d'you *mean* by John Bull?'

'I mean,' said de Wet, 'the British Government could not possibly allow such a thing.'

Phillips stood up and turned to face the Reform Committee.

'It seems to me, gentlemen, that we have little choice in this matter. The overriding factor is the safety of Jameson and his men. If there were no other reason at all, we would have to accept Kruger's ultimatum in order to ensure that. We have the assurance of the Government and Her Majesty's representative that our grievances will be considered – provided we first lay down our arms. There are alternatives, of course, but you know what they are and what they'll mean for Jameson and for this town that we've created here on the bare veld. I don't think we need consider that proposition any further. With the assistance of my colleagues,' he indicated the other principals in the front row, 'I've drafted a resolution agreeing to accept the conditions of the ultimatum and informing the President that the citizens have been instructed to lay down their arms. We also draw the Government's attention to the presence of armed burgher forces in the vicinity of the town, with a request that they be removed in order to avoid provocation at this very difficult time. It's not going to be easy persuading the people to hand in their arms – especially if there are armed Boers all round the town. Have you any ideas how we should proceed, Sir Jacobus?'

'It might be a good idea if we called a mass meeting so that I could explain the situation myself and appeal to them to hand in their arms right away.'

'Very well,' Phillips agreed. 'We'll call a meeting for noon today. In front of the Rand Club.'

It was fortunate, perhaps, that the first edition of *The Star* was on the streets before twelve o'clock. The populace, snapping up the papers hungrily, read the blunt notice:

'The Reform Committee notify hereby that all rifles issued for the defence of life and property in town and the mines are to be returned at once to the Central Office in order to enable the Committee to carry out the agreement with the Government upon the faithful observance of which so much is dependent.'

There followed a recapitulation of the events of the night and morning and the telegram to the British Agent from the High Commissioner. Sir Jacobus de Wet added his signed assurance that as soon as arms were laid down Jameson and his men would be handed over to the High Commissioner.

As news of the noon meeting percolated through the crowded streets, there was a general convergence on the Rand Club. By midday the club building was like a rocky island in a sea of humanity which overflowed from Loveday Street into Fox and Commissioner Streets.

When the British Agent appeared on the balcony he was greeted with as many boos as cheers. But the crowd had come to find out what was happening and what was expected of them; they grew silent as Sir Jacobus began to speak.

'As most of you know, I am the Agent of the British Government in Pretoria and you can accept it, therefore, that I have nothing but the best interests of Johannesburg and its people at heart. It is because of that that I tell you this morning to lay down your arms and allow the negotiations between the High Commissioner and the President to continue uninterrupted by any noises from here.

'I think I can say that I am better aware of the position than most of you listening to me today, and I feel it my duty to point out to you that you will be exposing the town and all its inhabitants, including the women and children, to the gravest risks if you do not comply with the terms of the ultimatum. I must warn you that Johannesburg is defenceless and that the President is having the greatest difficulty in restraining his commandos from attacking it —'

The reaction of the crowd was clearly revealed in the shocked expressions on upturned faces, and in shouted protests.

'What d'you mean, *defenceless*?'

'We're not afraid of a bunch of backveld farmers!'

'Go back to Pretoria – tell Paul Kruger to come and *get* our rifles – if he can!'

Behind the balcony Phillips and Farrar and one or two others held a swift consultation.

'The bloody old fool!' Bailey said. 'If he thinks he can *frighten* them into giving up their arms, they'll never do it!'

Angry and unhappy, de Wet persisted in his warnings of the fate that would befall them when the Boers attacked the town.

'We've got to stop him,' Phillips said, 'before they start marching on Pretoria.' He turned to Sir Sidney Shippard.

'Sir Sidney, will you say something to them? Jameson's life may depend on this mob outside here. Try and make them see reason. Appeal to them. George, get de Wet off that balcony. *Pull* him off, if you have to.'

Farrar slipped up behind the Agent and whispered in his ear. Sir Jacobus, a little lost and bewildered by this time, shook his head but did not resist when Farrar took him firmly by the elbow and propelled him off the balcony while the crowd below laughed and cheered. This was Shippard's moment, and he was not the sort of man to fail to take advantage of it.

He waited on the balcony for the cheering and the jeering to stop, his arms outstretched as though to include all the limits of the crowd within the circle of his sympathy and advice.

'Men – and women – of Johannesburg!' he called out to them. 'As a representative of Her Majesty you know I cannot express my true feelings at this time. You must also know that I sympathize deeply with you all in your struggle for what I believe to be your just rights.'

He paused to let the rumble of approval drift away down Commissioner Street.

'Let me just say that although I cannot officially take my place alongside you, that is where I would like to be. Now we have to consider our position in the light of all the recent developments. There's no need for me to remind you that Jameson and his brave men are prisoners in Pretoria; but there is, perhaps, some need to remind you that their lives are in great danger. They are, in fact, hostages for your good behaviour. I know well enough what you'd like to do: you'd like to march straight from here to the Boer capital, and it may be that you'd reach it – though as a man of some military training I would not rate your chances very high —'

He held up his hand to stop the shouted disagreement, grinning back at their anger.

'All right, all right: you'll reach Pretoria. But what d'you think you'll find there? Jameson and his followers lined up to cheer you in? I'll tell you what you'll find – only their corpses!'

He let this sink deep in, watching the quick change of emotion on those upturned faces.

'The Boer Government have made one condition for their safety. Only one. You must give up your arms. It is not surrender. You will be delivering them up to the High Commissioner, *your* High Commissioner. And in return, Jameson and his men will be delivered. And not only Jameson and his men, but all those men who have led this movement and who, let me assure you, are in no way responsible for its unfortunate ending. No, not its ending, for I do not believe it will end until it has achieved its objectives —'

The cheers and applause reached up to him, for him. Now he could end it; now he could leave it to them.

'And so, my friends, I – whose heart and soul are with you – say again: give up your arms! Give up your arms to your High Commissioner. You'll be surrendering nothing of value. What is of value is that Johannesburg, this city you have built, should grow on in greatness and prosperity. Give up your arms and go back to your work and your homes. You will never regret it!'

The moments of indecision, the essential inspiration of rebellion, were past. Long lines of men formed up leading to the Reform Committee's headquarters. Messengers cycled furiously to the outposts, calling in the perimeter defenders and the patrols.

Around the corner of Commissioner Street another meeting was being held in front of the Government Buildings. Over a thousand loyal burghers who had stayed on in their ramshackle homes in Johannesburg were addressed by Commandant Schutte and the Mining Commissioner. They were told that all the Uitlander arms would be given up within the next few days, and that their only duty now was to await the outcome of events in an orderly and quiet manner and to resume their ordinary day-to-day lives without giving provocation to any.

By Wednesday morning nearly every weapon issued to the Uitlanders by the revolutionary committee had been handed in. The Landdrost in Johannesburg was able to report to his Government that he had counted 1,814 rifles and three Maxim machine-guns. The reaction was swift and unexpected: Kruger sent an urgent communication to the

High Commissioner, complaining that the terms of the ultimatum had not been complied with; he was issuing orders that Johannesburg should be attacked that day.

The Reform Committee propaganda had succeeded too well. Kruger and every member of his Government believed that there were 20,000 armed men in the town, and that fewer than 2,000 of them had surrendered their arms. This left in being a force which could still outnumber the Boer forces at that time gathered against them. Of course, there was still Jameson and his men, and Kruger did not hesitate to remind Robinson of their position. As long as he had Jameson he didn't need any artillery.

Robinson, however, was not to be bluffed or frightened. He knew the exact total of men under arms in Johannesburg. It was just over 2,700, and of these almost 1,000 had weapons which they possessed before any thought of revolt had entered their minds. He pointed out to Kruger that the ultimatum concerned only guns and ammunition for which no permit of importation had been obtained, and that the onus of proving that weapons were being deliberately concealed lay with the Transvaal Government. He added, ominously enough to impress Kruger that he meant it:

'If, before this is done, Mr President, any hostile step is taken against Johannesburg, I should consider it a violation of the undertaking for which I have made myself personally responsible to the people of Johannesburg, and I will be compelled to leave the issue in the hands of Her Majesty's Government. I hope I make myself clear to Your Honour.'

He had made himself clear, all right. The order to mount an attack on Johannesburg was countermanded, and it was arranged that a number of republican officials would accompany the British Agent on a tour of the town and adjacent mines to inspect all the hiding-places where it had been freely reported by informers that arms were concealed.

In the evening the 'Zarps' emerged from their seclusion in the gaol on the top of Hospital Hill, and took over police duties from Trimble's men as peacefully as the interchange of roles had occurred eight days before.

That Wednesday night the revolution came to an end. For eight days the population had been organized for rebellion. Fewer than 3,000 had actually been armed, but another 17,000 males had been put on what was virtually a military footing. All this had taken place in a vast mining-camp overcrowded with every human element, good and bad and probably more bad than good. Yet not a single act of violence had been committed, not a single civilian had been killed or injured, not a single policeman had been hit on the head or kicked on the shins. The 'Zarps' had taken a week's holiday and Trimble's substitutes had taken their place. Now the 'Zarps' were back on duty. The Government had not fired one shot at Johannesburg and Johannesburg had not fired one shot at the Government.

The truth was that in all the conflicting interests and ambitions only one man, Jameson, had been ready for a fight. Deservedly, he'd got one. For both Rhodes and Chamberlain the fight was less important than the timing, and the time was not yet ripe. The Uitlanders were only prepared to fight if the fighting would leave their citadel of gold undamaged and firmly in their possession.

Paul Kruger recognized the skirmish at Doornkop as the beginning of a war that was inevitable, the only answer to a situation that had become impossible. Kruger did not want a war at that moment, because he and his country were not ready for it. First let the burghers be fully equipped for war – not just against a handful of border filibusters or a conglomeration of millionaires and miners; but war against an Empire, the greatest and most potent Empire in the world. Oh, they could have their war – but at a moment of his own choosing.

As for Jameson, he had lost his significance with the surrender of Johannesburg. The Raid had been little more, from a military point of view, than a nuisance, and now the prisoners were a greater nuisance than ever. It was time to get rid of them – and to earn a few marks for magnanimous statesmanship.

Kruger's psychology, as usual, was sound. When Jameson and his followers were handed over to the High Commissioner for return to Britain for trial, the anger and hurt pride of the British people found a target in the Uitlanders who had failed Jameson; the Randlords who had refused to leave their heap of filthy gold when Jameson needed their help; the very same Randlords who had begged Doctor Jim to rescue their defenceless women and children from the brutal Boers.

CHAPTER TWENTY-SIX

Ther was little public sympathy for the Reform Committee either in South Africa or Britain when, late on Thursday evening, the President issued yet another proclamation, full of 'whereas I, Stephanus Johannes Paulus Kruger' and 'therefore I, Stephanus Johannes Paulus Kruger', and which rambled on infuriatingly for eight inconsequential paragraphs until it came to this:

'Now I therefore proclaim that all persons who have already laid down and given over the said arms and ammunition ... shall be exempted from all prosecution, and will be forgiven for the misdeeds that have taken place at Johannesburg and suburbs, except all persons and corporations who will appear to be the chief offenders, ringleaders, leaders, instigators and those who have caused the rebellion of Johannesburg and suburbs. Such persons and corporations shall have to answer for their deeds before the legal and competent courts of this Republic.'

When Lionel Phillips read the proclamation out to the inner circle of the Reform Committee, they were dumbfounded.

'The cunning old bastard!' Bailey growled. 'First of all he gets the High Commissioner to disarm us, then he waits for two days while he moves his blasted commandos and Zarps into position, then he issues *this*. You know what this is? It's not a proclamation. It's a warrant for our arrest!'

Bailey was right. All day the rumours flew around the town like gossiping sparrows: the whole Reform Committee was going to be arrested and shot ... only the ringleaders were going to be shot ... everybody who had taken up arms against the Government would be deported ... Kruger had a list of all the names given to him by Lionel

Phillips ... they were to be tried for high treason, and you know what the penalty for high treason is ...

Hays Hammond comforted his wife by telling her that he did not believe the authorities in Pretoria would dare to put them in gaol.

'Not after giving their recognition to the Committee,' he said, patting her reassuringly on the shoulder. 'After all, they've accepted us as negotiators on behalf of all the people of Johannesburg, and even promised to introduce some of the reforms we've asked for. Besides, Great Britain would never allow any harm to befall her subjects after commanding them to lay down their arms and guaranteeing their safety. It would be the worst sort of bad faith.'

'But we're not British, John.'

'Well, nobody's going to make an exception of me just because I'm an American. We've got a government, too, you know! Now, don't you worry. If there's anything behind these rumours, and some arrests are planned, it'll simply be a matter of form – a demonstration that Kruger and his executive are back in authority.'

Within ten minutes of their reading the proclamation, the Reform Committee knew that the arrests would be made that night. Everybody whose name was on the list given to Judge Kotze by the Uitlander deputation was to be taken away. Well, they had three or four hours in which they could do something about it. The population was disarmed and defenceless; the 'Zarps' were in control of the town and the commandos had been moved up to the outskirts; it was no use thinking of putting up a fight. But they could escape over the borders. There were a dozen different ways of getting out. In spite of the restrictions, scores of men, women and children were leaving Johannesburg every day. A Government official came secretly to the four ringleaders and offered them a safe conduct out of the Transvaal – on his own responsibility, he said.

Captain Younghusband, just back from Pretoria, came into the boardroom. Farrar and Rhodes questioned him about the state of public opinion in the capital.

'I'm afraid nearly all the rumours you've been hearing about your own fate are based on truth,' he told them. 'The Boers are after your blood. In a hotel in Pretoria at lunch-time I heard a number of their commandants demanding that each of the Johannesburg ringleaders should have a

324

hole drilled through him. That was the exact expression. Seriously, gentlemen, I think you've a good chance of being shot if you're taken to Pretoria. Your arrest, I assure you, will be no mere formality.'

Somebody suggested that they ought to disguise themselves and get across the Natal frontier. They could be out of danger in a few hours. The four men concerned – Phillips, Rhodes, Farrar and Hammond – discussed the idea briefly among themselves, and turned it down unanimously. They had started this; they would see it through.

At a quarter to ten on Thursday night the Republican Police, with seventy-two arrest warrants, moved in on the members of the Reform Committee. They were scattered all over Johannesburg. Some, like Frank Rhodes and Sam Jameson, were in their surburban homes; others were drinking with their friends in various pubs and hotels where business was back to normal; the largest and most distinguished group was in the Rand Club lingering over an after-dinner brandy, playing billiards or poker.

Hays Hammond waited alone with his wife in their room at Heath's Hotel. Like most of the others he had left word for the police where he would be during the evening. Below them the hotel dining-room was noisy and gay with an Australian banquet. Suddenly the revelry stopped and in the silence they could hear a voice calling out the names of the men wanted.

'That'll be the "Zarps",' Hammond said. 'They'll be up here soon. I think we'd better start getting a few things ready.'

Mrs Hammond busied herself packing a small suitcase with necessities and a few luxuries like eau-de-cologne and lavender water. She filled his jacket pockets with slabs of chocolate and sticks of barley sugar. Then they sat hand in hand, and waited for the knock on the door.

Colonel Rhodes was fast asleep when the banging finally dragged him out of the deep sleep of exhaustion. The young police lieutenant was polite and apologetic.

'Sorry about the noise, Colonel. We couldn't wake you up.'

'It's entirely my fault, Lieutenant. We've been a little short of sleep lately. Care for a drink?'

'No, thank you, sir. Some other time, perhaps.'

325

'Then make yourself comfortable while I get dressed. On second thoughts, would you mind filling this with some books for me to take along?'

He passed over an empty portmanteau.

'You'll find them in the library. Second door on the left down the passage. Doesn't matter which books. As many as you can get in.'

This demonstration of military preparedness was good strategy but bad tactics. As many of the other Reformers discovered, whose wives had filled their valises with toilet luxuries in heavy cut-glass bottles, and cans of exotic foods, it is a long walk from Pretoria station to the gaol.

Andrew Trimble was in his office, winding up the affairs of his private police force. In a corner of the room were stacked a dozen rifles handed in that day by the last of the sentries he had posted to guard the banks in the town. His mind was turning over the possibilities of escape. He didn't care much for being imprisoned and shot – and his own intelligence service had made it known to him that there was an excellent chance of this happening. He was well aware that he was a marked man; but first there were all these incriminating papers. And there were all the accounts of his expenditure to be collated. He reckoned he had until dawn...

The heavy footsteps coming up the stairs shortly before ten o'clock took him by surprise, but he welcomed the 'Zarp' officer pleasantly.

'Hullo, Doyle. It's nice to see you back on duty again. What can I do for you?'

'Mr Trimble, I have a warrant for your arrest.'

'A warrant for my arrest? Well, I can't say I'm altogether astonished. But you'd better let me see it. We policemen have got to observe all the formalities, eh?'

He took the proffered warrant and studied it carefully.

'Well, Doyle, it seems to be in order ... Wait a minute! "January 10"? It's not the tenth – it's the ninth! Somebody's made a mistake – or you're two hours early. Look for yourself.'

Doyle looked at the date, and said glumly:

'That's right enough, Mr Trimble. Those bloody fools in the office! What the hell do I do now?'

'Well, you can make yourself comfortable next door for a

couple of hours. You'll find a couch in there, and a drink in the cupboard. Make yourself at home.'

'Well, that's very kind of you, Mr Trimble, but I think I'd better go back to the office and get this put right. If they've made the same mistake on all the warrants...'

'I hadn't thought of that,' Trimble said. 'Yes, that's what you'd better do. I'll get on with my work in the meantime. Got a lot to do. See you later then, Doyle.'

'Yes. I'll be back soon. And Mr Trimble, don't try to get away. I've got my men all round the building.'

'Now why should I want to get away?' Trimble asked blandly – wondering how the devil he was going to reach the Natal border with every 'Zarp' in the countryside looking for him.

As Doyle left the room, one of the two policemen who had come up with him stepped close to Trimble and whispered urgently: 'You'd better make a run for it. They're going to have you shot.'

Trimble needed no further urging. The dramatic opportunities of the situation were just to his liking. From a locked trunk in a corner of the office he carefully selected one of his numerous disguises. Twenty minutes later an old, bearded Boer in slouch hat and long overcoat slipped out of the front door and saw, in the gloom, men standing at the heads of their horses, encircling the building. The old man paused on the steps, looked up at the sky; immersing himself completely in the histrionic possibilities, he murmured: 'I, Andrew Trimble, do solemnly and sincerely swear that I will not be taken alive but will fight unto the last drop of my blood, God help me!' Then he patted the two Webley revolvers in the pockets of his overcoat, and the two Lee-Metford bayonets concealed beneath it in his belt, and walked across to the waiting policemen.

'That is a nice horse,' he said fluently in 'the Taal'. 'Would you sell him to me?'

'If it was mine I would,' the policeman said. 'But it is not mine. It belongs to the Government. Therefore I cannot sell it to you.'

'Ah, yes. To the Government. All the best things belong to the Government. Except the gold mines. Now, why do not the gold mines belong to the Government? Then we could all have nice horses for nothing.'

'Perhaps they will soon – when this trouble is over.'

'It is a nice horse, truly!' said the old Boer, passing his hand over withers and flank as he edged along it. Then with a final, affectionate pat on its rump, he was gone into the night.

Two days later a very dishevelled Boer stepped from the Johannesburg train on to the station at the coal-mining town of Newcastle in Natal; and, to the astonishment of the station staff and other onlookers, proceeded to tear off his long, white beard.

When Lieutenants de Korte and Pietersen were detailed to make the arrests of all the Reformers on the list who happened to be in the Rand Club that night, they prepared a careful plan for surrounding the block and its exits. Then, with about twenty 'Zarps' stationed at strategic points, the two officers commandeered a carriage and drove up to the front door of the Club.

There they were met by Preston, the Head Porter – a fearless defender of the institution's privileges and exclusiveness.

' 'Ullo, Lieutenant!' he said cheerfully. 'Nice evening.'

'Not so nice as you might think, Mr Preston. Do you mind if we come in?'

'I didn't know you two were members?'

Pietersen waved a list of names in Preston's face, and a handful of official-looking documents.

'These are the names of some people we would like to see – and these are the warrants for their arrest. We believe that many of them are here, now, so —'

'I'm sorry, Lieutenant. This is a private club. You can only come in 'ere if you're a member, or at the invitation of a member. Them's the rules, and I 'ave to obey 'em.'

'Preston, you know what a warrant is? It gives us the right to enter and search the premises. And if you don't get out of the way damn quick there'll be a warrant out for you, too! Now, move aside.'

'Tell you what, Lieutenant. Come in and sit down. I think this is a matter for the chairman. I'll send for 'im.'

He showed the two policemen into the spacious entrance hall, where they refused his offer of a couple of plush armchairs. Then he walked across to where two page boys were staring curiously at the officers.

'Boy, tell Mr Buckland there's two police gentlemen want

328

to see 'im urgent in the 'all!'

He added in a whisper: 'Get 'old of Mr Bailey and Mr Farrar and the others and tell 'em the "Zarps" are 'ere to arrest the 'ole Reform Committee. Tell 'em to get to 'ell out by the back door!'

'And you can tell them,' said Lieutenant de Korte, who had sauntered over, 'that there are two of my men outside the back door and every other door.'

Preston shrugged his shoulders in resignation and disgust.

'Just go to the billiard room and the card room, boy, and let 'em all know the "Zarps" have come for 'em.'

Preston's good intentions would have been wasted. None of the Reform Committee wanted to evade arrest. Soon the hallway and entrance were filled with a jovial crowd insisting on being arrested and removed there and then to gaol. Many of them were carrying carefully prepared bags and packages; some who found they were not on the wanted list considered it an insult and clamoured to be arrested with the others.

The 'Zarps', who had been prepared for everything except this, now found themselves in a certain difficulty.

'We have only one carriage,' Pietersen said apologetically. 'We cannot take more than six of you to the gaol at a time.'

Dr Sauer pressed forward.

'My carriage is just round the corner. You can borrow that. At a shilling a mile, of course. Preston; send a page for my carriage. That'll take care of twelve of us, Lieutenant. The rest will have to wait until the carriages come back.'

'Thank you, doctor,' Pietersen said gravely. 'There are, I think, twenty-two of you present. We will do it in two journeys. Now if the first twelve gentlemen will step this way —'

'Just a minute, Lieutenant!' Abe Bailey said. 'We've got time for a night-cap. It may be a long time before we can get another one. Why don't you join us?'

The policeman shook his head, but said pleasantly:

'You can have ten minutes. And if I were you I wouldn't just *drink*. The arrangements up at the gaol are not very satisfactory.'

So the crowd of Reformers bustled into the bar for their Scotches and brandies, stuffing their pockets with bottles and cigars. Their hilarious mood did not change as they clambered into the coaches outside and clattered noisily through the night, up Hospital Hill to the gaol that was built like a fort above the town. Bailey's final gesture was to thrust a thick wad of notes into Preston's hands.

'You can bribe these Boers to do anything. As soon as you find out what's happening to us see that we're well supplied with food and drink. No champagne – unless you can get some ice to go with it. And Preston, we'll need some cricket gear; bats, pads and two or three balls. Let us all pray it won't be necessary to ask you to bring us some footballs.'

The round-up of the Reform Committee went on during the night until it was impossible to accommodate any more in the limited facilities of the gaol. Then those not already arrested – about twenty of them – were told they would have to wait until the following morning, when they should assemble at Park Station at ten o'clock to go by special train to Pretoria. Not only all the wanted men kept the appointment; they were joined by half a dozen others who insisted on accompanying the prisoners. Fred Hamilton, editor of *The Star*, sent several messages to police headquarters inquiring whether he was wanted by them. He then addressed a note to Lieutenant Pietersen at Park Station suggesting that somebody had better come and arrest him before it was too late. Pietersen replied that if he hurried he would be just in time to catch the train. Hamilton immediately hired a cab and rushed to the station, where after a brief argument at the entrance over the matter of a ticket, he was able to jump on the prison train as it was moving off.

The first batch of prisoners were the lucky ones. They were taken over to Pretoria at dawn and were slipped through the quiet streets to the prison before the townsfolk had become aware of what was happening. But by breakfast time the news had spread throughout the district that another consignment of Reformers would be arriving later that morning.

The second contingent had a foretaste of what was in store for them when, at every station at which the train stopped en route to Pretoria, bands of burghers and their families gathered to hurl abuse, mealie cobs and over-ripe peaches at the compartments in which the prisoners were packed.

330

By the time the train reached Pretoria a large and ill-tempered mob had gathered outside the station and pressed threateningly around the Johannesburgers as they formed up and marched off in a column towards the gaol. An inadequate mounted escort clattered in front and behind them, doing their best to clear a way through the hostile crowd. The first stone that came sailing over into the target of prisoners was the signal for a barrage of rock and refuse, and for a rush at the men from the Rand by those nearest them. Soon a wild fight had broken out, with the confusion increased by the desperate efforts of the escort to give protection to their charges. All they succeeded in doing was to trample half a dozen prisoners under the horses' hooves. As the temper and pressure of the mob mounted, the officer-in-command yelled at the prisoners to run for it. This they did, while the escort strove with some success to prevent pursuit. The Reformers arrived at the prison gates breathless and dishevelled; their precious packages were scattered along the road. Those not so fortunate were roughly handled by the crowd and spat upon by the womenfolk. One or two, beaten senseless, were brought in over the rumps of police horses.

There could not have been any among them who had thought they would ever be glad to hear a prison gate clang shut behind them. The howling of the mob beat in waves of angry sound against the walls of their captivity. In fact, there was double reason for this feeling of strange security. Lionel Phillips was one of several who had been warned that his life was in danger – not from the Boers, but from the Uitlanders. The Johannesburg mob was almost as disgusted with the Reform leaders as were the burghers of Pretoria, and there was genuine relief among their business and mining associates when all were safely locked away.

As far as the prisoners were concerned, the relief was short-lived. Pretoria gaol had been built by the British during their brief occupation and it was not intended to hold more than a score or so of African criminals, or white people of a comparative level. It was certainly not expected that the cells would have to hold more than sixty of Johannesburg's most prominent citizens – engineers, doctors, dentists, company directors, lawyers, school teachers, business men, hoteliers. The Young Men's Christian Association was well represented, and there was at least one Sunday School superintendent.

They were split up into small groups and herded into cells in which there was barely room for them to lie down alongside each other. Not that they wanted to; the floors were full of ordure, vermin and insects left behind by previous occupants. Many could not bring themselves to lie down at all until they literally dropped with weakness and fatigue.

Phillips, Farrar, Hammond and Frank Rhodes were put together in a cell ten feet by ten. The four canvas stretchers were in the same condition as the floor – but a little softer to lie on. The only ventilation was a narrow iron grille above the door. At six o'clock in the evening this door was locked, and not re-opened until six the next morning. As Hays Hammond was suffering from dysentery the nights could not have been called restful; but these four were better off than most of the others.

The imprisonment which had started on a note of celebration and hilarity – with one of the Rand Club members asking the head gaoler for the complaints book – ended in misery and the suicide of one of the prisoners.

Jameson and five of his officers were lodged in the same gaol. No contact was possible between the two groups, and Jameson gave no sign of wanting to have any. The six men were visited by Younghusband, who reported that the Doctor appeared to be the most crushed and broken man in the whole prison and that he and all his officers felt they had been deserted by the men who had sent for them.

With Johannesburg disarmed, the whole Reform Committee locked up and the Jameson raiders awaiting the disposal of his mercy, Kruger thought the time opportune to make an attempt to come to terms with the Uitlanders and bring them back into the Republican fold. He addressed a final appeal, 'to all the residents of Johannesburg', which appeared in the first edition of *The Star*:

'I, S. J. P. Kruger, State President of the South African Republic, with the advice and consent of the Executive Council, by virtue of Article 6 of the Minutes of the Council, dated January 10th, 1896, do hereby make known to all the residents of Johannesburg and neighbourhood that I am inexpressibly thankful to God that the despicable and treacherous incursion into my country has been prevented, and the independence of the Republic saved, through the courage and bravery of my burghers.

'The persons who have been guilty of this crime must naturally be punished according to law, that is to say, they must stand their trial before the High Court and a jury; but there are thousands who have been misled and deceived, and it has clearly appeared to me that even among the so-called leaders of the movement, there are many who have been deceived.

'A small number of intriguers in and outside the country ingeniously incited a number of the residents of Johannesburg and surroundings to struggle, under the guise of standing up for political rights, and day by day, as it were, urged them on, and when in their stupidity they thought that the moment had arrived, they (the intriguers) caused one Dr Jameson to cross the boundary of the Republic.

'Did they ever ask themselves to what they were exposing you? I shudder when I think what bloodshed could have resulted had a merciful Providence not saved you and my burghers. I will not refer to the financial damage.

'Now I approach you with full confidence; work together with the Government of this Republic and strengthen their hands to make this country a land wherein people of all nationalities may reside in common brotherhood.

'For months and months I have planned which changes and reforms could have been considered desirable in the Government and the State, but the loathsome agitation, especially of the press, has restrained me. The same men who have publicly come forward as leaders have demanded reforms from me, and in a tone and a manner which they would not have ventured to have done in their own country, owing to fear for the criminal law. For that cause, it was made impossible for me and my burghers, the founders of this Republic, to take their preposterous proposals in consideration.

'It is my intention to submit a Draft Law, at the first ordinary session of the Raad, whereby a municipality with a mayor at the head, would be granted to Johannesburg, to whom the control of the city will be entrusted. According to all constitutional principles, the Municipal Board will be elected by the people of the town.

333

'I earnestly request you, laying your hands on your hearts, to answer me this question: After what has happened, can and may I submit this to the representatives of the people? My reply is, I know there are thousands in Johannesburg and the suburbs to whom I can entrust such elective powers. Inhabitants of Johannesburg, render it possible for the Government to go before the Volksraad with the motto "Forgotten and Forgiven".'

They were, on the whole, words of peace and surprising tolerance, but in order to emphasize that all was not yet forgotten or forgiven, Kruger ordered Cronje's Commando – the one that had defeated and captured Jameson – to parade through the streets of Johannesburg on Saturday morning. It was a studied insult which might have had violent consequences but which produced nothing more vehement from the Uitlanders lining the streets than a few ribald sarcasms, which were given even more ribald answers – to which the Afrikaans language is peculiarly well adapted.

The Government newspaper, *De Volkstem*, printed ominously an account of the Slagter's Nek affair, when four Cape farmers were hanged by the British for resisting arrest after flogging an African slave. As this had taken place eighty years before, readers were left to draw their own conclusions about the need for its publication at that particular moment.

The absence of demonstrable ill-feeling by the Johannesburgers at this sort of provocation was due less to the restraint of the populace than to their loss of confidence in their own leaders, and to the characteristic resilience of the town to shock and disaster. The whole impetus of Johannesburg was the making of money, and there was a desperate anxiety, after the Jameson Raid, to return to a condition of money-making as soon as possible.

This resilience was never better displayed than at this time. Early on Wednesday morning the speculators – predators and carrion – were back Between The Chains; High 'Change was resumed, all stocks being marked up for the first time in weeks. Barricades were removed, boards taken down from plate-glass windows. Customers flowed in and out of shops, offices and bars. In Market Square the drooping spans of oxen lay yoked and passive in the daybreak before their wagon-loads of produce, while the Boers and their womenfolk happily exchanged recent enmity for the friendship of Uitlander gold.

The commercial banks, to their great relief, found that more people were beginning to deposit money than take it out. At the beginning of the crisis there had been a rush to withdraw funds and to exchange paper currency for gold. One farmer had collected 8,000 golden sovereigns and, when warned by the cashier of the dangers he risked, said he was going to put it back deep in the earth of his farm – 'where it belonged', Fortunately in all the banks paper currency was well supported by gold, and there was no panic.

The Jameson Raid can be said to have ended officially when Lord Hawke's team of English cricketers arrived in Johannesburg; on January 13 they were taken out in carriages, before the day's play began, to inspect the scene of the battle of Doornkop and the very spot on which the white flag had been waved to signify Jameson's surrender.

In Pretoria the prisoners were allowed to receive visits from wives and relations, and to have their meals supplied – at their own expense – from the Pretoria Club. As it was reckoned there were about £30,000,000-worth of high-living Johannesburgers in gaol, the club's bar and kitchen takings for that month were the highest ever recorded.

The prisoners tried desperately, and successfully, to make the best of their miserable physical surroundings. They were sustained by the attitude and courage of their four leaders and by the knowledge that only a few hundred yards away Her Majesty's High Commissioner was negotiating for their release and a better deal for Johannesburg. That would make it all worthwhile.

On the morning of January 14, Sir Hercules Robinson called on Kruger. He was anxious to have this business concluded, so that he could get back to Cape Town. His mission, he felt, had been accomplished. He had come up to prevent fighting between Johannesburg and Pretoria, and to secure the best terms he could for Jameson and his men. Well, Johannesburg was not now in a position to fight, and the Boers had undertaken not to; the price of this arrangement was the surrender of Jameson and his force to the Imperial authority for trial. No one could have made a better job of a bad situation – in spite of Chamberlain's querulous cables.

Robinson was well-pleased with himself, and that little doctor – what was his name? Veale – had done his leg more good than all the specialists of London and Cape Town put together. But there was urgent business to be settled in Cape Town. Who was going to succeed Cecil Rhodes? The thought of an Africa without Rhodes brooding over it was beyond Robinson's comprehension. There would be an inquiry, of course. As for the Reform Committee, they'd have to submit to justice by trial. After all, they had committed or were ready to commit an act of rebellion against the Government of a friendly State...

The President and the High Commissioner settled themselves into cool, cane chairs on the wide stoep. Two old men together, respecting each other's age, position and opinion. For ten minutes they chatted perfunctorily about weather, crops and cattle, while the coffee cups were filled and refilled and pipe-smoke drifted away towards the Market Square and Robinson tried to conceal his distaste as the President spat meditatively into a hydrangea bush flowering in all its midsummer glory. Christmas bushes, they called them, up on the high-veld.

Kruger, his throat and mind now clear of superfluities, turned to the interpreter sitting between the two men. Jabbing the stem of his pipe at Robinson in a characteristic gesture, he said carefully:

'Tell him that, in my opinion, there is every reason for thinking that the complications at Johannesburg are approaching an end and that there need be no longer any fear of further bloodshed.'

'I am glad to hear Your Honour using such words,' Robinson responded more directly. 'They coincide with my own impression. As far as I am concerned there are only three matters outstanding. One is the arrangements to be made for handing over Dr Jameson and his force; the second is the matter of the Johannesburg prisoners; the third concerns assurances already given respecting the demands of the Uitlanders.'

His Honour stared up at a corner of the roof as the interpreter concluded his wholly unnecessary translation.

'Tell him,' said Kruger again, 'that the arrangements for Jameson are his business, not mine. They will be handed over when there is someone to hand them over to, and when a suitable escort is made available to take them down to the ship at Durban. As he may know, our gaol accommodation is a little overcrowded at the moment, and I do not want to keep them longer than I have to. But nor do I want them running loose all over the Transvaal. As far as the Johannesburg prisoners are concerned I do not consider this is any way the business of the British Government.'

Kruger jabbed his pipe three times towards the High Commissioner.

'Tell him we have documents proving that there was a widespread plot to seize the Government of the Republic and even the person of the President and to incorporate my country with the British South Africa Company. He knows what I mean by that, and perhaps I do not have to tell it to him. As to the third point, the Volksraad have already agreed in principle to the appointment of a municipal council for Johannesburg, and I have already made known this intention to the people. But they must first prove that they can be trusted to handle their own affairs. In any event, nothing can be done until the results of the trials are known.'

Robinson nodded glumly as the translation proceeded. There was nothing he could do to alter the course of events. Kruger had right on his side and – at the place where it mattered at the moment – might. Better make the best of a bad job.

'I am sure I can rely on Your Honour and the Government of the Republic to ensure that the prisoners have a fair trial, and that you will respect the obligation to consider the grievances of the Uitlanders. As for Jameson and the others, the Governor of Natal and the General Commanding the garrison at Durban have arrived in Pretoria to arrange their transport and escort. I am glad of your cooperation in this matter.'

He waited a few seconds for the interpreter, and then added:

'Mr President, I feel my continued stay in your capital will serve no useful purpose, and I propose to return on tonight's mail train to Cape Town. If there is anything further you think I might accomplish by staying on ...'

Kruger held up his hand. Now for the first time he looked straight at Robinson as he talked.

'There is no need for you to stay, Your Excellency. I understand your anxiety to get back. I will make arrangements for a special coach to be attached to the Cape train. I would like to take this opportunity of thanking you for myself and on behalf of my Government for the help you have given in preventing further bloodshed and on the manner in which you have fulfilled the object of your visit. Your efforts, I may say, were the subject of a vote of thanks in the Volksraad last night.'

He heaved himself to his feet with one hand pressing heavily and familiarly on the bible on the table beside him. Then the two old men moved towards each other and shook hands. There was nothing more to be said beyond the mumbled compliments and good-byes.

CHAPTER TWENTY-SEVEN

By the end of the month all the members of the Reform Committee except Phillips, Farrar, Frank Rhodes, Hammond and Percy FitzPatrick had been released on bail of £2,000 each and on condition they did not leave Pretoria. But Hammond's physical condition had deteriorated rapidly as his dysentery worsened.

The preliminary examination of the whole Committee began on February 3 and dragged on interminably throughout the month. The proceedings were officially described by the State Prosecutor as 'fishing for evidence', and as everybody knew that this preliminary performance would have no effect whatever on the subsequent trial, all concerned soon became bored stiff with the whole business. Besides, they had something else to absorb their attention.

On Sunday, February 16, a train of eight trucks each filled with dynamite was shunted gently into a goods siding at Braamfontein station. This was the nearest rail point to the magazines over the Braamfontein ridge where the concessionaires stored their dynamite before delivery to the mines. There was a brief argument between the yard foreman and the consignee's representatives, who pointed out that it was useless unloading any of the cases, as the magazines were already filled beyond their capacity; the dynamite would have to stay where it was until storage space could be found for it. They were making daily deliveries to the mines, so it would not be long before they unloaded.

There were 2,300 cases on that train, each holding 60 lb of dynamite. For three days they lay there in the February sun – the hottest sun of the year, in Johannesburg. Around them life in the densely-populated slum districts of the township – the Brickfields and the coloured locations of Fordsburg and the 'Malay location' – pursued its hungry, dishevelled course.

On Wednesday afternoon a gang of labourers arrived at Braamfontein station with their mule wagons to begin unloading the dynamite. One wagon had already been loaded and dispatched to the magazines when it became necessary to move the trucks to another part of the siding. The busy little shunting engine came bustling up and backed with the confidence of long familiarity towards the coupling. A little fast, perhaps...

It was fourteen minutes past three. Mrs van der Merwe was standing at the threshold of her tumble-down house in Fordsburg with one infant in her arms suckling at a copious breast; another child clung to her skirts for support. Next-door, her neighbour was working at a sewing machine set in the shade of an improvised front porch. They filled the space between them with the ceaseless, universal gossip of housewives everywhere...

The Circuit Court was in session in Government Square. Mr Justice de Korte had just taken his seat. The public gallery grew silent as the two reporters at the Press table opened their notebooks and the prisoner took the stand to give evidence. An official handed him a Bible: 'Do you swear that the evidence...'

Out at the Marist Brothers School a class was in the new gymnasium, equipped by public donation, getting instruction from a Hollander just out from Amsterdam in the intricacies of movement on horizontal bars, vaulting horse and rings. Other boys were slashing and poking at each other with single-sticks and fencing foils...

Over in the newly laid-out Agricultural Showground, about a mile from Braamfontein Station, a labourer was making a hole for one of the trees that were being planted to make avenues of shade in a land where nearly all the shadows, except at dawn and sunset, were man-made. And in the smart suburb of Doornfontein, at exactly the same moment, little Jacky Hammond was digging a hole in the garden...

Around the dynamite trucks the Kaffirs and coloured men and mule drivers paused in their labours while the shunting engine came fussing up. A split second later, as the couplings hit, earth and sky exploded in a roaring cataclysm of disintegration. It was fifteen minutes past three.

Mrs van der Merwe, in mid-sentence, surveyed herself incredulously. She was lying on her back on the floor of a house which, for some reason, had collapsed all round her. Her legs were a mangled mess and one arm had completely disappeared. The other couched the baby still sucking furiously at the nipple between its lips. Of her daughter there was no trace. Mrs van der Merwe was dead when they found her. The baby kicked up hell when they pulled it gently from the breast.

In the Circuit Court a glass chandelier crashed down on the Bench in the same moment as the roar of the explosion came into the room on the blast of air that shattered windows and shook and rattled the building; Mr Justice de Korte beat the reporters to the street, in spite of the burden of wig and gown. The prisoner was last seen heading for the open veld – bible still clutched in his hand. This was the truth, the whole truth and nothing but the truth; he was never going to tell another lie.

At the showground the labourer felt rather than heard the explosion, and looked up startled at the strange, whirring noise that seemed to fill the sky. He fell on his face in the trench he was digging, heard the thud just before the earth about him quivered. After a minute filled with prayer he raised his head above the level of the trench, ducked quickly at what he saw, and then came up again rubbing his eyes in disbelief. Not ten yards from him, partly buried in what had been an empty piece of ground, lay the wheels and axle of a railway engine. (Later railway officials fenced off the spot and put a little tablet on the uppermost wheel recording the disaster.)

Little Jacky Hammond was also down in his trench. He would soon reach the gold that his father was always searching for under the ground. You couldn't dig a hole like this without finding *something*. He put his spade in deep and felt the earth shake as a great roar filled the air. He looked with astonishment at the upright spade and then clambered out, fearful and proud, to rush to his mother: 'Mummy, mummy! I've dug up hell!'

As the glass sprayed over the boys in the Marist Brothers gymnasium they heard the distant detonation and made a hectic rush for the door – with the instructor in the lead. As they came into the open they looked up in sudden fear to where the sun had turned to a dull red disc behind a mushroom of dense smoke and dust that was still rising above the township but beginning to lean away from the wind and drift over the crests of the Witwatersrand. One of the Brothers came hurriedly over and shepherded them into the chapel where they were immediately joined by the rest of the school in spontaneous if uncomprehending prayer. Two of the boys, more curious than the rest, slipped out of the door and sped away towards that writhing pillar of doom. They soon found themselves in one of many streams of people and vehicles converging on the scene of the explosion.

The first panic reaction to the combination of noise, blast and concussion brought the whole population into the streets. The terror they shared was of a volcanic eruption right under Johannesburg. Then the cry went up that the Boers were shelling the town, to be supplemented by rumour that the gasworks had blown up. Then, as the column of smoke rose above the town, the news spread that the dynamite magazines at Braamfontein had exploded. Within ten minutes, as panic subsided, there was a concerted move towards Braamfontein, and soon every cab and cart in the town and thousands on foot were hurrying to the base of the smoke.

The ramshackle suburb of Braamfontein and the even more disreputable flimsiness of the coloured locations had been almost obliterated. Where ten minutes before had stood the homes and shops, warehouses and factories of a teeming working-class district, there was now nothing but scattered sheets of corrugated iron, shattered glass, grotesque piles of timber. Whole roofs had been lifted and dropped untidily hundreds of yards from the homes they had once covered. Through the wreckage wandered battered and bewildered men and women; only the dead lay unaware and silent.

Where Braamfontein Station had once stood there was a great hole in the earth 250 feet long, 60 feet wide and about 40 feet deep. At each end of it twin sets of rails were contorted upwards; of train or trucks, wagons, mules or men there was no sign.

When the awe-stricken crowd drew close they found themselves sinking ankle-deep in loose earth as if all the ground within fifty yards of that gaping, smouldering hole had been overturned by some swift, invisible plough. Then, standing on the edge of the pit, they saw the full horror of what had happened.

Shattered fragments of wood and iron, rock and machinery, lay inextricably mixed up with mangled chunks of flesh, all battered and charred to a state in which it was almost impossible to recognize white from black, human from mule. The two boys from Marist's found a Hottentot's head perched crazily on top of a twisted paling. They could see daylight through the wide nostrils, for skull and brains had gone. They ran back to school with retching stomachs, heaving with horror and bursting with the unbelievable stories they would tell their friends.

The first shock and bewilderment spent, Johannesburg made its usual rapid recovery, and soon its capacity for organization and improvisation, and the genuine compassion which lay beneath the rugged surface, were expressing themselves in a score of rescue operations in which all the resources of the town were employed to succour the wounded and homeless and recover the dead. The hospital was soon overflowing; the Wanderers Club was turned into a second infirmary, and the roller-skating rink proved very suitable for a morgue.

In the evening a meeting was held at the Rand Club to form a Relief Committee. Before sundown £4,000 had been subscribed, and when the members of the Stock Exchange held a meeting on the following afternoon the total was soon carried past £100,000. The Government added £25,000 and the Netherlands Railway Company £10,000. This latter contribution was regarded in Johannesburg as conscience money – particularly when it was discovered that the truck into which the shunting engine had backed had been loaded with detonators.

When the news of the disaster reached Pretoria, Paul Kruger was as shocked and distressed as any Uitlander at the extent and violence of the explosion. In addition to instructing the Executive to arrange immediate assistance, he made a personal visit to the scene of the tragedy on Thursday morning.

News of his coming spread rapidly through the devastated town so that several thousand people were at Park Station when his train arrived. They formed a solemn avenue along the few hundred yards which separated the presidential coach from the nauseous pit of death. Kruger stood on the edge of it, silent and tight-lipped, while the known details of the accident were explained to him. Then,

343

speechless, he turned away to the carriage waiting to take him around the stricken area and on to the hospital and the improvised wards at the Wanderers.

Braamfontein, Fordsburg and the Brickfields had caught the full blast. They were chiefly slum areas housing natives and half-castes and 'poor-white' Africaners living on the decrepit fringes of Johannesburg's gold-plush society. The shattered streets and alleys were now peopled only by huddled groups of homeless and bereaved, or by sad, solitary figures moving among the ruins, scratching among the rubble, in hopeless search for some loved one who had simply disappeared. It was not always hopeless. One little girl was found three days after the explosion, beneath the tumbled framework of her home, rolled up in a length of carpet and suffering from a cut finger. She complained of being thirsty and hungry.

Kruger, on his way past the long rows of beds each bearing mangled and burnt but still living flesh, was obviously moved by deep compassion. He stopped frequently to mutter a few words of consolation or a quick prayer, or hastily to wipe his eyes with a large bandana handkerchief. It was clear from the simple, sincere speech he made at the end, thanking all those who had contributed so much to the work of healing and rescue and recovery, that he was conscious of the gulf that had been bridged in this calamity between people of all races and colour.

The President's comment was of typical simplicity. 'Blessed are the merciful,' he said, 'for they shall receive mercy.'

The quality of mercy was a little strained as the time of the Reformers' trial approached. The President's greatest difficulty lay in finding a suitable judge. The Chief Justice and his associates had been deeply involved in all the matters concerned with the Jameson Raid, and two of them had been members of the commission which had received the Uitlander deputation – an occasion which had provided such vital evidence against the accused. There was, in fact, no suitable Transvaal judge available.

But did Kruger and his executive, or any other burgher of the republic, want an unbiased judge? In spite of the *Grondwet*, or Constitution, the line between judicial and legislative functions was very roughly drawn. The Volksraad, by majority resolution, frequently took decisions which they considered should have the immediate effect of law – even when they were contrary to the articles of the *Grondwet*. The Courts then had to decide, if appealed to, whether the hasty resolutions of the Raad or the articles of the *Grondwet* were paramount.

The Courts, in most cases, tried to maintain the authority and independence of the law. The Boer legislators, including their leaders, often had great difficulty in recognizing and acknowledging the absolute independence of the Courts, and were frequently in conflict with them.

So that although Kruger was concerned with the appearance of impartiality in the trial of the Uitlanders, it never entered his head that the presiding judge should be completely unbiased, any more than that he should be biased in favour of the prisoners. In this restricted field it was almost inevitable that Kruger should find his solution in the sister republic of the Orange Free State, and in the middle of April it was announced that Mr Gregorowski, the State Attorney on Bloemfontein, would preside at the trial.

Judge Gregorowski made no attempt to conceal the fact that, given the opportunity, he would see that armed rebellion against the State would get the punishment it deserved. A rumour flashed around the Witwatersrand that the first question he had asked of his Transvaal colleagues was: 'Do you have a black cap in Pretoria?'

The Reformers themselves, as a result of the preliminary proceedings, were confident that the charge of high treason could not be sustained. It was not until the Transvaal State Attorney, Mr H. J. Coster, revealed to Advocate Wessels, the defence counsel, the nature of the evidence accumulated against the accused, that they began to realize what they were up against.

Major Bobby White's dispatch-box, captured at Doornkop, contained not only a copy of the letter to Jameson but diaries, orders of the day, copies of all messages to and from Jameson, and code-books and cipher keys. When Coster then produced a file of Lionel Phillips' correspondence taken from his desk at Hohenheim, Wessels could see that the game was up and a successful defence impossible.

Whatever instructions were given to the State Attorney, they are not on record; but there was no doubt that first and foremost the trial of the Reformers was a political instrument, and Kruger's political purpose could certainly not have been served by the mass execution of over sixty Uitlanders who included the heads of some of the most important mining and finance houses in the world.

He wanted the guilt of the Uitlanders on a charge of high treason established before the bar of world opinion. Whatever Judge Gregorowski's sentence was, the presidential prerogative could subsequently be employed. Defence counsel and prosecutor had a long conference . . .

The trial was fixed for April 24 in the Market Hall at Pretoria. A week before this date Mrs Phillips came on one of her regular visits to the cottage where three of the ringleaders, joined by FitzPatrick, were confined. Hays Hammond, seriously ill with dysentery, had been permitted to go down to the more amenable climate of Cape Town on bail of £20,000 – for which Barney Barnato acted as surety.

'When Mrs Phillips arrived she could see that an intense discussion was going on in the dining-room between the prisoners and their counsel. Among them was Mr James Rose-Innes, Q.C., leader of the Bar in the Cape Colony, who had been briefed to appear on behalf of the Imperial Government. Eventually Phillips left the group and came out on to the veranda where his wife was waiting.

'Listen, Florence,' he said gravely. 'You reproached me before because I couldn't tell you everything. Now there's something which I think you ought to know. We've decided that the four principal prisoners are to plead guilty.'

'Guilty!' Mrs Phillips was aghast. 'Guilty to high treason?'

'I'm afraid so, my dear. We know now the nature of the evidence against us. It's overwhelming. There'd be no sense in disputing it. Not only Bobby White's papers but all my own correspondence, taken from my desk at home.'

'But you *can't* plead guilty, Lionel! They'll hang you, or shoot you!'

Phillips shook his head and smiled. Then he put his arm about her waist.

'It's not as bad as that, my dear. But what I tell you now is in absolute confidence. You must not breathe a word of it to anyone. Otherwise we'll end up in a noose.'

He kissed her gently on the cheek as she dabbed away with her handkerchief.

'Now listen carefully, Florence, and you'll understand our predicament. There are four indictments – and they've been served on all the accused. The first concerns the invitation to Dr Jameson to invade the Transvaal; the second accuses us of inciting the people of Johannesburg to assist him; the third is to do with the distribution of arms and ammunition; lastly, there's a charge of forming and arming our own police force.'

'But don't you see, if you plead guilty —'

'Wait till I've finished, my dear, then I think you'll understand. We are faced with three options. We can plead not guilty to all the indictments and enter a long-drawn-out trial before a hostile judge and jury in which every statement in our defence would be regarded as another attack on the State; the second choice would be to refuse to plead at all, and the third is to plead guilty and take a short cut on the best terms we can get to what is virtually a prearranged conclusion.'

'Prearranged? How d'you mean, prearranged?'

'That's what we've just been discussing. Wessels and Coster have had a meeting, and the State Attorney has made him an offer. If we four – that is the four who signed the letter to Jameson – agree to plead guilty to the first indictment, he'll withdraw counts two, three and four. In that case he'll ask the rank and file – that's what he called them – to plead guilty to three and four, and withdraw the first two charges. After very careful consideration – and a good deal of argument, let me say – it seemed to us that a plea of guilty would be best for all concerned; and especially for the remaining sixty-three who'd then only receive a nominal punishment. There's also the fact that in doing so we would not be compelled to offer testimony incriminating Dr Jameson, who has still to be tried.'

'Why should you worry about Jameson?' Mrs Phillips burst out. 'He and his officers have done nothing but incriminate you from the moment this affair started! Don't do it, Lionel! *Don't* plead guilty! It's just another trap for you, like the one you walked into before!'

'You're being selfish, Florence. This is a unanimous decision – in the interests of all. Look, I must go now. There's still a great deal to be discussed. You'll feel better about this when you've had time to think it over.'

Mrs Phillips walked sadly away, unable to check the tears

that were both for the present and the future. Percy Fitz-Patrick ran after her to the gate, comforting her with what words he could find.

'But don't you *see*, Percy?' she pleaded desperately. 'They intend to hang the four of you!'

CHAPTER TWENTY-EIGHT

No court in Pretoria was large enough to hold all the prisoners at one time, let alone the crowds of burghers and Uitlanders who were determined to make of the occasion a Roman holiday. Above all other interests, the Johannesburgers wanted to get the affair over. Almost every prominent man in the mining, commercial and professional life of the town was involved directly or indirectly in the trial. No part of the community could function efficiently as long as so many of its leaders were in prison, on bail or dashing to and fro between the Witwatersrand and the capital.

Not the least of their worries was the possibility of confiscation of property as part of the punishment; but they reassured themselves with the thought that so much overseas capital was invested in the Rand that Kruger would not dare to appropriate any of it. Taking their lives was one thing; taking their money was quite another – and it would less easily be forgiven.

There was only one building in Pretoria large enough to stage the trial: the great brick and galvanized-iron construction of the Market Hall. The Government went to a great deal of trouble to convert this vast cubic void, redolent with all the smells of the farmyard, into a court-room worthy of the majesty of the Law and the historic event.

A wooden platform, one foot high and about fifteen yards by thirty yards, covered the concrete in the centre of the hall. A balustrade was erected all around the perimeter, and against the wall of the building a canopied dais for the judge was hammered into place.

In the enclosed rectangle of the platform were placed the seats and tables for prosecuting and defence counsel and their assistants, a row of school desks for the Press and chairs for the jury and distinguished spectators. Several ranks of benches in a sort of pen indicated where the sixty-three accused would be seated. Outside the exclusive arena more rows of flat benches provided accommodation for the public. Two enormous glass chandeliers, suspended from the top of that cavernous dome, added a touch of incongruous splendour to the drab tin and woodwork.

The prisoners made a brief formal appearance on Friday, April 24, to be arraigned, after which an adjournment was made until Monday to permit the arrival of Hays Hammond and one or two others from Cape Town.

An hour before the trial began fifty armed troopers of the Republican Police were marched down from their barracks and disposed inside and outside the market buildings. Within another half-hour the interior of the hall was filled with a noisy, colourful mob all pressing and jostling for the favoured seats. The womenfolk of Johannesburg and Pretoria were out in force, with new hats and dresses bought specially for the occasion, vying with each other for the attention of friendly barristers or court officials to secure chairs near judge or prisoners. The latter filed noisily in, exchanging jovial greetings with friends who filled the hall beyond the enclosure, and grabbing at newspapers and letters which were handed to them despite the guards' disapproval.

A deep voice shouted above the din – its words unintelligible but its meaning plain. In sudden silence the door from the market-master's office opened; the diminutive Judge Gregorowski stepped on to the dais, and, after bowing to the counsel clustered before him, perched himself under the heavy canopy. Wives and friends of the accused saw a lean, saturnine face, hooked nose, hairless head sunk between narrow shoulders – a vulture waiting for its prey. They shuddered ...

The whole world of the Republic, it seemed, had grown still and silent, watching for the judge's nod that would set the drama moving. Alas, the selection of the Market Hall as the scene of the trial had been governed only by considerations of space, and not acoustics. With the first three prosecuting words of the State Attorney it became obvious that this great *cause célèbre* would be audible only in the narrow square of judge, counsel and newspapermen – enough for history but nothing for public understanding and entertainment. And perhaps not enough for justice; neither jury nor prisoners were close enough to hear, and had to be fed with passed-back morsels of evidence and argument.

It cannot be said that this made a great deal of difference to the packed rows of the Reform Committee. The air of boredom with which they had confronted their accusers ever since their arrest persisted in the courtroom. Most of them read books or papers, and the solemn air crackled with the rustling of newsprint and stimulated conversation. But the boredom was not entirely artificial. All the accused knew of the deal that had been made between Dr Coster, the State Attorney, and their own defending counsel. Their complacency was only momentarily shaken by reports of extensive preparations being made – chiefly with carbolic powder – at Pretoria gaol for the reception of a large number of prisoners.

The first formal procedure was the arraignment of Hays Hammond, followed by Hans Sauer and Woolls-Sampson, who had been absent on Friday. Hammond pleaded guilty to the charge of high treason and the other two to the charge of lese-majesty in terms of the indictment and in conformity with the action of all their fellow-prisoners.

With the agreement of the defence the proceedings of the preliminary examination were handed in unread, and the first witnesses made their brief statements as to the finding of Bobby White's dispatch-box and other incriminatory documents left by Jameson at the scene of the Doornkop surrender. Telegraph officials from Pretoria, Johannesburg and Cape Town handed in copies of all messages which had passed between the various persons concerned in the development of the conspiracy. It was only when the Cape Town clerk produced telegrams originating with the British South Africa Company that Advocate Wessels raised his first objection, claiming that the accused could not be held responsible for the acts of the British South Africa Company or what it said to Jameson. After hearing argument from both sides the judge ruled that any telegrams which might have passed between Jameson and the Chartered Company, having reference to the inroad, were admissible. The telegrams were handed in, but not read.

Albert Fleishack, chief of the civil department of the State Attorney's office, put in what he described as a copy of the letter sent by the leaders of the Reform Committee to Dr Jameson.

FLEISHACK: 'This letter was found on the person of Major

White in gaol.'

GREGOROWSKI: 'Did he not make any effort to conceal or destroy it?'

FLEISHACK: 'On the contrary, Your Honour. I may say that the State Attorney's Department has made every effort to obtain the original letter, without success. I have good reason to believe it is in England. Major White has certified that this is a correct copy.'

WESSELS: 'Are you certain that that is a correct copy?'

FLEISHACK: 'Yes.'

WESSELS: 'How do you know?'

FLEISHACK: 'Because it is certified.'

WESSELS: 'Did you see the original?'

FLEISHACK: 'No.'

WESSELS: 'Then the only reason you have for stating that it is a true copy is because White told you so?'

FLEISHACK: 'That is correct.'

WESSELS: 'Thus of I were to go and write the greatest nonsense in the world, and signed it, and informed you that it is a correct copy of a certain letter you would come and swear that it was a correct copy?'

FLEISHACK: 'No.'

WESSELS: 'As a matter of fact all you know is that White told you that the document was a copy of the original letter sent to Jameson. Can you guarantee the contents?'

GREGOROWSKI: 'Do you dispute the accuracy of the copy, Mr Wessels?'

WESSELS: 'No, Your Honour, we do not dispute the accuracy, but it is absolutely certain that the original document did not contain a date. This has a date and there are one or two other discrepancies, so we cannot admit it.'

GREGOROWSKI: 'The letter will be admitted, but the Court will bear in mind what you have said regarding the date. It is a question, Mr Wessels, of intent rather than time.'

The State Attorney then told the judge that, in view of the accused's plea, he would not call any further evidence. 'I ask Your Honour to punish the accused according to the law, taking into consideration the great seriousness of the crime they have committed, and the heavy punishment provided therefor according to the old Roman–Dutch Law.'

To the disinterested prisoners, busy with their letters and

352

newspapers and the latest Stock Exchange information passed freely from the public enclosure behind their backs, it seemed that the State Attorney was carrying out his part of the bargain and had even appeared to be anxious, during his presentation of the prosecution's case, not to stress the guilt of the Reform Committee overmuch.

Advocate Wessels, too, was satisfied that Dr Coster was faithfully conducting the case in the spirit of the arrangement made between them – until he uttered those last words: 'and the heavy punishment provided therefor according to the old Roman–Dutch Law'.

The effect on Wessels was immediate. He sat bolt upright in his chair and looked across at the State Attorney in astonishment and anger. Then he had a murmured consultation with his legal associates on the defence side and, with heads nodding agreement all round him, rose to suggest to the judge that it seemed an opportune moment for the Court to adjourn for lunch. Mr Gregorowski, after a brief look at his watch, said loudly:

'The Court will adjourn until three o'clock this afternoon,' and stepped down from the dais amid the shouts of the ushers and officials and the commotion of scraping chairs.

Wessels had two hours in which to meet the sudden challenge of those words. If the accused were to be found guilty under the terms of the Roman–Dutch Law instead of the Thirty-three Articles which the Volksraad had adopted to modify that Law for the uses of the Republic, then the prisoners could, quite literally, get it in the neck. By the time the Court reassembled, a new pile of precedent and authority was stacked in front of the defence counsel.

'Proceed, Mr Wessels,' said the judge.

'Your Honour, I will be as brief as possible but the case is of such an involved nature that I cannot give you any hope of finishing within the hour . . .'

Judge Gregorowski raised his eyebrows.

'In spite of the plea, Mr Wessels?'

'In spite of the plea, Your Honour. The accused's case rests on two written statements – one prepared and signed by the four leaders of the Reform Committee, the other by the remainder of the accused. With the Court's permission I will read them in English.'

He looked up to get the judge's quick sanction and began

reading the document signed by Phillips, Farrar, Rhodes and Hammond:

'For a number of years endeavours have been made to obtain by constitutional means the redress of grievances under which the Uitlander population labours. The new-comers asked for no more than is conceded to immigrants by all the other Governments in South Africa under which every man may, on reasonable conditions, become a citizen of the State, whilst here alone a policy is pursued by which the first settlers retain the exclusive right of government ...'

The statement went on to recapitulate the events leading up to Jameson's raid and the interchange of messages and deputations between the Government, the Reform Commit-tee and the High Commissioner: The declaration ended:

'We admit responsibility for the action taken by us. We practically avowed it at the time of the negotiations with the Government when we were informed that the services of the High Commissioner had been accepted with a view to a peaceful settlement. We submit that we kept faith in every detail in the arrangement. We did all that was humanly possible to protect both the State and Dr Jameson from the consequences of his action. We submit that we have com-mitted no breach of the law which was not known to the Government at the time; and that the earnest consideration of our grievances was promised. We can now only put the bare facts before the Court and submit to the judgment that may be passed upon us.'

Mr Wessels stopped and looked across at Dr Coster, who shook his head and motioned the defence counsel to con-tinue. Wessels picked up another sheet of paper.

'The declaration of the remaining members of the Re-form Committee, Your Honour, merely states — I quote: "We have heard the statement made by Mr Lionel Phillips and his associates and we fully agree with what they have said. We have worked with these gentlemen, and the only object all had in view was to use their utmost endeavours to avert bloodshed but at the same time to obtain the redress of what we consider very serious grievances." That is the defence case, Your Honour, and I do not propose to call any other evidence.'

He sat down, while the judge looked across to the State Attorney.

'Any questions, Dr Coster?'

'In the circumstances, Your Honour,' Dr Coster said, scarcely bothering to stand up, 'I do not think cross-examination necessary to assist the Court's decision. The plea and the statements confirm the guilt of the accused.'

Judge Gregorowski nodded his acceptance and indicated to Advocate Wessels that he should continue. Wessels had a few words with Mr Rose-Innes, sitting next to him; then he took a sip of water, and began:

'May it please Your Honour. Here we have a case in which Phillips, Farrar, Hammond and Rhodes plead guilty to a charge of high treason on the first count. The others have pleaded guilty to lese-majesty – in these circumstances a much less serious charge. Before I deal with details of the charges, so as to speak in mitigation of sentence, I would like to discuss the question of the law so that we may see not only what the law is, but *which* law it is.

'According to the broad Roman–Dutch Law, lese-majesty could be extended to a very considerable charge, but if our own local amendments – incorporated in the Thirty-three Articles – make provision for charges of high treason, it is not necessary for the Court to go to the Roman–Dutch Law for an interpretation.'

Mr Wessels opened two of the volumes before him, and quoted from Moorman and Voet in support of his contention that if the local laws imposed a lesser punishment for a serious crime than the Roman–Dutch Law, the law imposing the lesser punishment should be applied.

'In this country,' he went on, 'legislation has been enacted providing a penalty for high treason. The Court, however, is obliged when administering the law to inquire into the intention of the legislative when enacting it. When the States of Holland took over the Roman Laws and adopted them, crimes against the person of the sovereign or the State were punished in a most barbarous manner. In Holland it was the opinion of eminent jurists that these barbarous punishments were not in accordance with civilized ideas, and they were accordingly modified very considerably. In May, 1837, for instance, the punishment of confiscation of goods – even in cases of lese-majesty – was abolished.

'Now, Your Honour, whatever people might say about Afrikaners, no one could charge them with being a bloodthirsty race. They deprecate the older forms of punishment

355

and desire to be known as a peaceful and moderate people. This is surely proved in the Thirty-three Articles, which provide for a fine of five hundred rix-dollars in cases of conspiracy with foreign Powers against the State, or for acting in a treasonable manner. In these terms sentence of death cannot be passed in cases of high treason. In addition, the Volksraad has expressed itself in these Articles against outlawry and the confiscation of property.

'I submit, Your Honour, that seeing that the legislature has repeatedly declared itself against capital punishment, against outlawry and against confiscation of property in cases of high treason, it was the intention of the legislature that a milder form of punishment should always be applied.'

The four ringleaders had been leaning forward ever since Wessels had begun his address, straining to catch every word. Apart from shuffling feet and whispered comment or translation, the court-room was quiet for the first time during the trial. Hammond nudged Phillips.

'Say, Lionel, look at that guy from the Executive Committee.'

Members of the Government had chairs reserved for them immediately below and to the right of the judge, facing the jury. There was Mr Wolmarans staring at these burghers with a knowing smile on his face and shaking his head slowly all the way through defence counsel's speech.

'D'you think we ought to protest?' Phillips asked.

'Wouldn't do any good,' Hammond replied. 'Gregorowski's shaking his head, too.'

They shrugged their shoulders and devoted their attention again to their advocate. He had just finished reading out the first count of the indictment.

'What does it contain? It states that the accused had transaction with Jameson with a view to his coming into the country. It does not show that Jameson was an administrator or representative of any other country, or was in any official capacity. Jameson came in as a private citizen, but was in command of certain armed men. The clause in the Thirty-three Articles referring to treason deals specifically with conspiracy with foreign Powers. In this case the conspiracy took place with a private individual and therefore the form of punishment as applied to those conspiring with foreign Powers could not be applied. Only a lesser form of punishment would be appropriate.

'I observe that this argument does not appear to impress Your Honour – nor some of our distinguished guests.'

Here Mr Wessels looked deliberately at the members of the Executive Committee before proceeding.

'Those Thirty-three Articles adopted by an enlightened Volksraad in the early days of our Republic have never been repealed and are therefore in full force. They have, in fact, frequently been quoted by me in various cases before the highest courts in the case of Ruthven *v.* the State that in cases of that description Article Thirty-one of the Thirty-three Articles will always be applied in cases of treason.

'It is true that the basic Roman–Dutch Law enacts heavy penalties, including confiscation of property, but on page one hundred and twenty-six of the Local Laws you will find that the Volksraad repudiated these penalties altogether and said they did not consider that this punishment met with the approval of members. They said, in effect, that banishment and a fine of five hundred rix-dollars was the most stringent punishment they could tolerate. This was in the case of men conspiring with foreign Powers to assault the independence of the State. I submit it is nonsense to contemplate heavier punishment for those guilty of a lesser crime.'

'Mr Wessels,' Judge Gregorowski interrupted, 'I am under the impression that in this case the accused did conspire with a foreign Power to come into the country and take away the independence of the country.'

'With respect, Your Honour, that is not so. The State says that it accepts the plea that the accused conspired with Jameson to come into Johannesburg, but that did not imply that he was a foreign Power or that he was to attack the independence of the State. On the contrary, everything showed that there was no intent against the State. The telegrams put in this morning, and all the other evidence, in fact, show that the leaders of the Reform Committee did everything they could to prevent Jameson coming in. It is true that they were responsible to some extent because they had set the ball rolling, but they were not responsible for the battle of Doornkop.'

After a brief discourse on the Gold Law and the question of confiscation (which, he argued, the State could properly waive) Mr Wessels moved on to the grievances of the Uit-

357

landers and the conditions of their existence which they felt had become intolerable.

'Why did they conspire with Jameson? I admit it was an unfortunate move, but the people of Johannesburg genuinely believed they were being oppressed. They thought that by means of an armed demonstration in the town they would be able to draw attention to their grievances and obtain the redress which they had failed to obtain by constitutional means. There was no question of a conspiracy with the Chartered Company. Whatever the intention of Cecil Rhodes might have been, or that of the Company or Jameson, the Reform Committee had nothing to do with it. Those people might have been using the accused for their own ends, but the accused did not know it – at least, not at that time. They probably know it now.'

He looked across at the four ringleaders as if for acquiescence, but their faces remained non-committal, conceding nothing to this alien justice. Wessels went on determinedly:

'Phillips, Farrar, Hammond and Francis Rhodes are four of the most important men in Johannesburg. They were known throughout South Africa as men of experience, influence and intelligence and possessed of immense wealth. They had everything to lose by conspiring with the Chartered Company. Their interests were far from being identical. The name of Cecil Rhodes alone was enough to turn the people of Johannesburg against any movement with which he was connected, and they would have done anything rather than extend the control of Rhodes and his group to the Transvaal.

'If the accused had had the intentions which were imputed to them they could have imported twenty-five thousand rifles as easily as twenty-five hundred, and armed twenty-five thousand men. With such a force they could virtually have controlled the affairs of this country. But they did not want to overthrow the Government; they wanted justice! They had actually sworn allegiance, thanks chiefly to the accused Hammond, to the Transvaal flag. What these men did after the events of that fateful weekend is well known. The Government, far from punishing them indiscriminately, owes them a debt of gratitude for preserving law and order on the Witwatersrand and safeguarding the mines and property which are the very life-blood of the Republic.

358

'I will end by saying that I sincerely believe that these men, under the President's proclamation, are not liable to any punishment. It is not the desire of the Government that they should be severely punished. The prisoners have been under arrest for three and a half months, and the anxiety, trouble and expense to which they have been put are alone sufficient punishment. The banishment of these people will throw out of work hundreds of thousands of men and women; they employ half the population. A heavy penalty can do no good whatsoever. On the contrary it will be a source of danger and will make permanent martyrs of the prisoners.

'Your Honour, the sword of justice is entrusted to your hands. You can use it in two ways. You can use it severely and cause bitter feeling and a revival of race hatred; or you can use it mercifully and thereby restore to this unhappy land its former peace and happiness.'

He sat down to a burst of spontaneous applause which the judge tried in vain to hammer into silence with his gavel. When order was restored it was seen that the State Attorney was standing, impatiently trying to attract the judge's attention. All through defence counsel's address he had been displaying a mounting agitation and disapproval, and he now gave every indication of being a very angry prosecutor. Before he could begin speaking, however, Wessels had risen quickly to his feet.

'Your Honour, if it is my learned friend's intention to again address the Court, I must protest that in all my experience I have never known such a thing to happen except in the most exceptional circumstances. I have been pleading for mercy and it is unheard of that an attorney for the State should get up, as it were vindictively, to press home the charge.'

Judge Gregorowski smiled.

'Perhaps these circumstances could be considered exceptional. Continue, Dr Coster.'

'Counsel for the defence has given his interpretation of the law; now I will give mine. He has quoted from various authorities, but has omitted Van der Linden – the real authority for the administration of justice in this country. According to Van der Linden the punishment for sedition is death.'

The State Attorney had begun quietly enough, but with

each word his voice seemed to grow louder until it rose to a loud shout on the word 'death', which he emphasized by banging his hand on the table, like the blade of a guillotine falling. Now restraint seemed to desert him; he left his chair and began pacing the narrow space between judge and jury, punctuating a torrent of words with fierce gestures.

The rapid flow of Dutch was only decipherable by those in his immediate vicinity, but enough was audible for judge and Press to gather that he considered Jameson a bandit and freebooter, and that it was a more serious offence to conspire with freebooters than with a foreign Government. He demanded punishment in terms of the Roman–Dutch Law, and frequent use of the phrase *hangen by den nek* left those who could hear him in no doubt of the sort of punishment he was asking for. Fortunately the prisoners were all out of earshot, but not so Mrs Phillips, who covered her face with her hands as the dreadful meaning of those four words burned into her brain. Advocate Wessels could only stare at the State Attorney in astonishment and disgust. The tirade came to an end when Judge Gregorowski asked him to express an opinion on the question of confiscation of property. Dr Coster returned to his place at the table and took a long swallow from a glass of water. The dramatics were over, but not his ill-temper.

'There can be no two ways of reading the special article in the Gold Law regarding confiscation, Your Honour. It stipulates confiscation for the crime committed by the accused, and confiscation I ask for. My duty here is strictly to interpret the Law to the Court. It is for the Court to apply the Law. The Executive Council, under the President, is there for the purpose of reducing the sentence if they consider such sentence too severe. I can only demand that the accused be punished with the full severity of the law – and the Court is well aware what that punishment is.'

Dr Coster sat down abruptly, his face flushed and grim. There were a few seconds of uncertain silence in which the gallows-thought hung heavy in the air. Then the judge cleared his throat noisily.

'I wish for time to peruse the documents handed in during the course of the trial. I will therefore adjourn the Court until eleven o'clock tomorrow morning.'

He tucked a bundle of notes under his arm, bowed briefly and was gone. In the general hubbub which followed, the

State Attorney walked quickly from the Market Hall, avoiding the accusing eyes of Advocate Wessels.

The prisoners' equanimity had not been seriously disturbed. The ringleaders anticipated a stiff prison sentence which would be terminated in a few weeks' time by arrangement with the State Attorney when they were put over the border. After that it was simply a matter of time and the right number of petitions before they'd be back in Johannesburg again. As for the other fifty-nine, all they hoped was that the fines would not be so heavy that their friends and public subscriptions could not afford to pay them. They all drove off to Court next morning laughing and joking. But their gaiety, forced or natural, did not survive the journey to the improvised court-house. Something was about to happen in Pretoria. All the approaches to the Market Square and the square itself were thronged with armed and mounted burghers, State Artillery troops, mounted and foot police. All doors of the court-room were guarded and everybody who entered was thoroughly searched.

The vast hall was packed. The babel of speculation increased to a bewilderment of question and answer as over the heads of the crowd was passed a dock brought from the criminal court across the square. It was placed alongside the judge's dais, where it stood black and cavernous, like an empty sepulchre. Standing on guard beside it in full uniform was the bulky figure of the head gaoler – the one man in all Pretoria whom the prisoners hoped they would never see again. A loud knocking on the door of the market-master's office heralded the arrival of Judge Gregorowski; he came into the sudden silence with hunched shoulders and watchful eyes.

He took one swift look along the ranked faces of the prisoners, gave a half-smile to the members of the Executive at his elbow, nodded to the State Attorney and sat down. The crisp rustle of papers on his desk emphasized the stillness of the room. He spoke quickly, without preamble:

'I have considered carefully the statements made by all the accused and so pointedly laid before the Court. The Thirty-first Article of the Transvaal Law has been quoted in support of Counsel's contention that the only penalty for high treason is banishment and a fine of five hundred rixdollars. As regards that, I must say that there are only a few cases of high treason on record. In Van der Linden it states that the old Roman–Dutch Law should be applied unless special provision was made by Act of Volksraad. I do not think that Article Thirty-one has reference to cases where a foreign foe has actually been brought into the country by the action of the inhabitants. Therefore I think the punishment as laid down in the Thirty-three Articles cannot apply. When the law refers to the ordinary punishment, it means the old punishment under the Roman–Dutch Law. The State, in this case, is at liberty to punish the accused under the local laws or the Roman–Dutch Law.

'As far as contravention of the Gold Law is concerned, under which the accused are liable to confiscation of all their property, I am of the opinion that the Court has nothing to do in the case before it with the Gold Law, and therefore need not consider the question of confiscation. If the State is under the impression that I am wrong in such an opinion, and that they need not have made specific mention of that charge in the indictment, I am prepared to reserve that point for the decision of the full Bench.

'I have said all that I consider necessary regarding the facts and the law in this case, and it is now my duty to go to the mournful task of passing sentence on the accused according to the crimes to which they have pleaded guilty.'

As he finished speaking, Judge Gregorowski nodded to the head gaoler, who beckoned to the guard at the end of the prisoners' enclosure. He tapped each of the four ringleaders on the shoulder and, as they stood up, escorted each one across the platform to the dock in front of the judge. Phillips led the little procession; Hays Hammond, drawn and haggard from his illness, was accompanied by his doctor. The big hall was so quiet that each footfall of the four accused sounded like the stamp of a sentry. Outside, a native herd-boy was calling his oxen to the yoke, every syllable of the familiar names coming in through the open windows like memories of a different world. As the four men lined up in the dock, Judge Gregorowski spoke again:

'The four accused, Lionel Phillips, George Farrar, Francis Rhodes and John Hays Hammond, have pleaded guilty to the crime of high treason. The other accused have pleaded guilty to the lesser crime of lese-majesty. The facts appear from the evidence at the preliminary examination, and owing to that I have no hesitation in accepting their plea.

362

'It is apparent that the accused conspired with Dr Jameson to come into this country in order to come to their assistance the moment the contemplated rising took place in Johannesburg. Dr Jameson was only too willing to come in, and he came forward with the intent to oust the people of the South African Republic. His inroad was attended with the most regrettable consequences and the loss of a great deal of blood. This invasion, fortunately, was repelled by the valour and the pluck of the burghers of this Republic. Were it not for the accused this inroad would never have taken place, and this lamentable flowing of blood would have been avoided.

'Four of the accused admitted their responsibility but said as an excuse that their position was unbearable and that as soon as they heard that Jameson had come in prematurely they made every attempt to get him to return but it did not avail. It further appeared that they had guaranteed Jameson financially. The accused also said that after Jameson entered the country they acted purely for their own defence as they feared they and their town would be attacked by the Government, and therefore they armed the townspeople. What should they have done?

'The answer is not far to find. They, as inhabitants of the country, should have given the Government every assistance in maintaining the freedom and independence of the State and should have assisted in repelling Jameson in his invasion.

'The remainder of the accused say in one breath they are not responsible for Jameson's inroad, and in another announce that they will have to stand by Jameson and support him in his action. What must we say as to the conduct of the Reform Committee? They remained neutral as regards helping the Government in repelling Jameson from coming into the town. The Republic itself was endangered. They acted very wrongly indeed by helping an enemy against the country of their adoption. They were as guilty of high treason as were the leaders. That is not only Roman–Dutch Law, but also the Law of this State.'

In a completely unemotional voice Judge Gregorowski addressed himself to the first man in the dock.

'Lionel Phillips, it is my painful duty to pass sentence of death upon you. I am only applying the punishment which is meted out and laid down according to the law, leaving it to His Honour the State President and the Executive Council to show you any mercy which may lie in their power. May the magnanimity shown by His Honour and this Government to the whole world during the recent distressing events be shown also to you. I have nothing to do with that, however. I can only say that in any other country you would not have a claim on the mercy of the State.'

He paused while he fiddled around under his gown and pulled out a piece of black cloth which he perched, a little awry, on his gleaming baldness. The four men in the dock stood rigidly at attention, staring straight at the judge. He was almost smiling when he went on:

'The sentence of the Court is that you be taken from this place where you are now and be conveyed to the gaol at Pretoria, or any such other gaol in this Republic as may be appointed by law, to be kept there till a time and place of execution shall be appointed by lawful authority; that you be taken to the place of execution to be there hanged by the neck until you are dead. May Almighty God have mercy on your immortal soul.'

A sigh filled the silence of the hall, and a low murmur of unbelief rippled round the inner circle of the court. The bored mask fell from the faces of the nearest prisoners; they looked at each other in dismay while those in the back rows exchanged apprehensive whispers.

Only the four men in the dock retained their impassivity as one by one their doom was translated by the interpreter. It was too much for that official; having pronounced the death sentence three times in mounting distress, he broke into sobs as he confronted Hammond, and had to be comforted by the condemned man's doctor.

Judge Gregorowski went on in his level tones, ignoring the tears, the thud and commotion as a woman fainted, and the hoarse ejaculation of the Dutch sergeant guarding the prisoners: 'My God! He is like a dog: he has bitten and chewed and guzzled!'

The judge made a sign to the head gaoler, who beckoned four State Artillery troopers. They formed a small square into which the ringleaders stepped from the dock to be escorted in silence through the crowd, still struck dumb by the sentences, out to the coach waiting to take them to prison.

Gregorowski wrote busily for half a minute, then ordered the remaining accused to stand up. He smiled broadly at them and then, like a naughty schoolboy, put his hand over his mouth and wiped the grin away before he addressed them.

'The sentence of the Court is that you be kept in the Pretoria gaol, or any other gaol in the Republic as by law may be appointed, for a term of two years, and that each and all of you be fined two thousand pounds sterling, or in default of payment undergo a further period of one year of imprisonment at the expiration of the two years already mentioned; and that after the expiration of the period of your sentence that each and every one of you shall be banished from out of this Republic for a period of three years —'

'It's a bloody shame!' a voice shouted from just behind the prisoners, and a policeman moved swiftly through the crowd. The judge went on:

'I have only to add that the confirmation of the banishment of three years will rest in the hands of the Executive. Remove the prisoners.'

'Just a minute, judge!' The loud voice called with such authority that Gregorowski paused in the act of leaving the Bench. A brisk figure strode past the guards and through the stunned group of barristers. It was Barney Barnato.

'You know who I am, Gregorowski. And I know you! You were always a rotten lawyer, and you've got worse since you were promoted. You know why you're here? Because no decent man would take on this sort of job. So they found *you*. The only man low enough to do the job the Government wanted doing! You should have stayed in your tin-pot court in Bloemfontein, where you only had Kaffirs to deal with. Kaffir lawyer, that's what you are!'

As he went on he became more and more excited, waving his arms and gesticulating rudely at Gregorowski. At last Advocate Wessels moved across and caught his arm, whispering an urgent entreaty into his ear. Barnato paused, looked around wildly for a moment as though uncertain where he was, then nodded to Wessels and wiped bubbles of foam from the corner of his mouth.

Gregorowski, who had stood on the edge of the dais as though nailed to the spot by the hammer of Barnato's words, now shouted back at him:

'Mr Barnato, you are no gentleman!'

'Mr Gregorowski,' Barney answered, 'you are no judge!'

The slamming of the office door was the only answer he got. The sharp bang seemed to release the tension in the crowded hall. People started to applaud Barnato, the hand-clapping mingling with tears and laughter. Some of the prisoners raised a cheer above the bewilderment in which the crushing sentence had left them. Then they were rapidly herded together and led from the building to be formed up in fours outside and marched through the town to the gaol. Barnato came to the entrance to call after them:

'Don't worry, boys – I'll have you out of there in no time!'

'Good old Barney!' they yelled back to him, before the escort closed around them and they disappeared in the dust of Market Square.

The news of the trial and sentences was flashed around the earth, and it seemed as though the whole English-speaking world united to make the cause of the condemned men its own.

In the House of Commons Chamberlain read to anxious members a cable he had just sent, through the High Commissioner, to President Kruger: 'Her Majesty's Government have just learned that sentence of death has been passed on the chief leaders of the Reform Committee. They can feel no doubt that Your Honour will commute this sentence and they have assured Parliament of their conviction that this is Your Honour's intention.'

In Washington the House of Representatives referred to a committee a resolution requesting Secretary of State Olney to intervene on behalf of the condemned men and of John Hays Hammond in particular. Olney himself cabled the State Secretary in Pretoria: 'Understand sentence of death on Hammond and other sentences on American prisoners accompanied by understanding they will be commuted. Should like assurance on that point.'

Naturally enough, the emotional reaction to the events in that Pretoria court expressed itself most fiercely in Johannesburg. The whole populace, including the many who had turned against the Reform Committee for letting Jameson down, became united in revulsion against the severity of the sentences and the obvious relish of the judge in passing them. In all this, the most vociferous and effective protests came from Barney Barnato.

366

Throughout all the period of impending crisis, Barnato had stayed in England. He was on the crest of the wave. He had made small fortunes for thousands of investors, and his own great wealth and flamboyance concentrated popular attention on him far more than on other Randlords who were at that time beginning to set up expensive establishments in Park Lane and Newmarket. Barnato did not want a home in Park Lane – or anywhere else, for that matter – but Robinson had one, and so did Beit. So he would have to have one, too: bigger and more sumptuous than theirs. Robinson was buying expensive paintings; so did Barnato. He hung a picture by Sydney Cooper – *Group of Sheep* – on the wall in his study, 'because one of the poor blooming sheep looks exactly like me'. He bought racehorses and had Lord Marcus Beresford as his turf manager.

Suddenly, out of this blue sky, the bolt came crashing down on the glittering Johannesburg stock market. It was the Day of Atonement in September, 1895. With the Jews observing their solemn ritual of *Yom Kippur*, the stock exchanges all over the world were enjoying their quietest day. Without notice, thousands of gold shares were thrown on to the Paris markets. No buyers were about, and prices fell heavily. Cables flashed round the world: men left their devotions and golf matches and streamed to exchange and bourse to find out what was happening. No one could give an answer: but prices fell steadily as big financiers unloaded their holdings. By the time the general public read the news in the morning papers, the bottom had fallen out of the market, shattering thousands of little golden dreams.

Rumours of revolution in the Transvaal added to the panic rush to sell, and people to whom Barnato had been an idol now began to point to him as the man responsible for the sudden collapse. He had the inside information and was getting out before the collapse was complete. Barnato reacted characteristically. He knew nothing at that stage about the Reformers' plots; but he did know that every gold share he held was intrinsically sound no matter which government was in power in the Transvaal. The gold was there beneath the Witwatersrand; nothing could change that. He started buying shares to the limit of his resources – and that stopped the slide. By November prices were rising again, and a very relieved City of London decided on a unique honour to the man who had rescued them.

The Lord Mayor himself gave a banquet at the Mansion House 'to felicitate Mr Barnato on his recent courageous, honourable and successful efforts to avert a financial crisis'. When a newspaper regretted 'that the last official gesture of Sir Joseph Renals should be this curious honour to a financier on account of some Stock Exchange operation', Sir Joseph expressed his firm conviction that Mr Barnato had averted a panic in which many thousands of people would have been completely ruined; he considered it right that such an honourable action should be recognized.

But Barnato soon discovered that the rumours were based on fact. To start with there was Lionel Phillips' speech at the opening of the new Chamber of Mines building. There it was, in *The Times* and all the other London newspapers:

'It is a mistake to imagine,' Phillips had said, 'that this much-maligned community which consists, anyhow, of a majority of men born of free men, will consent indefinitely to remain subordinate to the minority in this country.'

That was the sort of thing which undid all the good work he was doing in London. He sent cables to his Johannesburg office instructing them not to get mixed up in any political situation. He was angry and disappointed when he learned that his nephew, Solly Joel, had become a member of the Reform Committee.

He valued his good relations with Kruger and consistently justified the old President's attitude to the new population. 'If I had a company going on all right and shareholders satisfied,' he told his City friends, 'd'you suppose I'd do anything that would bring in a lot of fresh shareholders if I didn't need their money?'

He was also hurt and annoyed that this great conspiracy had been conceived and executed without his knowledge and without consulting him. He was as shocked as the rest of the financial world at the news of Jameson's Raid. But when the revolution failed so dismally and the Reformers (including his nephew) were all thrown into prison, he decided that he would have to do something to get them out of their trouble. Solly Joel's mother in England begged him to do all he could for her son. It was a decisive appeal, and Barnato returned to Johannesburg in time for the trial.

His first act on reaching the Transvaal was to put up the £20,000 guarantee for Hammond's bail when his ex-associate was allowed to go to Cape Town for his health. When Hammond came back to Pretoria to stand trial, Barney was plainly astonished.

'Why didn't you skip back home to America?' he asked. 'They could never have touched you there.'

'What about your twenty thousand, Barney? You'd never have touched that again either.'

'I thought you'd have more sense ... Twenty thousand pounds? You and me could make that much in London in a few days!'

When the Reform prisoners had been marched off, Barnato continued his tirade outside the entrance to the market buildings. He was quickly surrounded by a crowd of burghers and Uitlanders with a fringe of police and troopers. It is more than likely that had anybody laid hands on Barnato at that moment it would have started the revolution which Rhodes and Jameson had failed to provoke. Perhaps the Boers did not understand his machine-gun-like imprecations; the police, most of whom were Hollanders or Germans, almost certainly did not. In any case, this was no ordinary Uitlander. This was Barney Barnato – a friend of the Republic and, more important, a friend of Paul Kruger.

Barnato had made his personal and voluble demonstration. Now he was prepared to back up his words with deeds. He hurried back to Johannesburg on the first train, to be welcomed as a hero by a lusty crowd 'Between the Chains'. He made a brief and hectic speech and spent half an hour in close conference with his associates in his office. Then he went back to Pretoria. To friends who warned him of the danger he was in of being arrested on charges of contempt of court, he replied curtly, 'Let them try!'

But not all Johannesburg saw in Barney an heroic figure. The more conventional Randlords had always tended to regard him with suspicion and a certain distaste – plus envy. In the past year or two, as the prolonged drinking bouts began to show their effect on his health and behaviour, they doubted his sanity. More than one Johannesburger, on that Pretoria morning after the trial, turned away from Barney's exhibition with a disgusted 'He's drunk, again ...'

There was another aspect of the situation he was creating which caused serious concern among members of the Reform Committee and their friends. It was expressed in two telegrams which arrived at the offices of *The Star* on Wednesday morning from Pretoria. One was from a prominent financier who requested that his name be withheld. It read:

'Every effort is being made here today for relief, but let them keep quiet, and muzzle that gas-bag Between the Chains for a day.'

Carl Jeppe, the member of the Volksraad for Johannesburg, also wired: 'You may expect satisfactory news, and that before night; but for Heaven's sake prevent any threats or disturbance.'

By the time those telegrams were sent, Barnato had already had an interview with Kruger. He had cooled down by the time he reached the capital and was able to appreciate that however much Judge Gregorowski had merited his abuse he had, in fact, been guilty of contempt of court, which was inexcusable. He was ready to acknowledge it.

When he was shown into the familiar voorkamer of Kruger's house the President spurned his outstretched hand and, without waiting for him to be seated, told him bluntly, 'You are lucky that I have received you. It is against advice and only because of our good relations in the past that I am able to allow it. Mr Barnato, your behaviour this morning was not only an insult to the judge, it was an insult to the State and to me personally.'

'It was never meant as such, Mr President,' Barnato said humbly. 'My first duty is to apologize to you as President and, through you, to Judge Gregorowski and the court. I was shocked at the harshness of the sentences – and my behaviour was due to shock.'

'In that case, I accept your apology. Shall we say, you were not yourself this morning.'

Kruger had been told that Barnato looked as though he had been drinking too much.

'I am grateful, Your Honour. But that does not alter my opinion that the sentences were not only harsh, but wicked!'

Kruger raised his eyebrows. He knew where all the wickedness in the republic was concentrated. He strummed his fingers on the leather binding of the bible on his lap.

'The sentences were in accordance with the law. The law is not wicked, Mr Barnato.'

'Well then, they are worse than wicked – they are foolish. You cannot carry them out. If you did, your republic

370

wouldn't last twenty-four hours. There would be no Reform Committee to hold back the Uitlanders, and they would get immediate support from England – and America, too. Every mine and every business enterprise on the Witwatersrand would close down overnight. And *then* where would your republic be?'

'The Uitlanders, and you yourself, Mr Barnato, are too fond of money to do a thing like that. You ask where would we be; I ask where would *you* be?'

'You don't believe me? Very well then, Mr President, I'll prove it to you. Unless the death sentences are commuted and the Reform Committee released from gaol in two weeks, I will shut down every single one of my companies in the Transvaal.'

Kruger stared back at him stonily, annoyance struggling with his disbelief.

'Do you realize what that'll mean?' Barnato went on. 'I employ twenty thousand white people and nearly a hundred thousand Kaffirs. If I close down I'll throw out of work more white people than you have burghers. My companies spend fifty thousand pounds a week in this republic, which would be lost to you. Already, as a result of this crisis, the production of the gold mines has dropped by twenty million. D'you want to ruin your country?'

It was far from a rhetorical question. Barnato's figures were exaggerated, but he was not addressing a board meeting. And for all his flamboyance, his boasts were never empty. He saw the disbelief in Kruger's eyes.

'Mr President; I mean what I say. Wait and see!'

'I do not make the laws, Mr Barnato. Nor can I break them. But what you have said will be reported to the Executive Committee. And now, you understand, I have a very busy evening ahead of me...'

Barnato went straight back to Johannesburg where he had another long session with his managers and secretaries. The next morning all South Africa was startled to see this announcement in the newspapers:

PRELIMINARY NOTICE
SALE OF VALUABLE LANDED PROPERTIES

Notice is hereby given that all our landed properties in the South African

Republic will be sold by public auction
on Monday, May 18th, 1896.
Barnato Brothers.

A telegram went off to the Secretary of the De Beers
Consolidated Mines in Kimberley:

'As Life Governor, I desire you to immediately close
down mine for one day, in consequence of the terrible sentence passed on the Reform Committee.'

Nobody bothered to correct his split infinitive.

The Star sent a reporter round to interview Barnato. He
found Barney on the steps of the Consolidated Investments
building.

'Is it true, Mr Barnato, that you intend to close down all
your companies and dispose of your interest in them if the
Reform Committee are not released?'

'Absolutely!' yelled Barnato, and disappeared into his
office.

Johannesburg was ready to make Wednesday a day of
mourning. On Tuesday evening an emergency meeting of
the Mercantile Association decided unanimously to close all
premises the next day, and on Wednesday morning the
members of the Stock Exchange decided to suspend business
as a mark of protest against the sentences.

In spite of the tension, the atmosphere in the town was
one of restraint. There was a general awareness that any
sort of physical demonstration against the authority of the
State would have the worst possible consequences for the
prisoners. A few hotheads contemplated blowing up the
Government buildings in Johannesburg and Pretoria; but
they received no popular support. The Uitlanders were prepared to wait for the commutation of sentence which they
were convinced the President would order.

At ten o'clock on Wednesday morning the news that
everybody had been confidently awaiting was announced:
the death sentences had been commuted.

There cannot be much doubt that the Government never
had any intention of putting the four ringleaders to death,
and it is ridiculous to suggest that Barnato's interview with
Kruger was in any way decisive. Early on Wednesday
morning the State Secretary in Pretoria cabled a reply to
Olney in Washington.

'There was no question of any understanding between

Judge and Government before death sentence was pronounced, but before receipt of your cable Executive Council had resolved to let mercy go before justice and not to apply death sentence.'

It was to be many days before the Executive announced the terms on which the death sentence had been commuted ... days of frustration and growing irritation along the Witwatersrand, of hardship and hunger for the prisoners, dark despair for the womenfolk who waited. Then one Saturday morning one of the prisoners, inconsequential in himself but more sensitive to his circumstances than the rest, brought his imprisonment to an end by cutting his throat. He was buried in Johannesburg, where 10,000 men followed the coffin and Mr Darragh, Rector of St Mary's, referred in his funeral oration to the judicial murder that had taken place.

The Government were shocked into action. A number of prisoners ill with typhoid and other diseases of confinement, exposure or malnutrition were immediately released. The Executive finally announced the new sentences : fifteen years imprisonment for the four ringleaders, and terms of from three to twelve months for the remainder.

Again the country was staggered by the unyielding severity of the Boer Government, and pressure to secure more reasonable terms was renewed and increased. It soon became apparent to the prisoners that they were being used as pawns in Kruger's devious game with the Colonial Office and public opinion.

It was public opinion which finally forced Kruger's hand – that and the blunt refusal of the prisoners to co-operate in any petitions to the Government acknowledging their guilt and begging for clemency. With his back to the wall of his own intransigence, Kruger conceded half the victory. He ordered the release of all the prisoners – except Phillips, Farrar, Hammond and Francis Rhodes.

CHAPTER TWENTY-NINE

The first telegram announcing the release of the Reform Committee arrived in Johannesburg just before eleven o'clock on the morning of Saturday, May 30. It soon appeared that everybody in Pretoria who knew anybody on the Rand was determined to be the first to break the glad news; the telegrams came in a flood.

Suddenly, for the first time in many months, the whole town was smiling. Strangers met in the street, slapped each other on the back and went off together to have a drink. Every corner was a meeting-place where laughter and jubilation answered inquiry and stimulated the need for fresh information and purpose. To satisfy these there was, as usual, a general and spontaneous movement towards The Chains and the Stock Exchange.

Though the share market had remained remarkably firm throughout the crisis, there had been little activity for months. Now the big hall of the Exchange was filled with excited members shouting the news to each other and reflecting the excitement in new and higher prices for all stocks. A reporter who interviewed the chairman of the committee was told happily: 'Shares which I hold that were worth twenty-five pounds a few minutes ago are worth a hundred now.'

At noon the chairman was called to the telephone in his office and came back to the rostrum to announce officially that at that very moment the prisoners were being released from Pretoria gaol. Cheering filled the hall and rolled out with the news into the crowded streets where it echoed and re-echoed up and down the canyons of the town. In the Stock Exchange the chairman called for three cheers for Paul Kruger and other members of the Government. There was an enthusiastic response, though there could not have been many in Johannesburg earlier that morning who could

374

have imagined they would ever cheer Kruger again.

Unwilling to let the moment pass without more formal recognition of it, members began shouting for Barney Barnato. He needed no great persuasion to get up on the rostrum. He stood there beaming and elated, waiting for the noise to stop.

'Well, my friends!' he began. 'It's nice to hear you cheering the Government of this country. It's a long time since you've been able to do that – and I hope it won't be the last.'

The renewed cheering made him pause. His manner grew suddenly solemn as he went on:

'Fifty-six of the prisoners have been released on payment of a fine of two thousand pounds and an undertaking not to interfere in the politics of this country for a period of three years, on pain of banishment. I am sorry to have to tell you that the order for release does not include the four leaders of the Reform movement.'

He held up his hand to quieten the quick booing.

'Also Mr Woolls-Sampson and our old friend Karri Davies have refused to sign the conditions demanded of them, and will have to stay in gaol. I understand they consider that it was the British High Commissioner who got them into this mess and that it's up to him to get them out of it without conditions. I must say I fail to appreciate their attitude, even though I admire their courage. However, I have every reason to believe that all those still imprisoned will be out before long.'

He gave the crowd a large wink as he said this, leaving a clear impression that he was not only privy to the innermost thoughts of President Kruger but had had a considerable influence on them.

'Good old Barney!' they shouted up at him, and cheered him all the way out of the Stock Exchange and on his clamorous way 'Between the Chains' and on to Commissioner Street. They formed a surging, singing mass behind him as they moved solidly down to Park Station to welcome the returning prisoners on the afternoon train from Pretoria.

All South Africa rejoiced at the release of the Reform Committee, and practically every community in the subcontinent stepped up its pressure on the President to secure the freedom of the four leaders. Petitions poured into Pretoria from towns and villages where public meetings had been held to urge clemency. Deputations were elected to make personal representations to Kruger, and within two weeks this widespread local agitation had coalesced into a great national movement concentrated on persuading Kruger and his Executive to make the magnanimous gesture that would give Phillips, Farrar, Hammond and Frank Rhodes their freedom.

Municipal and citizen delegations converged on Pretoria from every province and district in the country, including the neighbouring Boer republic of the Orange Free State. Even the Afrikaner Bond, the Cape nationalist movement which had become bitterly disillusioned with Cecil Rhodes and his ideals for a united South Africa, sent a deputation of members of the Legislative Assembly under J. H. Hofmeyr to plead for clemency.

On the morning of Thursday, June 11, over 100 mayors, including the first citizens of every major town in South Africa, were gathered in Pretoria to decide on a joint approach to the President. In the middle of their discussion a messenger arrived to tell them that the four prisoners had been released. With the news, which received a standing ovation from the assembled delegates, came the text of the Executive's resolution. Mr Hofmeyr read it out to them:

'With regard to the prisoners Phillips, Francis Rhodes, George Farrar and J. H. Hammond, the imposed imprisonment of fifteen years upon each and every one of them will be mitigated, and in place of the above punishment there will be imposed on each and every one of them a fine of £25,000 sterling or in default of payment fifteen years' imprisonment; further, the sentence of banishment remains in force, and will commence immediately upon the release of the prisoners from custody. The execution of the banishment portion of the sentence will not be enforced against those prisoners who, after having paid the above-mentioned fine, or after the period of the subsidiary terms of imprisonment, shall have in writing given their word of honour that they will in future neither directly or indirectly interfere with the internal or external politics of the South African Republic, and that they will always conduct themselves as orderly and obedient inhabitants of this State; with this condition, however, that upon him who, according to the judgment of the Executive Council, has broken his word of honour as above-mentioned, the life-long banishment will be imposed.'

When the murmurous comment, accompanied by much nodding of heads and hand-shaking, had died down, Mr Hofmeyr pointed out that the purpose of their mission had been accomplished.

'I would not like you to think that you have played no part in this decision, but I do not believe that there is anything to be gained in emphasizing this aspect of the situation. I propose that a delegation be appointed to give formal expression of our gratitude to the President; and as for the rest of us ... well, we can all go home.'

In Johannesburg the crowd had been gathering at Park Station since dawn. All shops and places of business had been closed to honour the occasion but there was no lack of opportunity for obtaining appropriate stimulation or for quenching the sunrise thirst which afflicted so many of the inhabitants.

By ten o'clock a huge and immensely jovial crowd surrounded the tracks and platforms of the rail terminus. All the way from Jeppestown through Doornfontein the cheers of embankments of men and women mingled with the snorting and hissing of the locomotive as it rounded the long bend into Park Station. Long before the train stopped, the spontaneous welcoming committee was running alongside the coach from which Phillips and Farrar, accompanied by their wives and Percy FitzPatrick, could be seen waving their hats and handkerchiefs. Frank Rhodes, as an Imperial officer, had not been able to give the undertakings asked for; he had been met at the prison gates by an escort who took him to the Transvaal border at the Vaal River. Hays Hammond, still very weak, had been released and gone straight to his home the night before.

The cheers reached their climax as the train pulled up at the platform, drowning the long, whistled response of the engine-driver. There was a concerted rush to the carriage occupied by the two men, neither of whom was allowed to set foot on the ground. They were lifted bodily from the train on to the shoulders of the jubilant Johannesburgers and borne in triumph to the entrance, where a light Victoria cab was awaiting them. This was soon festooned with well-wishers anxious to shake the two leaders by the hand or thump their backs.

For the two heroes – a trifle unused to such enthusiastic company – it was becoming more of an ordeal than a welcome. But it was far from over. The horses were quickly unharnessed and their places taken by a score of men who set off at a brisk trot up Eloff Street, dragging the carriage and most of the cheering crowd with them. They did not stop running until they reached the throng gathered 'Between the Chains'. There Phillips and Farrar were again lifted shoulder-high and carried through the shouting, back-slapping crowd into the Stock Exchange.

A short speech from Phillips, carefully non-political, and they were heaved into their carriage again and dragged to Farrar's office. Outside, a crowd of several thousand jammed the length of Simmonds Street, shouting for the two Reformers. Eventually Farrar, deeply moved, came to the balcony window to thank them again for the warmth of their reception. As the crowd began to sing 'For he's a jolly good fellow' he backed hastily into the room to hide the tears that rolled down his cheeks.

The local newspapers splashed the event in the biggest type that Victorian restraint permitted them. Other news items of the same day drew much less interest.

'The criminal sessions for the Witwatersrand District ended today and Judge Ameshoff indicated that the Court had dealt with more cases than ever before. The district surgeon had informed him that barely a day passed without his having to hold a *post-mortem* examination, and in almost every case the victims were suspected of having died by treachery . . .'

The dynamite Commission reported that no one was to blame for the Braamfontein explosion, as they were of the opinion that it might have been caused by a box of dynamite falling off a truck on to the rails; 'and who could be blamed for that?'

Nor could many people spare attention for the paragraph recording that the site of Messrs Store Brothers' warehouse, recently burned down, had been sold to the Anglo-Austria Boot Company for £35,000. Nine months before, the same site together with extensive buildings had been bought for

£20,000. There was, after all, nothing extraordinary in such quick appreciation. Hadn't Solly Joel just paid £40,000 for six stands, at the corner of Eloff and Commissioner Streets, which had been offered to the Sanitary Board as a site for the new Town Hall for £24,000? And that was exactly ten times the amount the stand owners had paid a few years previously. It was easy to multiply by ten; nowhere did it seem more easy than in Johannesburg.

BOOK THREE

The War

CHAPTER THIRTY

A little unsteadily, Barney Barnato climbed the companion-way to the boat-deck of the mail steamer *Scot*. It was June 2, 1897, and the emotional farewell scene at Cape Town docks had been made more hectic than usual by the fact that the *Scot* was carrying the official South African delegation to Queen Victoria's Jubilee celebrations.

Up the steps behind Barney came Solly Joel, with the doctor's last words still echoing in his ears ...

'You'll have to keep an eye on him all the time, you know. Make him cut down on the whisky, but keep his spirits up – if you see what I mean. If he goes on at this rate you'll have a case of D.T.'s on your hands. I mean that, Solly; your Uncle Barney is heading for an institution or the grave if he doesn't slow down and get himself under control. The sea voyage should put him right – but only you and Mrs Barnato can do it. He'll need watching.'

From the boat-deck the two men looked back along the turbulent wake of the ship. A winter nor'-wester was coming in from the Atlantic, piling up dark clouds against the ramparts of Table Mountain, obliterating the noble brow of Lion's Head.

'A pity about the weather,' said Solly. 'This is the most wonderful panorama in the world, on a clear day.'

'D'you realize, Solly, it's only ten years since I made that speech to them at the St Andrew's Day banquet? I remember the exact words ... "I look forward to Johannesburg becoming the financial Gibraltar of South Africa." All that, in ten years!'

He turned, and his gaze moved from the mountain across the level expanse of the Cape Flats to where the Blaauw-berg and the Matroosberg progressed in giant steps up to the high plateau of the interior. Once you stood on the edge of the Karroo, Barnato thought, if you could see far enough there was nothing between you and the lengthening range of mine-dumps, the man-made cliffs of Johannesburg. He said suddenly to his nephew, 'Remember those two blue-gum trees, Solly?'

'Blue-gum trees? There are millions of blue-gum trees. Which —'

'Come off it – you know damn well which I mean! You slid down them often enough. Those two blue-gums in front of Sylvia Villa at the railway end of Rissik Street. The most expensive tarts in South Africa. Very exclusive. D'you remember that night when the "Zarps" came busting in?'

'Look at that, Barney,' Joel exclaimed hurriedly. 'There's a sight we won't see for very much longer!'

A ship under sail came bowling in from the Atlantic, running before the nor'-wester faster than the steamship pressing into it. Even as they watched they could see men swarming aloft, sails crumpling as the vessel made ready for entering port. A signal lamp flashed from ship to ship in the early gloom.

'The lights will just be coming on in Johannesburg,' Barnato said. 'Electric lights. Ah, if only I'd been able to get that electricity concession in '89! It wouldn't have taken *me* six years to put up the first electric street lamp at the corner of President and Rissik. And I could have talked old Kruger into letting me run electric trams instead of those horse-drawn contraptions.'

He snorted his amusement and contempt.

'Horse-drawn trams in the richest city in the world! The world's greatest gold producer, ten years after the reef was struck – that's progress for you, Solly. Sixty thousand whites and sixty thousand Kaffirs! What was that latest valuation of Johannesburg, Solly? It came out just before we left.'

Joel rattled it off.

'Total rateable value of twenty million pounds, of which stand values amounted to sixteen million, compared with five-and-a-half and three million respectively in 1895.'

Barney nodded approvingly, his eyes still fixed on the coastline now beginning to merge with sea and sky, and night creeping up across the continent.

He hadn't done too badly by Johannesburg. He had set the pace all right, and much of what Johannesburg had become was due to the faith he had kept in the golden reefs when others all around him were losing theirs. He'd kept on telling them: *the gold's there, all you've got to do is dig it up . . .*

Of course, it was more than a digging operation. It was above all a financial matter, and he had seen sooner than most that the money would have to come chiefly from London and Paris – London for respectability, Paris for speculation. And he had wanted it to flow through *his* hands. London and Paris; Rosebery and Rothschild; Johannesburg Consolidated Investment, Barnato Consolidated Mines, the Barnato Bank, Mining and Estate Corporation . . . Ah, those were the days! When his name was on everybody's lips – usually in champagne. And when, during six months of 1894, he had seen the value of Witwatersrand shares quoted on the London Stock Exchange rise from £20,000,000 to £60,000,000. But it wasn't enough for some people to make fortunes. They wanted the vote. For what? To vote themselves a bigger share of the money they were making, that's what. And nobody recognized the strong hands that were pushing them along to disaster – Cecil Rhodes'! Political rights for Uitlanders? My foot! Political power for Rhodes: his dream of empire. And they hadn't even consulted him, Barnato, the man who'd made Johannesburg for them. They hadn't trusted him; hadn't valued his opinion enough to ask him for it. He would have told them to drop the whole business of the Jameson Raid. They would have got all the things they wanted by waiting for them. Did they think he was less patriotic than the Germans and Americans on the Reform Committee? Or was it all an attempt to ruin him? Was that why Phillips and Beit had thrown their shares on the market? *To ruin him?* Johannesburg Consolidated had fallen from £7 to £3 a share, the Barnato Bank from £4 to 30s.

'Why should they want to ruin me, Solly?' he asked suddenly. 'I saved them. If it hadn't been for me —'

Joel put an arm round his uncle's shoulders.

'It's getting cold, Barney. Let's go down and get ready for dinner. The others'll be wondering where we are.'

It had been a bad year for Barnato. He had reached the pinnacle of material success and found, like many another, how dreary was the view from the top. He thought of himself alongside his great contemporary and old rival, Cecil Rhodes. He knew he was cleverer than Rhodes; he never ceased to be aware that he lacked the stature of Rhodes.

What was the difference? That, too, was not difficult to answer when you thought about it. Rhodes needed all the wealth of Africa to make of Africa a monument to Rhodes and the British race. What had Barnato done with his millions? He had put up a few buildings in Johannesburg, and a great house in Park Lane that he never wanted to live in. They had named a park after him, but nobody had ever thought of naming a country after him. Rhodesia. Well, Rhodes had come crashing down. The vacuum of his departure was too big for any one man to fill. But why not Barney Barnato? He was as good as Rhodes any day! There was a Matabele rebellion on in Rhodesia; the white settlements were in danger of being engulfed by the black waves of the Matabele *impis*. He'd do a little empire building himself . . .

Barnato started immediately to work out a plan of campaign. He would raise and equip an expeditionary force of 150 mounted men, a machine-gun section, an ambulance and medical unit, and 200 native auxiliaries. He approached several experienced soldiers to take command of his force, and discussed with them the best route to Bulawayo to protect that town from the imminent rebel onslaught. (That's what Jameson would have done . . .)

Someone told him that he had better inform the Cape and British Governments of his intentions. He sent off enthusiastic cables to Cape Town and Whitehall. The replies he got caused him to drop all his plans abruptly.

Plunged into bewildered gloom by these rebuffs, Barnato looked at himself more and more critically. He was a failure. Everybody could see he was a failure! Barnato stepping into the shoes of Rhodes and Jameson? It was a joke, the whole world was laughing at it! His business interests had been neglected while he pursued his brief dream of glory, and when he went to pick up the reins again he became obsessed by fears that his rivals were bent on his ruination. Always a heavy drinker, but always for the shared pleasure of it, he now took seriously to the bottle.

The process of disintegration in that sparkling but erratic brain was rapid. His obsessions pursued him through the alcoholic maze of his days and caught up with him at night. He would wake screaming from tormented dreams, rush out into the street and batter on the door of a neighbour's house, shouting 'Let me in! Let me in! They're after me!'

His family persuaded him to leave Johannesburg for the calmer atmosphere of Cape Town, where he recovered sufficiently to attend the Legislative Assembly, of which he was still a Member. He even made an eloquent contribution to a debate on the finance bill, speaking with great force against subsidized shipping rates and in favour of free competition. He was not yet daft enough not to perceive that monopoly tendencies in the South African shipping industry would increase costs for the gold industry and every other Johannesburg undertaking.

But the lucid, intelligent intervals in the delirium of his mind grew rarer and rarer. Doctors advised a return to England on the off-chance that there he might find a security denied him in South Africa. Barnato would not hear of it. It was another ruse by his enemies to destroy him. They wanted to throw him to all those shareholders in London who'd lost their money buying Barnato shares! Besides, many of them were his friends who had only invested their capital on his advice. He couldn't face them: he would rather be dead! Yes, that was it: rather be *dead*!

His desperate wife summoned Solly Joel from Johannesburg. Barney had always regarded Solly more as son than nephew, and had complete confidence in his judgment in everything from complicated financial transactions to the odds against a racehorse winning. Joel came down from the Rand immediately. There was a brief family council with the doctors and then he went to see Barney with the plan ready in his mind.

'Barney,' he said enthusiastically, 'I've got some great news for you. You know that the Cape delegation to Queen Victoria's Jubilee celebrations is leaving on next Friday's mailboat? Well, the Chamber of Mines in Jo'burg wants you and me to go along with them as representatives of the mining industry. What d'you think of that?'

It was a whopping great lie, but it worked. Barnato, his vanity always susceptible to the complimentary gesture, was overjoyed. Perhaps he'd been wrong about his rivals on the Witwatersrand. Queen Victoria's Jubilee: and Barney Barnato in the front row!

'I'll tell the wife to start packing,' he said.

The voyage was a great success. Barnato recovered his good spirits, and the lapses into delirium became fewer and

fewer. One of his family was always by his side, and Solly
Joel, as unobtrusively as possible, kept the drink away from
him. The conspiracy of abstention was shared by all the
distinguished passengers with whom Barney mixed, including Sir Gordon Sprigg, new Prime Minister of the Cape,
and Sir Henry de Villiers, the Chief Justice.

One of the reasons for Barnato's improvement was the
loss of contact with the business and financial world in
which his every thought and decision had become a distortion, at the mercy of every market fluctuation. Conversation centred chiefly on the Jubilee celebrations which lay
ahead and the summer pastimes to which they were steaming from a Capricorn winter – cricket at Lord's and the
Oval; racing at Newmarket and Goodwood. Perhaps even a
share in the honours that were sure to be dished out on such
a memorable anniversary. There was a merry birthday party
when the Barnato son and heir, Jack, reached the age of
three.

Yet, as the slow days went past, it was clear that all was
not well. Some subtle alchemy was at work in that unpredictable mind. Joel found him one morning before breakfast
in the writing-room, staring at the calendar from which he
had just torn the previous day's dead page. The twin black
verticals of eleven looked back at him, full of dark meaning.

'Hullo, Barney. Speeding up the passing days?'

'June 11, Solly. Remember that date? It's exactly one
year ago that I got Lionel Phillips and the others out of
gaol. I got them out, and what did they do for me? Tried to
ruin me, that's what. After all I did for them! If it hadn't
been for me —'

'Now, Barney, *nobody's* trying to ruin you!'

'You don't know, Solly. You don't *know* what they're up
to. Just wait till we get to London, and I'll show you one or
two things that'll open your eyes!'

He jabbed with his finger at the new day on the calendar.

'One year ago today,' he said, quietly and fiercely. 'And
they'd still be rotting in Pretoria prison if I hadn't got them
out!'

As the ship approached Madeira, Barnato's manner became more and more strange. Each morning before breakfast he seemed to make a point of being first in the writing-
room so that he could tear the date off the calendar to
reveal the new day. Joel was puzzled at the constant queries

about the time of arrival at Madeira, and puzzlement changed to concern when Barney, half a dozen times a day, would work out small calculations revealing the exact number of hours left before the ship dropped anchor at the lovely Portuguese island.

'What're you up to, Barney?' Solly asked him lightly. 'Running a sweepstake on the time of arrival, or something?'

'That's a good idea, Solly! I'll mention it to the captain at dinner tonight. But it's not that. We'll collect the English mail and papers at Madeira. And there's bound to be a cable or two from London. I tell you, Solly, I'm not exactly looking forward to hearing what my friends must be thinking of me. And even less to seeing them. If my friends are like that, how d'you suppose all those other shareholders must be feeling? *Thousands* of them. You know why they bought those shares? Because they were *Barnato* shares. That was good enough for them. *Now* look at them! What about the Queen? What must *she* be thinking of me? She's probably a shareholder, too. My God, Solly, suppose she is!'

'Come off it, Barney. None of your friends have turned against you. The market collapse had nothing to do with you. Why d'you think the City gave you that dinner party? Your shares'll recover like everybody else's. And quicker than most. You wait till Madeira, and see what good news is waiting for you.'

But Barney only shook his head and paced the decks endlessly on the arm of nephew or wife, mumbling deep thoughts, inconsequential figures. Gone was the gaiety and bright conversation of the preceding days; Joel redoubled the vigilance with which he surrounded his uncle.

One morning, twelve days out from Cape Town, Barnato went early into the writing-room on his self-imposed duty of changing the calendar. He ripped off the useless 13 and dropped it into the waste-paper basket with a brief comment to Joel about throwing away another bit of bad luck.

'June 14, Solly. Just one more day.'

'Just one more day to what?' Joel asked disinterestedly. He was getting used to the morning ritual.

'We're due at Madeira some time tomorrow afternoon, aren't we?'

'Yes, that's right, round about three o'clock. But —'

'Then that makes it just one more day, doesn't it?' Barnato said, and went mumbling down to the saloon.

Joel made up his mind he would not let Barney out of his sight until the *Scot* had sailed from Madeira. He prayed that whatever news was awaiting them there would all be good. But at lunch-time his fears seemed groundless. Barnato was in cracking form, insisting on champagne all round and inviting Sprigg and De Villiers to share a bottle of brandy in the smoking-room when the meal was over. The conversation was animated and intelligent, dominated by the quick wit and ready reminiscence of Barnato. Still exuberant, he thumped Joel on the back:

'Come on, young feller; a dozen times round the deck. You youngsters nowadays don't know what exercise means. When I was your age I used to think nothing of ...'

The two drifted out of earshot. Sprigg looked quizzically at the Chief Justice. De Villiers shrugged and shook his head.

'What can you make of him?' he asked helplessly.

'I don't know,' said the Prime Minister. 'I only hope he comes back to South Africa as cheerful as he is now. The House still needs characters like Barnato – whichever way they vote.'

Outside on the promenade deck Barnato stepped briskly round, his hand hooked in the arm of his reluctant nephew. At the end of half an hour Joel had had enough.

'We've had too big a lunch, Barney. This can't be doing us any good. I know it's not doing *me* any good. Sit down for a bit and let that brandy settle.'

He flopped into a deck-chair, put his feet up and his head back. Barnato asked urgently:

'Solly! What's the time?'

Astonished at the sudden change of tone, Joel sat up straight in his chair.

'What on earth –?'

'Never mind that. Just tell me the time; the exact time.'

Anxious to humour the moods of his uncle, Joel pulled his watch from his waistcoat pocket and looked at it carefully.

'Thirteen minutes past three.'

Barnato looked wildly round for a few seconds. Then he put one hand on the rail and, without a word, vaulted straight from the deck into the sea. With a yell Joel leapt to his feet and made a wild grab. He managed to clutch a

390

handful of clothing, but he could not hold it against the momentum of the fall. He saw and heard the splash at the same time as he heard the shout of 'Man Overboard!' echoing round the ship; saw Mr Clifford, the fourth officer, ripping off his jacket and shoes and plunging over the side after Barnato. Joel could see the dark form of his uncle in the frothy wake of the steamer. Barney was swimming. But he was swimming away from the ship. A good two hundred yards separated him from the fourth officer who was trying desperately to reach him.

Bells clanged down in the engine room; commands were shouted down from the bridge; the upper decks pattered with running feet. A lifeboat swung out on its davits on the lee side and, as the ship turned and lost way, was lowered gently into the water with sailors ready at the oars and the ship's doctor in the stern.

Joel hurried to the end of the promenade deck, but looked in vain in the choppy sea for any sign of the two men. Every railing was lined with passengers, their interest fixed on the plunging lifeboat. Soon that, too, was barely discernible in the motion and the spray and the bright path of the sun's reflection. After an interminable half-hour the boat could be seen making its slow way back to the ship. Breathlessly the whole ship waited. Even the steam seemed muted in the silent engines. Then a great cheer went up as two sodden figures could be seen lying in the stern sheets. But on one of them the doctor was working feverishly, applying artificial respiration, and the cheers died to a murmur of uncertainty and speculation. Mrs Barnato turned away, unable to bear the suspense any longer. Joel gripped her hand and murmured comforting, meaningless phrases. One of the prostrate figures sat upright and there was a gasp when the passengers recognized Fourth Officer Clifford. As the lifeboat came alongside, the doctor looked up at the captain, and shook his head.

If Barnato had lived, if he had kept himself alive for another twenty-four hours, he would have found the letters and cablegrams he was expecting at Madeira. They would have told him of the upward turn in the market, that his shares were in big demand and his shareholders waiting to give him an enthusiastic welcome.

But Barnato was dead. With him died something of Johannesburg.

CHAPTER THIRTY-ONE

The great adventure had failed. Johannesburg and the Uitlanders returned as quickly as they could – and that was
overnight – to their essential purpose in South Africa:
making money. The source of money – without working for
it – was the Stock Exchange, and to the Stock Exchange the
populace turned, filling again the space 'Between the
Chains' for consolation and reward.

They found little of either. The over-inflated balloon had
been punctured by the bullets of Doornkop; as the confidence of the overseas financial world expired, the golden
fabric collapsed. Simmer and Jack crashed from 560s. to
42s. 6d.; Rand Mines, in spite of the magic names of Wernher and Alfred Beit, stood at 300s. compared with a boom
price of 910s.; and Consolidated Goldfields, Cecil Rhodes'
Group, fell from 397s. 6d. to 67s. 6d.

The flurry of recovery in share prices on the release of
the Reform leaders was an emotional celebration which
subsided as soon as the celebration ended. The interest of
London and Paris was concentrated on the political aftermath of Jameson's Raid, manifest in the trials of reformers
and raiders, and in the committees of inquiry initiated in
Cape Town and London. Until fear of war had been removed from the Transvaal and political stability restored,
there would be little speculative money available from Europe, and even less investment capital.

Yet in June, 1895, less than ten years after Harrison's
historic stumble, the Witwatersrand headed the list of the
world's gold producers. Production during that year totalled
2,278,000 ounces with a value at ruling prices of £7,840,000.
In spite of the Raid and its depressing after-effects – particularly the withholding of capital for development – the
following year saw an increase in both output and value. By
the end of 1897 total production from the Witwatersrand

had risen to 3,035,000 ounces, with a money value of £10,584,000. Dividends kept pace with output, rising from a distributed £1,444,000 in 1894 to £2,817,000 in 1897.

The depression which followed the Raid was completely unrelated to the output and potential of the golden reefs. By the autumn of 1895 there were 311 companies on the Witwatersrand connected with gold-mining, its development and exploitation – and the exploitation of the public. Those who were interested in the latter objective quickly disappeared when the crash came, and though the financial strength of the industry can be said to have gained considerably from the departure of these 'trust' companies, nothing was potent enough to restore public and investment confidence.

The sensitivity of the whole South African share market to rumour and extraneous influences, its susceptibility to manipulation by the exclusive few who held majority shares, was vividly demonstrated by fluctuations in the price of Rhodes' Chartered Company stocks. In October, 1895, when it was freely believed that Britain was moving towards the annexation of the South African Republic, 'Charters' £1 shares shot up to £8. The combination of price and political possibilities proved irresistible to the principal shareholders – as can be seen from the following transactions . . .

Earl Grey, a director of the British South Africa Company, owned 19,271 shares in July, 1895, and during the next six months disposed of 5,903 of them for a profit of £27,612; Lord Gifford, one of the original petitioners for the charter, sold all except 1,013 of his 10,610 shares at a profit of £38,388; another director, Sir Horace Farquhar (later Lord Farquhar), reduced his holding during the same period from 17,589 shares to 2,357, leaving himself a surplus of £60,928. All this was insignificant compared to the operation carried out by the principal partners, Alfred Beit and Cecil Rhodes. Between July, 1895, and the following March, Beit disposed of 114,880 of his 122,376 shares, and Rhodes reduced his holding from 166,057 to 29,463. Beit showed a profit of £459,520 and Rhodes £546,376.

Johannesburg itself had become the biggest town in the sub-continent, and it was clear before the century ended that along the ridges of the Witwatersrand would be concentrated the greatest assemblage of Europeans in the whole of Africa. A counting of white heads in April, 1890, showed

393

that there were in the town 6,502 males and 3,829 females. An attempt at a more scientific census in 1896 revealed a total population of 102,000, of whom more than half were European.

The urban spread to accommodate the constant increase in population had overflowed the fashionable suburbs of Doornfontein and New Braamfontein, Jeppestown and Ophirton, and the wealthy were establishing themselves in magnificent, many-roomed mansions along the high ridges of Houghton and the Berea and among the blue-gum plantations of the Saxonwald – where the Ecksteins had hoped to find gold but where the value of surface property was later to match that of the underground reefs.

Politically, the Uitlanders had been shorn of leadership and inspiration by the terms of banishment threatened against all the ringleaders. That the Pretoria Government had every intention of applying these strictly was demonstrated in the case of Lionel Phillips. Together with Fitz-Patrick, Phillips had gone to England to try to persuade Dr Jameson to acknowledge that he had invaded the Transvaal against their instructions. In this they were unsuccessful, and when Sir John Willoughby attacked the Reform Committee in an article in the magazine *Nineteenth Century* Phillips made a spirited reply in the next edition. The Executive Council in Pretoria deemed this a breach of his undertaking not to take part in political activities, and a decree of banishment was issued against him. It was a convenient precedent for the Government and an effective warning to all the Reformers.

But if the Uitlanders had lost their political impetus and Paul Kruger had emerged triumphant over Cecil Rhodes, the dream persisted in another man's will and ambition. Joseph Chamberlain, now the most powerful man in England, had taken up the Uitlander cause, though not on their behalf. His opinion of the Johannesburgers and the President was revealed in what he called 'A Statement of Policy, 1896':

'The Boers believe that we gave way because we were afraid of them, and they have been intolerable ever since . . . I cannot feel the least sympathy with either Kruger or his antagonists. The former is an ignorant, dirty, cunning and obstinate man who has known how to feather his own nest and enrich all his family and dependants. The latter are a lot of cowardly, selfish, blatant speculators who would sell their souls to have the power of rigging the market...'

The failure of the Raid and of the Uitlanders to rise had not diminished Chamberlain's determination to establish the Queen's suzerainty over the whole of Southern Africa, and especially over the golden treasure-house of the Transvaal. He wanted the South African Republic as badly as did Rhodes.

He finally got it; but he could never have done so by the means he used if he had not been interpreting in his own will the will of the great bulk of the nation he represented. The mood of the British people immediately after the Jameson Raid was accurately and execrably expressed in rhyme by the new Poet Laureate, Alfred Austin, in his poem *Jameson's Ride*.

The fact that *The Times* saw fit to publish this doggerel on January 11, 1896, was a positive demonstration of the attitude of a great London newspaper towards events in South Africa. Marching alongside Chamberlain, it was a potent force for the war which was to engulf the Boer republic; *The Times* gave to the Poet Laureate's inspiration a stature which it did not deserve, and soon the music-hall stages of England were active and noisy with khaki-clad, sun-helmeted, jodhpurred characters reciting *The Ballad of Jameson's Ride*...

'Wrong! Is it wrong? Well, may be:
    But I'm going all the same.
Do they think me a Burgher's baby,
    To be scared by a scolding name?
They may argue and prate and order;
    Go, tell them to save their breath:
Then, over the Transvaal border,
    And gallop for life or death!

'Let lawyers and statesmen addle
    Their pates over points of law:
If sound be our sword, and saddle,
    And gun-gear, who cares one straw?
When men of our own blood pray us
    To ride to their kinsfolk's aid,
Not Heaven itself shall stay us
    From the rescue they call a raid.

'There are girls in the gold-reef city,
    There are mothers and children too!
And they cry, "Hurry up! for pity!"
    So what can a brave man do?
If even we win, they'll blame us:
    If we fail, they will howl and hiss.
But there's many a man lives famous
    For daring a wrong like this!'

– and so on, for five more terrible verses.

The imperial acquisitiveness of Victorian Britain was not
the only impulse behind Chamberlain and the people. There
was a strong suspicion that if Britain did not establish her
hold on the Transvaal, the Germans or the French almost
certainly would. The intense continental rivalry of these
three Powers was reflected in the golden mirror of the
South African Republic and, as far as Germany was concerned, it was concentrated in a dark beam of mistrust and
jealousy by the Kaiser's telegram to Kruger. Chamberlain
wrote to the Prime Minister:

'My dear Salisbury,
    I think what is called an "Act of Vigour" is required to
soothe the wounded vanity of the nation. It does not matter which of our numerous foes we defy, but we ought to
defy someone . . .'

Chamberlain's policy passed the test of contemporary
British morality and conscience because it was based on a
concept that the British race was the best in the world and
the British way of life the best for the world. Each wandering Briton was a missionary propagating the gospel of the
Pax Britannica, and Joe Chamberlain was their archpriest.
From his Whitehall pulpit he sermonized an enthusiastic
congregation, read homilies on behaviour to the President
of the South African Republic. He tried to get the High
Commissioner in the Cape to persuade Kruger that war
would be the outcome if he continued to refuse to redress
the grievances of the Uitlanders or even to discuss them.
This communication ended:

'You will have seen by my speeches and answers in the
House of Commons that I have endeavoured to quiet the
angry feeling which largely prevails, but I admit that my

396

patience is nearly exhausted.'

He followed this up with a suggestion that the garrisons in the Cape and Natal should be increased 'in view of the Matabele rising'.

Sir Hercules Robinson refused to subscribe to any policy that he thought would lead inevitably to war. He urged Chamberlain to wait and see what measures of redress President Kruger would propose, and the effects of the pressure of public opinion in England and South Africa on the Republic's attitude.

Chamberlain decided to wait. He put on a public face of reason and restraint, but he had already decided by the end of 1896 that the Britannic version of peace in South Africa could only be imposed by war. It was necessary to have a *casus belli*, of course; and because they were the English it was necessary to have a good one, one that would stand up to the judgment of history.

The trial and sentence of the Reformers for crimes of which they were undoubtedly guilty was hardly a *casus belli*, nor was Paul Kruger's blunt refusal to go to England to discuss Uitlander grievances: the Uitlanders, in Kruger's uncomplicated logic, had no citizen rights, therefore they could have no grievances.

Chamberlain knew well enough that every Utilander on the Witwatersrand was a potential cause of war. He realized that Kruger could be relied on to give them none of the political concessions they demanded – which would have given them the Republic without a war, but which would not have given the Republic to Britain. The Colonial Secretary had no intention of watching a Kruger republic being exchanged for an Uitlander republic. Between them, Kruger and the Uitlanders would provide the moment in which he could act. In the meantime the mouth of his public face was able to rebuke the war party in England – including *The Times* and the *Observer* – with these words to the House of Commons.

'In some quarters the idea is put forward that the Government ought to have issued an ultimatum to President Kruger; an ultimatum which must have led to war. Sir, I do not propose to discuss such a contingency as that. A war in South Africa would be one of the most serious wars that could possibly be waged. It would be in the nature of a civil war. It would be a long war, a bitter war and a costly war, and it would leave behind it the embers of a strife which I believe generations would hardly be long enough to extinguish. Of course, there might be contingencies in which a great Power has to face even such an alternative as this, but to go to war with President Kruger in order to force upon him reforms in the internal affairs of his State with which successive Secretaries of State, standing in this place, have repudiated all right of interference – that would have been a course of action as immoral as it would have been unwise.'

Politicians, and particularly Cabinet Ministers, have always known that sincere self-delusion is an essential factor in deluding the populace. There is no reason to think that Joseph Chamberlain did not believe every word he spoke to the House of Commons that day.

The Colonial Secretary, it can be said, viewed the outcome of the Cape Parliament's inquiry into the raid with some trepidation. Its findings that the whole movement had been financed and engineered from outside the Republic, and that the director of the conspiracy was Cecil Rhodes, brought him considerable relief. But it was a finding which suggested strongly that Rhodes should be in the dock alongside Jameson and his officers at the trial which was imminent.

If Rhodes was placed on a criminal charge, thought Chamberlain, there was no knowing where revelation would stop. Fortunately, Rhodes was out in Africa dealing with the Matabele rebellion. Even more fortunately, Jameson and his colleagues had decided they would say nothing at all that would incriminate Rhodes or the Imperial Government. Thus, although the best counsel in the land – Sir Edward Clarke and Edward Carson – were engaged for them, their explicit instructions not to make use of any incriminating messages that would compromise Rhodes or the Colonial Office made an effective defence impossible.

Counsel's task was further complicated by the curious attitude of the principal accused. He refused to co-operate in any attempt to acquit him or ease his punishment. It was as though the enormity of his offence and the disastrous results of it to the man he worshipped, Cecil Rhodes, had placed a burden on his conscience which could only be exculpated by the ordeal of trial and punishment.

Even then the Lord Chief Justice had considerable

difficulty in persuading the jury to reach a unanimous verdict of 'guilty' – a verdict which he was obviously determined they should reach. Few of the legal observers of the trial doubted that this sort of misdirection of the jury would form the basis of a successful appeal; but when Sir Edward Clarke intimated that he intended to ask for a new trial, Jameson flatly refused to allow him to proceed any further. In the same mood of melancholy abstraction in which he had endured the whole trial he heard the Chief Justice's final words ...

'The sentence of the Court therefore is that: as to you, Leander Starr Jameson, and as to you, Sir John Willoughby, that you be confined for a period of fifteen months' imprisonment without hard labour. That you, Major Robert White, have seven months' imprisonment without hard labour. That you, Colonel Grey, you Colonel Henry White, you Major Coventry, have each five months' imprisonment without hard labour.'

To the people of Johannesburg, 1896 was the year of the great hang-over, the morning-after in which the excesses of the night-before were regurgitated in the Cape parliamentary inquiry and the trial of Jameson. Each was part of the essential cleansing process, and each brought relief.

The Boers of the republic were aware only of the insult to themselves in the sentences on the raiders. They could have killed Jameson and all his men one by one at Doornkop, and the world would have justified their actions. They could have lined the whole gang up against a wall and shot them, and still been justified. Jameson and his filibusters had committed the ultimate crime against the State, and had been punished by a few months' imprisonment. If they had raped a Kaffir girl instead of a republic, they would not have got off so easily.

To Paul Kruger, the personification of Afrikanerdom, the sentences represented an act of contempt for his race and his Republic which he was determined to efface. Never able to understand the concept of the superiority and independence of the Courts, he saw only the deliberate intention to humiliate. It was perhaps the final disillusion, the final destruction of his belief in the integrity and good faith of Britain and her Queen. He began to convert every spare ounce of Uitlander gold into armaments, and ordered the transformation of the gaol above Johannesburg into a strong fortress. Appropriations for the republic's military expenditure rose from £28,000 in 1894 to £87,000 in 1895; in 1896 it soared to £495,000.

To Cecil Rhodes – in England at the time of the Cape Committee of Inquiry, and in Matabeleland at the time of the Jameson hearing – the trial was but the overture to the Commission of Inquiry which the Opposition was demanding in the House of Commons and which *The Times* was trying vainly to thwart: 'These men have done wrong ... but they undoubtedly erred from excess of zeal for what they thought the interests of Empire in South Africa and of their fellow-subjects in Johannesburg ... nothing much of importance remains to be discovered, and only new discoveries would justify further stirring up of the muddy waters which are now, happily, subsiding.'

It was undoubtedly excess of zeal which caused *The Times* to err in every fact it advanced. Neither the interests of the Empire nor the Uitlanders of Johannesburg were paramount; a great deal remained to be discovered, and the muddy waters, unhappily, were only beginning to be stirred up – never to subside.

On to the stage now sauntered for its brief moment the obscure figure of Bouchier Francis Hawksley, Rhodes' solicitor, not to conduct the orchestra but with a discreet baton in his hand with which, on behalf of his formidable client, he was determined to call the tune ... a baton loaded cosh-like with the weight of Chamberlain's complicity in the Rhodes plot. And there was no doubt in Chamberlain's mind at whose head the cosh was aimed.

Rhodes' plan was straightforward and uncomplicated by alternatives. He was guilty, but not according to his own definition of guilt. The only way he could keep the dock empty was by threatening to overcrowd it. Only in this way could he prevent the inquiry of the Select Committee becoming the preparatory examination of his own trial. Rhodes' secret weapons were a number of telegrams which Hawksley revealed once to Chamberlain and thereafter steadfastly refused to divulge to the Select Committee.

Chamberlain saw enough in the telegrams to appreciate that their publication would reveal his own complicity. Never at any time did that complicity rest heavily on his conscience, but he could anticipate the full political consequences if it could be proved. He offered his resignation to the Prime Minister after drafting a memorandum on the compromising messages. It was not accepted – and the deal was made with Cecil Rhodes, who had held back the telegrams concerned for just such a purpose. It was less of a deal than an arrangement between two businessmen turned politicians – a cartel to protect mutual interests against cutthroat competition.

The Colonial Secretary had no difficulty with his own political colleagues. The purpose of the Opposition was to associate Chamberlain and the Government with Rhodes and the Chartered Company, to discredit the one group by discrediting the other.

In giving Chamberlain their tacit support the Tory Cabinet were keeping themselves in power. Even this would not have been enough to save either the Colonial Secretary or the founder of Rhodesia if what they had done and were doing had run counter to public opinion. The public were ninety-nine per cent behind Joe Chamberlain, and Rhodes expressed the situation exactly when, on returning to England soon after Jameson's Raid, he reported, 'I found all the busmen smiling at me when I came to London, and then I knew I was all right.'

The House of Commons, having accepted a Select Committee composed entirely of politicians, did not see anything irregular in appointing the Colonial Secretary as a member of an inquiry whose essential purpose was to establish or disprove the complicity of the Colonial Office in the events in the Transvaal. It is partly explained by the fact that Sir William Harcourt, the leader of the Opposition, was after Rhodes and the Chartered Company, not Chamberlain and the Government. Whatever the reason, Chamberlain was in the happy position of not only being a witness but a judge of his own actions.

The Select Committee began its sessions in London on February 5, 1897. It obtained answers or evasions to 9,862 questions – very few of which were deliberately intended to embarrass or compromise the Colonial Secretary. Simultaneously Rhodes escaped serious embarrassment. It also became apparent during the course of the inquiry that the intention of the British Government was to sustain the Uitlanders in their position of grievance, and to support the anti-Kruger factions in the republic and in the rest of South

Africa.

At the end of it all they produced a majority report – without the aid of Hawksley's hidden telegrams – which formally censured Rhodes without offering any suggestion of punishment and which reproached the Imperial officers concerned for 'a grave dereliction of duty'.

The case against Chamberlain and the Colonial Office had been covered up more effectively than it had been pressed – with, as *The Contemporary Review* put it, 'an audacious disregard of the principles which guide all ordinary tribunals'.

It had become for the time being a contest of will and of bluff between the new force in South Africa, Krugerism, and Imperialism – personified in Joseph Chamberlain and represented from 1896 onwards by the South African League, which soon had branches functioning in every major town in the sub-continent as well as in England, and which in Johannesburg became the natural successor to the banned Reform Movement.

Kruger, determined on the integrity of his Republic, tried to ensure it by making an Afrikaner state of the whole of South Africa. It was an appeal to brotherhood and ultimate nationhood which few Dutch-speaking inhabitants could resist. The powerful Afrikaner-Bond, though led by moderate and far-seeing men who had given their support to Rhodes' ideal of a united South Africa within the British association, had turned from Rhodes in disgust after the Jameson Raid, and switched their allegiance to Kruger.

The Colonial Office became doubly concerned that it would not only be the Transvaal and its gold that would be lost, but the strategically vital ports of Cape Town and Simon's Town. The Colonial Secretary himself was further disturbed by the news that a group of Rand mining magnates headed by Joseph Robinson and including George Albu and Adolph Goerz had broken away from the Witwatersrand Chamber of Mines to form a separate organization which they called The Association of Mines of the South African Republic. Robinson, whose enduring dislike of Rhodes and Beit gave all his words and actions the taint of being pro-Boer, was probably inspired in this break-away move by the same impulse. What worried Chamberlain was the association of the Goerz and Albu groups in this development; both were financed and virtually controlled as far as policy was concerned by German banking houses which, at that time, were making a deliberate assault on the financial fortress of the Sterling area. It was very much part of the German Government's plans to become a colonial power rivalling England – and there was no part of the world they would rather have as a colony than the golden Transvaal. Kruger was fully alive to the negotiating advantages this gave him in his relations with the Colonial Office.

The cumulative effect on Chamberlain was to induce him to take the positive line in South Africa that he had always intended to take. Retiring Colonial Office officials in Cape Town and Pretoria were replaced by men far less well-disposed towards the republic than their predecessors had been, and the ailing de Wet was succeeded as British Agent in the Boer capital by Conyngham Greene, formerly a diplomatic representative at The Hague.

It was essential to Chamberlain's ultimate purpose to increase Britain's military forces in South Africa. He was able to persuade the War Office that there was a serious risk that President Kruger might be 'pushed into launching an attack on the Empire', and produced an intelligence report showing that in the middle months of 1896 the republic had imported, chiefly from Germany, fifty field and position guns, twenty-six Maxims and 45,000 rifles. The fact that this was an exaggeration did not deter the Colonial Secretary. He justified the need for troop reinforcements in a report to the Cabinet in November in which he stressed the importance of strengthening the loyalty and morale of British subjects in the country, and of demonstrating to the Boers the determination of the Government to maintain all the provisions of the Convention. 'A display of strength,' he ended, 'always impresses them.'

Though he did not get the troops for another seven months, it was clear by the end of 1896 that both Chamberlain and Kruger had set their ships of State on collision courses that would end in war. Chamberlain proceeded with determination but with a sort of restraint which he believed was civilized and essentially British; Kruger obstinately, perversely and sometimes blindly but with a profound faith in himself, the destiny of his Republic and the brotherhood of the new Afrikanerdom; plus the hope – a vain one – of the support of Britain's continental rivals.

Chamberlain waited for the mistakes which he was provoking Kruger into making and which would provide in due course the opportunity for military intervention. His contempt for the Uitlanders did not prevent him making the most of their existence and their cause. At one stage he contacted Lionel Phillips in London with the suggestion that 'the mining magnates of Johannesburg could, if they chose, bring matters to a satisfactory issue by closing the mines and that, in this case, the Transvaal Government would be obliged to make concessions in order to secure their revenues'.

It was not an idea likely to appeal to Phillips or the mining magnates, who were just as intent as the Transvaal Government on 'securing their revenues'. Chamberlain, who was less interested in concessions to the Uitlanders than in the cession of the whole country to the Crown, did not press the point, and the idea almost certainly got no further than the boardroom of Wernher, Beit.

Towards the close of 1896 Kruger, sustained by the rightness of his cause and the favourable forces of world public opinion, secured passage through the Volksraad of three highly contentious bills. The Aliens Expulsion Law provided that any alien who was considered by the President and Executive to be a danger to the public peace and good order could be summarily expelled from the republic; the Press Law empowered the Executive to prohibit the distribution of printed publications whose contents were deemed to be in conflict with public morals or dangerous to the order and peace of the republic; the Immigration Law, which came into force on January 1, 1897, was designed to obtain the registration of all foreigners and to check the influx of undesirable immigrants.

Chamberlain regarded each of these measures as an attack on the suzerainty of the Queen; he declared them to be a breach of the London Convention.

CHAPTER THIRTY-TWO

Kruger saw his visit to President Steyn of the Orange Free State as the first step in his ambition to make of all South Africa an Afrikaner republic; and it was taken for granted that the outcome of that Bloemfontein meeting would be a formulated alliance between the two states. But not all the Free Staters were happy about this. The views did not go unexpressed. The Bloemfontein Dutch newspaper *De Burger* greeted the neighbouring President with some frank words:

'We have written a great deal over the matter, and people know we are in favour of joining with the Transvaal provided the latter is freed from the British yoke. Our burghers must clearly understand that in the event of the Free State joining hands with the Transvaal it means that this free Republic places itself under the suzerainty of Great Britain. If the Free State wishes to place itself under that hated yoke, well and good – but the consequences?

'Then again the most recent legislation in the Transvaal is so despotic and so irritating, not alone towards the Uitlanders but towards the free burghers of the Orange Free State, that it becomes simply dangerous; for it means that our burghers, and even our women, are obliged like the Kaffirs to carry passes in the Transvaal...'

Not all comment was as impartial. Anti-Government newspapers in the Transvaal had seldom had greater opportunity for attacking Krugerism, nor made less responsible use of it. The President's arrival in Bloemfontein on March 10 provided fresh scope for comment, which was nowhere more critical than around the bar of the Rand Club.

Since so many members had been Reformers, whose freedom was now conditional on their undertaking to abstain from political activity for three years, conversation on contentious subjects affecting the republic and the Uitlanders was always restrained or muted. The embargo did not apply on this Thursday morning to R. J. Pakeman – who had taken over the editorship of *The Star* on the imprisonment of Hamilton – nor to Francis Dormer, now resident in Cape Town as a director of the Argus Printing and Publishing Company, who had added *The Star* to their expanding group of newspapers. Dormer was on a visit to Johannesburg to guide editorial policy through what was seen as a critical and provocative time for the Uitlander Press.

'Compare Kruger with Gladstone? Why, it's sacrilege! I'm not exactly a Gladstone man myself, but what Gladstone has to say sounds like the words of a giant intellect alongside the drivel of this Pretoria understudy of his – if you choose to regard him as such. Make a note of that for your next leader, Pakeman. Make it strong! We must do everything we can to destroy this image of a great man. We must try by every means to weaken his position in Bloemfontein during this week. Rub it in: Kruger's an anachronism. *Say it*, Pakeman!'

He stopped just long enough to swallow two mouthfuls of champagne and emit a well-mannered belch.

'As for the President's address yesterday at Bloemfontein, it's a lot of unmitigated twaddle. Don't mess about with euphemisms, Pakeman. Make sure that we mean *twaddle*, nothing else ... Have you got a piece of paper?'

He scribbled busily for a few seconds, using his free hand to lift the glass to his lips between phrases.

'Here you are, Pakeman. Here's your penultimate paragraph. I say penultimate becaue I think you might well add a more sober conclusion to balance what I think I may term its irreverence. I'll read it out for the benefit of those members who, unhappily, fail so often to purchase *The Star*.'

With a theatrical flourish of his champagne glass, now empty, he declaimed:

' "It is really to be hoped that at today's banquet President Kruger will disprove the aspersion cast on him by Mr Cecil Rhodes that he drinks nothing but water and coffee – a mixture which is known to retard development – and that he will give his brain at least sufficient artificial stimulus to infuse into his post-prandial homily a few dashes of common sense; would that he could also add a little humour, but we fear that no amount of Drakenstein could imbue Paul Kruger with so much saving grace as that." There, how d'you like that?'

Pakeman joined in the general laughter; but he looked far from happy.

Down in Bloemfontein the two Presidents went into secret session from which they emerged briefly for a public banquet. Kruger was massive alongside his compact colleague, impressive behind his customary blue-green sash and the insignia of five orders. President Steyn did not dwell long on his response to the toast of 'The Free State'.

'I know that all present,' he began, 'are as anxious as I am myself to welcome and honour the great South African patriot and statesman who, for the past fifteen years, has made South African history. As you are all aware, President Kruger has come here in connection with the question of closer union. It is sometimes asked why should the Free State unite more closely with the Transvaal? I think the question is wrongly proposed. We have two republics of the same blood, language and religion. The real question is: why should we *not* unite?'

The applause which greeted this remark turned to cheering and shouting as Steyn faced Kruger and bowed and indicated him with open, expressive hand to the assembly, giving him ungrudgingly and publicly the seniority in the homely aristocracy of Afrikanerdom. Kruger nodded, content to have this genuine tribute from his compatriots.

Then he rose slowly, as though those great shoulders were supporting too much of decision and responsibility. He leaned on the table with bowed head, while the thunder of the ovation poured over him. He took that large handkerchief from his pocket, wiped his eyes with a quick, ashamed gesture, and held up his hand – the one with the thumb missing – until the cheering stopped. By the time he had finished his formal thanks for the welcome his deep voice was filling the silence.

'Although the object of my visit is to promote the union of the Transvaal and the Orange Free State, I want to tell you that in my opinion this often-heard call for a United South Africa is a fraud...'

He looked deliberately around the room as he said this, quelling the murmurs of surprise and disapproval.

'And I will tell you why I believe it is a fraud. It is a fraud because a United South Africa would be a State in subjection to another State!'

This time he paused to listen to the hear-hears of assent, the shouts of agreement.

'As for what I myself have done, I have only to thank my burghers and officials for my achievements. When the Jameson Raid took place, they were the ones who shot the Englishmen so nicely through the head. I myself did some shooting in the War of Independence, and took good aim. I know that sometimes my bullet missed the target – but this was not often.' He joined in the loud laughter that guffawed across the table-cloths.

'During that Jameson Raid I knew that the Free State was prepared to help the Transvaal in its trouble. What I want to do now is to consolidate the feeling of fraternity made manifest at that time, and to bind the two republics together in the bonds of brotherhood. I know that my dear friend, your President, does not disagree with me in this matter and, speaking on behalf of my own people – and I know that I echo their sentiments – I venture to express the hope that President Steyn may long be spared to guide the policy of the Free State.

'Mind you,' he was quick to cut off the applause, turning towards where the British Agent was sitting on the other side of Steyn, 'while speaking in this strain I want to remind you that by no means have I come here to work against or to speak against Her Majesty's representative...'

He turned back to the crowded dining-hall before he added: 'That old woman has got a very quick temper!'

Again he laughed with them, as though sharing a familiar camp-fire joke.

While Chamberlain was pondering the implications of Conyngham Greene's report on the Bloemfontein meeting, with its warning that the Kruger Government intended to make use of its new alliance by assuming that any treaties with foreign Powers made by the Orange Free State would be operative also for the South African Republic, Kruger himself was studying, in mounting anger, a sheaf of cuttings from *The Star*, which he had found on his desk when he returned from Bloemfontein. He sent for Dr Leyds.

'What think you, Doctor?' he said gruffly, waving the leading article which Dormer had composed in the Rand Club. 'Does this give us grounds for acting against *The Star*?'

'It cannot be regarded as anything but a gratuitous insult to the Head of State, Your Honour, and you could on those grounds take action against the editor and proprietors. But...'

Leyds hesitated. From long experience he knew the deliberate obstinacy of the old man across the table. His touchiness wherever the dignity of the President was concerned was notorious – and this newspaper attack was on a very low, personal level.

'But *what*, Doctor?'

'Any action you take against the Press will be scrutinized by every newspaper in the world, for each one of them will see its own rights involved. If you will forgive me for saying so, Your Honour, it must not be thought that any action which may be taken is inspired by your personal feelings.'

He waited anxiously for the reaction. Kruger puffed meditatively on his pipe. At last he said: 'I see your point, Doctor. What do you suggest?'

'That we do not make specific mention of any particular article. The cumulative effect of all that writing is to stir up a section of the population against the Government. I would say that without any doubt the attitude of *The Star* is dangerous to law and order. That gives us sufficient grounds for action.'

Kruger picked up Dormer's editorial and read it through again. Leyds watched anxiously as he saw the angry colour spreading over the sallow face. The printed column disappeared as Kruger's huge hand crumpled it into his fist. He thumped the table hard.

'They must be punished. Draw up the Order. It must be made operative from ten o'clock tomorrow morning. I will sign it when it is ready. In the meantime see that the necessary steps are taken to serve the Order on the editor and to prevent the appearance of tomorrow's edition of *The Star*. And each one thereafter for three months. I will take full responsibility before the Raad.'

Before ten o'clock on the morning of March 24 Pakeman and Dormer were served with the Executive Committee's Order suspending publication of *The Star* for three months with immediate effect. When the Order was delivered, Dormer at once sent a telegram to the British Agent in Pretoria:

'Transvaal Executive resolved this morning suppress *The*

409

Star three months on grounds dangerous to law and order stop My company composed British subjects claim protection from loss under London Convention which secures access to Courts Press Law deprives us of and invoke intervention High Commissioner stop Copy official intimation will be supplied you by post stop Your advice earnestly solicited as to proper course to adopt in meantime stop Managing Director, Argus Company.'

The Argus Company, in fact, did not need any advice. They knew exactly what course they would take – proper or otherwise. There was no question of defying the Government's edict. *The Star* went, temporarily, out of existence. In the same moment another newspaper was born, with Francis Dormer as editor. That afternoon the citizens of Johannesburg and the mining towns all along the main reef were startled and delighted to hear the newsboys rushing through the streets shouting '*Star* closed down! *Comet! Comet!*'

It was an enterprising move by Dormer and his associates, in the best traditions of democratic journalism. But although *The Comet* soared along the Witwatersrand its sponsors were grievously disappointed in Chamberlain and the Colonial Office, whom they had expected to leap to the defence of one of the most sacred principles of the British way of life. All they got, from the Colonial Office, was an off-hand comment from the Permanent Under-Secretary:

'It is, of course, ridiculous for President Kruger to be so thin-skinned, but the Bloemfontein article is coarsely offensive.' A broad hint was given the Argus Company that they should seek their redress in the Courts.

The company had not waited for this advice either. On the day *The Star* was banned, their lawyers had filed suit in Pretoria. Three weeks later, on April 14, it was *The Star* and not *The Comet* which was first with the news of Judge Ameshoff's verdict:

'In the application of the Argus Printing and Publishing Company to have set aside the order of the President suspending *The Star* for three months, the High Court this morning has given judgment setting aside the order of the State President with costs. The receipt of this news was hailed in *The Star* by a spontaneous burst of applause from the employees.'

The judgment was, in fact, based on the simple premise

that the Press Law invoked by the President referred to matter which had already appeared in the Press, and did not confer on the President the power to prohibit the publication of news or comment which was still to be printed and which, until it appeared, could not be said to have any effect on public order.

No self-respecting judge could have evaded such a decision in law. Nevertheless it was a courageous enough judgment in all the circumstances, and one which both elevated the Transvaal Bench in the eyes of the world and fortified Kruger's resolve to make the judges subservient to the President. The time would come.

Meanwhile Kruger had other things to think of. Chamberlain continued his policy of patient provocation – even to the extent of staging a small naval demonstration in Delagoa Bay. By the middle of 1897 it was being said that war between the two Afrikaner republics and Britain was inevitable.

Kruger began to play his cards badly. His Executive compiled and submitted to the British Government a detailed claim for damages and compensation resulting from the Jameson Raid. On March 15 the claim was received by the House of Commons, where it was shown to total £1,677,938 3s. 3d., made up as follows:

£1,000,000 for moral damages;
£136,733 for military expenditure;
£28,243 for widows and children of five burghers killed and to comfort the wounded;
£462,120 as compensation for burghers called up;
£36,011 19s. 1d. for expenses incurred by the Orange Free State.

A list of minor items added up to the balance of £14,830 4s. 2d.

The claim was more than justified morally and in international law, but it did not stand up to the close scrutiny it received in the Commons. There was a charge of £2,422 for shoeing horses, and two of the five men killed on whose behalf widow's pensions were claimed were shown to have been unmarried. But it was the absence of goodwill which really caused the claim to be rejected out of hand. As *The Times* put it: 'A lack of generosity on the one side and of

411

honesty on the other destroyed any hope of settlement and greatly increased rancour between the two sides.'

South Africa, and the Transvaal in particular, now dominated Chamberlain's thoughts and actions. From the very beginning he had steadfastly, if secretly, pursued his objective – the acquisition of Kruger's republic. Early in April he told the War Office that precautionary military measures had become 'a matter of pressing importance'. Before the end of that month the War Office was able to inform him that the British garrison in South Africa would be reinforced immediately by a battalion of infantry and three batteries of field artillery. These reinforcements were sent to Natal – as near to the Transvaal border as they could get without constituting an act of aggression.

Above all, the Colonial Secretary needed at the Cape a man who would represent his policy effectively. In March he had announced the appointment of Sir Alfred Milner, fresh from considerable administrative success in Egypt, as the new High Commissioner in South Africa. At Milner's farewell dinner at the Café Monico in London on March 27 – only a few days after the announcement of the treaty between Kruger and Steyn – Chamberlain included these remarks in his speech:

'It may be true that there are eminent persons in South Africa who have aspirations for an independent federation of States in which Dutch influence would be predominant, and which would look for sympathy and support rather to the continent of Europe than to this country. If such an aspiration exists, in my opinion it is incompatible with the highest British interests.'

Kruger's reaction was typical of the difficult, devious game he was playing. His actions and intentions had been strongly influenced by his conversations with President Steyn and his contact with Free State opinion. He was, apparently, willing to forestall the ultimate provocation by giving way on all matters except those – like the franchise – which might affect the independence of the republic.

Early in May the Volksraad, against the wishes of a considerable number of members, agreed to a repeal of the Immigration Law. And he let it be known that a measure was being prepared which would amend the Expulsion Law so that only those persons would be banished who had been found guilty of subversive activity. At the same time he began construction of a ring of forts on the hills surrounding Pretoria, and stepped up his defence budget for 1897 to a record £614,000 – £120,000 more than in 1896, and seven times that of 1895.

The people of Johannesburg felt rather like the ball in a football match – kicked around by both sides. It was a football loaded with dynamite. They rejoiced at what they called Kruger's climb-down over the Immigration and Expulsion Laws, and celebrated the departure of every troopship for the Cape and Durban. But they would rather have celebrated a rise in share values or a return of prosperity to the town. Although the level of gold production was still rising and most of the producing mines were maintaining their profits, the political uncertainty hung like a dark cloud over the town, constantly threatening disaster, discouraging enterprise and progress.

This period of depression, hardship and discontent found its worst expression in an alarming growth of the illicit liquor trade all along the Witwatersrand, and in the already widespread theft of raw gold. Both were natural hazards in a developing mining industry with a floating, exploitable labour population, but by 1897 they had become almost as well organized, if not quite as profitable, as the industry itself.

In that year an official Government Commission revealed that the annual loss to the mines caused by the theft of gold amounted to £750,000, or about ten per cent of the total output. The industry had long been urging that they should themselves supervise and control any organization formed to deal with the detection and suppression of the thieving and illicit buying of gold. The Commission not only supported this request but added, rather pointedly considering it was a Commission composed chiefly of pro-Government officials, that '... it would remove the blame from the present administration, viz., that these thefts can be practically carried on with impunity.'

It was an opinion shared by the whole Uitlander population. Belief in the impunity of gold stealers was based on the long-standing Boer conviction that the earth and everything in it belonged to the republic and that it was therefore impossible for any burgher to steal what rightfully belonged to him.

There was quick confirmation of this argument even

while the Commission was taking evidence on the subject. Anticipating the Commission's recommendation and the Government's probable inaction, the City and Suburban Mining Company formed their own detective force. They succeeded in arresting two notorious gold thieves, with raw gold in their possession, and handed them over to the authorities for punishment.

To nobody's great surprise one of the prisoners escaped from custody in the court-house, and the other was sentenced to six months' imprisonment. When President Kruger remitted three-quarters of this, the hostile Uitlander Press erupted in bitter condemnation, inevitably comparing the President's attitude to this known gangster with his attitude to the two Reformers, Woolls-Sampson and Karri Davies, who had been in gaol since the Jameson Raid more than a year before.

In 1896, as a result of organized agitation by the Chamber of Mines, by every Church in the country, and by scores of public petitions, the Volksraad was induced to pass legislation, in spite of Kruger's opposition, prohibiting altogether the sale of liquor to natives on the Witwatersrand. A total abstainer himself, Kruger realized that the liquor concession was a valuable asset for the State and a valuable market for his farmers' grain. When a deputation of liquor dealers waited upon him to complain of the severity of the prohibition law, he denounced it as immoral because, by restricting the sale of intoxicating drink, it deprived a number of honest people of their livelihood.

Few remained honest enough not to cash in on the fabulous profits that were to be made from the liquor trade among the Kaffirs as soon as it became illicit. Highly organized gangs took over the direction and control of the liquor trade. The chain of supply stretched from the Eerste Fabriek distillery near Pretoria, and from the port of Delagoa Bay, through the licensed wholesalers and retailers to the shebeens, eating houses and touts who dealt directly with the mine-workers and other urban labourers.

Although traffic and trade in illicit liquor was continuous, day and night, drinking and drunkenness reached their peak on Sunday...

It is two o'clock on Sunday morning. At every street corner of every block containing a bar the European and native pickets are out, scrutinizing every passer-by, checking

414

the credentials of every potential customer. There is not much fear of informers, for the informer's price can always be topped; and there is not much fear of the 'Zarps', who are not immune to bribery and who have long conceded the hopelessness of trying to reach the men at the top through arresting the men at the bottom.

It is between two and four o'clock on Sunday morning that the salesmen buy their forty or fifty bottles at 4s. a bottle – it has originally cost 4s. a dozen – with an extra bottle thrown in for every dozen bought. With this cargo concealed about their persons or in rolls of blankets, the salesmen head for the open veld or the mine compounds – where a bottle to the Kaffir policeman at the gate ensures entry. Retail prices vary between 6s. and 15s. a bottle, depending not so much on demand, which is consistently high, as on supply, which is variable. By dawn the first contacts have been made, perhaps at the foot of some koppie or in the bed of a donga, and, responding to the efficient telepathy of the nefarious, a steady stream of individuals converge across the veld from various mines like bees returning to a hive from a world without honey.

The early assignation is the last attempt at concealment. Once the bottles have been sold, drinking is done progressively openly, and by noon the veld is dotted with drunken groups and prostrate natives, their colourful blankets and tribal ornaments making incongruous and tragic contrast with the boots and bottles of an industrialized civilization. The salesmen hurry back to Fordsburg and Braamfontein for new supplies to cope with the mid-afternoon rush from churches and Sunday schools. It was a well-known phenomenon that natives in contact with civilizing and missionary influences readily dropped their aboriginal virtues in favour of the vices of superior example. If the Bible was part of the process, so was drink; they adopted both with equal sincerity and enthusiasm.

Nightfall brings out the thieves, flitting from drunk to drunk for the meagre cash that is left over from a day's orgy. And the bottle collectors are picking up the empties in hundreds of dozens for exchange next morning at canteens and stores at the rate of two bottles for a box of matches, a bun or a handful of peanuts. Nobody picks up the booze-soaked bodies. Those who can, stagger back to the mine-compounds at the end of the day. The rest litter the veld, to be kicked or beaten into wakefulness next morning by the boots and *sjamboks* of police and compound staff.

It is a serious problem in economics for the mining industry, as well as a grave social and moral problem for the republican community. Unable to work at all on Monday and only able to give fifty per cent efficiency on Tuesday, the great majority of mine labour was only capable of providing three-and-a-half days' work a week. But what the mine-owners lost, the farmers gained in increased demand for their grain. In Paul Kruger's view that was no cause for grief.

CHAPTER THIRTY-THREE

In Johannesburg, gloom and depression were forgotten in the preparations for Queen Victoria's diamond jubilee celebrations. This was an Empire-wide celebration, spanning all the continents and climates of the earth, as people of every race and colour, creed and language, acknowledged the rotund little old woman at Windsor who personified the majesty and might of the greatest imperial experiment in the history of man.

For Johannesburg it was far more than a jubilee occasion. It was a physical demonstration that Britons, wherever they may be, never, never shall be slaves. Its organizer, W. Y. Campbell, proclaimed that the inspiration of the whole pageant was to be 'Britons, hold up your heads!'

An executive council of British subjects was formed to prepare for the event. It consisted of seventy-two prominent Uitlanders, including Abe Bailey, Percy FitzPatrick, George Farrar, Solly Joel and almost every English-speaking Reverend in town. An early problem was whether President Kruger should be invited to the celebration. They debated it earnestly.

'You remember what he said when we asked him over to that Queen's birthday dinner and dance in 1889, George?' Bailey said to Farrar.

'Ah, yes. He turned it down flat.'

'Not only turned it down flat. I knew this would be coming up, so I asked Pakeman to let me have a copy of the reply as it appeared in *The Star* that week. Listen to this: "Sir,

In reply to your favour of the 18th instant requesting me to ask His Honour the State President to consent to his name being used as a patron to a ball to be given at Johannesburg on the 26th inst. I have been instructed to inform you that His Honour considers a ball as Baal's service, for which reason the Lord ordered Moses to kill all offenders;

and as it is therefore contrary to His Honour's principles, His Honour cannot consent to the misuse of his name in such connection. F. Eloff, Private Secretary." '

'Well, in that case,' Campbell said, 'there's no need to embarrass him by sending an invitation. I'll explain the situation to old von Brandis. We'll ask him along.'

In spite of its theme, the whole polyglot community co-operated in the tribute to Britain's queen; French and German businessmen competed with English, Scots and Welsh in the festive patriotism with which they decorated buildings and shops. On orders from Pretoria all Government buildings in Johannesburg were closed for the day, and Kruger added the culminating gesture of goodwill by releasing Woolls-Sampson and Davies. They had been in prison for thirteen months – a period which had been recorded week by week in the *Cape Times* by the following announcement: 'Today Messrs Sampson and Davies complete the ... week of their imprisonment in Pretoria gaol for the crime of not signing a petition.'

The great day dawned cold and bright. 'Real Queen's weather,' they all called it. Every mine along the Witwatersrand sent its contingent of Europeans and Africans to swell the dense crowd which lined the pavements and balconies and filled Von Brandis Square, where the historical procession formed up before starting its circuit of the town. Even for Johannesburg, well used to excesses of all kinds, it was a fabulous pageant.

At the head of the column twelve mounted police rode abreast clearing a broad swath through congested streets and avenues of bunting, evergreens and banked flowers. Behind the mounted police marched the combined bands of the Wanderers Club, their blaring brass setting an appropriate tempo and tone for a procession which included 2,000 school-children and groups representing every industry, shop and activity in Johannesburg. Frank Fillis had turned out his entire circus, including a 'Britannia tableau', and this was followed by an historical pageant recapturing Britain's story through the ages.

A procession within the procession was provided by the mining industry. Thirty-six mines contributed to this display, which was preceded in the processional column by 200 Zulus in full war-dress.

The Jubilee procession was more than three miles long

and took an hour and a half to pass a given point. The meticulous timing of the organization was demonstrated when the twelve mounted police clanked into the eastern side of Von Brandis Square just as the last of 150 cyclists pedalled out at the tail of the column on the western side. The only untoward incident was when a lady holding a sheaf of wheat fell off the Castle Brewery lorry in Pritchard Street; it was taken as a compliment to the brew.

The high-light of the occasion was the unfurling of the Union Jack from the flag-post in front of the grand-stand at the Wanderers Ground, which was packed solid with the densest congregation of men and women ever assembled in Johannesburg. It was for them, and for the town they had created, a significant moment – far more than a celebration of Victoria's sixty years on the throne. It was their recovery from the humiliation of the Jameson Raid. They saluted their Queen with one hand and thumbed their noses at Kruger with the other. The committee had told them: 'Britons, hold up your heads!' And on this day they were doing exactly that.

Mr Campbell jerked the rope. The wind caught the folds of red, white and blue cloth as they were released; simultaneously the massed bands blared out the first notes of the National Anthem. Every masculine hat in that vast throng was removed, and 'God Save the Queen' rolled out majestically as human voices overwhelmed the trumpets and trombones.

The Uitlanders had got back their self-respect.

Johannesburg went back to work the next day with renewed vigour and purpose; but the display of patriotism did nothing to increase international confidence in the stability of the Witwatersrand mining industry, and share values stayed as depressed as the jobbers and dealers and other operators were soon to become. The Rand Club found itself short of new members because, for the first time, political and patriotic motives were influencing the election of applicants.

Two other events of importance made 1897 a memorable year for Johannesburg and the Uitlanders. Early in May the Government announced the appointment of an Industrial Commission ostensibly to inquire into the depressed state of the mining industry and to suggest means of curing it. Kruger's concern, it can be assumed, was not for the financial difficulties of some of the companies nor for the fall in income of the Rand millionaires. He was confronted with a quite novel situation for his administration; it seemed likely that the revenue from the Uitlanders would no longer continue to support the expenditure of the State. Record spending on armaments unfortunately coincided with a rinderpest epidemic which killed over 300,000 cattle and a drought which made it essential to import food to feed burghers and natives, and donkeys – immune to rinderpest – to provide farmers with draught animals to replace their oxen.

It was a situation which provided plenty of scope for the opportunists who peopled the corridors of Government buildings in Pretoria. A syndicate lost no time in securing a contract for supplying donkeys – the Government taking all risk of loss. The animals were bought in Ireland and South America at one-sixth of the contract price, and the syndicate, pleading that they had insufficient capital, were paid a cash advance equal to three-quarters of the contract figure. It was a satisfactory arrangement, giving them an unsecured advance of £450 for every £100 they had to spend.

The partnership then approached the President with the very reasonable suggestion that the donkeys from South America would have to travel on the upper decks of ships where ventilation was better. This would make the charter vessels top-heavy and there would be a real risk of ship and donkeys foundering in bad weather unless sufficient ballast was carried. What better idea than to fill the holds with corn, which the country so badly needed? They got that contract, too.

Fortunately for the syndicate concerned, Johannesburg and Pretoria became far more engrossed in the report of the Industrial Commission than in the brief pleasures of what was known as 'the donkeys and mealies scandal'. This report was a surprising document.

Kruger's ancient and, on the whole, well-founded suspicion of the Rand's mining magnates had helped to convince him that their own inefficiency, greed and anti-Republican attitude was the chief cause of the depression in the industry. He felt sure that the investigations of the Industrial Commission would reveal this to the world and justify much of the legislation which had hitherto been regarded as oppressive. So confident was he of the outcome that he agreed that five representatives of the mining industry should be added to the six Government officials appointed under the chairmanship of Schalk Burger, a highly respected member of the Executive Council.

These five men immediately assumed the same rights as those exercised by the Government members, and as they were the only experts on the economic and technical problems of the industry, it is not surprising that they dominated the Commission's inquiry – and ultimately, its report. The proceedings and recommendations were published by the Witwatersrand Chamber of Mines in a volume of over 700 pages. As an intended indictment of the men and organizations who ran the gold mines it backfired badly as Kruger discovered in the first paragraph:

'Your Commission are pleased to state that at present there exist all the indications of an honest administration and the State, as well as the mining industry, must be congratulated upon the fact that most of the mines are controlled and directed by financial and practical men who devote their time, energy and knowledge to the mining industry...'

It went on to criticize the improper application of the Liquor Law and the Gold Law relating to the theft of gold; it recommended a reduction of import tariffs and railway rates, and strongly advised the establishment of a joint mining board composed of nominees of Government and the industry 'so that the Government representatives should have the benefit of the experience of men whose daily occupation it is to look closely into all the affairs appertaining to the mines'.

Nor did the Commission shirk handling the explosive issue of the dynamite concession – still the principal grievance of the mine-owners for the simple reason that no other single item affected their profits so adversely. The subject was dynamite in any context, and there was general approval, except in Government circles, when the Commission not only recommended that the concessionaires' contract should be cancelled but that their books should be examined to ascertain whether the Government was being defrauded of its proper share of the profits.

The new High Commissioner, Sir Alfred Milner, received the report in Cape Town and was startled into writing that 'it shows a breadth of view, a liberality of judgment, and a force of expression which, if of genuine Boer origin, give me quite a new idea of the *niveau intellectuel* of the Boer'.

It was even more startling for Kruger and his executive associates than for Milner. They succeeded in postponing action indefinitely by appointing a Volksraad committee – whose report in October virtually rejected, in the nicest possible way, all the Commission's recommendations.

To the Uitlanders this was a bitter blow. Gloom and depression settled over the Witwatersrand, replacing the elation of the Jubilee month. Nevertheless, that event had left its influence on the vast British section of the community, whose desire for some form of positive action found expression in the increased and more hostile activity of the South African League. The League paid lip service to its objective of promoting good government and amicable relations in the country, but its members proclaimed more and more emphatically the gospel of what was known as Primary Principle 'A':

'This League affirms most strongly its unalterable resolve to support the existing supremacy of Great Britain in South Africa, and binds itself to oppose any attempts that may be made to weaken or destroy this supremacy.'

When this was propounded by a considerable section of the Transvaal's Uitlanders, the Boers could be forgiven for describing it as treasonable.

But the President's handling of the Industrial Commission also had its repercussions in the Volksraad, where opposition to him and to the Executive was shown more freely than ever before. There was every indication that a strong liberalizing influence was at work within the Volksraad and in the country. The danger was that Uitlander pressure on the citadel of the republic would unite the opposing elements against the common enemy.

This was not unrecognized by the men on the spot. So that when Chamberlain, constantly on the look-out for the cause that would foster his intentions, sent an instruction to Milner – soon after the publication of the Industrial Commission's findings – to inform the Pretoria Government that the dynamite monopoly was a breach of the London Convention, Milner locked it away in a drawer, thought about it for a month and then sent for Conyngham Greene and Percy FitzPatrick.

*

Sir Alfred Milner was a man of quick but penetrating judgment. He seldom changed an opinion or an intention, and it was fortunate for Chamberlain's plans for South Africa that Milner's ambitions as High Commissioner coincided so closely with those of the Colonial Secretary.

Milner came to South Africa with a pretty good idea of what he wanted to do with the South African Republic. His overall mission − self-defined − was to unite the sub-continent within the Imperial orbit. Before he could accomplish this, Kruger's ramshackle republic would have to be eliminated. It could be eliminated by an Uitlander franchise, or it could be eliminated by war. In either case the end would be the same. Milner was an administrator, a proconsul, not a warrior. He would have preferred the franchise to a war. But the choice was not his: it was Kruger's.

Milner did not rush straight up to Johannesburg from Cape Town when he landed. He let it be known that the colonies of the Crown had first call on his services ... the Republic could wait. But he demanded the most detailed reports from Conyngham Green, and he kept in close touch with Uitlander opinion. Gradually the idea gained strength in his mind that the Boers would provide their own solution to the problem of the Transvaal. The Industrial Commission's report and the reaction to the Volksraad's disregard of it convinced him that opposition to Kruger was mounting and that Oom Paul would be defeated in the presidential election at the beginning of 1898.

When Milner met Greene and FitzPatrick in Cape Town, Greene's choice of an opening gambit could not have suited the High Commissioner better.

'Percy,' he said, almost as soon as they were seated round Milner's big desk, 'why have I not been approached by the English section of the Rand community over the Industrial Commission's report − in the same way as the French, German and Dutch communities have approached their consuls?'

'I thought you'd take me up on that, Conyngham. As a matter of fact most of us thought the introduction of the political element into the controversy at this stage would only help Kruger to rally the Volksraad to the old cry of foreign interference.'

'Forgive me for interrupting, Mr FitzPatrick,' Milner said. 'But you can hardly fail to introduce a political element to a dispute with the Pretoria Government. It is, after all, a denial of the Uitlanders' political rights, plus a misuse of governmental powers, which is at the bottom of all difficulties in the Transvaal. Mind you, I'm inclined to agree with the English section's attitude.'

'Let me say,' Greene interjected, 'that my information from people who know the character of the Boer better than I do is that we must not rule out the possibility of something very like a revolution taking place in the Transvaal – not among the Uitlanders, but among the anti-Kruger burghers. Feeling's very strong. The least that could happen, I imagine, is that Kruger will find himself out as President in January, and Joubert or Schalk Burger in his place.'

'Well, I don't know about a revolution,' FitzPatrick said, 'but I do believe that if you give the Boers enough rope they'll hang themselves.'

'It reminds me,' Milner told them, 'of the Colonial Secretary's remark on getting Mr Greene's report on the crisis between Kruger and the judges at the beginning of the year. "*Quos Deus*," was all he said. He left it to us to fill in the missing words. Whom God wishes to destroy he first makes mad. What you have said, Mr FitzPatrick, expressed in a different way. I agree with you that for Kruger's régime to be overthrown from within, and preferably by his own countrymen, would be an ideal solution. My only criticism is that it may never happen and that the present state of affairs will be prolonged indefinitely. That is not how I see my mission in South Africa.'

He held up his hand as FitzPatrick was about to say something.

'One moment. I think I'd better put you in the picture more fully before we proceed to further suggestions. About a month ago I received a dispatch from Mr Chamberlain with instructions to inform Pretoria that the dynamite monopoly was a breach of the London Convention. The inference was clear that if the situation was not amended other steps would be taken. That dispatch has never left this drawer.'

He opened a drawer beside him and pulled out an official-looking envelope. He fluttered it at them.

'Here it is. However, I have had another communication from the Colonial Secretary in which he suggests that you,

424

Mr Greene, should contact Dr Leyds and make him aware that the Imperial Government considers the dynamite monopoly a breach of the Convention but is delaying taking further steps until the President's reaction to the Industrial Commission's report is revealed. The expectation, of course, was that the President's reaction would be favourable. We now know that it is not. In the light of these recent developments have you any suggestions to make, Mr Greene?'

'I would say the time has arrived, Your Excellency, to present the original dispatch.'

'Mr FitzPatrick?'

'Well, Sir Alfred; may I say that we in Johannesburg never expected anything from the Industrial Commission, so that we're not as disappointed as we might have been that we're not going to get it. I prefer to regard Kruger's attitude and the Raad's rejection of the recommendations as a few more inches of rope. My feeling is that we should continue to give them enough to make a noose with.'

Milner nodded slowly.

'I'm inclined to agree with you. You convince me of the wisdom of allowing the bitter quarrel which seems to be springing up among the Boers themselves to develop itself. This will form the basis of my reply to the Colonial Secretary. In any case, I believe the monopoly is doomed and it would be a great pity for the growth of the opposition party to be prejudiced by any visible encouragement from us.'

Conyngham Greene looked far from satisfied.

'As I have said, Sir Alfred, I accept the possibility of a revolt against Krugerism from the Afrikaners themselves. What I am uncertain about is whether it would be better to do nothing that would prejudice them – as you have pointed out – or to give them encouragement in such a way that it would, in fact, encourage them to take action.'

'Let me say,' Milner replied, 'that I am thinking in terms of British Government action that would be construed as imperialist intervention. For the same reason I do not want the South African League to take any positive steps. If this becomes an issue of nationalism and patriotism we are likely to undo all the progress that has already been made, and Kruger will be confirmed in his extremist policies. What about Johannesburg, Mr FitzPatrick? Ultimately, I believe, Johannesburg must decide the future of the Transvaal. How long are you prepared to endure a state of economic and political stagnation?'

'Well, as Your Excellency knows, the only state of depression recognized in Johannesburg is a depressed Stock Exchange, and that's almost unendurable.'

They laughed together as FitzPatrick went on.

'I am pledged not to take any political action that's prejudicial to the republic. I would find it difficult to reconcile my conscience with my visit to you, Sir Alfred, if I thought that what I have to propose is not in the best interests of the republic. It is, indeed, a scheme which I have every intention, with your approval, of making known to the Pretoria Government.'

'This is most interesting, Mr FitzPatrick. Please go on.'

'You will appreciate that the chief interest of the big mining houses on the Witwatersrand is the maintenance of a satisfactory business position. In the case of my own firm, Wernher, Beit, this represents custody of a capital investment of over a hundred and fifty million pounds from all the countries of Europe and from America. So you'll understand the patriotic motive is not paramount.'

Milner scribbled enigmatic doodles on the blotting-paper before him and nodded brief acceptance.

'As Wernher himself put it to me,' FitzPatrick went on, 'our interests in the Transvaal are so great that we can always feel that what's best for the country will be best for us. It was with those thoughts in mind that I decided to approach the Government with a practical proposition which, if accepted, might produce an atmosphere in which the outstanding political problems could be solved – and I had in mind, first and foremost, the franchise.'

FitzPatrick fumbled around for a match for the pipe he now pulled out of his pocket. Impatiently, Milner pushed a box over to him, and an ashtray. Greene uncrossed and crossed his legs again as they waited. FitzPatrick blew out a long, meditative turmoil of smoke.

'My proposal is that Wernher, Beit – and the others if they wanted – should attempt to clear up the differences between the mining industry and the Government by a cash settlement to be mutually agreed on an assesssment by valuators ...'

He held up his hand as both Milner and Greene framed the obvious questions.

'The matters which I believe to be capable of settlement on a cash basis are the dynamite monopoly, the Netherlands Railway concessions, the Liquor concession and the complicated business of mining rights where surface titles are involved. There are three monopolies involved, each of which we regard as iniquitous, rapacious, and inconsistent with decent government and reasonable mining development. I am not myself concerned with the question of profits in this case, but I can understand it would have its appeal in some quarters. My idea is to remove these factors from the sphere of political dispute. They have a cash value to the Government and to us which is assessable. We would be buying a considerable asset and, I hope, political peace.'

'It would cost a great deal,' Milner murmured. 'Have you any idea how much?'

'None, at the moment. Five millions? Ten millions? It would be cheap at almost any price.'

'And are Wernher, Beit prepared to pay out ten million pounds?'

'It can't be a solo effort. It must be a co-operative approach, and the money would be raised in the same way. The Chamber of Mines, perhaps. But Wernher, Beit would, I think, be prepared to give a lead and if necessary underwrite the agreed amount.'

Milner made a few notes on a piece of paper. He looked up at Greene.

'What do you think?'

'It's certainly a novel idea. I don't know how Kruger would react – or the Volksraad. If they get it into their heads that the mining magnates are trying to buy them out of their republic it could easily make things worse instead of better.'

'You will indeed have to be very careful in your approach, Mr FitzPatrick,' Milner said. 'Have you anyone in mind?'

'I've given that matter considerable thought. There's a young Afrikaner – they're talking about him as the next State Attorney. Cambridge degree. Used to be a great Rhodes supporter, but the Raid changed all that. Now he's hitched his wagon to Kruger's span. His name is Smuts, Jan Smuts. You've heard of him?'

'Yes, I've heard a good deal of Smuts. He may be your man. But watch out. He's intelligent, shrewd and exces-

427

sively ambitious. He is also a completely disillusioned man – and there's nothing like a shattering disillusion to warp judgment or influence intention. One other thing, Mr Fitz-Patrick; you understand that at no stage in any negotiations you undertake is the sanction of the British Government or myself to be hinted at. This is an approach exclusively on behalf of the mining industry.'

A few minutes later, as FitzPatrick and Greene walked away from the High Commissioner's residence, Greene said suddenly, 'You know, Percy, I've a strong feeling that the last thing Milner or Chamberlain want is for Kruger to be defeated in the election.'

'Why on earth should you think that? If Burger and the Progressives get power, half the problem will be solved. There'll be reduced taxation on the mines, and franchise concessions that'll enable us to have a say in our government.'

'And that'll help to keep the republic intact?'

'Of course it will! What —'

'The whole point, Percy! That's why I believe Chamberlain would prefer Kruger to be re-elected. There'll be no concessions from Kruger.'

'But that'd lead to intervention —'

'Exactly,' said Conyngham Greene.

FitzPatrick returned to Johannesburg just in time to read that Kruger had decided to give Johannesburg its own council, or *Stadsraad*. In October, 1897, the Sanitary Board that had supervised the emergence of the town from mining-camp to metropolis passed into the rubbled history of the Witwatersrand. In giving Johannesburg a town council to replace the Board, Kruger was at pains to let it be known that he was implementing the promises given to the Uit-landers at the time of the Jameson Raid. But he took away far more than he gave. He gladly handed over to them responsibility for public safety, order and morality, yet retained control of the police force; he let them elect twenty-four members to the council, but insisted that at least one of the two representatives of each ward should be a burgher of the State; the burgomaster was a Government appointment and had a power of veto. The effect was to ensure that the 2,000 Boers and officials in Johannesburg had a permanent majority in the Stadsraad over the representatives of more than 40,000 adult male Uitlanders. As a result, Johannesburg could never accept the Stadsraad as anything but an instrument of Pretoria; instead of alleviating Uitlander grievances, it became another one.

On the eve of the Transvaal's presidential elections Chamberlain revealed the sort of hand he was holding and the sort of game he was going to play. He sent through Greene a dispatch rejecting a Volksraad appeal for Swiss arbitration on points of difference between the two governments over interpretation of the 1884 Convention. His blunt reason: 'A suzerain Power cannot submit to arbitration on matters at issue between herself and her vassal.'

If there was a moment in which war between Great Britain and the South African Republic became inevitable, it was the moment when Paul Kruger read this dispatch handed to him by the British Agent. Its first consequence was a resounding victory for Kruger in the elections. Out of a total vote of 18,609 he obtained 12,858. Schalk Burger could total only 3,750.

Now Kruger, confirmed in his destiny by the confidence of his people, could see only one way out, and he began to move deliberately towards it. He could not see that Joseph Chamberlain, just as deliberately, had set him on that path.

The Uitlander attitude to the election and its result reflected only the varied ambitions and selfish interests of the Johannesburg community. The mining magnates decided to support Burger. This was not because they wanted him to win – they did not think he would ever be able to carry the Volksraad against Kruger – but because if he polled enough votes Kruger might feel compelled to sanction some of the reforms the mining industry desperately needed.

When the mining magnates supported anything, they did it with the only weapon they knew how to use: money. They suggested to the third man, Joubert, that he withdraw his candidature – for a small consideration. When this was rejected they concentrated on persuading as many as possible of Joubert's and Kruger's supporters to vote for Burger. This cost them, according to the Pretoria newspaper *De Volkstem*, £50,000 – in spite of the law prohibiting canvassing, election committees and other forms of wire-pulling.

The ultra-British section of the populace and the South African League, though they had no vote, exerted all their influence in Kruger's favour. They felt, with Chamberlain, that the best chance of destroying the republic was for a re-elected Kruger to continue his policy over the brink of war.

Kruger, who preferred a visible enemy, went out of his way in his inaugural speech to castigate the capitalists and speculators of the Witwatersrand, without mentioning the League. He welcomed all foreigners 'who are obedient to the laws of the land', and with a sure eye on the future not only of his republic but of all South Africa, he addressed his final appeal to the next generation:

'And now, dear children, a short word to you. Stand firm by God's Word. Keep to the language in which your fathers and forefathers, whom God led out of the wilderness, prayed to Him. It is a good thing to learn foreign languages, especially those of your neighbours; but let any foreign language be, to you, only a second language.'

Thus he identified and fixed in firm ground the anchor to which succeeding generations of Afrikanerdom were to cling through all the storms and adverse winds of the twentieth century.

The strength of Paul Kruger's position was further demonstrated, even before the announcement of his election triumph but coincident with his own awareness of it, by his dismissal of Chief Justice Kotze. He did this under Law 1 of 1897 – the very law which had caused Kotze to dispute the Presidential authority.

Milner waited hopefully for the reaction that would unite all the democratic forces in South Africa against the Transvaal dictatorship. He was disappointed. The Johannesburg branch of the South African League passed a resolution stressing the dangers to Uitlander interests in a State in which the judiciary had been made subservient to the Executive, and calling upon the British Government to intervene in protection of their threatened rights and liberties. It was sent to Conyngham Greene in Pretoria, who duly dispatched it to Chamberlain with a copy to the High Commissioner.

The Cape Bar sent a mild and appropriately judicious protest; and that was all.

Milner realized that a policy founded on an expectation that the Boers would hang themselves if given enough rope was misconceived. The hanging would have to be done for them. He wrote to Chamberlain: 'There is no way out of the political troubles of South Africa except reform in the

Transvaal or war. And at present the chances of reform are worse than ever. The Boers quarrel bitterly among themselves but it is about jobs and contracts, not politics!'

To Lord Selborne he revealed his mind even more plainly: 'The delusion under which most of us, including myself, laboured has been dispelled by the election and by the desertion of Kotze by even the most progressive of his fellow-burghers. Two wholly antagonistic systems – a mediaeval race oligarchy and a modern industrial State – cannot live permanently side by side in what is after all one country. The oligarchy has got to go, and I see no signs of its removing itself. In the fight for the establishment of the principle of equality, if it comes to a fight, we shall have to rely on British forces alone . . .'

When Dr Coster, the State Attorney who had prosecuted the Reform Committee, resigned his office as the result of a dispute with Kruger, that young barrister whom Milner had discussed with his visitors at Cape Town – Jan Smuts – was appointed in Coster's place on June 2, 1898.

CHAPTER THIRTY-FOUR

There was nothing very unusual about Tom Jackson Edgar. He was bigger than most, stronger than most, got drunk just as often, and he had a terrible temper; but he was a well-behaved citizen by Johannesburg standards, and generally respected. Nothing he ever did in his life could have caused his name to be remembered by history, yet by his death he changed history. If there are descendants of Tom Jackson Edgar in South Africa today, they could with some truth boast to their friends: 'My grandfather started the Boer War.'

It was one week to Christmas, 1898, and Johannesburg with its facility for anticipating festive occasions had begun celebrating the previous weekend. By midnight on Sunday, when the more respectable bars closed their doors, the streets were full of small, voluble groups, ineffectual fights and erratic navigation homeward. Tom Edgar was not drunk. He'd had a fair amount of whisky and beer. But he was not drunk – just bad-tempered. He headed, a trifle unsteadily perhaps, for his room in Florrie's Chambers at the corner of Anderson and Frederick Streets; his wife would be waiting up for him, and the thought of the nagging that lay ahead played on his irritability and his conscience.

At the entrance to Florrie's three or four other inmates of the rooming-house had gathered in the darkness, reluctant to leave the comradeship of controversy for the bachelor loneliness of their beds. It was Foster's dog that came sniffing around them.

'*Voetsak!*' Foster said loudly, and gave it a shove with his boot that sent it scampering off into the night. As Edgar came up to the doorway of the passage that divided Florrie's Chambers, he heard the contemptuous dismissal and came lurching over.

'Who do you *voetsak*?' he asked angrily.

'I was not speaking to you. Mind your own business!'

Edgar's big fist swung up through a quarter-circle that ended on the point of Foster's jaw. He went down in a crumpled heap. One of his companions bent quickly.

'My God,' he said as he straightened up, 'I think you've killed him! What did you want to do that for? He was *voetsakk*ing his dog. I'm going to fetch the police!'

The man went into the middle of the intersection of the roads and started yelling for the police. Edgar, after a swift look down at the prostrate, motionless figure, hurried up the passage and into his room. As he locked the door behind him his wife got out of bed and came across to him.

'What's happened, Tom? Why are they shouting for the police? Are you in trouble?'

'Now ~~don~~'t worry, Bessie. Get back into bed. I'll handle this.'

'But what's all the noise about?' Mrs Edgar persisted, as the sound of running footsteps and a crescendo of voices came through the window. She lay down on the bed and her husband went to the wardrobe and groped around inside. When he stood upright again he had in his right hand a short bar with an iron nut at the end.

'One of those drunks along the passage insulted me, so I hit him. That's when they started yelling for the police. You know what those "Zarps" are like...'

A loud hammering on the door punctuated the terse commands to 'Open up! It's the police!'

'I'm not opening anything!' Edgar yelled. 'You come back in the morning. And bring a proper warrant with you.'

They heard the voice say, 'Try the window. If you can't get in there we'll have to break down the door.' There was a pause of a few seconds, then they heard scratching and pushing at the window. Mrs Edgar pulled the bed-clothes up to her neck, her eyes wide and frightened. Edgar stood poised in the middle of the room, ready to move in either direction.

Outside in the passage four policemen gathered. Foster lay unmoving where he had been felled. Across the street a small group collected in pyjamas and nightgowns. One of Foster's friends was urging the police to break down the door and arrest Edgar.

Constable Bart Stephanus Jones leant against the door of Edgar's room and felt it give a little.

433

'This won't take a lot of breaking,' he said to the policemen behind him. 'Give me a hand, Muller. Just get behind me and shove.'

'You look out – hey, Jones? That man can be dangerous, and he's as strong as an ox.'

'I'll take care of that,' Jones said, and patted his holster. 'Now, you ready? Then push!'

At the first heave the door splintered open. Jones glimpsed a large man silhouetted above him with raised arm, then felt the blow on the side of his face. He caught another blow on his forearm as his right hand flew to his revolver. He saw Edgar's arm lift again, the knobbed bar at the apex of its swing. He pulled the trigger.

The flash and detonation were simultaneous with the look of shock and astonishment that appeared on Edgar's face. His hand went up to the left side of his chest; he stared stupidly at the blood seeping through his fingers. Then he lurched through the doorway and pitched on his face in the passage. A blur of white went past Jones as Mrs Edgar rushed to her husband and crouched sobbing beside him; blood spread slowly across the floor. They lifted her gently off, and one of the policemen turned Edgar over. He was dead, all right. They picked the iron bar out of the pool of blood and gave it to Jones. 'You look after this carefully, hey? It's going to be your best witness.'

'Thanks, Muller. You three stay here. I'm going back to the charge office to make a report. I'll tell the District Surgeon and the Field-Cornet to come along right away. Don't let anybody touch anything; and keep your mouths shut.'

Jones – who stated he was a grandson of Queen Victoria's coachman – was arrested on a charge of murder; but after hearing an account of the affair from police officials, the Public Prosecutor, Dr Krause, reduced the charge to culpable homicide and released Jones on bail of £200.

It was just the opportunity the Johannesburg branch of the South African League was waiting for. With the enthusiastic assistance of *The Star* and other organs of Uitlander opinion, an Edgar Committee was formed. Its members visited all persons, other than the police, who had been in any way associated with, or witnesses of, the incidents at Florrie's Chambers. On December 22 *The Star* published a series of affidavits, sworn before the British Vice-Consul, all of which indicated that Edgar had been shot without provocation as soon as Jones had burst open the door. The following morning a weekly review, *The Critic*, published an article accusing Dr Krause of racial bias in the exercise of his duties, thus violating his oath of office.

At the same time British subjects in Johannesburg were summoned by leaflet and newspaper announcement to a protest meeting, to be held in the Market Square outside the Post Office, in order to support a petition which was to be sent to the Queen through the Consul. In the face of this uproar the acting British Agent in Pretoria had an interview with Jan Smuts, the new State Attorney, who ordered the re-arrest of Jones on a charge of murder. The vice-consul in Johannesburg was told to avoid anything in the shape of a public meeting outside the Consulate, as satisfaction in the Edgar case had been given.

But the South African League were not to be put off. Edgar was only a symbol of something far more significant. Besides, they had already drawn up their petition, and obtained 5,000 signatures to it. To the Queen it must go.

At three o'clock on Saturday afternoon Market Square began to fill. By 3.30 there were reckoned to be nearly 5,000 people before the Post Office. But they were not all British subjects, and the entire detective force of the town was distributed among the crowd. A small group of burghers, easily distinguishable, kept up a running exchange of insults with the Englishmen who surrounded them. As these became more personal and intimately slanderous, the good temper of the afternoon disappeared, and it was not long before one of the Boers got a punch on the nose. Soon fists and sticks were flailing, and the crowd began to close in angrily on the cluster of burghers. The detectives and police immediately formed a protective circle around them and shepherded them through the iron gates at the entrance to the Post Office.

At this stage Mr C. D. Webb, chairman of the Johannesburg branch of the League, stood up on a wagon and reminded the crowd that public and open-air meetings were not allowed in the Transvaal and that they must respect the law like true Britishers.

'The intention is,' he told them, 'that you should accompany the committee in a quiet and orderly manner to the Consul's office, where the deputation will present the petition which has been prepared. I desire that the police and detectives I see around shall have no objection to raise against your behaviour. The policy of those who run Johannesburg has always been that the public must cry under and act the little lamb business. Now the time has come when British subjects have got justice on their side. The Vice-Consul has sent a message saying that he is ready to receive the deputation, so let us go.'

The members of the Edgar Committee then climbed into a carriage, but before they could drive off the crowd unyoked the horses and pulled the vehicle, singing and cheering, to the Standard Bank Buildings in Commissioner Street. There a dozen committee men headed by Messrs Wybergh, Webb and Dodd of the South African League went upstairs to the consulate.

By the time the Vice-Consul and the deputation appeared in the french windows, Commissioner Street was jammed by a mass of 6,000 people. It was made clear to Dodd that there could be no speeches and that he would be limited to reading the petition. Dodd took the rolled document in his hand and stepped to the edge of the balcony. He had to wait for the cheering and one verse of 'Rule, Britannia' to stop before he could make himself heard. Then he turned to the Vice-Consul, and announced:

'I am here today to present to you the following petition to Her Gracious Majesty the Queen – whom God preserve – with regard to the shooting of Edgar. I will now read the petition.'

What he read was a thirteen-point indictment of the republican police and republican oppression, the gist of it being concentrated in Point 7: 'During the past few months this antagonistic attitude of the police has assumed a much more serious and aggressive aspect. Without warrant they have invaded private houses and taken the occupants into custody on frivolous charges; violently arrested British subjects on the streets on unintelligible charges; and generally displayed towards Your Majesty's subjects a temper which undoubtedly tends to endanger the peace of the community . . .'

The megaphone voice of Dodd rolled on over the shouts of the crowd, sometimes submerged by cheers. Finally he came to the summing-up:

' "We humbly represent to Your Majesty that we, your

436

loyal subjects resident here on the Witwatersrand gold-
fields, are entirely defenceless since the police are appointed
by the Government and not by the municipality; we have no
voice in the government of the country; there is no longer
an independent judiciary to which we can appeal; there is
therefore no power within this State to which we can have
recourse with the least hope of success, and as we are not
allowed to arm ourselves our last resource is to fall back on
our status as British subjects."

'That is all, gentlemen. Now I must ask those who would
like to authorize the dispatch of this petition to signify their
assent by holding up their hands.'

Hands, hats, papers and coloured neckscarves broke the
mobile surface of the crowd. There was not one in all those
thousands who did not give his assent with upraised arm.
There was none who dared not give it.

Unfortunately for the South African League, Sir Alfred
Milner was in England at the time of these occurrences and
his deputy as High Commissioner at the Cape was the
newly-appointed commander-in-chief in South Africa,
General Sir William Butler. He was liberal and pacific in his
assessment of the South African situation, and was inclined
to agree with those who judged Rhodes and the Uitlanders
as the principal menaces to peace in the country.

When he received the Edgar petition, Butler returned it
to the Agent at Pretoria explaining that he could not trans-
mit it to the Queen because its contents had appeared in the
Press before it had been presented. It was a technical cover
for his privately-expressed opinion: 'I'll see them damned
first!'

Webb and Dodd accepted the technicality but were determined, in spite of the re-arrest of Jones, that their grievances should be brought to the personal notice of the
Queen. Nor were they discouraged in any of their intentions when the Pretoria Government ordered their arrest
for infringements of the laws against public meetings. They
were released on bail of £500 each. It was a tactical error on
Kruger's part, for all the branches of the South African
League, as though waiting for this signal, immediately
summoned meetings in protest against 'this and similar outrages against British subjects in the Republic'. They resolved
that 'further toleration of this condition of affairs on the
part of the Imperial Government must affect the peace of

the country and lead to the contempt and degradation of every British subject throughout South Africa unless remedied by Imperial intervention'.

It was in the last few words that they revealed themselves. Intervention it was they were after. But words were not enough. Within a week of the arrest of Webb and Dodd, the Johannesburg branch of the League had called a public meeting of protest in the Amphitheatre – a large enclosure in which circuses and similar performances were held. The Amphitheatre had never seen anything – circus or prize-fight – like the show that was put on during the afternoon of Saturday, January 14.

To make sure that another technicality would not be employed to prevent the meeting, Wybergh had seen Smuts and received an assurance that provided it was a meeting of residents in a public hall there could be no legal objection. Nor could there be any legal objection if the meeting was attended by loyal burghers of the Republic. Early on Saturday morning the foremen in charge of the gangs constructing the Main Reef road received their instructions: they were to select groups of 'ware Afrikaners' and arrange transport to take them to the Amphitheatre in Johannesburg by 2 p.m. There they would receive further instructions from an official of the Public Works Department.

There was no lack of recruits, particularly when it was known that they were to be paid two hours earlier than usual and get a free ride into town. Acting Road Inspector Papenfus had great difficulty in explaining to squads of Russian labourers that their services were not required.

Thus it was that at half-past one the men who were preparing the seating in the sawdust ring of the Amphitheatre were mildly surprised to see a collection of about 100 Boers in the street outside. There they were addressed briefly by one of the Landdrost's clerks, and told to report to the police station. During the next half-hour other cart-loads of road-workers were redirected until more than 300 men were gathered behind the charge office. Mr Brocksma, the Third Public Prosecutor, told them briefly they were to go down to the Amphitheatre, occupy as many seats as they could and, at a signal from himself and the plain-clothes policemen who would be with them, break up the meeting. The foreman of each gang received more specific orders, so that each group went independently to the meeting-place, stopping joyfully at pubs on the way.

Soon after three o'clock, as the doors of the Amphitheatre were opened, the Afrikaners rushed a side door and occupied all the seats immediately below the box from which the speeches were to be delivered. The only opposition they encountered was from a solitary doorman; the bulk of the Uitlander population, their loyalties torn between patriotism and the Roodepoort races, had gone to the latter.

The Boers behaved themselves with unexpected decorum while the hall was filling and while the prospective speakers and their lady guests took their seats in the box. There was a minor distraction when the canopy above this reservation collapsed under the weight of a number of embryo Uitlanders, precipitating them amid much screaming and squealing on to the hats and laps of the ladies below. Only when Mr W. Wybergh, chairman of the meeting, came forward to the rim of the box, did the Afrikaners erupt. Poor Wybergh never got further, that anybody could hear, than, 'Ladies and gentlemen, we are met today —'

He struggled on valiantly, but it was a pantomime performance on a silent screen as hooting and booing from the near burghers competed with counter-cheering from the other occupants of the ring and the public galleries. He was seen to turn and indicate Joseph Dunn, editor of *The Critic*, who was due to propose the first resolution to be submitted to the meeting. As soon as they saw him coming forward the Boer party began to sing the *Volkslied*, and the unfortunate Dunn, conceding the anthem the respect due to it, felt compelled to stand to attention above the hostile crowd almost at his feet. As the last stanzas rolled away into brief silence he spoke quietly: 'The resolution I have to propose reads as follows – "That this meeting of British subjects —"'

It was the last anybody heard of Joe Dunn's speech – or any other speech. A free fight developed at the side entrance where the outraged doorkeeper had finally found a solitary burgher of his own size and weight. It was like a small match set to a powder-keg. The one fight turned into three, then into ten; suddenly the whole arena was a swirling mass of punching, kicking, cursing humanity.

In a few minutes Uitlander resistance was overwhelmed and the ring cleared of all except Afrikaners. But there were still plenty of Britishers in the galleries and boxes. One group of sun-hardened workmen began breaking up chairs to hurl the legs, seats and arms at the enemy. Immediately every chair in the place was being splintered to provide missiles, and the air was filled with flying timber.

In the main box the conveners of the meeting held a hasty consultation and then shepherded their guests and womenfolk out of harm's way. Their example was followed by most of the audience who, once outside, sought help from mounted and foot police in vain. They were met by a smiling indifference, with invitations to make affidavits and name the men by whom they had been assaulted.

Inside the Amphitheatre a handful of Uitlanders whose valour had become the better part of their discretion were well occupied in hurling the wooden missiles back at the Boers. With such a congested target and from the advantage of their own dispersion they had a tactical superiority which was proving highly effective, especially as such a dense fog of sawdust and powdered earth was rising from the circus ring that those in it could hardly breathe, let alone see.

There was a spontaneous rush outwards from the centre, and soon the last Uitlander outposts were being cleared from the battlefield as mopping-up parties of roadmen roamed through the boxes, galleries and passages of the building, smashing up furniture and fittings when human opposition had evaporated.

In ten minutes it was all over. A tall foreman, beard falling over a blue flannel shirt, came to the front of the League's box and yelled, 'Come on boys, it is finished! The *rooineks* have run away, like they did at Majuba. Let us go home!'

The battle of the Johannesburg Amphitheatre was, it can be said, the first Afrikaner victory of the Boer War. As for Constable Jones, he was finally indicted for culpable homicide and acquitted – very properly, on the evidence.

In England Milner fumed at Butler and, as soon as he returned to the Cape, reviewed the Edgar case in a dispatch to Chamberlain. It was his opinion that the trial supported the Uitlander belief that they could not expect impartial justice from the courts of the Republic and that the verdict had created an alarming situation.

Chamberlain was only too eager to accept Milner's conclusions. His minute on this dispatch began: 'The case is a bad example of the treatment British subjects are liable to in this semi-barbarous community . . .' He also claimed £4,000 compensation for Edgar's widow on the ground that there 'appears to have been a clear miscarriage of justice on the criminal trial'.

Thus the grandson of Queen Victoria's coachman passed from the limelight of history having cast in it, for his brief moment, a longer, darker shadow than many of her own imperial offspring.

Throughout the agitation over the shooting of Edgar many of the mining magnates had demonstrated a pronounced unwillingness to associate themselves with the attitude of the South African League. In a situation in which the whole structure of their great industry and their share of the profits was dependent on the goodwill of the Government – as they have been ever since – this was reasonable enough. But at the time they were far more concerned with serious developments connected with the dynamite monopoly.

The report of the commission inquiring into the operation of the monopoly had been suppressed by Kruger, and never came before the Volksraad. Instead, at the end of 1898 the Executive made the astounding proposition that in return for a comparatively insignificant reduction in the price of dynamite to the mines it was intended to ask the Raad to prolong the monopoly for a further fifteen years, to condone all past breaches of contract and to prohibit cancellation for future breaches during the period of extension. The Raad postponed a decision until February, but there was little doubt they would then agree to it.

Milner learnt of this while still on leave in England. He and Chamberlain, in direct touch with each other, regarded the dynamite dispute as a vital step on the road to physical intervention in the affairs of the Republic. As usual, Her Majesty's Government could not appear to take an initiative that would appear to a critical and watchful world as aggression. In their talks together neither Milner nor Chamberlain had any doubts where the answer to this problem lay.

'It is getting more and more obvious,' Milner told the Colonial Secretary, 'that if we allow Kruger's concessions policy to continue unopposed, the administration of the Transvaal will eventually be undertaken by us burdened by these monopolies to such an extent that we will only get the shell of the nut.'

'The kernel having gone into the pockets of Kruger and his accomplices, eh?'

'Exactly, sir. What we must do is to get those Rand magnates busy. They're frightened to death of offending the President. Can't you get the Agent in Pretoria to prod them a little?'

'I was coming to that, Sir Alfred. We have already been in touch with the Agent on the lines you suggest. He has consulted the president and prominent members of the Chamber of Mines. You know what their reply was? I'm quoting from memory, but this is the gist of it. They told him that no further protest against the dynamite decision was contemplated until the Raad had acted, and that no direct appeal from them to Her Majesty's Government could be expected as long as the Transvaal Government regarded such an appeal as treason, and as long as there was no evidence of any intention on our part to give them protection. So you see, if we want the mining houses to move we've got to make it clear that we'll support them. It cannot be a secret arrangement: to be effective it must come out in the open that we are in alliance with the magnates on this issue. That, as I am sure you appreciate, can have significant consequences.'

'Would you not say, perhaps, that they were desirable consequences?' Milner suggested. He got Chamberlain's quick nod of approval, and went on: 'I believe we should instruct the Agent to tell the Chamber that a strong but moderate protest from them would receive the Colonial Secretary's support, if the protest is made public.'

Chamberlain pondered this in silence for a few minutes as the clatter of traffic in Whitehall came through the window closed against the bitter January air.

'Very well,' he said at last. 'I am willing to take the risk of this course. It's almost like 1896 again, isn't it? Thank heaven there's no Dr Jameson loose in Bechuanaland! I will arrange the sending of a dispatch protesting officially, in the name of this Government, against the extension of the monopoly. It seems to me it is a contravention of several articles of the London Convention. I believe it would be proper to make the protest in such terms.'

Towards the end of January the annual meeting of the Witwatersrand Chamber of Mines heard its president, W. Rouliot, criticize the Government's intention to extend the dynamite concession. Moving a resolution offering the Goverment a loan of £600,000 for the purpose of compensating the monopoly for its capital expenditure in the event of cancellation, he went on to express approval of the Colonial Secretary's dispatch protesting against the monopoly, thus making public – as Chamberlain had anticipated – that the Randlords were now in league with the Colonial Office against the administration of the Republic.

In the meantime the State Secretary in Pretoria had rejected Chamberlain's charge of contravention of the London agreement on grounds of irrelevance. For good measure he added that even if the argument was relevant it was for the Government of the Republic to decide what was best for itself.

Although there was still some hope that the Volksraad would not agree to the extension of the dynamite monopoly, not many people were under any illusions as to what was happening or in which direction event and circumstances were being steered. Percy FitzPatrick, who had never had any doubts as to the extent of Kruger's domination over the Volksraad, was convinced that a totally different policy must be pursued in a totally different direction if imperial intervention was to be avoided. He saw more clearly than most that this would not only mean war between the Transvaal and Great Britain, but that it would tear South Africa in half for generations. He was determined to do what he could to prevent such a catastrophe.

Jan Smuts, a man of increasing and beneficent influence in the presidential circle, was his man. FitzPatrick and Smuts had got to know each other well during the young barrister's rather unprofitable sojourn in Johannesburg. They liked and respected each other, and FitzPatrick did not share the general opinion that twenty-eight was rather too young an age for the State Attorney of the South African Republic. He was enormously impressed by the sincerity and determination revealed in those aesthetic features; the vivid blue eyes could sparkle with warmth and humour, or glint like blue ice or, at other times, withdraw behind an opaque veil when communication was unwanted. If anybody was to introduce the progressive changes which the republic and the mining industry required, this – thought FitzPatrick, as he outlined the scheme he had propounded to Milner – was the man.

Smuts heard him out in silence, finger-tips pressed together, head tilted back with the eyes staring into some vision of the future, in what was to become a characteristic pose. The clean firm line of the chin was not yet accentuated by the goatee beard that was to become so familiar in the years ahead. When FitzPatrick had finished, Smuts said carefully in that clipped, rather high-pitched voice:

'I think it is necessary for me to say in the first place that I acknowledge unreservedly that I regard this as the first genuine effort on the part of the leaders of the mining industry on the Witwatersrand to bring about a real settlement. Now, let us take some of the specific issues you mention.'

He scribbled two or three words on a writing-pad and went on.

'The liquor traffic, for instance. This, I know, is a blot on the administration. We all know what the problems are. And we know there are difficulties as far as the President is concerned. He is a very strong man, but he wants to do what is best. And he hears a lot of things that you and I don't hear. You have to remember there are a number of people who are hangers-on, who have personal interests to serve of which he knows nothing; and there are times when they make it very difficult to carry out what we all know ought to be done. But it will be done, Mr FitzPatrick – it will be done.'

He took a quick look at the pad before him as FitzPatrick wondered whether he should say something. Smuts gave him no chance.

'Now, this dynamite business. Most people would ridicule any suggestion that there is a connection between the dynamite monopoly and the independence of the republic. You and I know there is none; even that our independence would be strengthened if there were no such thing as a dynamite concession. But that's not the practical point. There are some very plausible people interested in dynamite. I won't mention any names, but they have access to

444

the President and to some of his advisers and they seem to have persuaded him that cancellation of the dynamite monopoly would produce such an effect that it would alienate many who are our powerful supporters.'

'That is an argument,' FitzPatrick said quickly, 'that I have never been able to understand. How can —'

'The republic has need of friends. And may need them more than ever in the years to come. Or should I say that it must appear that we have powerful friends? But be patient, Mr FitzPatrick. Just tell your friends to be patient. We will get these reforms by degrees. Above all you must learn to be patient with the President. He is a great man and a great leader. But he is also an old man and beset by difficulties and by numbers of people whom he trusts but who are not his true friends.'

FitzPatrick then shifted the discussion to political matters, the familiar arguments for Uitlander rights and expectations. As he spoke he could see the eyes of the man opposite reflecting his mental withdrawal. They flickered with interest when FitzPatrick suggested a round-table conference to discuss a practical settlement with the mining industry of the proposals he had made – a settlement which would undoubtedly improve the political situation. But the quick gleam became steely when the Johannesburger went on to include the Imperial Government in the scope of the conference to try to reach an agreement on questions of suzerainty, immigration and citizenship. Smuts held up one hand to stop the words and said firmly: 'That, of course, is impossible.'

'But why?' FitzPatrick asked, surprised at the sudden hardness.

'It will be inconsistent with the dignity of an independent State to discuss its internal affairs with another Power.'

This, thought FitzPatrick, is the republic's answer to Chamberlain ... two completely irreconcilable points of view.

'At some time or other, Mr State Attorney,' he put his thoughts into words, 'you will have to get around a table and talk it out. If we don't make a supreme effort to reach a settlement, you must realize the alternative is war.'

'Yes, I realize it. I think the position is very threatening.' Smuts stood up and threw his arms wide, then he moved

445

his hands through an arc in front of him until they came together with a loud smack.

'I seem to see two great thunderclouds approaching, and when they meet there will come the crash – and the deluge.'

He stood there for some seconds, his eyes closed, his hands slowly clenching into fists. Then his head drooped sadly as his arms fell to his side. FitzPatrick said urgently:

'D'you know what such a war means? It will extend from the Zambesi to three oceans. It will divide the races and the States. It will split us from one end to the other. Every community will be divided. Families will be divided: father against son, brother against brother. God alone knows where the thing will end. It'll bring utter ruin to South Africa. And you'd risk all this for something which is nothing more than vanity – something which is inconsistent with your dignity? That's all it is!'

Smuts said softly: 'Yes, I know what it means.'

'Your dignity! Your independence! Good God man, you know England; you were educated in England. You know what the Empire means. In six months you'll have no dignity left. You'll have no independence. No State. Nothing! What kind of madness is this?'

FitzPatrick was pacing up and down the room, making emphatic gestures with his hands as he erased dignity, independence and the republic from the future. Smuts was smiling as he sat down.

'Yes, Mr FitzPatrick, I know England. Better perhaps than you think. I lived and studied there. Yes, I know England. Not in six months, my friend, not in six years. You may take the cities and the mines, for we would not face you there. But for six or seven years we would hold out in the mountains where your armies would be no larger than the space we allowed you to fight in. And long before six years are up there will be a change of opinion in England. Other things will crop up. The people will become weary and lose interest. There will be another general election and the Liberals will come into power.'

He got up from his chair again and came close to Fitz-Patrick.

'And this time,' he said slowly, 'we shall get all we want.'

He turned his back on his visitor and moved across to the window from where he could see the Magaliesberg ranging away to the westward. Mountain and veld, heat and

446

drought, disease and distance ... these were the allies of the Boers. The English would have to fight all of them together. And together they could not be eliminated. They could not be conquered by men and guns.

CHAPTER THIRTY-FIVE

Once again the dapper, red-bearded figure of Edouard Lippert was seen slipping in and out of the headquarters of the mining houses. His mission was high-principled; his motives, as usual, not quite on the same level. He made it known quickly that he was an emissary of the Government of the Republic, and that his objective was a meeting between representatives of the Executive and the mining industry to discuss not only a settlement of the differences and difficulties between them, but 'peace between the Government and the whole Uitlander population'.

The Rand magnates approached the proposition warily. Long experience of negotiations with Kruger had made them doubtful of any altruistic inspiration, and these doubts were not lessened by Pretoria's choice of Lippert as an intermediary – particularly when it became known that his own reward for the maintenance of the dynamite monopoly would be a settlement of £150,000.

By the beginning of February all the principal actors were gathered on stage. Milner was back in Cape Town and Conyngham Greene had returned to Pretoria – having travelled out on the same ship as the High Commissioner. Dr Leyds was in Pretoria after a tour of European capitals in search of money and of support other than friendly assurances. It was the failure of this mission, coinciding with the outburst of patriotic emotion occasioned by the Edgar affair and the activities of the South African League, which prompted Kruger to try to make his peace with the Rand capitalists. Peace, perhaps, was the wrong word for his aim, which was an alliance with the magnates against the Uitlander eruption and the Imperial Government.

The terms which Lippert brought from Pretoria were strictly a business proposition, but they revealed the concern of the Boer Government and, more significantly, the weakening of their position. The initial approach was made on the basis of a memorandum submitted by Lippert to Fitz-Patrick and George Rouliot, like FitzPatrick a member of the Wernher, Beit firm. There were nine main headings: cessation of Press agitation against the Republic in South Africa and Britain; support of the Government's attitude on the immigration of Asiatics; settlement of the dynamite question; support for a loan if required by the administration; repudiation of the South African League; appointment of a State Financier with full authority in the Executive on all questions of finance; no new taxation of the mining industry until the Financial Adviser's proposals had been placed before the Government; sale of 'undermining' rights to the owners of surface rights at a moderate valuation; extension of the franchise rights by reducing the qualifying period for Uitlanders.

The immediate conclusion on the part of the Randlords, Milner and the Colonial Secretary was that Kruger and his Executive were hard-pressed. Milner's chief worry was that Chamberlain would take a non-committal line, and allow the mining houses to make a deal in their own interests and not in the interests of the whole Uitlander population – on which, Milner saw quite clearly, the case for intervention would depend.

As the negotiations proceeded through March it soon became apparent that the Government were intent on bribing the mining houses with the offer of reduced charges for dynamite in exchange for acceptance of the other demands in the memorandum. It was also apparent that the industry's representatives had perceived this; they were just as intent on getting their demands met on the franchise question, in exchange for those other concessions.

On March 15 a dinner was held at the Rand Club, attended by twenty-four of the most prominent English businessmen and industrialists. They included the presidents of the Chamber of Mines and the Chamber of Commerce, and all the committee members of the South African League.

Percy FitzPatrick was the principal speaker; after detailing the origins and the course of the negotiations, he summarized the situation:

'Naturally, gentlemen, I have been in the closest touch with the British Agent and the High Commissioner from the moment Lippert made his first approach, and I do not think I am revealing any secrets when I tell you that the position is being closely studied in Whitehall, and that our attitude in these negotiations is very largely the attitude of the Colonial Secretary. The consensus of opinion among all on this side is that the whole affair is a "spoof" on the part of Kruger and the Executive with a view to frustrating the legitimate aims of Her Majesty's Government in the Transvaal. To accomplish this they seek to sow dissension among the Uitlanders by splitting the mining houses from political organizations like the South African League – whom we are pleased to see represented here tonight – and by offering a solution of the dynamite question as a bribe to prevent agitation for our rights as citizens and Englishmen. I am sure Mr Rouliot will agree with what I have been saying.'

FitzPatrick sat down to loud applause. As the port bottle went round, Rouliot, who voiced no objection to this erasure of his French nationality, expressed the approval of the mining industry of Mr FitzPatrick's conduct of the talks.

'These talks,' he added, 'are still in progress between myself and several other gentlemen at this table representing the Chamber of Mines on the one side, and Dr Leyds with Messrs Reitz and Smuts on the other. I can tell you now that we intend to co-opt a number of prominent citizens to report on the franchise question so that we can fairly represent the views of the whole community and show the Government that their attempts to divide us have failed. I may say that we all regard the franchise problem and not the dynamite monopoly as the most significant factor in our talks with the Government. I agree with Fitz that the real motive of the Government is not among the subjects listed for negotiation. As he says, they are trying to "spoof" us. What I believe we should do now is continue these negotiations in the friendliest and most reasonable spirit in order to induce Kruger to show his hand. I trust this meets with your approval.'

Approval was quick to come in the table-thumping and loud hear-hears which ended Rouliot's brief speech. The dinner party broke up with a final injunction from FitzPatrick that everything they had heard was in the strictest confidence. The editor of *The Star* nodded his head in glum assent.

In Heidelberg the delegates to a conference called by the

Burghermacht – a sort of citizen defence force – were surprised to learn on the morning of Friday, March 17, that they would not be able to hold their afternoon meeting; the Good Templars' Hall was required by President Kruger for a discussion with the public on the latest political developments.

Kruger travelled across to Heidelberg in the State coach attached to one of the trains to Johannesburg. It was detached at Germiston, and he completed the journey to Heidelberg in a Cape cart behind four horses. Thirteen years before, he had come to Heidleburg in a Cape cart on his return from Barberton and the low-veld...

He looked about him. Had all this happened in thirteen years? Was this the Promised Land into which their God had led them – this land of brick and tin and steel, man-made koppies of rubbled earth obliterating the veld where once the Voortrekkers had grazed their cattle and shot the teeming herds of antelope? Was this smoke and noise-filled obscurity the same air that had once filled their lungs with its clean inspiration as they listened to the silence? Those old Boers at Potchefstroom had seen the future clearly when they had prohibited the prospectors. But they had not been able to prevent the monstrous rape of the republic; and now the republic had brought forth this. Was it worth fighting for? Why did they not pack their wagons, inspan their oxen and trek?

Because there was nowhere to go. The British had encircled them; locked them in their republic. That was Rhodes' idea. Cecil Rhodes. Kruger had broken him at Doornkop. Was Rhodes going to triumph after all?

Here in Heidelberg he was among his own people. Most of them had come with him across the Vaal River; many of the young men had been conceived in the lurching wagons rolling across the plains of the Orange Free State. From his seat above them on the platform he looked them over. Fifteen years ago he would have talked with them about their cattle and the crops, about the need for rain and the coming move to winter grazing. Now he had to talk a very different language – but this also was one that they all understood. 'Now about this dynamite business; I'm not going to talk history. Most of you know what the position is. Let me put it to you this way. Supposing a man had a nice farm with well-cultivated and fertile soil and then decided to get mealies from his neighbour because he could get them cheaper that way than by growing them himself; the result would be that the farm would be useless for in the event of a quarrel with the neighbour his supplies would be cut off and next day he would have nothing. That is the case with our dynamite factory – the principal factor in connection with our independence. If we have a quarrel with England and she closed her ports to us, where would we be without our factory? We have to import some things for the manufacture of dynamite because the sulphur and saltpetre are still in the rocks and *krantzes* of our country and would be very expensive to get out. I tell you that the factory could make me a million Martini-Henry cartridges if I wanted them. That is what I mean by independence! But it is not something you get in a day.

'The State wants to take over the factory, but the contract still has four years to run. In that time the dynamite company would pay to the State about one million pounds – enough to take over the plant and other assets. I do not want to break the contract, for that would damage our credit. Already the contractors for the new wool factory say they are having difficulty in raising capital because of the threat of State interference in the dynamite contract. So you see, it is not a simple matter of doing what the gold mines want us to do. But let me say, also, that if the company is agreeable we would expropriate as speedily as possible.'

The discussion now became general, with Kruger shrewdly fending off inquiries about profits per case and the amount taken by the concessionaries. Finally, Mr E. P. A. Meintjies spoke up.

'Oom Paul, I would like to ask whether I am to understand that in order to bring all the disputes to an end your object is to have the factory taken over and placed in the hands of the State?'

As the President's tall hat nodded in vigorous assent the whole audience clapped its appreciation. Kruger held up his hand for silence. He had got over the most difficult part. He had no worries when he talked about votes for Uitlanders in front of his burghers. But there were one or two Uitlanders in the hall: he hoped they would not question him too deeply.

'Now, friends,' he began, 'in regard to the franchise:

what the law says is that after two years an Uitlander can vote for the Second Raad, and two more years gives him the right to be a member of that body. In another ten years he can become a full burgher, provided two-thirds of the enfranchised burghers in his district approve.

'Now, I know that in most countries the period is five years, but you must remember that when this fourteen-year law was made there were only twelve thousand full burghers in the whole Transvaal, while there were so many newcomers that giving the franchise to everybody would have meant giving away the country to the Uitlanders! Today there are approximately forty thousand burghers, and because of this I intend to propose to the next session of the Raad a reduction of five years in the period of qualification – making nine years in all. But I want the election of the President to remain in the hands of the old burghers and their descendants.'

Kruger, who was now reputed to have a very convenient deafness, had a fine ear for crowd noises; he was rather surprised, as the murmur of comment reach him, to sense the half-note of doubt and questioning. Perhaps there were more Uitlanders than he had thought in the hall. A man stood up and introduced himself, in fluent Afrikaans, as Chatterton.

'Mr President, is your proposal to be retrospective? Supposing a man were naturalized seven years ago, that is after he had the right to vote for the Second Raad, would he have full burgher rights immediately the law came into force?'

'Yes; that is the position.'

'And would it have to be done, Mr President, with the approval of two-thirds of the burghers?'

'Exactly. That is what the law says.'

Chatterton was about to point out that as the law was going to be altered in one respect it could be altered in another, but he saw Kruger looking past him and heard the next question suggesting it would be a good idea to have special representatives for Johannesburg and the gold-fields, as under the present restrictions on voting their representatives were returned chiefly by the police force stationed in the district.

Kruger smiled a little grimly with the reluctant laughter. 'The people of Johannesburg,' he said, 'are like a man who wants a second wife while his first wife is still living. And that, as you know, is not allowed by the law. Now I have some more important news for you people of Heidelberg. Your request for a windmill and reservoir has been approved, and will be constructed on a piece of Government land near the mining office . . .'

The President's speech made, on the whole, a favourable impression in all parts of South Africa – except in Johannesburg, where Uitlander reaction was that they had heard too many of Kruger's promises to take them seriously. In the House of Commons on the following Monday night Sir Ellis Ashmead-Bartlett made a lengthy speech detailing the grievances of the Uitlanders and accusing the Government of failure to look after the interests of British residents in the Transvaal. He urged them to take action to secure full redress of these grievances.

Chamberlain was quickly on his feet.

'What is it that the honourable member wants the Government to do? Does he wish the Government to insist on reforms – and if they are not granted that we should go to war with the Transvaal? I see the honourable member nodding his head, but is he sure that is what the Uitlander population want? Does he not remember a recent speech by the president of the Witwatersrand Chamber of Mines asking us not to go on nagging the Pretoria Government? They are naturally concerned about what would happen to the mining industry if war broke out.

'At the same time,' he went on, 'there is a good deal of truth in the honourable member's complaints. President Kruger, three years ago, made certain promises. None of these has yet been fulfilled. The grievances of the Uitlanders have increased rather than diminished. As far as I can see the latest promises made by the President at Heidelberg are entirely illusory, and I think that his suggestions for remedying the situation both in regard to the franchise and the dynamite monopoly are not of the slightest value. I can assure the House that the Government is watching the position very carefully . . .'

Whatever Chamberlain said in the House of Commons or in public, Milner knew the Colonial Secretary's real intentions. In their talks together they had arrived always at the same conclusion – that the South African Republic must disappear, in the interests of the Transvaal itself and of British dominion over the sub-continent. It would have been in the worst of taste (especially for a Balliol man) to have mentioned the golden reefs of the Witwatersrand, but both men must have wondered privately just how great British interest in the republic would have been if it did not contain the greatest treasure hoard in the world.

The one thing Milner did not want was the establishment of a new form of the republic in which the new population would merge with the old in the construction of a new State. He saw the danger in the capitalist talks, and insisted constantly to the Uitlander negotiators that any settlement contemplated was the prerogative of Her Majesty's Government and not of the people most concerned. It was also quite clear that in this Her Majesty's Government consisted of himself and Chamberlain.

FitzPatrick agreed whole-heartedly, and it was largely because of this influence that the mining houses and the Johannesburg representatives combined to stress the essential factor of the franchise in their negotiations with the republic. As Milner and FitzPatrick had foreseen, it was the one rock on which any hope of agreement with Kruger would founder.

On March 27 the capitalist committee sent their reply to the Government's proposals, addressed to the State Secretary. Attached to it was a memorandum on the franchise problem drawn up by FitzPatrick and H. C. Hull – both ex-members of the Reform Committee. The report itself described the franchise as 'the vital point upon which a permanent and peaceful settlement must hinge'; the memorandum asked that all legislation dealing with the franchise since the Volksraad session of 1890 should be annulled, and that the Raad should legislate 'to restore and confirm the status prior to 1890 and thus satisfy the indisputable claims of those who settled in this country under certain conditions from the benefits of which they could not properly be excluded'.

At the same time FitzPatrick reassured Milner that Kruger would find the whole thing unacceptable.

'Let's hope it turns out that way, then,' Milner replied. 'When are you sending your reply?'

'I'm taking it over to Pretoria myself. They've asked for delivery by hand. In the interests of secrecy, no doubt. I'm to deliver it personally to Reitz.'

A few days later, when FitzPatrick stepped out of the noon train on to the platform of Pretoria station, the precious envelope in his breast-pocket, he was astonished and dismayed to see Paddy Falconer advancing towards him with outstretched hand. Falconer was the correspondent in the Transvaal of the *Cape Times* and the London *Times*. At that moment the reporter was the last person FitzPatrick wanted to see or be seen with, as he was well aware that all his movements and contacts were under observation. His worst fears were confirmed when Falconer shook his hand warmly and said: 'Sure, Mr FitzPatrick, I knew you wouldn't let me down, and me meeting every train from Johannesburg since breakfast time!'

'How d'you mean, let you down? I don't know what you're talking about.'

'Why, the letter, to be sure! The one in your pocket for Mr Reitz. As one Irishman to another, Mr FitzPatrick —'

'You can cut out that blarney, Paddy. It won't get you anywhere. But you'd better come with me in the cab.'

On the long downhill run from the station FitzPatrick pulled the envelope out of his pocket and displayed the heavy seals.

'So you see, Paddy, I couldn't show you the report even if I wanted to. And I'm sworn to secrecy. I've been entrusted with the task of delivering this to the Secretary of State; it's a waste of time discussing it any further.'

Falconer used every argument of reason and emotion to persuade FitzPatrick to divulge the contents of the letter, but the Johannesburger would have none of it. At last Falconer said, 'You know, I don't get paid much for this job, and you can't do anything here without money. If I had fifty pounds, or even twenty-five, I'd have that damned letter, or a copy of it, by tonight. I'd have the biggest scoop that's ever been made in this country, and do the biggest service to a cause in which we both believe. But every penny I could scrape together has gone on train fares for my wife and child, who've had to go to the coast on doctor's orders.'

'What d'you mean, you'd get the letter if you had the cash?'

'You know as well as I do. There's nothing you can't buy here. They've filled their offices with a lot of jackals and spies; smart Hollanders of a low class who are there because they'll do the dirty work. They're as ready to sell their employer as anybody else. If I had the money, I'd have that letter tonight!'

'I'm sorry, Paddy, I can't help you. But – tell you what: you come round to my office in a couple of hours. We'll have a cup of tea.'

Falconer jumped off the cab as it rounded the corner of Market Square and headed for the Government Buildings.

There FitzPatrick was greeted by one of the secretaries and taken straight to the office of Francis Reitz. The State Secretary, normally the most courteous and kindly of men, was excited and brusque to the point of rudeness. He did not stand up to greet his visitor, and when the letter was handed to him he said crossly:

'I am acquainted with its contents, Mr FitzPatrick. I do not think we have anything to discuss.'

Then he threw the envelope, unopened, into a drawer which he slammed shut in a noisy gesture of dismissal.

'In that case, Mr State Secretary,' FitzPatrick said, 'I will wish you good day.' He turned and left the room without another word passing between them. If Reitz did know the contents of the letter, which was quite possible, then he had some reason to be upset.

When Falconer came to the firm's office, FitzPatrick sent out for a tray of tea and biscuits and described his reception by the State Secretary.

'That does not surprise me at all,' Falconer said when FitzPatrick had finished. 'I suspected all along that the whole thing was a political manoeuvre on the part of the Government. Now, if the report doesn't suit them, it's quite certain they won't publish it. Your Committee can't reveal it without a serious breach of confidence. Pretty soon you'll find the word going round that all you capitalists were interested in was financial advantages for yourselves and that the Government had rejected your proposals in the interest of the people – including the Uitlanders.'

'We were not altogether unaware of that, Paddy. But even so it doesn't warrant a breach of confidence on my part – as you've said yourself. You know, Paddy, I'm very concerned about your family. They need a better holiday than you can afford to give them. And you look as though you could do with one, too. Why don't you go and join them – no, don't interrupt. Look, you've worked hard in the common cause, and run to a good deal of expense too. That's not right. I'd look on it as a privilege if you'll let us help you to get away for a while and enjoy yourself with your family as you deserve.'

FitzPatrick picked up a bulky envelope lying near his hand, passed it across the table to Falconer.

'But Mr FitzPatrick ... I'm most grateful, but I can't leave Pretoria now. I just can't!'

'You know what Reitz did with that letter when I gave it to him, Paddy? He just pushed it into a drawer at his right hand. The top right-hand drawer ...'

Next day Falconer crossed the border. The day following that the full story of the capitalist negotiations filled the columns of the *Cape Times* and of *The Times* in London. Kruger and Reitz were furious. Under Kruger's direction the State Secretary wrote a long letter to Rouliot and his associates in which he denied that Lippert had ever been an agent of the Government and insisted that throughout the negotiations he, Leyds and Smuts had acted on their own initiative and not on behalf of the Executive.

'In conclusion,' he ended his letter, 'I wish to refer to one matter which has caused me much pain. It was clearly and distinctly agreed by you all as well as by us that both sides would treat this matter as confidential and secret. What has happened? On April 3, while I was yet giving your letter earnest consideration and had taken all measures to keep it secret, the contents of the same appeared in the London *Times* and in the *Cape Times*. This has caused me to doubt (I admit it with regret) your good faith. Thinking, however, of the great interest as it were in the balance and believing that you never, for private or party purposes, intended to play with the true and lasting interests of all sections of the community, I cannot help thinking that the reply has been published through one of your subordinates and regret that the publication has not been immediately repudiated by you publicly as a grave breach of faith. Owing to the publication of your reply there exists no further reason for secrecy and I shall hand my reply to the Press.'

The Johannesburg committee retaliated by publishing all the correspondence that had passed between the negotiating bodies, including the minutes and memoranda of both sides.

The publication of these proceedings had a considerable

effect on public opinion in South Africa and overseas. In Johannesburg the South African League – busy preparing a second petition to the Queen, with Milner's full approval – called a public meeting to endorse the attitude and actions of the capitalist negotiators. The Government refused permission to hold an open-air assembly, and when the organizers announced their intention of booking a hall for the purpose, the Johannesburg Landdrost had the building condemned as unsafe. Milner made the most of the consequent uproar by suggesting that the Uitlanders should resort to holding a number of small meetings at different localities along the Witwatersrand. When Reitz heard of this he forestalled the enemy by himself giving permission for a series of small indoor meetings.

By this means, and by the employment of well-paid canvassers, the League was able to obtain the signatures of 21,000 British subjects on the Queen's petition. When Kruger retaliated with a counter-petition protesting against foreign intervention in the affairs of the republic, signed by 23,000 Uitlanders, Greene's comment was that it should not be taken seriously as the signatures were obtained under various forms of duress and influence.

Milner himself transmitted the second petition to London at the end of March, and decided that the time had come to take more direct and active steps – with or without the approval of Whitehall or Westminster – towards the destruction of the republic. He placed his faith in the Uitlanders to provoke a situation which would compel a slow-moving British Government to act. More and more often he used one of his favourite expressions – 'we must get things forrarder!' – and told the Uitlanders through Greene 'to keep pegging away'.

On May 5, in response to a covert invitation from Chamberlain, Milner cabled to the Colonial Office a 2,200 word review of the position in the Transvaal. Johannesburg was full of rumours. They crystallized, as usual, in the Rand Club where the bar whispered wheezily with inside information and where the new editor of *The Star* could be seen nursing a black eye received during an encounter in his office with an over-patriotic Afrikaner from Krugersdorp.

There was only one man in Johannesburg who knew what the Milner telegram contained. That was Percy Fitz-Patrick; part of his role was to leak certain bits of it, to sustain the Uitlanders in their new attitude of defiance and to give them hope for the future. Anything that FitzPatrick said in the Club would, he knew, be sure to find its way to the Stock Exchange and eventually to the old man on his bungalow stoep in Pretoria.

'I can, as a matter of fact, tell you something of the contents,' he told lunchtime guests who had been plying him with questions. 'Greene gave me the gist of it. It's hot stuff. Typically Milner. There's no nonsense about that man. He's said some pretty straightforward things about the police; "harsh and arbitrary" I believe was the term he used. He referred to the Uitlanders suffering from the effects of chaotic local legislation and of incompetent and unsympathetic administration. He's demanded that we have a share in the government of the Transvaal; and then comes the best bit. I liked it so much I wrote it down. Listen to this: "The case for intervention is overwhelming. The spectacle of thousands of British subjects kept permanently in the position of helots, calling vainly to Her Majesty's Government for redress, does steadily undermine the influence and reputation of Great Britain and the respect for the British Government within the Queen's dominions." '

As FitzPatrick paused, loud expressions of approval and excitement rose above the clatter and conversation that filled the dining-room. Faces turned towards FitzPatrick; several members left their tables and came over, full of food and curiosity, to the group in the corner.

'There's more to come,' they heard FitzPatrick say, and even the waiter paused to listen. 'Of course, I haven't been able to make a full copy. There's over two thousand words in that telegram. But this is how it ends:

' "I can see nothing which will put a stop to this but some striking proof of the intention of Her Majesty's Government not to be ousted from its position in South Africa. And the best proof alike of its power and its justice would be to obtain for the Uitlanders in the Transvaal a fair share in the government of the country which owes everything to their exertions." '

Jubilant 'hear, hears' rumbled round the room, mingling with calls to the waiters for fresh drinks and bottles of champagne. Soon the whole dining-room was drinking toasts to the Queen and to Sir Alfred Milner – God bless 'em! The British lion had growled in Johannesburg. Was any other noise necessary to frighten those Boers to death?

Not everybody in the Rand Club responded with the same enthusiasm. The representatives of the big international mining groups raised their glasses in acknowledgment, but their thoughts were on output figures from the gold mines – which were surpassing all previous records. Average monthly production during 1898 had run at 300,000 ounces. There were seventy-four producing mines employing 10,000 whites and 90,000 natives. There was a yearly wage bill of £3,000,000, a dividend distribution of £5,000,000, and an expenditure on stores which was greater than that of the Transvaal Government. They were only beginning the vast development of the deep levels and, as methods of extraction improved, the golden flow from the bowels of the Witwatersrand would continue to swell with each new tribute from the underground streams. True, working costs were high – up to thirty shillings a ton – due to the ridiculous monopoly system.

But it did not need a war to change a monopoly to a competitive business. All it needed was a little common sense. Some of them remembered, too, that Kruger and his Boers were not frightened of lions; they had been fighting them all their lives.

CHAPTER THIRTY-SIX

Every other issue in the South African Republic was now subordinate to British paramountcy. Chamberlain virtually eliminated all hope of a compromise when he informed Milner that 'it is a great thing to be able to say that the majority of the people, as I believe, recognize that there is a greater issue than the franchise or the grievances of the Uitlanders at stake, and that our supremacy in South Africa and our existence as a great Power in the world are involved in the result of the present controversy'.

Here was the plot laid bare. Here was the culmination of the years of surreptitious planning that had been so rudely interrupted by the Jameson Raid. Power politics with all its chicanery and dissimulation and high-level hypocrisy had replaced the straightforward, high-motivated deceit of Cecil Rhodes – who had also wanted the Transvaal for the Empire. At last Chamberlain and Milner were able to join hands in public.

There was still a need for appearances – not on behalf of the British, who were 'rarin' to go', but in deference to the judgment of a watching world. Compromise had been eliminated; but it must not be thought that compromise had been rejected by the Colonial Secretary. The opportunity for superficial vindication of Britain's intentions was provided by the second Uitlander petition addressed to the Queen early in 1899. Chamberlain drafted a reply for the approval of the Cabinet which, in its indictment of the Pretoria Government and its demands for redress of Uitlander grievances, was only one step away from an ultimatum. That one step Chamberlain was determined to take.

War, and civil war, stared South Africa in the face. Men of good will on both sides tried desperately to avert the final tragedy. They persuaded the British Government to agree to a conference between Milner and the two Presidents of the sister Boer republics. It was held in Bloemfontein between May 31 and June 5. Milner presented demands to Kruger which he knew were unacceptable. The atmosphere of the discussions was adequately and truthfully summed up by the old man when he cried out bitterly: 'Ah, it is our country you want!' The pathos bounced off Milner's hardness like tears off a granite rock. Kruger finally proposed arbitration in his search for a solution to the franchise question that would not destroy the independence of his beloved land. Milner's words rang like a death knell across the Transvaal.

'This conference is at an end,' he said abruptly to the two Boers, 'and there is no obligation on either side arising out of it.'

The charade was over. And while the talking was going on in Bloemfontein, troopships were steaming full speed ahead for Durban. Milner had even suggested the dispositions.

'We want an overwhelming force,' he wrote to the British Government. 'It may be 10,000 men – to be sent out to Natal. And Laing's Nek on the republican frontier to be occupied. This forward position once assured, we should have a means of pressure which should be irresistible.'

Young Jan Smuts saw the situation clearly. He wrote to Merriman down in the Cape: 'The situation is being forced from the outside in order by an armed conflict to forestall or defeat the work of time. It fills me with a savage indignation to think that the work of those who are spending their life-blood for South Africa is to be undone in a moment by academic nobodies who fancy themselves great imperial statesmen.'

The Boers in the Volksraad watched the war marshalling along the borders of their country. Could they prevent it by relaxing the franchise qualifications? They agreed hurriedly to concede a seven-year retrospective period and to give the Witwatersrand four additional Members in the Raad.

The immediate reaction from Whitehall was a request for a further meeting between Milner and Kruger in Cape Town, provided the right of the British Government to interfere in the internal as well as the external affairs of the republic was acknowledged. Kruger found himself pressed beyond endurance.

'It is our interest to keep the peace,' he rumbled, 'and we

have tried hard to do so; but if our independence is to go, it must be taken from us by force.'

A thousand miles from Johannesburg, the *Cape Times* wrote: 'We have come to the point when the gun must be loaded and the aggressive combination calling itself the Afrikaner nation must be made to believe it is loaded even by its discharge, if no other way succeeds.'

More than one gun was being loaded. The republic's expenditure on armaments had been increasing rapidly each year and now, with German pressure on Portugal easing the situation at the port of Delagoa Bay, the railway line to Pretoria rumbled unceasingly with the passage of trains full of field-guns, rifles and ammunition. On distant farms the word went round and fathers and brothers, uncles, nephews and sons packed their saddle-bags with biltong, filled their bandoliers with bullets, kissed their wives and daughters good-bye and rode into the capital.

In Johannesburg, and all along the Witwatersrand, families began looking up steamer schedules; trunks and portmanteaux were pulled down from attics and box-rooms, and servants started packing household treasures. The ticket clerk at Park Station suddenly found himself confronted with daily queues for advance bookings to Delagoa Bay, Durban and Cape Town, and asked the station-master urgently for assistance. Mine managers studied the daily production figures anxiously; output slowly dropped as European workers trickled away. They made their plans for maintenance of the mines in the event of a shut-down, and tried to explain to their thousands of Africans why it might become necessary for them all to go back to their homes. Small parties of Zulus and Basutos, Shangaans, Swazis and tribesmen from Portuguese East could be seen setting off each day along the dusty cross-country tracks, their blanketed belongings slung over their shoulders, new boots suspended round their necks.

The meaningless words and surreptitious preparations of August changed stridently to threats and strategic disposals for war in September. Troopships rode at anchor in Table Bay and in the roadstead at Port Natal, and Chamberlain informed Milner that all preparations for an expeditionary force were being proceeded with.

In Britain the propaganda machine was in full blast, receiving unexpected but almost violent stimulation by the publication of FitzPatrick's book *The Transvaal from Within*. It was a classic of the Uitlander case which became the war party's bible – with almost as many picturesque inaccuracies treated as gospel. It was quoted by the Colonial Secretary in Commons' debates, and Lord Rosebery described it as 'an appalling record of the way in which the Government of the Transvaal was carried on and the subjection to which it reduced our fellow-countrymen there'.

Kruger saw the slow massing of his enemies on the frontiers, he saw the troopships leaving Southampton and Plymouth and cleaving their way through the Atlantic with all the potent instruments for the destruction of the republic in their holds and cabins. Milner and Chamberlain, he knew, would carry on the fight with words until they had assembled an overwhelming force; then they would strike. Should he await the inevitable, and be inevitably overwhelmed? His generals and his commandos knew the answer. They shouted it at him so that even his deafness could not prevent him hearing. Their only chance of saving the republic was to strike first. Every day meant another thousand *rooineks* to be fought. Let them strike at once! Let them drive the redcoats back into the sea: then all South Africa would be theirs. There was not an Afrikaner in the whole country who would not join them after the first victorious battles. The British armies would be invested in a hostile land. They would not be able to move forwards, backwards or sideways without encountering an enemy. But, they urged Kruger, strike first and strike hard!

Kruger heard them, and smoked his pipe and sipped his coffee and stared at the pass in the Magaliesberg through which the road ran to Johannesburg. If the *rooineks* came, that was the only way in. His eyes shifted to the left, to where the earthworks of his new fort glowed red against the still yellow grass and weathered rock of the mountain. They had chosen a good place for it, truly. But if the English got that far would the fort be any use to the Boers? They could not hold the towns or the plains against the vast armies that would be poured into South Africa from all corners of the Empire. His burghers were right. And what was it that clever young man Jan Smuts had told him? That the two republics must take the offensive from the start: that they must invade Natal and capture Durban. There was a thing! If they won the first few battles, Smuts said, the reluctant

European Powers might intervene against England. They were all frightened of England; but if a handful of backveld farmers could show them there was no need to be ...? A far-seeing young man, was Smuts. What was that about weakening the British position in India and Egypt, and the Russian Tsar moving troops down to the Afghanistan border? There was no doubt about it. The republic must attack the British Empire. And Jannie Smuts must be made a general.

Smuts himself had noted in a memorandum on the situation in September: 'South Africa is on the eve of a terrible blood-bath, from which our people will emerge either as an exhausted remnant – woodcutters and water-carriers for a hated race – or as victors, founders of a United South Africa, of one of the greatest empires of the world, an Afrikaner republic stretching from Table Bay to the Zambesi.'

When Smuts wrote this did he see, for one fleeting second, the massive figure and imperial head of Cecil John Rhodes standing before him? Did he recognize the words?

Business came to a standstill in Johannesburg; the thunder of the batteries crushing gold-bearing rock dwindled to spasmodic throbbing as, one after another, the mines had to cease operations, their staffs and workers joining the steady exodus from the Transvaal.

Milner had been told by Rhodes and FitzPatrick (now in England enjoying the enormous success of his book) that Kruger would 'bluff right up to the canon's mouth' but that he would then throw in his hand. Milner did not want him to stop bluffing. He wanted war because he believed that only a victorious war would solve permanently the problems of South Africa. There was never any doubt about the victory – and a quick one it was going to be.

The newspapers announced that 10,000 reinforcements were on their way from India and Britain and that a complete army corps would back them up. With typically casual cynicism Milner persuaded the British Cabinet not to deliver the ultimatum they had already prepared 'until the reinforcements now on their way are in position on the frontiers of the republic'.

A few days later he telegraphed again urging them to delay the ultimatum still further 'as events of next few days may supply us with a better one than anybody can compose.

The ultimatum has always been a great difficulty as unless we widen the issue there is not sufficient cause for war...'

The Boers, too, had prepared an ultimatum. Kruger, with time against him, wanted to present it and start fighting. President Steyn of the Free State would not allow this.

'Oom Paul,' he said to his senior partner, 'I think we should wait for the British terms. When they are made public it will strengthen our cause in the eyes of the world. Besides, the supply arrangements for the commandos on the Natal border are not yet complete.'

Chamberlain told his Cabinet colleagues that the Boers might make an ultimatum unnecessary by taking the offensive. 'If so,' he added, 'the Lord will have delivered them into our hands – at least as far as diplomacy is concerned.'

Kruger curbed his impatience, although it was reported to him that the Gordon Highlanders and other regiments had arrived at Durban and were *en route* to the frontier. It was plainly suicidal to postpone the Boer attack much longer. But he was waiting for October 9. On that day a delegation from Pretoria called on President McKinley in Washington to seek United States support in the coming struggle against England.. Reitz brought Kruger the news with grim face. The President of the United States had declined to receive the Boer delegation, as his Government did not acknowledge the right of the South African Republic to conduct foreign affairs. The President further announced his determination to avoid complications.

Old Kruger nodded his head sombrely. They were alone, then. His burghers against the full might of the British Empire. So let it be. God would guide them again to the Promised Land, as He had done before. They needed no other ally. He lifted his great, tired head and his eyes gleamed with sudden decision.

'Mr Reitz. You have the ultimatum to the British Government ready?'

'Yes, Your Honour. It is ready.'

'Then see that it is presented to the British Agent this afternoon.'

'This afternoon, Your Excellency?'

'This afternoon. At once. And inform President Steyn.'

Reitz hurried back to his office. He sent for Hoytema, one of the Foreign Department assistants, and handed him an envelope with instructions to take it to Conyngham Greene immediately. Then he sent a wire to Bloemfontein informing Steyn that he had given the British Government forty-eight hours in which to give an undertaking that all troops would be withdrawn from the Transvaal border, that all troops landed in South Africa since the Bloemfontein Conference would be evacuated and that no further troop-landings would occur.

No need to give Steyn any further information or instructions. The common purpose was acknowledged, the common plan defined. He would know what such an ultimatum meant. By Wednesday night the two Boer republics would be at war with Great Britain.

There were only two ways in which their republic could be destroyed, Reitz thought; they could give it away by giving the Uitlanders the franchise, or they could have it taken away.

It was not going to be easy to take.

After a night of wild rumour Johannesburg read the story of the ultimatum on Tuesday morning in *The Diggers' News*. The leading article of the day was devoted to a eulogy of President Kruger, whose seventy-fourth birthday it was.

There was little cheering or demonstrating in the Uitlander citadel. Indeed there were not many left to cheer – except in the Boer section of the town, where now, for the first time since the golden discovery, burghers outnumbered Britons. The great exodus had reached its climax during the previous week. Special trains had been laid on by the railway company, and they were departing from various stations along the Witwatersrand every few hours for the ports around the coastline of the whole sub-continent. Each train was the last one out. It became necessary to reserve some of them for women only and some, consisting of open goods trucks, for men only.

By Monday night the peak of the exodus had passed. Only the mail train was full to bursting point, including among its 150 passengers the last of the mining magnates who had decided to go. The slow train to Cape Town, consisting of three ordinary carriages, two covered trucks and four open wagons, took away 350 passengers.

After the Europeans came the Kaffirs. As the mines ground slowly to a halt the disposal of thousands of unemployed natives became an urgent problem. The mining companies were not interested in feeding or paying them when there was no work for them to do. It was the Government's business – let the Government sort it out!

The Government had made up its mind to continue to operate as many gold mines as it could. It was entirely a question of manpower – and know-how. For this they needed Uitlanders, most of whom were bound to be British and therefore enemy. But not every Briton, and certainly not many of the other aliens, were pro-British in their quarrel with the republic, and a considerable number expressed their willingness to stay. In this way six mines were kept in production.

This solved a small part of the Kaffir question. The rest, in their thousands, were told they had to go home. Some walked, some went in ox-wagons, and for the remainder the Government laid on long trains of cattle and grain trucks. The movement reached its climax on the Monday, when five goods trains, each of twenty-two trucks jammed with native mine-workers, passed through Pretoria on their way to the Eastern Transvaal and Moçambique.

The anti-Boer Press in South Africa and in Britain made the most of the mad scramble to get away from the Rand by printing highly-coloured accounts of hardships and brutalities inflicted on the fleeing Uitlanders. The Archbishop of Cape Town joined in with a public condemnation of the 'dastardly and brutal outrages now being daily inflicted by armed men on the unhappy, defenceless passengers, male and female, who are escaping for their lives or being ruthlessly driven forth from their homes'.

Milner added official misinformation in a communication addressed to the President of the Free State, whom he was trying hard to pry apart from Kruger:

'The prolonged negotiations have hitherto failed to bring about a satisfactory understanding, and no doubt such an understanding is more difficult than ever today after the expulsion of British subjects with great loss and suffering.'

No one could expect the Boers to be polite and considerate of the British Uitlanders at this stage, but the charges of brutality against refugees did not stand up to investigation. If there was any during the exodus it occurred when men, desperate to get away, pulled women off the trains to make room for themselves. Nor, as Milner well knew, was there any question of expulsion. The refugees were all voluntary evacuees and the Pretoria Government was anxious that Britons with expert knowledge should stay behind. Several hundred availed themselves of this opportunity and were required only to make a very mild form of undertaking:

'I, the undersigned, a British subject, declare hereby under oath that I, during my stay in the South African Republic, will behave myself in a quiet, calm and submissive manner, and that I will remain obedient to the laws and the authorities of the country and that neither directly nor indirectly will I do aught, nor cause anything to be done, against the independence of the country and people of the Republic. So truly help me, God.'

Most of them also joined unpaid the Town Special Police, although it is difficult to say whether this was through a sense of duty to the community or because of the excellent rations that were issued at a time when the whole of Johannesburg was suffering a serious food problem.

As a job it was no sinecure. The town was in imminent danger of being taken over by riff-raff and criminals who since the days of Ferreira's Camp had formed an ever-increasing section of the population. They occupied abandoned suburban houses of the rich departed, sold the furniture on the open market, and lived luxuriously from larders and cellars and the produce of well-tended vegetable gardens. Poultry featured daily on their menu.

Johannesburg died slowly and peacefully. *Vierkleurs* fluttered from mastheads and windows instead of the gay bunting of defiant imperialism; in place of the constant rumble of traffic there was a clattering of hoof-beats on macadam as the slouching, slouch-hatted Boer commandos rode south to tomorrow's war, their waistcoats quartered with full-charged bandoliers.

The Stewards of the Turf Club, not surprisingly, announced the abandonment of the Spring Meeting; Phillips' Monster Sweepstakes regretted that their next lottery would take place, 'due to circumstances beyond our control', on the Port Elizabeth Handicap instead of the Johannesburg Spring Cup.

In the excitement of preparing for war, Smuts had not overlooked the small item of the recent output of the mines. He sent Lieutenants Oosthuizen and Muller, with a picked squad of the State Artillery, across from Pretoria to call on each of Johannesburg's banks. From these they commandeered a total of forty-six cases of gold bullion, weighing 45,288 ounces.

Wednesday had come too soon for many Johannesburgers unwilling to believe that some last-minute miracle would not intervene to prevent the war. When the Pretoria Government announced the conditions of martial law which would be proclaimed in the town in the event of a rejection of the ultimatum, it provoked another rush to the railway stations of hundreds from whom the last hope had been removed. (Among the last to leave on the midday train for Cape Town was Mr Jimmy Sinclair, an employee of the French Bank and South Africa's greatest cricketer.) Now the railway lines were burdened with other trains, loaded not with refugees but with armed burghers headed for frontier *laagers*.

At four o'clock on the afternoon of October 9, 1899, the Republics of the Transvaal and the Orange Free State were at war with Great Britain. Kruger's orders went out from Pretoria to his generals. Boer commandos crossed into Natal and the Cape Colony.

CHAPTER THIRTY-SEVEN

Under martial law the first act of the Tribunal of War and the newly-appointed Military Governor, Commandant Schutte, was to order the expulsion in commandeered trains of all 'disreputable characters', of whom the police, on Smuts' instructions, had already prepared a list. With them to the borders went the Cape Coloureds who were not in regular employment or who were of doubtful character. All British subjects who had no desire to stay, or who could not get the necessary permit, were politely invited to accept a free train-ride to Natal or the Cape. In this way Smuts relieved the Boer command of any concern about the enemy within; they would need every man and every bullet in the republic for the enemy without.

The 'disreputable characters' raised no objections to their expulsion once they had read the edict prohibiting the sale of drink in Johannesburg. In vain hotel and saloon proprietors appealed direct to Kruger to allow them to sell liquor to familiar friends and permanent residents. Kruger told the deputation who came to see him: 'During the coming weeks many of my burghers will be passing through Johannesburg on commando. I cannot afford to have them getting drunk. There must be no liquor available in Johannesburg.'

He relented only once, when an old man called Nathan Cohen, accompanied by a young Rabbi, asked him for permission to consume the wine prescribed by Jewish law for the nuptial ceremony. Within half an hour of this request being granted a dozen other weddings were announced, and applications made to Pretoria for a similar concession. They were, alas, refused; the weddings, so far as is known, did not take place.

By the time the expulsions were over the great exodus had drained Johannesburg of all but 1,000 Britons. For a time most of the stores and shops kept their doors open.

The advertising space they bought in the newspapers was devoted to saying, rather despairingly, that they were still in business. But gradually, as stocks dwindled and windows emptied of goods, merchants no longer bothered to open their doors in the morning; the plate-glass windows gazed blankly back at curious backvelders on their way to war.

The pubs, denied liquor and customers, could think of no reason to stay open, and the hotels found they could not profitably survive on board and lodging alone. There were no staff to serve meals, and pretty soon no meals to serve. Slowly the blinds and curtains were drawn over the once-bright lights of a town that had never gone to bed. Dust and dirt blew in from the surrounding veld and mine-dumps; soon, as the spring rains began to fall, the streets sprouted grass and weeds, and Boer ponies grazed on meadows that had been parks and squares. The Chains drooped disconsolately outside a silent Stock Exchange, with nothing between them except the ancient ordure of long-departed cab-horses.

But it was the dim pulse of the mines that told the remaining inhabitants that Johannesburg was on the brink of death. The great heart-throb of the stamp batteries had dwindled to this reluctant palpitation murmuring its epitaph for golden days gone by. Only the Rand Club rose superior to environment – though it made its bargain with circumstance by admitting to honorary membership the senior officials of the Republic. It did not, in fact, have any option in the matter.

Every day brought rumours from the battlefields, but few of these brought cheer or hope to Her Majesty's subjects still in Johannesburg. They had given an undertaking to the Boer authorities, and they were, for the most part, faithfully fulfilling it. Down at Begbie's Iron Foundry, commandeered by the Government at the start of the war, they were even turning out shells for the Boer artillery.

Six months went by, and still the Transvaal was inviolate; the Uitlanders strained their ears in vain for the distant argument of guns that would herald the advent of Lord Roberts' army.

At 5.30 p.m. on April 25 – that was the time the electricity was switched on at the power station – Johannesburg rocked to a violent explosion on its southern outskirts. On the eastern and western ends of the Reef they heard and felt the thud of the detonation, and looked to the south in search of guns and troops. In Johannesburg itself the first uncomprehending panic was followed by reports that the Boers were shelling the town; women grabbed their children and pushed them under beds and tables, waited fearfully for the next salvo.

It never came. Instead, the billowing, green-hued smoke drifted through the streets just ahead of the news that Begbie's factory had been blown up. It was Braamfontein in miniature all over again: that gaping hole in the ground filled with unsightly remnants; the column of odious smoke wreathing among shattered buildings and houses; the screams and groans, shouted orders as help came running. Cabs brought doctors and nurses; from the mines came work-gangs with picks and shovels to burrow into the rubble. When it was all over they counted twelve men dead, and fifty-six seriously injured.

When Kruger was told of the explosion, and that it was probably sabotage caused by placing dynamite so that it would be detonated when the mains current was switched on, his anger at the act and the damage it had done the Boer war potential left no room in his heart for compassion.

'These *verdomde* Englishmen!' he stormed, spitting his contempt at his feet. 'They're all the same! Rhodes, Jameson, Chamberlain, Milner, Begbie – what's the difference? They'll all *verneuk* you if they can!'

He turned to Reitz.

'These spies and murderers must be found and punished. And all the Britishers must get out of the Transvaal. Immediately! Tell Schutte to see to it. No, not Schutte: he's too soft, too friendly with the Uitlanders. Make Krause commandant. But get rid of those damn Englishmen, before they blow us all up!'

Poor old Kruger: he knew that his days, and the days of his republic, were numbered. He could not stop Roberts reaching Johannesburg. And after Johannesburg, Pretoria. The *Vierkleur* would come down, and the Union Jack would fly once more over the Boer capital. But that would not end the war. The Boers did not need a capital to fight a war. They carried their capital and their parliament with them. In the saddle. But he was too old for the saddle: he would have to go. When Roberts crossed the Vaal River – that would be the time. Then the others – Botha, Smuts, de la Rey, Joubert – could carry on the fight. Kruger slowly shook his great, buffalo head. Perhaps they would know better than he when to stop. But could it ever stop? It must go on until the Republic was born again. It was God's will! Not Chamberlain's, not Milner's. His hands fingered lovingly the familiar pages of the bible on his knee. Yea, though I walk through the valley of the shadow...

The pavement bystanders of Johannesburg, always sensitive to change, were the first to notice it. Something was different. But what? Suddenly they knew. The commandos were clattering through the town again. But they were going north. Grim, silent, weary. No more jibes and jeers for the Uitlanders. Their ears were too full of the noise of battle; their eyes too full of the unending streams of men and animals, weapons and wagons, that seemed to stretch from Bloemfontein all the way back to Cape Town. Their minds went ahead of their tired ponies to their farms and families. Had they got the mealie crop in yet? The cows would be heavy with calf and bulging udders. *Hemel!* It was a long time since they had seen a woman. Johannesburg? Was that what they had been fighting for? This blasphemy? The *rooineks* could have it...

Late one evening towards the end of May, the southerly wind boomed faintly. Early next morning the citizens climbed to the top of the ridges behind the town and looked out across the flats to Heidelberg and Klipriviersberg. Would they come today? Tomorrow?

They couldn't come too soon for the Uitlanders – British or Swedish, French, German, Italian or Russian. Dr Krause's resources for discipline and order were strained to the utmost. He depended now almost entirely on the civilian 'specials'. An advertisement in *The Diggers' News* signed by one O'Reilly called for volunteers for an Irish Scouting Force to continue the fight against the British invaders. Everybody knew O'Reilly, and everybody knew that his 'Irish Scouting Force' was nothing but a cover for organized gang war with military objectives limited to safes, bullion deposits and other forms of Uitlander wealth. Fortunately, O'Reilly assaulted an American citizen by the name of Murphy who had refused to volunteer, and was quickly arrested and thrown into gaol before he had time to collect the replies to his advertisement.

Krause was under strong pressure from the desperate burghers who were all in favour of a scorched-earth policy in front of the advancing British. High on their list of priorities was the destruction of the Rand's gold mines. In preventing this the Commandant had the support of Botha and Smuts, now back in Pretoria organizing the dispositions of Boer forces which would carry on the fight for another three years before capitulation.

As far as Dr Krause was concerned, if the Boers were not going to defend Johannesburg then the sooner it was occupied by the British the better for all concerned. In the Landdrost's office he consulted with Pretoria and the retreating commanders. The town was indefensible for an army that depended so much on its mobility for success and survival; and it was of no tactical significance. They told Krause he must make the best deal he could with the enemy. Time was needed for the withdrawal of the retreating commandos. Let him trade with the British for time. In exchange for what? In exchange for the gold mines intact. If time was not to be bartered, the mines would be destroyed. And what would have been the use of this war, if the gold mines were destroyed?

It was a fair question, and on May 29 Dr Krause rode out to Germiston to put it personally to the Commander-in-Chief, Lord Roberts. He offered the complete surrender of Johannesburg. Then he put forward his conditions. No British forces to enter the town until May 31 – in return for the mines undamaged. Otherwise . . .

Roberts did not want to fight his way through the streets of Johannesburg. He was not interested in gold mines himself; he had his eye on Pretoria and the end of the war. But he knew what the Rand gold meant to the City of London and to the vast capitalist structure behind the war effort. He nodded briefly to Krause, and held out his hand.

On the same day on the western flank of the town – at Doornkop, on the ridges where the Boers had compelled Dr Jameson to surrender – General Ian Hamilton and the Gordon Highlanders had fought one of the briskest actions of the war. The Boers had been put to flight, and Hamilton was anxious to let Roberts know his position and the result of the day's fighting. Unaware of the arrangements made that day between Krause and the commander-in-chief, he was waiting for authority to attack the town.

Civilians who came out of Johannesburg in their eagerness to welcome the advancing British gave conflicting accounts of the situation, but it was apparent that Boer forces
were still in occupation in some strength, though obviously
preparing to withdraw.

Among these civilians was a young Frenchman on a bicycle, who gave his name as Lautré. He assured his ques-
tioners that it would be easy to cycle right through Johannesburg and out the other side to where Roberts had established his headquarters. He offered to guide anybody they
cared to send. Hamilton accepted the offer. His choice of
courier was a young officer, recently of the South African
Light Horse; he was also war correspondent of the London
Morning Post, and he had made it known that he wanted to
get back to the main headquarters to telegraph his reports of
the fighting.

The two of them set off on their bicycles on the new
surface of the Main Reef road, and, as darkness fell, came
unchallenged past the smoke-stacks of Langlaagte mine and
into Johannesburg. They had to get off their bikes and walk
up the short, steep rise that led to the town-centre. Hearing
behind them the clip-clop of a trotting horse, they began
talking volubly in French – an accomplishment which
would have astonished the reporter's public school French-
master had he not been close enough to recognize familiar
stanzas from *La Marseillaise*.

An armed Boer rode up alongside, reining-in his horse to
match their pace. They continued three abreast through the
centre of the town where the lights were now on in most of
the hotels and where dim groups could be seen clustered on
verandas and street corners. Then they were out in the trees
and gardens of the eastern suburbs and their silent com-
panion suddenly put spurs to his horse and cantered north
into the night. Ten minutes later the two men met a party
of British soldiers strolling casually into Johannesburg.

'Where are you off to?' the reporter asked, sensing a
story.

'We're going to town to get a bit of grub and a bit of
booze, like. Bit of skirt, too, if we're lucky.'

'You're more likely to get a bullet through your stomach: the place is still full of Boers!'

'What's that, guv'nor? Blimey, we thought Johannesburg

had surrendered! 'Ere – you ain't one of these spies, are yer? What's yer name?'

'This is my friend, Monsieur Lautré, a French resident of Johannesburg, and I am the correspondent of the *Morning Post* – which you probably don't take. My name's Winston Churchill.'

At ten on the morning of May 31, 1900, Lord Roberts entered Johannesburg. On his left rode Lord Kitchener on a white charger; on his right the small, drab, civilian figure of Dr Krause, as forlorn in all that military finery as his forlorn pony. As they passed through the first shuttered streets only a handful of lounging natives and disconsolate burghers stared curiously and unemotionally at the passing cavalcade. But the pavements thickened with people as they approached the town-centre and the court-house where arrangements had been made for the formal surrender ceremony.

Behind Roberts rode his headquarters staff and bodyguard. Behind that marched a company of the Grenadier Guards, followed by the kilt-swinging Argyll and Sutherland Highlanders. The rear of this selectively impressive procession was brought up by four great siege guns; and how glad the citizens must have been when they saw them that the combatants had agreed not to fight for Johannesburg.

Now the crowds began to respond to the occasion; irrespective of nationality they began to cheer and wave, the unexpected welcome reaching a crescendo as Roberts came into the cleared space in front of the court-house. The balcony of the building was filled with officials and their ladies, while the polyglot population, in which the wide-brimmed felt hats of burghers and their children clearly outnumbered the bowlers and trilbys of the Johannesburgers, clustered ten-deep under the blue-gum trees around the square. Englishmen at last dared to raise their voices; sporadic shouts of 'Well done, Bobs!' and 'We're slaves no longer!' were gravely acknowledged with a white-gloved salute from the Commander-in-Chief.

They reined-in their horses at the base of the flag-pole from which the four-coloured flag of the Republic still gleamed in the bright winter sunlight. Lord Settrington, one of Roberts' aides, stepped forward and untied the cord at the foot of the pole. As the flag dipped slowly in surrender they raised their hands in the tribute of a salute – Roberts, Kitchener, all the officers. Dr Krause took his hat off and bowed his head as though he was standing at a graveside into which a beloved corpse was being lowered. The tears fell unashamedly, splashing on the leather of his saddle. Suddenly, as Settrington's fingers slipped, the flag came crashing down the pole: like a guillotine on the bowed head of Afrikanerdom. A sigh rose from the crowded square, rustling the slim leaves of the eucalyptus trees.

Captain Bleksley of the town police – formerly the efficient head of the sanitary department – stepped forward and handed Roberts the keys of the safe in Corporation Buildings where the local authority had its headquarters. It was a prosaic act of submission which the Field-Marshal acknowledged by asking all officials to remain at their posts and fulfil their duties until further orders.

Then Lord Settrington, still blushing furiously, unfurled a silken flag which had been made specially for this surrender by Lady Roberts. The Guards and Highlanders presented arms and, as the fife band struck up 'God Save the Queen', the Union Jack was hoisted jubilantly to the top of the mast. Roberts himself stood up in his stirrups and called for three cheers for Her Majesty.

In a corner of the square a uniformed Free Stater, his war over, watched the ceremony impassively. When he refused to remove his hat as the anthem was being played, a small civilian alongside attempted to knock it off. The man was pushed away by an off-duty Guardsman.

'Leave 'im alone,' the soldier growled. ' 'E fought for *'is* flag. *You* fought for none!'

Life returned to Johannesburg gradually, but gratefully. It was less of a reincarnation than an awakening, tousle-headed and red-eyed, from a troubled sleep. First all the trappings of twilight were removed. Down came the boards and shutters, up went the blinds, and the town looked out again on the world. Not quite the world it had known, but a familiar world of busy streets, hotels and bars and shops. In final recognition of the return of normality the wagons rolled again across the veld through the night with their oblations for the ritual of the dawn market.

From his stall in the Market Hall a Boer baker, back in

the money again, presented each passing 'Tommy' with a loaf of bread. He had believed too literally in his own side's propaganda that the supply lines of the British forces had been cut and that the soldiers were starving.

Once more the trains came panting round the Doornfontein curve or trundled cautiously through the bush and koppies of the Western Transvaal where commandos were still riding, raiding. Most of the trains carried the men and material of war which Roberts, and later Kitchener, were to need for a long time to come; but every now and then a mail train would pull in to Park Station and off-load its cargo of returning Uitlanders.

Uitlanders? Mine-workers and engineers, storekeepers and clerks, lawyers and doctors, spivs and crooks and gamblers, they saw the Union Jack waving over the station and from every building the length of Eloff Street; they read the official notices, printed for the first time that any of them could remember in English only, and ending with the triumphant slogan of imperialism established – GOD SAVE THE QUEEN.

Uitlanders? They stood on the platform and said the name over to themselves, wondering. It was not the South African Republic they had come back to: the Republic was dead. They were Uitlanders no longer.

On both counts, they were wrong.